The Bérenger Plays

Eugène Ionesco

Translated by Donald Watson
and Derek Prouse

T0352478

CALDER

CALDER PUBLICATIONS
an imprint of

ALMA BOOKS LTD
Thornton House
Thornton Road
Wimbledon Village
London SW19 4NG
United Kingdom
www.almabooks.com
www.calderpublications.com

'The Killer' first published in French as *'Tueur sans gages'* in 1958;
'Rhinoceros' first published in French as *'Rhinocéros. Pièce en trois actes et quatre tableaux'* in 1959; 'Exit the King' first published in French as *'Le Roi se muert'* in 1963; and 'A Stroll in the Air' first published in French as *'Le Piéton de l'air'* in 1963.
'The Killer' (1960), 'Rhinoceros' (1960), 'Exit the King' (1963) and 'A Stroll in the Air' (1965) first published in these translations by John Calder (Publishers) Ltd.
This edition first published by Calder Publications in 2019
'Tueur sans gages' © Éditions Gallimard, Paris, 1958
'Rhinocéros. Pièce en trois actes et quatre tableaux' © Éditions Gallimard, Paris, 1959
'Le Roi se muert' © Éditions Gallimard, Paris, 1963
'Le Piéton de l'air' © Éditions Gallimard, Paris, 1963

Translation of 'The Killer', 'Exit the King' and 'A Stroll in the Air'
© Donald Watson, 2019
Translation of 'Rhinoceros' © Derek Prouse, 2019

Cover design by Will Dady

Printed and bound by CPI Group (UK) Ltd, Croydon, CR0 4YY

ISBN: 978-0-7145-4848-7

Contents

The Bérenger Plays

THE KILLER*

*First produced in Paris by José Quaglio at the
Théâtre Récamier on 27th February 1959*

Characters, Voices, Silhouettes

BÉRENGER, an average, middle-aged citizen
THE ARCHITECT, of ageless, bureaucratic age
ÉDOUARD, thirty-five, thin, nervous, darkly dressed, in mourning
THE KILLER
DANY, young typist, conventional pin-up
MOTHER PEEP
THE CLOCHARD, drunk
THE OWNER OF THE BISTRO (THE PATRON), middle-aged, fat,
    dark and hairy
THE CONCIERGE (preceded by THE VOICE OF THE CONCIERGE),
    typical concierge
THE DRUNK IN TOP HAT AND TAILS
THE OLD GENTLEMAN WITH THE LITTLE WHITE BEARD
FIRST POLICEMAN (1ST POL.)
SECOND POLICEMAN (2ND POL.)
THE ECHO
FIRST OLD MAN (1ST O.M.)
SECOND OLD MAN (2ND O.M.)
THE GROCER
VOICE OF THE CONCIERGE'S DOG
A MAN'S VOICE
SECOND MAN'S VOICE
TRUCK DRIVER'S VOICE
CAR DRIVER'S VOICE
SCHOOLMASTER'S VOICE
FIRST VOICE FROM THE STREET
SECOND VOICE (GRUFF) FROM THE STREET
THIRD VOICE (PIPING) FROM THE STREET
FOURTH VOICE FROM THE STREET
FIRST VOICE FROM BELOW
SECOND VOICE FROM BELOW

4

VOICE FROM THE RIGHT
VOICE FROM ABOVE
VOICE FROM THE LEFT
SECOND VOICE FROM THE LEFT
WOMAN'S VOICE FROM THE ENTRANCE
SILHOUETTE OF A MOTORCYCLIST ON HIS BICYCLE
POSTMAN'S VOICE (preceding the POSTMAN himself, if desired)
VOICES OF THE CROWD

Stage Directions

Several of these parts may be played by the same actors. Moreover, it is probable that all the voices in the second act will not be heard. Any cuts required may be made in the first half of Act II: it will all depend on the effectiveness of these voices and their absurd remarks. The director can choose those he likes. He should, however, try, if possible, to obtain stereophonic sound effects. In the second act it is also better to have the greatest possible number of figures appearing in silhouette on the other side of the window, as on a stage behind the stage. In any case, after the curtain has risen on the second act, some voices and sounds around the empty stage are indispensable – at least for a few minutes – in order to continue and, in a way, intensify the visual and aural atmosphere of street and city; this is first created at the end of Act I; it fades after the arrival of Bérenger and returns again in force at the start of Act III, to die right away at the end.

A few cuts could also be made in Act I, according to the power of the actor playing the part and his natural capacity to "put it over".

Bérenger's speech to the Killer at the end of the play (pp. 98–112) is one short act in itself. The text should be interpreted in such a way as to bring out the gradual breaking-down of Bérenger, his falling apart and the vacuity of his own rather commonplace morality, which collapses like a leaking balloon. In fact, Bérenger finds within himself, in spite of himself and against his own will, arguments in favour of the Killer.

5

Act One

No decor. An empty stage when the curtain rises. Later there will be, on the left of the stage, two garden chairs and a table, which the ARCHITECT will bring on himself. They should be near at hand in the wings.

The atmosphere for Act I will be created by the lighting only. At first, while the stage is still empty, the light is grey, like a dull November day or an afternoon in February. The faint sound of wind; perhaps you can see a dead leaf fluttering across the stage. In the distance the noise of a tram, vague outlines of houses; then, suddenly, the stage is brilliantly lit; a very bright, very white light; just this whiteness, and also the dense vivid blue of the sky. And so, after the grisaille, the lighting effects should simply be made up of white and blue, the only elements in the decor. The noise of the tram, the wind and the rain will have stopped at the very moment the light changes. The blue, the white, the silence and the empty stage should give a strange impression of peace. The audience must be given time to become aware of this. Not until a full minute has passed should the characters appear on the scene.

BÉRENGER comes on first, from the left, moving quickly. He stops in the centre of the stage and turns round briskly to face the ARCHITECT, who has followed him more slowly. BÉRENGER is wearing a grey overcoat, hat and scarf. The ARCHITECT is in a summer-weight jacket, light trousers, open-necked shirt and without a hat; under his arm he is carrying a briefcase, rather thick and heavy, like the one ÉDOUARD has in Act II.

BÉRENGER: Amazing! Amazing! It's extraordinary! As far as I can see, it's a miracle... (*Vague gesture of protest from the* ARCHITECT.) A miracle, or, as I don't suppose you're a religious man, you'd rather I called it a marvel! I congratulate you most warmly: it's a marvel, really quite marvellous – you're a marvellous architect!...

ARCHITECT: Oh... you're very kind...

BÉRENGER: No, no. I *want* to congratulate you. It's absolutely incredible: you've achieved the incredible! The real thing is quite beyond imagination.

ARCHITECT: It's the work I'm commissioned to do – part of my normal duties – what I specialize in.

BÉRENGER: Why, yes, of course, to be sure – you're an architect – a technician and a conscientious civil servant at one and the same time... Still, that doesn't explain everything. (*Looking round and staring at several fixed points on the stage:*) Beautiful – what a magnificent lawn – that flower-bed!... Oh, what flowers, appetizing as vegetables, and what vegetables, fragrant as flowers... and what a blue sky – what an amazingly blue sky. How wonderful it is! (*To the* ARCHITECT:) In all the cities of the world, all cities of a certain size, I'm sure there are civil servants, municipal architects like you, with the same duties as you, earning the same salary. But they're nowhere near achieving the same results. (*Gesture of the hand.*) Are you well paid? I'm sorry – perhaps I'm being indiscreet...

ARCHITECT: Please don't apologize... I'm fairly well paid – the scale is laid down. It's reasonable... It's all right.

BÉRENGER: But ingenuity like yours is worth its weight in gold. And what's more, I mean the price gold fetched before 1914... the real thing.

ARCHITECT (*with a modestly disclaiming gesture*): Oh—

BÉRENGER: Oh yes it is... You're the town architect, aren't you?... *Real* gold... After all, today gold has been devalued, like so many other things – it's paper gold...

ARCHITECT: Your surprise, your—

BÉRENGER: Call it my admiration; my enthusiasm!

ARCHITECT: Very well, your enthusiasm, then, touches me very deeply. I feel I must thank you, dear Monsieur... Bérenger. (*The* ARCHITECT *bows in thanks, after first searching one of his pockets for a card that doubtless bears the name of* BÉRENGER, *and as he bows he reads the name off the card.*)

BÉRENGER: Genuinely enthusiastic, quite genuinely. I'm not the flattering kind, I can tell you.

ARCHITECT (*ceremoniously, but unimpressed*): I am very highly honoured.

BÉRENGER: It's magnificent! (*He looks about him.*) I'd been told all about it, you see, but I didn't believe it... or rather, I wasn't told a thing about it, but I *knew,* I knew that somewhere in our dark and dismal city, in all its mournful, dusty, dirty districts, there was one that was bright and beautiful, this neighbourhood beyond compare, with its sunny streets and avenues bathed in light... this radiant city within a city which you've built...

ARCHITECT: It's a nucleus which is, or rather, was, in theory meant to be extended. I planned it all, by order of the City Council. I don't allow myself any personal initiative...

BÉRENGER (*continuing his monologue*): I believed in it, without believing; I knew without knowing! I was afraid to hope... hope – that's not a French word any more, or Turkish, or Polish... Belgian perhaps... and even then...

ARCHITECT: I see, I understand.

BÉRENGER: And yet, *here* I am. Your radiant city is *real*. No doubt of that. You can touch it with your fingers. The blue brilliance of it looks absolutely natural... blue and green... oh, that grass, those rose-pink flowers...

ARCHITECT: Yes, those pink flowers really are roses.

BÉRENGER: Real roses? (*He walks about the stage, pointing, smelling the flowers, etc.*) More blue and more green things, too... the colours of joy. And what peace, what peace!

ARCHITECT: That's the rule here, Monsieur... (*He reads off the card:*) Bérenger. It's all calculated, all intentional. Nothing was to be left to chance in this district; the weather here is always fine... And so the building plots always fetch... or rather, always used to fetch, a high price... the villas are built of the best materials... built to last, built with care.

BÉRENGER: I don't suppose it ever rains in these houses?

ARCHITECT: Definitely not! That's the least you can expect. Does it rain in yours?

BÉRENGER: Yes, I'm afraid it does.

ARCHITECT: It oughtn't to, even in your district. I'll send a man round.

BÉRENGER: Well, I suppose it doesn't really rain *inside*. Only in a manner of speaking. It's so damp, it's as if it *was* raining.

ARCHITECT: I see. Morally speaking. In any case, here in this district it never rains at all. And yet all the walls and all the roofs of the buildings you can see are damp-proof. It's a habit, a matter of form. Quite unnecessary, but it keeps up an old tradition.

BÉRENGER: You say it *never* rains? And all these things growing? This grass? And not a dead leaf on the trees, not a faded flower in the garden!

ARCHITECT: They're watered from below.

BÉRENGER: A technical marvel! Forgive me for being so astonished, a layman like me... (*With his handkerchief he is mopping the sweat from his brow.*)

ARCHITECT: Why don't you take your overcoat off? Carry it on your arm – you're too hot.

BÉRENGER: Why yes... I'm not at all cold any more... Thank you, thanks for the suggestion. (*He takes off his overcoat and puts it over his arm; he keeps his hat on his head. He looks up, with a gesture.*) The leaves on the trees are small enough for the light to filter through – but not too big, so as not to darken the front of the houses. I must say, it's amazing to think that in all the rest of the town the sky's as grey as the hair on an old woman's head, that there's dirty snow at the pavement's edge, and the wind blowing there. When I woke up this morning I was very cold. I was frozen. The radiators work so badly in my block of flats, especially on the ground floor. They work even worse when they don't make up the fire... So I mean to say...

(*A telephone bell rings, coming from the* ARCHITECT's *pocket; the* ARCHITECT *takes a receiver from it and listens; the telephone wire ends in his pocket.*)

ARCHITECT: Hullo?

BÉRENGER: Forgive me, Monsieur; I'm keeping you from your work...

ARCHITECT (*to the telephone*): Hullo? (*To* BÉRENGER:) Not a bit... I've kept an hour free to show you the district. No trouble at all. (*To the telephone*:) Hullo? Yes. I know about that. Let the assistant manager know. Right. Let him hold an investigation if he insists. *He* can make the official arrangements. I'm with Monsieur Bérenger, for the visit to the radiant city. (*He puts the machine back in his pocket. To* BÉRENGER, *who has taken a few steps away, lost in admiration*:) You were saying? Hey, where are you?

BÉRENGER: Here. I'm sorry. What was I saying? Oh yes... Oh, it doesn't really matter now.

ARCHITECT: Go ahead. Say it anyway.

BÉRENGER: I was saying... oh yes... in my district, especially where I live, everything is damp: the coal, the bread, the wind, the wine, the walls, the air, and even the fire. What a job I had this morning, getting up. I had to make a big effort. It was really painful. I'd never have made up my mind if the sheets hadn't been damp too. I never imagined that, suddenly, as if by magic, I should find myself in the midst of spring, in the middle of April – the April of my dreams... my earliest dreams...

ARCHITECT: Dreams! (*Shrugging his shoulders.*) Anyhow, it would have been better if you'd come sooner, come before—

BÉRENGER (*interrupting him*): Ah yes, I've lost a lot of time, that's true...

(BÉRENGER *and the* ARCHITECT *go on walking about the stage.* BÉRENGER *should give the impression he is walking through tree-lined avenues and parks. The* ARCHITECT *follows him, more slowly. At times* BÉRENGER *will have to turn round to speak to the* ARCHITECT *in a louder voice. He should appear to be waiting for the* ARCHITECT *to come closer. Pointing to empty space*:)

BÉRENGER: *There's* an attractive house! The façade is delightful – such a wonderfully pure style. Eighteenth century? No, fifteenth or the end of the nineteenth? It's classical, anyway, and then it's so neat, so smart... Ah yes, I've lost a lot of time – is it too late?... No... Yes... No, it may not be too late – what do you think?

ARCHITECT: I haven't given the matter much thought.

BÉRENGER: I'm thirty-five years old, Monsieur, thirty-five... Actually, to tell the truth, I'm forty... forty-five... perhaps a little more.

ARCHITECT (*consulting the card*): We know. Your age is on the card. We have files on everyone.

BÉRENGER: Really? Oh!

ARCHITECT: It's quite usual – we have to have them for the record – but don't worry: the code provides no penalties for that kind of prevarication, not for vanity.

BÉRENGER: Thank goodness for that! Anyway, if I only admit to thirty-five, it's certainly not to deceive my fellow citizens – what's it matter to them? It's to deceive myself. In this way I act on myself by suggestion – I believe myself to be younger, I cheer myself up...

ARCHITECT: It's only human, only natural. (*The pocket telephone rings; the* ARCHITECT *takes it out again.*)

BÉRENGER: Oh, what nice little stones on the paths!

ARCHITECT (*to the telephone*): Hullo?... A woman? Take a description of her. Write it down. Send it to the statistics department...

BÉRENGER (*pointing to the corner of the stage on the left*): What's that over there?

ARCHITECT (*to the telephone*): No, no, no, nothing else to report. All the time *I'm* here, nothing else *can* happen. (*He puts the receiver back in his pocket. To* BÉRENGER:) I'm sorry – I'm listening now.

BÉRENGER (*as before*): What's that over there?

ARCHITECT: Oh, that... It's a greenhouse.

BÉRENGER: A greenhouse?

ARCHITECT: Yes. For the flowers that can't get used to a temperate climate – the flowers that like the cold. We've created a wintry climate for them. Now and again we have a little storm...

BÉRENGER: Ah, everything's been thought of… yes, Monsieur, I could be sixty years old, seventy, eighty, a hundred and twenty – how do I know?

ARCHITECT: Morally speaking!

BÉRENGER: It can be interpreted physically too. It's psychosomatic… Am I talking nonsense?

ARCHITECT: Not particularly. Like everyone else.

BÉRENGER: I feel old. Time is, above all, subjective. Or rather I *used* to feel old. Since this morning I'm a new man. I'm sure I'm becoming myself again. The world's becoming itself again; it's all thanks to *your* power. Your magic light…

ARCHITECT: My electric light!

BÉRENGER: …Your radiant city. (*He points quite nearby.*) It's the power of those immaculate walls covered with roses, your masterpiece! Ah, yes, yes, yes!… Nothing's really lost – I'm sure of that now… Now, in fact, I *do* remember, two or three people did tell me about the smiling city; some said it was quite nearby, others that it was far away, that it was easy to get to, hard to find, that it was a district specially reserved—

ARCHITECT: Not true!

BÉRENGER: —That there was no means of transport—

ARCHITECT: Nonsense. There's a tram stop over there, at the end of the main thoroughfare.

BÉRENGER: Yes, of course, of course! I know *now*. For a long time, I tell you, I tried consciously or unconsciously to find the way. I would walk right to the end of a street, and then realize it was a dead end. I'd follow a wall or a fence until I reached the river far from the bridge, away beyond the market and the gates of the town. Or else I'd meet some friends on the way who hadn't seen me since our army days; I'd be forced to stop and chat to them until it was too late and I had to go home. Still, what does it matter now? I'm *here*. My worries are over.

ARCHITECT: It was really so simple. You only had to drop me a line, write an official letter to the municipal offices, and one of my departments would have sent you all the necessary information by registered post.

BÉRENGER: Why yes, I only needed to think of that! Oh well, no good crying over lost years...

ARCHITECT: How did you set about finding the way today?

BÉRENGER: Pure accident. I just took the tram.

ARCHITECT: What did I tell you?

BÉRENGER: Took the wrong tram – I meant to take another – I was sure it wasn't going the right way, and yet it *was,* by mistake – a lucky mistake...

ARCHITECT: Lucky?

BÉRENGER: No? Not lucky? But it *was*. Very, very lucky.

ARCHITECT: Oh well, you'll see for yourself – later.

BÉRENGER: I've seen already. I'm firmly convinced.

ARCHITECT: Anyway, remember you must always go as far as the terminus. Whatever the circumstances. All trams lead this way: it's the depot.

BÉRENGER: I know. The tram brought me here, to this stop. Although I hadn't been here before, I recognized everything at once – the avenues and the houses all blossoming, and you, looking as if you expected me.

ARCHITECT: I'd been informed.

BÉRENGER: It's such a transformation! It's as though I was far away in the south – two or three thousand miles away. Another universe, a world transfigured! And just that very short journey to get here – a journey that isn't *really*, since you might say it takes place in the same place... (*He laughs; then, embarrassed:*) Forgive me – that wasn't very funny.

ARCHITECT: Don't look so upset. I've heard worse. I'll put it down to your state of bliss...

BÉRENGER: I've no mind for science. I suppose that's why, in spite of your very pertinent explanations, *I* can't explain how the weather can always be fine here! Perhaps – this may have made it easier for you – perhaps it's a more sheltered spot? And yet it's not surrounded by hills to protect it from bad weather! Besides, hills don't chase the clouds away or stop it raining – everyone knows that. Is it that there are bright, warm waves of air coming from a fifth point of the compass or some third stratum of the upper air? No, I suppose there aren't. Everyone would know about it. I'm really stupid. There's no breeze, although the air smells good. I must say it's odd, Monsieur – it's very odd!

ARCHITECT (*giving the authoritative information*): I tell you, there's nothing unusual about it: it's a technical matter! So try and understand. You ought to have taken an Adult Education course. It's just that this is a little island... with concealed ventilators I copied from the ones in those oases that crop up all over the place in the desert, where suddenly out of the dry sand you see amazing cities rising up, smothered with dewy roses, girdled with springs and rivers and lakes...

BÉRENGER: Oh yes... That's true. You mean those cities which are also called mirages. I've read explorers' tales about them. You see, I'm not completely uneducated. Mirages... there's nothing more real than a mirage. Flowers on fire, trees in flame, pools of light – that's all there really is that matters. I'm sure of it. And over there? What's that?

ARCHITECT: Over where? Where? Oh, over there?

BÉRENGER: Looks like an ornamental pool.

(*By means of the lighting, the vague outline of an ornamental pool appears at the back of the stage just as he says these words.*)

ARCHITECT: Er... yes, it *is* a pool. You recognized it. It's a pool, all right. (*He consults his watch.*) I think I still have a few minutes.

BÉRENGER: Can we go and see?

ARCHITECT: You want to have a closer look? (*He appears to hesitate.*) Very well. If you insist, I'll have to show it you.

BÉRENGER: Or instead... I don't know what to choose... It's all so beautiful... I like ornamental pools, but I rather like the look of that flowering hawthorn too. If you don't mind, we can look at the pool later...

ARCHITECT: As you like.

BÉRENGER: I love hawthorn bushes.

ARCHITECT: You've only to make up your mind.

BÉRENGER: Yes, yes, let's go over to the hawthorn.

ARCHITECT: I'm completely at your service.
BÉRENGER: One can't see everything at once.
ARCHITECT: True enough.

(*The pool disappears. They walk a few steps.*)

BÉRENGER: What a sweet smell! You know, Monsieur, I... forgive me
for talking about myself... one can say anything to an architect;
he understands everything.
ARCHITECT: Do please carry on. Don't be shy.
BÉRENGER: Thank you! You know, I do so need another life, a new life.
Different surroundings, a different setting. A different setting – you'd
think that's not much to ask, and that... with money, for example.
ARCHITECT: No, not at all...
BÉRENGER: Yes, yes, you're too polite... A setting, *that's* just super-
ficial, an artistic consideration, unless it's – how shall I say – a
setting, a background that would answer some profound need
inside, which would be somehow...
ARCHITECT: I see, I see...
BÉRENGER: ...the projection, the continuation of the universe inside
you. Only, to project this universe within, some outside help is
needed: some kind of material, physical light, a world that is
objectively new. Gardens, blue sky or the spring, which corre-
sponds to the universe inside and offers a chance of recognition,
which is like a translation or an anticipation of that universe, or
a mirror in which its own smile could be reflected... in which it
can find itself again and say: that's what I am in reality and I'd
forgotten – a smiling being in a smiling world... Come to think
of it, it's quite wrong to talk of a world within and a world
without, separate worlds; there's an initial impulse, of course,
which starts from us, and when it can't project itself, when it
can't fulfil itself objectively, when there's not total agreement
between myself inside and myself outside, then it's a catastrophe,
a universal contradiction, a schism.
ARCHITECT (*scratching his head*): What a vocabulary you have. We
don't talk the same language.

BÉRENGER: I felt I couldn't go on living, and yet I couldn't die. Luckily it's all going to be different now.

ARCHITECT: Don't get too excited!

BÉRENGER: I'm sorry. I get carried away.

ARCHITECT: That's characteristic of you. You're one of those poetic personalities. Since they exist, I suppose they must be necessary.

BÉRENGER: Year after year of dirty snow and bitter winds, of a climate indifferent to human beings... streets and houses and whole districts of people who aren't really unhappy, but worse, who are neither happy nor unhappy, people who are ugly because they're neither ugly nor beautiful, creatures that are dismally neutral, who long without longings as though they're unconscious, unconsciously suffering from being alive. But *I* was aware of the sickness of life. Perhaps because I'm more intelligent or, just the opposite, *less* intelligent, not so wise, not so resigned, not so patient. Is that a fault or a virtue?

ARCHITECT (*showing signs of impatience*): Depends.

BÉRENGER: You can't tell. The winter of the soul! I'm not expressing myself clearly, am I?

ARCHITECT: I'm not capable of judging. It's not one of my duties. The logic department sees to that.

BÉRENGER: Perhaps you don't appreciate my lyrical side?

ARCHITECT (*drily*): Why yes, of course!

BÉRENGER: Well, you see: once upon a time there was a blazing fire inside me. The cold could do nothing against it – a youthfulness, a spring no autumn could touch; a source of light, glowing wells of joy that seemed inexhaustible. Not happiness; I mean joy, felicity, which made it possible for me to live...

(*The telephone rings in the* ARCHITECT'*s pocket.*)

There was enormous energy there...

(*The* ARCHITECT *takes the telephone from his pocket.*)

A force... it must have been the life force, mustn't it?

ARCHITECT (*holding the receiver to his ear*): Hullo?

BÉRENGER: And then it grew weaker and all died away.

ARCHITECT (*to the telephone*): Hullo? Fine, fine, fine!… Don't tell me that only happened yesterday!

BÉRENGER (*continuing his monologue*): Oh, it must go back… I don't know how long… a long, long time ago…

(*The* ARCHITECT *puts the receiver back in his pocket and shows fresh signs of impatience; he goes into the wings on the left and brings on a chair, which he sets down in the left-hand corner, where the greenhouse was supposed to be.*)

Must be centuries ago… or perhaps only a few years; perhaps it was yesterday…

ARCHITECT: I must ask you to excuse me: I'm afraid I must go to my office. I've some urgent matters to attend to. (*He goes off left for a moment.*)

BÉRENGER (*alone*): Oh… Monsieur, really, I'm so sorry, I—

ARCHITECT (*coming back with a small table, which he sets in front of the chair; he sits down, takes the telephone from his pocket, puts it* on *the table and lays his briefcase open before him*): It's for me to apologize.

BÉRENGER: Oh, no! I feel terrible about it!

ARCHITECT: Don't let it upset you too much. I have two ears: one for duty, and the other I reserve for you. One eye too, for you. The other's for the district.

BÉRENGER: It won't tire you too much?

ARCHITECT: Don't worry. I'm used to it. All right, carry on… (*He takes from his briefcase, or pretends to, some files which he lays out on the table and opens.*) I'm attending to my files, and to you, too… You were saying you didn't know how long ago it was this force died away!

BÉRENGER: It certainly wasn't yesterday. (*He goes on walking, from now on, round and round the* ARCHITECT, *who is plunged in his files.*) It's such an old story; I've almost forgotten; it might have been an illusion – and yet it can't be an illusion when I still feel the loss of it so badly.

ARCHITECT (*in his files*): Go on.

BÉRENGER: I can't analyse the feeling – I don't even know if the experience I had can be communicated. It wasn't very frequent. It happened five or six, ten times, perhaps, in my life. Often enough, though, to fill to overflowing Heaven knows what secret reservoirs of my mind with joy and conviction. When I was in a gloomy mood, the memory of that dazzling radiance, that glowing feeling, gave fresh life to the force within me, to those reasonless reasons for living and loving... loving what?... Loving everything wholeheartedly ...

ARCHITECT (*to the telephone*): Hullo, the supplies have run out!

BÉRENGER: Yes, I'm afraid they have, Monsieur.

ARCHITECT (*who has hung up*): I wasn't saying that to you – it's about my files.

BÉRENGER: It's true for me too, Monsieur: the reservoirs are empty. I'm not economically sound any more. My supplies of light have run out. I'll try and explain... I'm not imposing on you?

ARCHITECT: It's going in the record. That's my job. Carry on, don't mind me.

BÉRENGER: It happened as spring was ending, or perhaps in the very first days of summer, just before midday; it all came about in a way that was perfectly simple and perfectly unexpected as well. The sky was as pure as the one you've managed to cover your radiant city with, Monsieur. Yes, it happened in extraordinary silence, in a long, long second of silence...

ARCHITECT (*still in his files*): Right. Fine.

BÉRENGER: The last time I must have been seventeen or eighteen, and I was in a little country town... which one?... I wonder which it was?... Somewhere in the South, I think... It's of no importance anyway – the place hardly counts. I was walking along a narrow street, which was both old and new, with low houses on either side, all white and tucked away in courtyards or little gardens, with wooden fences, painted... pale yellow

– was it pale yellow? I was all alone in the street. I was walking along by the fences and the houses, and it was fine, not too hot, with the sun above, high above my head in the blue of the sky. I was walking fast, but where was I going? I don't remember. I was deeply aware of the unique joy of being alive. I'd forgotten everything; all I could think of was those houses, that deep sky and that sun, which seemed to be coming nearer, within my grasp, in a world that was made for me.

ARCHITECT (*consulting his watch*): She's not here yet! Late again!

BÉRENGER (*continuing*): Suddenly the joy became more intense, breaking all bounds! And then, oh! what indescribable bliss took hold of me! The light grew more and more brilliant, and still lost none of its softness; it was so dense you could almost breathe it; it had become the air itself; you could drink it like clear water... How can I convey its incomparable brilliance?... It's as if there were four suns in the sky...

ARCHITECT (*speaking into the telephone*): Hullo? Have you seen my secretary today? There's a pile of work waiting. (*He hangs up angrily.*)

BÉRENGER: The houses I was passing were like immaterial shades ready to melt away in that mightier light which governed all.

ARCHITECT: I'll make her pay a nice fat fine!

BÉRENGER (*to the* ARCHITECT): You see what I mean?

ARCHITECT (*vaguely*): More or less. Your story seems clearer now.

BÉRENGER: Not a man in the street, not a cat, not a sound – there was only me.

(*The telephone bell rings.*)

And yet I didn't suffer from being alone, I didn't feel lonely.

ARCHITECT (*to the telephone*): Well, has she arrived?

BÉRENGER: My own peace and light spread in their turn throughout the world; I was filling the universe with a kind of ethereal energy. Not an empty corner; everything was a mingling of airiness and plenitude, perfectly balanced.

ARCHITECT (*to the telephone*): At last! Put her on the line.

BÉRENGER: A song of triumph rose from the depths of my being:
I *was,* I realized I had always *been,* that I was no longer going
to die.

ARCHITECT (*on the telephone, mastering his irritation*): I must
say I'm very pleased to hear your voice, Mademoiselle. It's
about time. What?

BÉRENGER: Everything was virgin, purified, discovered anew. I
had a feeling of inexpressible surprise, yet at the same time it
was all quite familiar to me.

ARCHITECT (*on the telephone*): What do you mean by that,
Mademoiselle?

BÉRENGER: That's *it,* all right, I said to myself, that's *it,* all
right... I can't tell *you* what I mean by "it", but I promise you,
Monsieur, *I* understood quite well what I meant.

ARCHITECT (*on the telephone*): I don't understand you,
Mademoiselle. You've no reason to be dissatisfied with us –
I should say the boot's on the other foot.

BÉRENGER: I felt I was there at the gates, at the very centre of the
universe... That must seem contradictory to you?

ARCHITECT (*on the telephone*): One moment, please. (*To*
BÉRENGER:) I follow you, I follow you, don't worry, I get the
general idea. (*On the telephone*:) Hullo, yes?

BÉRENGER: I walked and ran and cried: I *am,* I *am, everything* is,
everything *is!*... Oh, I'm sure I could have flown away, I'd lost
so much weight; I was lighter than the blue sky I was breathing... The slightest effort, the tiniest little leap would have
been enough... I should have taken off... I'm sure I should.

ARCHITECT (*on the telephone, banging his fist on the table*): Now
that's going too far! What's made you feel like this?

BÉRENGER: If I didn't do it, it's because I was too happy; it didn't
even enter my head.

ARCHITECT (*on the telephone*): You want to leave the Service?
Think carefully before you resign. You're abandoning a brilliant career for no good reason! After all, with us your future
is insured, *and* your life... your life! You aren't afraid of the
danger!

BÉRENGER: And suddenly – or rather, gradually... no, it was all at once... I don't know, I only know that everything went grey and pale and neutral again. Not really, of course – the sky was still pure, but it wasn't the same purity; it wasn't the same sun, the same morning, the same spring. It was like a conjuring trick. The light was the same as on any other day: ordinary daylight.

ARCHITECT (*on the telephone*): You can't stand the situation any longer? That's childish. I refuse your resignation. Come and clear up the day's mail anyway, and you can explain yourself. I'm waiting for you. (*He hangs up.*)

BÉRENGER: There was a kind of chaotic vacuum inside me; I was overcome with the immense sadness you feel at a moment of tragic and intolerable separation. The old gossips came out of their courtyards and split my eardrums with their screeching voices, the dogs barked, and I felt lost among all those people, all those *things*...

ARCHITECT: She's a stupid girl. (*He stands up.*) Still, it's her own business. There are thousands more after her job... (*he sits down again*) and a life without peril.

BÉRENGER: And since then, it's been perpetual November, perpetual twilight – twilight in the morning, twilight at midnight, twilight at noon. The light of dawn has gone! And to think we call this civilization!

ARCHITECT: We're still waiting!

BÉRENGER: It's only the memory of what happened that's helped me to go on living in this grey city.

ARCHITECT (*to* BÉRENGER): You got over it, just the same, this... melancholy?

BÉRENGER: Not entirely. But I promised myself I wouldn't forget. I told myself that on the days I felt sad and nervous, depressed and anxious, I would always remember that glorious moment. It would help me to bear everything, give me a reason for living, and be a comfort to me. For years I felt sure...

ARCHITECT: Sure of what?

BÉRENGER: Sure I'd been sure... but the memory wasn't strong enough to stand the test of time.

ARCHITECT: But it seems to me...

BÉRENGER: You're wrong, Monsieur. The memory I've kept is nothing now but the memory of a memory, like a thought grown foreign to me, like a tale told by another, a faded picture whose brightness I could no longer restore. The water in the well had dried up and I was dying of thirst... But *you* must understand me perfectly – this light is in *you* too – it's the same as mine, because (*a broad gesture taking in empty space*) you have obviously recreated and materialized it. This radiant district must have sprung from you... You've given me back that forgotten light... almost. I'm terribly grateful to you. In my name and in the name of all who live here, I thank you.

ARCHITECT: Why yes, of course.

BÉRENGER: And with you, it's not the unreal product of an overheated imagination. These are real houses and stones and bricks and cement. (*Touching empty space.*) It's concrete, solid, tangible. Yours is the right system, your methods are rational.

(*He still appears to be feeling the walls.*)

ARCHITECT (*also feeling the invisible walls, after leaving his corner*): It's brick, yes, and good brick too. Cement: the best quality.

BÉRENGER (*as before*): No, no, it's not just a dream this time.

ARCHITECT (*still feeling the invisible walls, then stopping with a sigh*): Perhaps it would have been better if it had been a dream. It's all the same to me. I'm a civil servant. But for a lot of other people, reality, unlike dreams, can turn into a nightmare...

BÉRENGER (*who also stops feeling the invisible walls, greatly surprised*): Why, what do you mean?

(*The ARCHITECT returns to his files.*)

In any case, I'm glad my memory is real and I can feel it with my fingers. I'm as young as I was a hundred years ago.

I can fall in love again... (*Calling to the wings on the right:*) Mademoiselle, oh, Mademoiselle, will you marry me?

(*Just as he finishes this last sentence,* DANY *comes in from the right. She is the* ARCHITECT's *blonde secretary.*)

ARCHITECT (*to* DANY *as she enters*): Oh, so there you are! I've got something to say to you!

DANY (*to* BÉRENGER): Do give me time to think it over!

ARCHITECT (*to* BÉRENGER): My secretary, Mademoiselle Dany. (*To* DANY:) Monsieur Bérenger.

DANY (*absentmindedly, rather nervously, to* BÉRENGER): Pleased to meet you.

ARCHITECT (*to* DANY): In the Civil Service we don't like people to be late, Mademoiselle, or impulsive either.

BÉRENGER (*to* DANY, *who goes and sets her typewriter on the table, and fetches a chair from the wings on the left*): Mademoiselle Dany – what a lovely name! Have you thought it over yet? The answer's "Yes", isn't it?

DANY (*to the* ARCHITECT): I've made up my mind to leave, Monsieur. I need a holiday, I'm tired.

ARCHITECT (*sweetly*): If that's all it is, you should have told me. We can arrange something. Would you like three days off?

BÉRENGER (*to* DANY): It is "Yes", isn't it? Oh, you're so beautiful.

DANY (*to the* ARCHITECT): I must have a much longer rest than that.

ARCHITECT (*to* DANY): I'll apply to the Departmental Board; I can get you a week – half-pay.

DANY (*to the* ARCHITECT): I need a permanent rest.

BÉRENGER (*to* DANY): I like fair girls, with glowing faces, bright eyes and long legs!

ARCHITECT: Permanent? I see!...

DANY (*to the* ARCHITECT): I simply must do some different work. I can't stand the situation any longer.

ARCHITECT: Oh, so that's it.

DANY (*to the* ARCHITECT): Yes, Monsieur.

BÉRENGER (*to* DANY, *enthusiastically*): You said yes! Oh, Mademoiselle Dany...

ARCHITECT (*to* BÉRENGER): She's talking to me, not to you.

DANY (*to the* ARCHITECT): I always hoped things might change, but they're still the same. I don't see any chance of improvement.

ARCHITECT: Now think, I'm telling you again, think carefully! If you no longer belong to our organization, the Civil Service can no longer take you under its wing. Do you realize? Are you fully aware of the dangers that lie in wait?

DANY: Yes, Monsieur; no one knows more about that than I do.

ARCHITECT: You're willing to take the risk?

DANY (*to the* ARCHITECT): I am, yes, Monsieur.

BÉRENGER (*to* DANY): Say yes to me too. You say it so nicely.

ARCHITECT (*to* DANY): Then I refuse all responsibility. You have been warned.

DANY (*to the* ARCHITECT): I'm not deaf! I understand – you needn't repeat yourself!

BÉRENGER (*to the* ARCHITECT): Isn't she sweet! Delightful. (*To* DANY:) Mademoiselle, Mademoiselle, we'll live here, in this district, in this villa! We'll be happy at last.

ARCHITECT (*to* DANY): So you really won't change your mind? It's a crazy, headstrong thing to do!

DANY (*to the* ARCHITECT): No, Monsieur.

BÉRENGER (*to* DANY): Oh, you didn't say "No"?

ARCHITECT (*to* BÉRENGER): She said "No" to *me*.

BÉRENGER: Ah, that's all right, then!

DANY (*to the* ARCHITECT): I hate the Civil Service! I detest your beautiful district! I can't stand any more, I can't bear it!

ARCHITECT (*to* DANY): It's not *my* district.

BÉRENGER (*to* DANY, *who is not listening*): Give me your answer, beautiful demoiselle, Dany the magnificent, Dany the sublime... May I call you Dany?

ARCHITECT (*to* DANY): I can't stop you resigning, so you'd better go, but keep a sharp lookout. That's a piece of friendly advice I'm giving you – fatherly advice.

BÉRENGER (*to the* ARCHITECT): Were you decorated for your achievements in urban development? You should have been.

DANY (*to the* ARCHITECT): If you like, I'll finish typing the letters before I go.

BÉRENGER (*to the* ARCHITECT): If I'd been the Mayor, I'd have decorated you, all right.

ARCHITECT (*to* BÉRENGER): Thank you. (*To* DANY:) You needn't bother, thank you. I'll manage.

BÉRENGER (*smelling imaginary flowers*): What a lovely smell! Are they lilies?

ARCHITECT: No, violets.

DANY (*to the* ARCHITECT): I was only trying to be helpful.

BÉRENGER (*to the* ARCHITECT): May I pick some for Dany?

ARCHITECT: If you like.

BÉRENGER (*to* DANY): You don't know, my dear, dear Dany, dear fiancée, how I've longed for you.

DANY: If that's how you take it... (*In some irritation, she briskly puts her things in order and picks up her typewriter.*)

BÉRENGER (*to* DANY): We'll live in a wonderful flat, full of sunshine.

DANY (*to the* ARCHITECT): Surely you can understand I can't go on sharing the responsibility. It's too much for me.

ARCHITECT: The Civil Service is not responsible for that.

DANY (*to the* ARCHITECT): You ought to be able to realize...

ARCHITECT (*to* DANY): It's not for you to give *me* advice. That's *my* business. But I warn you again: watch your step.

DANY (*to the* ARCHITECT): I'm not taking advice from you either. It's *my* business too.

ARCHITECT (*to* DANY): All right, all right!

DANY: Au revoir, Monsieur.

ARCHITECT: Goodbye.

DANY (*to* BÉRENGER): Au revoir, Monsieur.

BÉRENGER (*running after* DANY, *who is making for the exit on the right*): Dany, Mademoiselle, don't go before you've given me an answer... At least, please take these violets.

(DANY *goes out.* BÉRENGER *stands near the exit, his arms hanging loosely.*)

Oh... (*To the* ARCHITECT:) You understand the human heart; when a woman doesn't answer "Yes" or "No", it means "Yes", doesn't it? (*Calling towards the wings on the right:*) You'll be my inspiration, my muse. I'll really work. (*While a slight echo is heard repeating the previous words,* BÉRENGER *moves two paces nearer the* ARCHITECT *and indicates the empty space:*) I'll not give up. I'm settling down here with Dany. I'll buy that white house, with the trees and grass all round – the one that looks abandoned by the builders... I haven't much money – you'll let me pay in instalments?

ARCHITECT: If you really want to! If you're not going to change your mind.

BÉRENGER: I'm determined. Why should I change my mind? With your permission, I want to be a citizen of the radiant city. I'll move in tomorrow, even if the house isn't quite ready yet.

ARCHITECT (*looking at his watch*): Twenty-five to one.

(*Suddenly, there is the noise of a stone falling a few paces from* BÉRENGER, *between him and the* ARCHITECT.)

BÉRENGER: Oh! (*Starts back a little.*) A stone!

ARCHITECT (*impassively, without surprise*): Yes, a stone!

BÉRENGER (*leans forwards and picks up the stone, then straightens up and inspects it in his hand*): It *is* a stone!

ARCHITECT: Haven't you seen one before?

BÉRENGER: Yes... of course... What? They're throwing stones at us?

ARCHITECT: A stone – just one stone, not stones!

BÉRENGER: I understand: they threw a stone at us.

ARCHITECT: Don't worry. They're not really going to stone you. It didn't touch you, did it?

BÉRENGER: It could have.

ARCHITECT: No, no, of course it couldn't. It *cannot* touch you. It's only teasing.

BÉRENGER: Oh, I see!... If it's only teasing, then I suppose I can take a joke! (*He drops the stone.*) I don't easily take offence. Especially in these surroundings, it takes a lot to upset you. She will write to me, won't she? (*He casts a rather anxious look about.*) It's so restful here, and intended to be that way. Almost a little too restful, don't you think? Why can't you see a single soul in the streets? We really are the only people out!... Oh yes, of course, it must be because it's lunchtime. Everyone's eating. But why can't we hear any laughter at table, any clinking of glasses? Not a sound, not a whisper, not a voice singing. And all the windows are shut! (*He looks round the empty stage, surprised.*) I didn't notice before. It would be understandable in a dream, but not when it's real.

ARCHITECT: I'd have thought it was obvious.

(*The sound of broken window panes is heard.*)

BÉRENGER: What's happening now?

ARCHITECT (*taking the telephone from his pocket again; to* BÉRENGER): That's easy. You don't know what it is? A window's been smashed. It must have been broken by a stone. (*The noise of another window being smashed;* BÉRENGER *starts back more violently. On the telephone:*) Two broken windows.

BÉRENGER: What's it all about? A joke, I suppose? Two jokes! (*Another stone knocks his hat off; he picks the hat up quickly and puts it back on his head.*) Three jokes!

ARCHITECT (*putting the telephone back in his pocket and frowning*): Now listen, Monsieur. You and I are not businessmen. We're civil servants, bureaucrats. So I must tell you officially, bureaucratically, that the house that looked abandoned really has been abandoned by the builders. The police have suspended all construction work. I knew this before, but I've just had it confirmed by phone.

BÉRENGER: What?... Why?

ARCHITECT: It's an unnecessary step to take, anyway. You're the only one who wants to buy any property now. I don't suppose you know what's going on...

BÉRENGER: What *is* going on?

ARCHITECT: Actually, the people who live in this district want to leave it...

BÉRENGER: Leave the radiant district? The people want to leave it...

ARCHITECT: Yes. They've no other homes to go to. Otherwise they'd *all* have packed their bags. Perhaps, too, they make it a point of honour not to run away. They'd rather stay and hide in their beautiful flats. They only come out when they really have to, in groups of ten or fifteen at a time. And even that doesn't make for safety...

BÉRENGER: What's so dangerous? Just another joke, isn't it! Why are you looking so serious? You're clouding the whole place over! You're trying to frighten me!...

ARCHITECT (*solemnly*): A civil servant doesn't make jokes.

BÉRENGER (*terribly upset*): What are you talking about? You're really upsetting me! It's you who just threw that stone at me... Morally speaking, of course! Oh dear, and I already felt I'd taken root in these surroundings! Now all the brilliance they offer is dead, and they're nothing more than an empty frame... I feel shut out!

ARCHITECT: I'm very sorry. Steady there!

BÉRENGER: I've a horrible premonition.

ARCHITECT: I'm so sorry, so sorry.

(*During the previous dialogue and what comes after, the acting should never lose a touch of irony, which should especially balance the poignant moments.*)

BÉRENGER: I can feel the darkness spreading inside me again!

ARCHITECT (*drily*): Sorry, very sorry, so sorry.

BÉRENGER: Please, you must explain. I was so hoping to spend a nice day!... I was so happy a few moments ago.

ARCHITECT (*pointing*): You see this ornamental pool?

(*The pool reappears, clearly this time.*)

BÉRENGER: It's the same one we went past already, just now!

ARCHITECT: I wanted to show you then... You preferred the hawthorns... (*He points to the pool again:*) It's there, in the pool, every day, that two or three people are found drowned.

BÉRENGER: Drowned?

ARCHITECT: Come and look if you don't believe me. Come on, come closer!

BÉRENGER (*accompanying the* ARCHITECT *to the place indicated, or right to the front of the stage, while the objects referred to appear as they are mentioned*): Go nearer!

ARCHITECT: Look! What do you see?

BÉRENGER: Oh, Heavens!

ARCHITECT: Come on now, no fainting – be a man!

BÉRENGER (*with an effort*): I can see... it's not true... Yes, I can see, on the water, the dead body of a little boy, floating in his hoop... a little chap of five or six... He's clutching the stick in his hand... Next to him the bloated corpse of an officer in the engineers in full uniform...

ARCHITECT: There are even three today. (*Pointing*) Over there!

BÉRENGER: It's a plant in the water!

ARCHITECT: Look again.

BÉRENGER: Good God!... Yes... I see! It's red hair streaming up from the bottom, stuck to the marble edge of the pool. How horrible! It must be a woman.

ARCHITECT (*shrugging his shoulders*): Obviously. And one's a man. And the other's a child. We don't know any more than that, either.

BÉRENGER: Perhaps it's the boy's mother! Poor devils! Why didn't you tell me before?

ARCHITECT: But I told you! You were always stopping me, always admiring the beautiful surroundings.

BÉRENGER: Poor devils! (*Violently:*) Who did it?

ARCHITECT: The murderer, the thug. Always the same elusive character.

BÉRENGER: But our lives are in danger! Let's go! (*He takes to his heels, runs a few yards across the stage and comes back to the* ARCHITECT, *who has not moved.*) Let's go! (*He takes flight again, but runs round and round the* ARCHITECT, *who takes out a cigarette and lights it. A shot is heard.*) He's shooting!

ARCHITECT: Don't be afraid. You're in no danger while you're with me.

BÉRENGER: What about that shot? Oh, no... no... You don't make me feel safer! (*He moves restlessly about and starts shaking.*)

ARCHITECT: It's only a game... Yes... Just now, it's only a game, to tease you! I'm the City Architect, a municipal civil servant; he doesn't attack the Civil Service. When I retire, it'll be different, but for the moment...

BÉRENGER: Let's go. Get away from here. I can't wait to leave your beautiful district...

ARCHITECT: There you are, you see – you *have* changed your mind!

BÉRENGER: You mustn't hold it against me!

ARCHITECT: I don't care. I haven't been asked to detail volunteers and compel them to live here by choice. No one's obliged to live dangerously if he doesn't want that sort of life!... When the district's completely depopulated, they'll pull it down.

BÉRENGER (*still hurrying round and round the* ARCHITECT): Depopulated?

ARCHITECT: People will decide to leave it in the end... or they'll all be killed. Oh, it'll take a bit of time...

BÉRENGER: Let's be off, quick! (*He goes round and round, faster and faster, with his head well down.*) The rich aren't always happy either, nor are the people who live in the residential districts... or the radiant ones... There are no radiant ones!... It's even worse than the other districts, in ours, the busy crowded ones!... Oh, Monsieur, I feel so upset about it. I feel shattered, stunned... My tiredness has come on again... There's no point in living! What's the good of it all – what's the good if it's only to bring us to this? Stop it – you must stop it, Superintendent.

31

ARCHITECT: Easy to say.

BÉRENGER: I suppose you *are* the police superintendent of the district too?

ARCHITECT: As a matter of fact, that is also one of my duties. It always is for special architects like me.

BÉRENGER: You're really hoping to arrest him before you retire?

ARCHITECT (*coldly annoyed*): Naturally, we're doing all we can!... Look out – not that way: you'll get lost! You're always going round in circles, going back in your own tracks.

BÉRENGER (*pointing quite close to him*): Ooh! Is that still the same pool?

ARCHITECT: One's enough for him.

BÉRENGER: Are those the same bodies as just now?

ARCHITECT: Three a day is a fair average – what more do you want?

BÉRENGER: Show me the way!... Let's go!...

ARCHITECT (*taking him by the arm and guiding him*): This way.

BÉRENGER: And the day started so well! I shall always see those people drowned; I shall always have that picture in my mind.

ARCHITECT: That's what comes of being so emotional!

BÉRENGER: Never mind, it's better to know it all, better to know it all!...

(*The lighting changes. Now it is grey, and there are faint sounds of the street and the trams.*)

ARCHITECT: Here we are! We're not in the radiant city any more; we've gone through the gates. (*He lets go of* BÉRENGER's *arm.*) We're on the outer boulevard. You see, over there? There's your tram. That's the stop.

BÉRENGER: Where?

ARCHITECT: There, where those people are waiting. It's the terminus. The tram starts off in the opposite direction and takes you straight to the other end of the town – takes you home! (*You can just see, in perspective, some streets beneath a rainy sky, a few outlines and vague red lights. The designer should see that* very gradually *everything becomes more real. The*

change should be brought about by the lighting and with a
very small number of props: shop signs and advertisements
should slowly appear one after the other, but not more than
three or four in all.)

BÉRENGER: I'm frozen.

ARCHITECT: You *are*. You're shivering.

BÉRENGER: It's the shock.

ARCHITECT: It's the cold too. (*He stretches out his hand to feel*
the raindrops.) It's raining. Half sleet, half snow.

(BÉRENGER *nearly slips over.*)

Be careful – it's slippery, the pavement's wet. (*He holds him up.*)

BÉRENGER: Thank you.

ARCHITECT: Put your overcoat on or you'll catch cold.

BÉRENGER: Thank you. (*He puts his overcoat on and fever-*
ishly ties his scarf round his neck.) Brr. Goodbye, Monsieur
Superintendent!

ARCHITECT: You're not going straight back home! No one's
expecting you… You've plenty of time to have a drink. Do you
good. Go on, let yourself go: it's time for that drink before
dinner. There's a bistro over there, near the tram stop, just by
the cemetery. They sell wreaths too.

BÉRENGER: You seem to be in a good mood again. I'm not.

ARCHITECT: I was never in a bad one.

BÉRENGER: In spite of—

ARCHITECT (*interrupting him, as the sign of the bistro lights*
up): Have to look life in the face, you know! (*He lays his hand*
on the handle of an imaginary door, beneath the sign of the
bistro.) Let's go in.

BÉRENGER: I don't feel much like it…

ARCHITECT: Go on in.

BÉRENGER: After you, Monsieur Superintendent.

ARCHITECT: No, please, after you. (*He pushes him. Noise of the*
bistro door. They come into the shop: this may be the same
corner of the stage where the imaginary greenhouse and then

the ARCHITECT'*s imaginary office was before. They go and sit
down on two chairs by the little table. They are doubtless next
to the big windows of the shop. In the event of the table and
chairs having been removed previously, a folding table can be
brought on by the* OWNER OF THE BISTRO *when he appears.
Two folding chairs could also be picked up from the floor of
the stage by* BÉRENGER *and the* ARCHITECT). Sit down, sit
down. (*They sit down.*) You *do* look cheerful! Don't take it to
heart so! If we thought about all the misfortunes of mankind
we could never go on living. And we must live! All the time
there are children with their throats cut, old men starving,
mournful widows, orphan girls, people dying, justice miscarry-
ing, houses collapsing on the tenants... mountains crumbling
away... massacres, and floods, and dogs run over... That's how
journalists earn their daily bread. Everything has its bright
side. In the end it's the bright side you've got to bear in mind.

BÉRENGER: Yes, Monsieur Superintendent, yes... but having been
so close and seen with my own eyes... I can't remain indifferent.
You may have got used to it – you with your two professions.

ARCHITECT (*slapping* BÉRENGER *on the shoulder*): You're too
impressionable, I've told you before. Got to face facts. Come
on now, pull yourself together – where's your will-power? (*He
slaps him on the shoulder again.* BÉRENGER *nearly falls off
the chair.*) You seem fit enough, whatever you say, although you
look so sorry for yourself. You're healthy in mind and body!

BÉRENGER: I don't say I'm not. What I'm suffering from doesn't
show – it's theoretical, spiritual.

ARCHITECT: I see.

BÉRENGER: You're being sarcastic.

ARCHITECT: I wouldn't dream of it. I've seen quite a few cases
like yours among my patients.

BÉRENGER: Yes, of course, you're a doctor too.

ARCHITECT: When I've a minute to spare, I do a little general
medicine; I took over from a psychoanalyst and was assistant to
a surgeon in my youth; I've also studied sociology... Come on
now, let's try and cheer you up. (*Clapping his hands.*) Monsieur!

BÉRENGER: I'm not as versatile as you.

(*From the wings on the left can be heard the voice of a clochard.**)

CLOCHARD (*off*): When I left the Merchant Navy
  I got spliced to young Octavie!
VOICE OF OWNER (*loud voice*): Be right with you, Monsieur
  Superintendent! (*Change of tone; still in the wings to the*
  CLOCHARD:) Get out of here – go and get drunk somewhere
  else!
CLOCHARD (*off, thick voice*): What's the point? I'm drunk already!

(*The drunken* CLOCHARD *appears from the left, brutally pushed
onstage by the* OWNER, *a dark fat character with great hairy arms.*)

  I got drunk at your place, paid for it – shouldn't have given
  me the stuff!
OWNER: I told you to get out! (*To the* ARCHITECT:) Glad to see
  you, Monsieur Superintendent.
ARCHITECT (*to* BÉRENGER): You see… We aren't in the beauti-
  ful district any more – people's manners aren't as good, to
  start with.
CLOCHARD (*still being pushed by the* OWNER): What you up to?
BÉRENGER (*to the* ARCHITECT): So I see!
OWNER (*to the* CLOCHARD): Off you go… Look, the
  Superintendent's over there!
CLOCHARD: Not doing anyone any harm! (*While still being
  pushed, he stumbles and falls full length, but picks himself
  up without protest.*)
ARCHITECT (*to the* OWNER): Two Beaujolais.
OWNER: Right, sir. I've got some of the real stuff for you. (*To the*
  CLOCHARD, *who is getting up:*) Get out and close the door
  behind you – don't let me catch you again. (*He goes off left.*)
ARCHITECT (*to* BÉRENGER): Still feeling depressed?
BÉRENGER (*with a helpless gesture to the empty air*): What do
  you expect?

(*The* OWNER *appears with two glasses of wine, while the* CLOCHARD *closes the door in mime and leaves the shop.*)

OWNER: Your Beaujolais, Monsieur Superintendent!
CLOCHARD (*going off right, still staggering and singing*):
    When I left the Merchant Navy
    I got spliced to young Octavie!
OWNER (*to the* ARCHITECT): You want a snack, Monsieur
    Superintendent?
ARCHITECT: Give us a couple of sandwiches.
OWNER: I've got a first-class rabbit pâté – pure pork!

(BÉRENGER *shows signs of wanting to pay.*)

ARCHITECT (*laying his hand on* BÉRENGER's *arm, to stop
    him*): No, no, not you! This is on me! (*To the* OWNER:)
    This is on me!
OWNER: Right, Monsieur Superintendent! (*He goes off left. The*
    ARCHITECT *takes a sip of the wine.* BÉRENGER *does not
    touch his.*)
BÉRENGER (*after a short pause*): If only you had a description
    of him.
ARCHITECT: But we have. At least we know how he looks to
    his victims. Pictures of him have been stuck on all the walls.
    We've done our best.
BÉRENGER: How did you get them?
ARCHITECT: They were found on the bodies of the drowned. Some
    of the people have been brought back to life for a moment,
    and they even provided other information. We know how he
    sets about it too. So does everyone in the district.
BÉRENGER: But why aren't they more careful? They only have
    to avoid him.
ARCHITECT: It's not so simple. I tell you, every evening there
    are always two or three who fall into the trap. But *he* never
    gets caught.
BÉRENGER: It's beyond me.

(*The* ARCHITECT *takes another sip of wine. The* PATRON *brings the two sandwiches and goes out.*)

I'm amazed... but you, Monsieur Superintendent, seem almost amused by the whole business.

ARCHITECT: I can't help it. After all, it is quite interesting. You see, it's there... Look through the window. (*He pretends to be pulling an imaginary curtain aside; or perhaps a real curtain could have appeared; he points to the left:*) You see... it's there, at the tram stop, he strikes. When the people get off to go home they walk to the gates, because they're not allowed to use their private cars outside the radiant city, and that's when he comes to meet them, disguised as a beggar. He starts whining, as they all do, asks for alms and tries to rouse their pity. The usual: just out of hospital, no work, looking for a job, nowhere to spend the night. That's not what does the trick – that's only the start. He's feeling his way; he chooses a likely prey, gets into conversation, hangs on and won't be shaken off. He offers to sell a few small articles he takes from his basket – artificial flowers, birds, old-style nightcaps, maps... postcards... American cigarettes, obscene little drawings, all sorts of objects. Generally his offerings are refused, his client hurries on, no time to spare. Still haggling, they both arrive at the pool you already know. Then, suddenly, the big moment arrives: he shows them a colonel's photo. This is irresistible. As it's getting rather dark, the client leans forwards to get a better view. But now it's too late. A close scrutiny of the picture is a disturbing experience. Taking advantage of this, he gives a push, and the victim falls in the pool and is drowned. The blow is struck; all he has to do now is to look for fresh prey.

BÉRENGER: What's so extraordinary is that people know and still let themselves be taken in.

ARCHITECT: That's the trick, you know. He's never been caught in the act.

BÉRENGER: Incredible! Incredible!

ARCHITECT: And yet it's true! (*He bites into his sandwich.*) You're not drinking? Or eating?

(*Noise of a tram arriving at the stop.* BÉRENGER *instinctively raises his head quickly and goes to pull the curtain aside to look through the window in the direction of the tram stop.*)

That's the tram arriving.

BÉRENGER: Groups of people are getting out!

ARCHITECT: Of course. The people who live in the district. Going home.

BÉRENGER: I can't see any beggars.

ARCHITECT: You won't. He'll not show himself. He knows we're here.

BÉRENGER (*turning his back to the window and coming back to the* ARCHITECT, *who also has his back to the window, to sit down again*): Perhaps it would be a good idea if you had a plain-clothes inspector permanently on duty at this spot.

ARCHITECT: You want to teach me how to do my job? Technically, it's not possible. Our inspectors are overworked – they've got other things to do. Besides, *they'd* want to see the Colonel's photo, too. There have been five of them drowned already like that. Ah... If we had the evidence, we'd know where to find him!

(*Suddenly a cry is heard, and the heavy sound of a body falling into water.*)

BÉRENGER (*jumping to his feet*): Did you hear that?

ARCHITECT (*still seated, biting his sandwich*): He's struck again. You see how easy it is to stop him! As soon as your back's turned, a second's inattention, and there you are... One second – that's all he needs.

BÉRENGER: It's terrible, terrible!

(*Muttering voices are heard, alarmed voices coming from the wings, the sound of footsteps and a police car's screaming brakes.*)

(*Wringing his hands*:) Do something, do something... Intervene, move!...

ARCHITECT (*calmly, still sitting, sandwich in hand, after another sip*): It's far too late now. Once again, he's taken us unawares...

BÉRENGER: Perhaps it's just a big stone he's thrown in the water... to tease us!

ARCHITECT: That *would* surprise me. And the cry?

(*The* OWNER *comes in from the left.*)

Now we'll know everything, anyway. Here comes our informer.

OWNER: It's the girl, the blonde one...

BÉRENGER: Dany? Mademoiselle Dany? It can't be!

ARCHITECT: It is. Why not? She's my secretary – my ex-secretary. And I gave her fair warning not to leave my staff. She was safe there.

BÉRENGER: Oh God, God, God!

ARCHITECT: She was in the Civil Service! He doesn't attack the Service! But no – she wanted her "freedom"! That'll teach her. She's found it now, her freedom. I was expecting this...

BÉRENGER: Oh God, oh God! Poor girl... She didn't have time to say yes to me!

ARCHITECT (*continuing*): I was even sure it would happen! Unless she'd gone right out of the district as soon as she left the Service.

BÉRENGER: Mademoiselle Dany! Mademoiselle Dany! Mademoiselle Dany! (*Lamentation.*)

ARCHITECT (*continuing*): Ah! People are so determined to have their own way, and above all the victims are so determined to revisit the scene of the crime! That's how they get caught!

BÉRENGER (*almost sobbing*): Ooh! Monsieur Superintendent. Monsieur Superintendent, it's Mademoiselle Dany, Mademoiselle Dany! (*He crumples up on his chair, in a state of collapse.*)

ARCHITECT (*to the* OWNER): Make the usual report – routine, you know. (*He takes his telephone from his pocket:*) Hullo?...

Hullo?... Another one... It's a young woman... Dany... the one who worked with us... No one caught in the act... Just suspicions... the same ones... yes!... One moment. (*He lays the telephone on the table.*)

BÉRENGER (*suddenly jumps to his feet*): We can't— We mustn't let things go on like this! It's got to stop! It's got to stop!

ARCHITECT: Control yourself. We've all got to die. Let the investigation take its usual course!

BÉRENGER (*runs off, slamming the imaginary shop door with a bang, which is, however, heard*): It can't go on! We must *do* something! We must, we must, we must! (*He goes off right.*)

OWNER: Au revoir, Monsieur! (*To the* ARCHITECT:) He might say goodbye!

ARCHITECT (*still seated, he watches him go, as does the* OWNER, *who is standing with his arms folded or his hands on his hips; then, as soon as* BÉRENGER *has gone, the* ARCHITECT *polishes off the rest of his wine and, pointing to* BÉRENGER's *full glass, says to the* OWNER): Drink it! Eat the sandwich too! (*The* OWNER *sits down in* BÉRENGER's *place. On the telephone:*) Hullo! No evidence! Close the case! Crime unsolved! (*He puts the telephone back in his pocket.*)

OWNER (*drinking*): Santé! (*He bites into the sandwich.*)

CURTAIN

Act Two

BÉRENGER'S *room. Dark and low-ceilinged, but lighter in the centre opposite the window. Near this long low window, a chest. To the right of it, a gloomy recess; in this dark patch, an armchair, French Regency style, rather knocked about, in which, as the curtain rises,* ÉDOUARD *is sitting silently. At the beginning of the act he is not visible; nor is the armchair, because of the darkness that reigns in* BÉRENGER'S *ground-floor room.*

In the centre, in the brightest part, a large table in front of the window, with notebooks and papers, a book, an inkstand and a fancy penholder like a goose quill.

A red worn-out armchair with one arm missing is a few feet to the left of the table. In the left-hand wall, more shadowy corners.

In the rest of the room you can make out in the half-light the shapes of old pieces of furniture: an old writing desk and a chest of drawers, with a threadbare tapestry on the wall above it; there is also a chair and another red armchair. Next to the window, on the right, a small table, a footstool and some shelves with a few books. On the top, an old gramophone.

At the front of the stage on the left is a door which gives onto the landing. Hanging from the ceiling, an old chandelier: on the floor, a faded old carpet. On the right-hand wall, a mirror in a baroque frame, which shines so little at the beginning of the act that it is difficult to tell what the object is. Beneath the mirror, an old chimney piece.

The curtains are not drawn, and through the window you can see the street, the windows of the ground floor opposite and a part of the front of a grocer's shop.

The decor of Act II *is very much constructed, heavy, realistic and ugly; it contrasts strongly with the lack of decor and the simple lighting effects of Act* I.

When the curtain rises the window lights the middle of the stage and the central table with a pale, yellowish light. The walls of the house opposite are a dirty grey colour. Outside the weather is dull; it is half snowing, half drizzling.

Sitting in the armchair in the darkest corner of BÉRENGER's *room, to the right of the window,* ÉDOUARD *is neither seen nor heard at the start of the act. He will be seen later, after* BÉRENGER's *arrival: thin, very pale, feverish-looking, dressed in black, with a mourning band round his right arm, a black felt hat, black overcoat, black shoes, white shirt with starched collar and black tie. Now and again, but only after* BÉRENGER's *arrival,* ÉDOUARD *will cough or clear his throat; from time to time he spits into a great white handkerchief with a black border, which he fastidiously returns to his pocket.*

A few moments before the rise of the curtain the VOICE OF THE CONCIERGE *is already heard coming from the left – that is, from the landing in the block of flats.*

CONCIERGE (*singing*): When it's cold it's not hot,
 When it's hot it's because it's cold!
 Oh dear, you can sweep as much as you like, it's dirty all day
 long, what with their snow and their coal dust.

(*Noise of a broom knocking against the door, then the* CONCIERGE *is heard singing again:*)

 When it's cold it's not hot,
 When it's hot it's because it's cold,
 When it's cold it can't be hot!
 When it's hot how can it be cold?
 What *is* it, then, when it's cold?
 Cold as cold, and that's your lot!

(*During the* CONCIERGE's *song there are sounds of hammering from the floor above, a radio blaring and trucks and motorcycles approaching and dying away; at one point, too, the shouts of children in the schoolyard during break: all this must be slightly distorted, caricatured, so the cries of the schoolchildren sound like dogs yapping; the idea is to make the uproar sound worse, but in a way that is partly unpleasant and partly comic.*)

MAN'S VOICE (*preceded by the noise of footsteps on the stairs and the barking of a dog*): Good morning, *madame la concierge*.

VOICE OF CONCIERGE: Good morning, Monsieur Lelard! You're late leaving this morning!

MAN'S VOICE: I've had some work to do at home. I've been asleep. Feel better now. Going to post my letters.

VOICE OF CONCIERGE: You've a funny sort of job! Always working with papers! Writing all those letters, you must have to think all the time.

MAN'S VOICE: It's not writing them that makes me think, but sending them off.

VOICE OF CONCIERGE: Yes, you've got to know who to send them to! Can't send them to *anyone*! Mustn't send them all to the same person, eh?

MAN'S VOICE: Still, got to earn your living by the sweat of your brow, as the prophet says.*

VOICE OF CONCIERGE: There's too much education these days – that's where things go wrong. Take sweeping: even that's not as easy as it used to be.

MAN'S VOICE: Still, got to earn your living anyway, to pay your income tax.

VOICE OF CONCIERGE: Minister in Parliament, that's the best job. They don't *pay* taxes, they *collect* them.

MAN'S VOICE: Even poor chaps like them have to earn their living, just like anyone else.

VOICE OF CONCIERGE: Yes, the rich are probably as poor as us, if there are any left these days.

MAN'S VOICE: Ah yes, that's life.

VOICE OF CONCIERGE: Ah yes, afraid so!

MAN'S VOICE: Ah yes, Madame.

VOICE OF CONCIERGE: Ah yes, Monsieur. It's a dog's life, and we all end up in the same place: a hole in the ground. That's where my husband is – forty years ago he died, and it's just like it was yesterday. (*A dog barks at the entrance.*) Shut up, Treasure! (*She must have clouted the dog with her broom, for you can hear his plaintive yelps. A door bangs.*) Go back in. (*To the* MAN, *presumably:*) Oh well, goodbye, Monsieur Lelard. Careful now: it's slippery outside – the pavements are all wet. Stinking weather!

MAN'S VOICE: I'll say it is. We were talking about life, Madame – we've got to be philosophical, you know!

VOICE OF CONCIERGE: Don't you talk to me about philosophers! I once got it into my head to be all stoical and go in for meditation. They never taught me anything, even that Marcus Aurelius. Doesn't really do any good. He wasn't much worse than you or I. We all have to find our own solution. If there is one, but there isn't.

MAN'S VOICE: Ah yes!...

VOICE OF CONCIERGE: And do without feelings too – how are we meant to find room for them? They don't enter into our account of things. How would feelings help *me* sweep my staircase?

MAN'S VOICE: I haven't read the philosophers.

VOICE OF CONCIERGE: You haven't missed much. That's what comes of being educated like you. Philosophy's no good, except to put in a test tube. May turn it a pretty colour, if you're lucky!

MAN'S VOICE: You shouldn't say that.

VOICE OF CONCIERGE: Philosophers! They're no good, except for a concierge like me.

MAN'S VOICE: You shouldn't say that, Madame – they're good for everyone.

VOICE OF CONCIERGE: I know what I'm talking about. You, you only read *good* books. I read the *philosophers,* because I've no money – the twopenny-halfpenny philosophers. You, even if you've no money – at least you can go to a library. You've got books to *choose* from... and what's the good of it, I ask you – you ought to know!

MAN'S VOICE: Philosophy, I say, is good for learning a philosophy of life!

VOICE OF CONCIERGE: I know all about the philosophy of life.

MAN'S VOICE: Good for you, Madame!

(*The broom knocks against the bottom of the door of* BÉRENGER'S *room.*)

VOICE OF CONCIERGE: Oh dear, oh dear, what a dirty house this is! It's the slush!

MAN'S VOICE: Plenty of that about. Oh well, I'm off this time – time's pressing on. Au revoir, Madame; keep smiling!

VOICE OF CONCIERGE: Thanks, Monsieur Lelard! (*The entrance door is banged violently.*) Oh, that's clever of him – silly fool will smash the door next, and *I'll* have to pay for it!

MAN'S VOICE (*politely*): Did you say something, Madame?

VOICE OF CONCIERGE (*more politely still, sweetly*): It's nothing, Monsieur Lelard: just chatting to myself, learning to talk! Makes the time go quicker!

(*The broom knocks against the bottom of the door of* BÉRENGER'S *room.*)

MAN'S VOICE: I quite thought you'd called me. Sorry.

VOICE OF CONCIERGE: Oh well, we all make mistakes, you know, Monsieur! Can't help it! No harm done. (*The front door is slammed violently again.*) He's gone this time. Tell him the same thing over and over again – he doesn't listen – him and his doors. Anybody'd think he was deaf! Likes to pretend he is, but he can hear all right! (*She sings:*) When it's cold, it's not hot. (*Yapping of the dog, more muffled.*) Shut up, Treasure! Ah, call that a dog! You wait, I'll knock hell out of you! (*You can hear the door of the* CONCIERGE'S *room opening. The dog yelps. The same door bangs again.*)

45

ANOTHER MAN'S VOICE (*after the sound of footsteps, in a slightly foreign accent*): Good morning, *madame la concierge!* Mademoiselle Colombine: she live here?

VOICE OF CONCIERGE: Can't say I know the name! There aren't any foreigners in the house. Only French people.

SECOND MAN (*at the same time the radio upstairs is turned up very loud*): But they told me she live on fifth floor this block.

VOICE OF CONCIERGE (*shouting to make herself heard*): Can't say I know the name, I tell you!

SECOND MAN'S VOICE: Please, Madame? (*Coming from the street on the right, the lumbering sound of a truck, which suddenly brakes a few seconds later.*)

VOICE OF CONCIERGE (*still shouting*): I tell you, I don't know the name!

SECOND MAN'S VOICE: This Number Thirteen, Twelfth Street?

VOICE OF CONCIERGE (*as before*): What street?

SECOND MAN'S VOICE (*louder*): This Number Thirteen—

VOICE OF CONCIERGE (*yelling*): Don't shout so loud. I can hear you. Of course it's Number Thirteen, Twelfth Street. Can't you read? It's written up outside.

SECOND MAN'S VOICE: Then it must be here Mademoiselle Colombine lives!

TRUCK DRIVER'S VOICE (*in the street*): Goddam learn to drive!

VOICE OF CONCIERGE: I know better than you.

CAR DRIVER'S VOICE (*in the street*): Don't you goddam me!

VOICE OF CONCIERGE: Oh, I see, Mademoiselle Colombine – perhaps you mean Monsieur Lecher's concubine?

TRUCK DRIVER'S VOICE (*in the street*): Bastard! Pimp!

SECOND MAN'S VOICE: Yes, that's it! Latcher!

VOICE OF CONCIERGE: Latcher, Lecher, it's all the same!

CAR DRIVER (*in the street*): Can't you be polite, damn you?

VOICE OF CONCIERGE: So it's the redhead you're after! If she's the one, *she* lives here, I told you she did! You want to say what you mean! Take the elevator!

TRUCK DRIVER (*in the street*): Son of a bitch!

CAR DRIVER (*in the street*): Son of a bitch yourself! (*Combined noises of the elevator going up, the radio, vehicles starting up again in the street, and then the splutter of a motorbike; for a split second you can see the motorcyclist through the window, passing in the street.*)

VOICE OF CONCIERGE (*loudly*): Don't forget to shut the elevator door after you! (*To herself:*) They always forget, especially foreigners! (*She sings:*)

Of course you never get on, if you stay in the same places,
But do you really get on, if you're always changing places?
(*The door of the* CONCIERGE'*s flat is heard banging — she has gone in; the dog yaps; her voice is more muffled:*) Yes, come on, my little Treasure! Who hasn't had his lump of sugar? Here it is — here's your sugar for you! (*Yapping.*) Take that!

(*The dog howls. In the street two people can be seen through the window, coming on from the left. Or possibly you just hear them talking, without seeing them. Two* OLD MEN, *both decrepit, who hobble along painfully, taking small steps and leaning on their sticks.*)

1ST O.M.: Terrible weather.

2ND O.M.: Terrible weather.

1ST O.M.: What you say?

2ND O.M.: Terrible weather. What *you* say?

1ST O.M.: I said "terrible weather".

2ND O.M.: Hang on to my arm, you might slip over.

1ST O.M.: Hang on to my arm, you might slip over.

2ND O.M.: I used to know some surprising people, very surprising.

CLOCHARD (*appearing from the right on the pavement opposite; he is singing*): When I left the Merchant Navy... (*He looks up at the windows; some coins could be thrown down.*)

1ST O.M.: What did they do, these surprising people?

2ND O.M.: They surprised everyone!

CLOCHARD: ...I got spliced to young Octavie!

1ST O.M.: And where did these surprising people surprise?

47

(*The* CLOCHARD *does as before.*)

2ND O.M.: They surprised in society circles... everywhere they
    surprised!
1ST O.M.: When did you know them, these surprising people?
CLOCHARD (*as before*): When I left the Merchant Navy...

(*Still looking up at the windows of the upper floors, he makes
off left and disappears.*)

2ND O.M.: In the old days, the old days...
1ST O.M.: Do you still see them sometimes?
GROCER (*coming out of the shop opposite, looking furious and
    gazing up at a first-floor window*): Hey, Madame!
2ND O.M.: Ah, my dear chap, there aren't any more nowadays,
    there aren't any more people who surprise... (*He is seen disap-
    pearing on the right, and you can hear:*) All that's gone. I only
    know two of them today... two surprising people...
GROCER: Hey, Madame! Who do you think I am?
2ND O.M.: ...only two. One of them's retired and the other's
    deceased. (*The* 1ST OLD MAN *disappears, too.*)
GROCER (*as before*): I mean... who do you think I am?
VOICE OF CLOCHARD (*singing*): The captain of the tanker.
GROCER (*as before*): Who do you think I am? I'm a shopkeeper,
    Madame, not a ragman! (*He goes back furiously to his shop.*)
VOICE OF CLOCHARD (*moving away*): Sent for me and said:
    If you want to get spliced to young Octavie
    You'd better leave the Merchant Navy...
VOICE OF 1ST O.M. (*moving away*): If there were any, you
    wouldn't notice. Surprising people don't surprise any more.

(*From the right the noise of breaktime, which has already been
heard quietly, redoubles in intensity. A school bell rings.*)

SCHOOLMASTER'S VOICE: Back to class! Back to class!
VOICE FROM THE STREET: We've fifty-eight delivery boys—

SCHOOLMASTER'S VOICE: Silence! (*Stamping of feet, shouting, noise of desks, etc., from the right.*) Silence! Silence!

VOICE FROM THE STREET: We've fifty-eight delivery boys!

(*The children in the school are silent.*)

SCHOOLMASTER'S VOICE: History lesson: the people's representatives came to the gates of the palace of Queen Marie Antoinette. And they shouted...

VOICE FROM THE STREET: We've fifty-eight delivery boys!

SCHOOLMASTER'S VOICE: They shouted: "We haven't any more cake, Your Majesty – give us cake." "There isn't any left, replied the Queen."

VOICE FROM THE STREET: We've fifty-eight delivery boys!

SCHOOLMASTER'S VOICE: "There isn't any left, why don't you eat bread?" Then the people grew angry and cut off the Queen's head. When the Queen saw that she'd lost her head, she was so upset she had a stroke. She couldn't get over it, whatever the doctors did. They weren't up to much at the time.

VOICE FROM THE STREET: We've fifty-eight delivery boys!

GRUFF VOICE (*in the street*): We were seven thousand feet up, when suddenly I saw the wing of our plane coming off.

ANOTHER VOICE (*thin and piping*): You don't say!

GRUFF VOICE: All right, I said to myself, we've still got one left. The passengers all piled up on one side of the plane to keep an even keel, and it went flying on with one wing.

PIPING VOICE: Were you frightened?

GRUFF VOICE: You wait... suddenly the second wing fell off, and then the engines... and the propellers... and we were seven thousand feet up!

PIPING VOICE: Phew!

GRUFF VOICE: This time I thought we'd had it... (*The voice fades:*) Really had it, no way out... Well, do you know what saved us? Give you three guesses...

VOICE FROM THE STREET: Our fifty-eight delivery boys waste too much time urinating. Five times a day, on average, they interrupt their deliveries to satisfy a personal need. The time is not deducted from their wages. They take advantage of this, so they've got to be disciplined; they can make water in turn once a month for four and a half hours without interruption. That will save all the coming and going, which sends up our costs. After all, *camels* store up water.

1ST VOICE FROM BELOW: I went to catch my train, find my compartment and sit down in my reserved seat. The train was about to leave. Just at that minute, in comes a gentlemen with the same seat and the same number as me. Out of politeness I gave my seat up and went and stood in the corridor. He hardly said thank you. I stood for two hours. In the end the train stopped at a station and the man got off. I went and sat down again, as the seat was mine in the first place. Again the train pulled out. An hour later it stopped at another station. And the same man gets in again and wants his seat back! Legally had he any right to it? It was my seat as well as his, but he claimed second occupant's rights. We went to law about it. The Judge said the man was entitled to extra privileges, because he was a blue-blooded critic, and it was only modesty made him conceal his identity.

ANOTHER VOICE FROM BELOW: Who was the gentleman?

1ST VOICE: A national hero. Harold Hastings de Hobson.*

2ND VOICE: How did he manage to catch the same train again?

1ST VOICE: He took a short cut.

VOICE FROM THE STREET (*closer*): We've fifty-eight delivery boys.

(*The two* OLD MEN *reappear in the street from the opposite direction – that is, from the left.*)

1ST O.M.: I was invited to the wedding reception, of course... I wasn't very satisfied because all I like is coq au vin...

2ND O.M.: They didn't serve any coq au vin?

1ST O.M.: They *did*. But they didn't tell me it was coq au vin, so it didn't taste right.

2ND O.M.: Was it really coq au vin?

1ST O.M.: It WAS coq au vin, but as I didn't know, the whole meal was ruined.

2ND O.M.: I wish I'd been invited instead of you. I *like* my dinners ruined. (*They go off.*)

VOICE FROM THE STREET: We've fifty-eight delivery boys!

VOICE FROM RIGHT: We must seriously raise the question of our finances.

VOICE FROM ABOVE: Has the problem been considered by the delegation of deputy delegates?

VOICE FROM LEFT: We must seriously raise the question of *their* finances.

VOICE FROM ABOVE: We must seriously raise the question of the finances of our delivery boys.

ANOTHER VOICE FROM LEFT: No, the problem's been solved by the delegate of the deputy delegation.

VOICE FROM RIGHT: After all, production is production! The whole basis of the problem must be re-examined.

VOICE FROM LEFT: With our overseers and our underseers, our visionaries and our viewfinders, we shall form an organizational basis, a common-funds committee.

VOICE FROM ABOVE: The seers and the underseers will form development committees for companies of contractors who will form special communities...

VOICE FROM RIGHT: There's the basic organizational principle and the organizational aspect of the superstructure.

VOICE FROM LEFT: What about our fifty-eight delivery boys?

VOICE FROM ABOVE: After work, we must organize leisure.

VOICE FROM BELOW: Concentrated leisure.

VOICE FROM LEFT: We must force the pace of leisure.

(*For some seconds thick fog darkens the stage: for a while the sounds from outside are muffled; all you can hear are vague snatches of dialogue.*)

VOICE OF CONCIERGE (*after a banging of doors in the entrance*): Oh, when the fog's mixed with the factory smoke, you can't hear a word! (*Strident whistle from a factory hooter.*) Thank God for the hooters!

(*The fog has lifted, and on the other side of the street, you can see the* CLOCHARD *singing:*)

CLOCHARD: The second in command
Sent for me and told me
To marry my Octavie
To marry my Octavie

(*The street sounds fade a little to facilitate the following scene.*)

And I'd be as good a slavey
As I'd once been in the Navy!

(*In the entrance a door is heard banging, while the* CLOCHARD, *still singing, looks up at the windows to catch the coins as they fall, takes off his battered old hat in general acknowledgment and comes nearer the window, advancing into the middle of the street.*)

VOICE OF CONCIERGE: Don't bang the door like that!
WOMAN'S VOICE (*in the entrance*): You bang it too, sometimes. I didn't mean to.
VOICE OF CONCIERGE: Yes, but with me it's because I don't know when I'm doing it.
CLOCHARD (*in the street, looking up at the windows*): Thank you, ladies and gentlemen, thank you! (*He starts muttering when there are no coins falling.*) They're a stingy lot, curse 'em!
VOICE OF CONCIERGE (*singing*): Cold as cold,
And that's your lot.
CLOCHARD (*while the* CONCIERGE *goes on singing the same refrain, he has crossed the street. A motorcyclist brushes past him from behind, travelling fast, and a voice is heard: "Stupid bastard!"*): As I'd once been in the Navy! (*He is right up to the window as he sings:*)
But keep a weather eye,
But keep a weather eye!

(*He looks through the window into* BÉRENGER*'s room, squashing his face and nose up against the glass.*)

CONCIERGE (*making her appearance on the pavement, which she is sweeping, singing away until she bumps into the* CLOCHARD): What are you doing here?

CLOCHARD: I'm singing!

CONCIERGE: You're dirtying the window panes! That's one of my tenants, and I'm the one has to keep them clean.

CLOCHARD (*sarcastically*): Oh! I beg your pardon, Madame. I didn't know. No need to get upset.

CONCIERGE: Go on, clear off and don't be a nuisance!

CLOCHARD (*still a bit cheeky and rather drunk*): I've heard that a thousand times before. You're not very original, Madame.

CONCIERGE (*threatening him with her broom*): I'll teach you to play the critic with me.

CLOCHARD: Don't trouble yourself, Madame; I'm going, Madame; I'm sorry! (*He moves off, still singing:*) When I left the Merchant Navy

I got spliced to young Octavie.

CONCIERGE (*still in the street near the window, she wheels round as the dog barks*): Shut up!... The postman! (*To the* POSTMAN:) Who's it for, Postman?

POSTMAN'S VOICE: Telegram for Monsieur Bérenger!

CONCIERGE: Ground floor, on the right.

POSTMAN'S VOICE: Thanks.

CONCIERGE (*waving her broom after the* CLOCHARD, *who is no longer visible*): Lazy old bugger! (*Shrugging her shoulders:*) If he's a sailor, I'm a tart!

(*The* POSTMAN *is heard knocking at* BÉRENGER*'s door, while the* CONCIERGE *sweeps the pavement.*)

Oh, all this dog's mess, I wouldn't let mine do it.

POSTMAN'S VOICE: No reply.

CONCIERGE (*to the invisible* POSTMAN): Knock louder. He's there.

POSTMAN'S VOICE: I tell you, there's no reply.

CONCIERGE: Don't even know how to knock on a door! (*She disappears into the entrance.*) Of course he can't have gone out. I ought to know his habits. He is my tenant. I even do his housework. Clean his windows!

POSTMAN'S VOICE: Try!

(*Loud knocking is heard, repeated several times, on* BÉRENGER'*s door.*)

VOICE OF CONCIERGE (*knocking at the door*): Monsieur Bérenger! Monsieur Bérenger! (*Silence, then more knocking.*) Monsieur Bérenger! Monsieur Bérenger!

POSTMAN'S VOICE: What did I tell you!

VOICE OF CONCIERGE: Well, I like that! He can't have gone out. Could be asleep, but that's not one of his habits! Knock louder! I'll go and look!

(*The* POSTMAN *goes on knocking and the* CONCIERGE *appears again outside the window; she glues her face to the window pane. Her face is naturally hideous, but with her nose squashed against the glass it looks even worse.*)

CONCIERGE: Monsieur Bérenger! I say, Monsieur Bérenger!

(*At the same time the* POSTMAN *is heard knocking at the door.*)

POSTMAN'S VOICE: Monsieur Bérenger! Telegram, Monsieur Bérenger!

CONCIERGE: Monsieur Bérenger, there's a telegram for you... fine state of affairs! (*Pause.*) Where on earth can he be? He's never at home! (*She raps on the window again, while the* POSTMAN'*s knocking continues.*) Some people go for walks, got nothing better to do, and we work our fingers to the bone!... He's not there! (*She disappears: she must be near the entrance, as you can see her arm brandishing the broom out of one corner of the window.*)

POSTMAN'S VOICE: If he's not in, he's not in. And you said he never went out!

VOICE OF CONCIERGE: I didn't! Give me the telegram – I'll give it to him! (*She disappears completely.*) I'm the one cleans his windows!

POSTMAN'S VOICE: I'm not allowed to give it to you. I can't.

VOICE OF CONCIERGE: That's that, then – keep it.

POSTMAN'S VOICE: I'll give it you anyway. Here it is.

CONCIERGE: Now I've got to keep a lookout for him! Oh dear!

(*Pause. The noises have suddenly ceased, after the dying fall of one last factory siren. Perhaps, too, the* CONCIERGE *has been heard for one last time, abusing her dog, which yelps as usual. A few moments' silence. Then, passing along the street, close to the window,* BÉRENGER *can be seen coming home. He has his overcoat on and is clutching his hat in his right hand; he is swinging his arm vigorously. He is walking with his head down. Once he has gone past the window his steps are heard in the entrance. Then his key turns in the lock.*)

VOICE OF CONCIERGE (*very polite*): Why, it's you, Monsieur Bérenger! Had a nice walk? You need some fresh air! Good idea!

VOICE OF BÉRENGER: Good morning, Madame.

VOICE OF CONCIERGE: If you've been for a walk, you must have gone out. Didn't hear you go. Why didn't you tell me – I hadn't got a key to do your room. How could I know? *I* was ready. Telegram came for you.

(*Pause.* BÉRENGER *has stopped opening the door to read the telegram.*)

I hope it wasn't urgent? I read it, you see. It's the old clothes man. Wants you, urgently. Nothing to worry about.

(The key is again heard grating in the lock. The door of BÉRENGER'*s room opens quietly. The* CONCIERGE *is heard angrily muttering words that are indistinguishable, then she bangs the door of her flat and the dog squeals. The figure of* BÉRENGER *can be picked out in the dim room. He advances slowly towards the centre of the stage. The silence is complete. He turns the electric light switch and the stage lights up.* ÉDOUARD *is seen in his corner, with his hat on his head, wearing his overcoat, his briefcase at his feet, clearing his throat. Surprised, first by the coughing, then almost at the same time by the sight of* ÉDOUARD *himself,* BÉRENGER *gives a jump.)*

BÉRENGER: Oh, what are you doing here?

ÉDOUARD (*in a thin, rather high-pitched voice, almost childlike, as he gets up coughing, picking up his briefcase, which he keeps in his hand*): Your place isn't very warm. (*He spits into his handkerchief. To do this, he has laid his briefcase down again and taken his right hand out of his pocket; this arm is slightly withered and visibly shorter than the other. Then, carefully and methodically, he folds his handkerchief again, puts it back in his pocket and picks up his briefcase.*)

BÉRENGER: You startled me... I wasn't expecting you... what are you doing here?

ÉDOUARD: Waiting for you. (*Putting his deformed hand back in his pocket.*) How are you, Bérenger?

BÉRENGER: How did you get in?

ÉDOUARD: Through the door, of course. I opened it.

BÉRENGER: How? I had the keys with me!

ÉDOUARD (*taking some keys from his pocket and showing them to* BÉRENGER): So did I! (*He puts the keys back in his pocket.*)

BÉRENGER: How did you get those keys? (*He lays his hat on the table.*)

ÉDOUARD: But... you let me have them for a while yourself, so I could come to your flat when I liked and wait for you if you were out.

BÉRENGER (*trying to remember*): I gave you those keys?... When?... I don't remember at all...

ÉDOUARD: You gave them to me all the same. How else could I have got them?

BÉRENGER: Édouard, it's amazing. Still, if you say...

ÉDOUARD: I promise you did... I'm sorry, Bérenger – I'll give them back if you don't want me to have them.

BÉRENGER: Oh... no, no... keep them, Édouard; keep them now you've got them. I'm sorry, I've a bad memory. I don't remember giving them to you.

ÉDOUARD: Well, you did... you remember – it was last year, I think. One Sunday when—

BÉRENGER (*interrupting him*): The concierge didn't tell me you were waiting.

ÉDOUARD: I don't suppose she saw me; it's my fault – I didn't know I had to ask *her* if I could come to your flat. I thought you told me it wasn't necessary. But if you don't want me here...

BÉRENGER: That's not what I mean. I'm always pleased to see you.

ÉDOUARD: I don't want to be in the way.

BÉRENGER: You know it's not that at all.

ÉDOUARD: Thanks.

BÉRENGER: It's losing my memory that upsets me... (*To himself:*) Still, the concierge oughtn't to have left the flats this morning!... (*To* ÉDOUARD:) What's wrong with you? You're trembling.

ÉDOUARD: Yes, I am. I don't feel very well. I'm cold.

BÉRENGER (*taking the sound hand in his, while* ÉDOUARD *stuffs the other in his pocket*): You've still got a temperature. Coughing and shivering. You're very pale, and your eyes look feverish.

ÉDOUARD: My lungs... they're not improving... after all the time I've had trouble with them...

BÉRENGER: And this building's so badly heated... (*Without taking his overcoat off he goes and sinks morosely into an armchair*

57

near the table, while ÉDOUARD *remains standing.*) Do sit down, Édouard.

ÉDOUARD: Thank you, thanks very much. (*He sits down again on the chest, cautiously setting his briefcase down nearby, within reach; he always seems to be keeping an eye on it. A moment's silence. Then, noticing how gloomy* BÉRENGER *is looking and how he is sighing:*) You seem so sad; you look worn out and anxious...

BÉRENGER (*to himself*): If that was all...

ÉDOUARD: *You're* not ill too, are you?... What's wrong? Has something happened to you?

BÉRENGER: No, no... nothing at all. I'm like that... I'm not cheerful by nature! Brrr... I'm cold too! (*He rubs his hands.*)

ÉDOUARD: I'm sure something's happened to you. You're more nervous than usual – you're quite jumpy! Tell me about it, if I'm not being indiscreet – it may help.

BÉRENGER (*getting up and taking a few excited paces in the room*): I've got good reason.

ÉDOUARD: What's wrong?

BÉRENGER: Oh, nothing... nothing and everything... everything...

ÉDOUARD: I should like a cup of tea, if I may...

BÉRENGER (*suddenly adopting the serious tones of a tragic pronouncement*): My dear Édouard, I am shattered, in despair, inconsolable!

ÉDOUARD (*without changing the tone of his voice*): Shattered by what; in despair about what?

BÉRENGER: My fiancée has been murdered.

ÉDOUARD: I beg your pardon?

BÉRENGER: My fiancée has been murdered – do you hear?

ÉDOUARD: Your fiancée? Since when have you been engaged? You never told me you were thinking of getting married. Congratulations! My condolences too. Who was she?

BÉRENGER: To be honest... She wasn't exactly my fiancée... just a girl, a young girl who might have been.

ÉDOUARD: Ah yes?

BÉRENGER: A girl who was as beautiful as she was sweet and tender, pure as an angel. It's terrible. Too terrible.

ÉDOUARD: How long had you known her?

BÉRENGER: Always, perhaps. Since this morning, anyway.

ÉDOUARD: Quite recently.

BÉRENGER: She was snatched from me... snatched away!... I... (*Gesture of the hand.*)

ÉDOUARD: It must be very hard... please, have you any tea?

BÉRENGER: I'm sorry, I wasn't thinking... With this tragedy... which has ruined my life! Yes, I've got some.

ÉDOUARD: I understand.

BÉRENGER: You couldn't understand.

ÉDOUARD: Oh yes I do.

BÉRENGER: I can't offer you tea... It's gone mouldy. I'd forgotten.

ÉDOUARD: Well, a glass of rum, please... I'm quite numb with cold...

(BÉRENGER *produces a bottle of rum, fills a small glass for* ÉDOUARD *and offers it to him while he says:*)

BÉRENGER: No one will ever take her place. My life is over. It's a wound that will never heal.

ÉDOUARD: You really have been wounded, poor old thing! (*Taking the glass of rum.*) Thanks! (*Still in a tone of indifference:*) Poor old thing!

BÉRENGER: And if that was all... if there was nothing but the murder of that unfortunate girl. Do you know the things that happen in the world – awful things – in our town – terrible things – you can't imagine... quite near here... comparatively close... morally speaking, it's actually here! (*He strikes his breast.* ÉDOUARD *has swallowed his rum, chokes and coughs.*) Aren't you feeling well?

ÉDOUARD: It's nothing. It's so strong. (*He goes on coughing.*) I must have swallowed it the wrong way.

BÉRENGER (*gently hitting* ÉDOUARD *on the back to stop him coughing and with the other hand taking his glass from him*):

I thought I'd found everything again, got it all back. (*To* ÉDOUARD:) Stretch your head up and look at the ceiling. It'll stop. (*He goes on:*) All I'd lost and all I hadn't lost, all that had been mine and all that had never been mine...

ÉDOUARD (*to* BÉRENGER, *who is still hitting him on the back*): Thank you... that's enough... you're hurting... stop it, please.

BÉRENGER (*going to place the little glass on the table while* ÉDOUARD *spits into his handkerchief*): I thought the spring had returned for ever... that I'd found the unfindable again, the dream, the key, life... all that we've lost while we've gone on living.

ÉDOUARD (*clearing his throat*): Yes. Of course.

BÉRENGER: All our muddled aspirations, all the things we vaguely yearn for, from the depths of our being, without even realizing... Oh, I thought I'd found everything... It was unexplored territory, magically beautiful.

ÉDOUARD: The girl was unexplored?...

BÉRENGER: No. The place. The girl too, if you like!

ÉDOUARD: You're always searching for something out of the way. Always aiming at something out of reach.

BÉRENGER: But I tell you, it wasn't. This girl...

ÉDOUARD: The answer is that it *is,* and so is *she* now. Your problems are so complicated, so impractical. You've always been dissatisfied, always refused to resign yourself.

BÉRENGER: That's because I'm suffocating... The air I have to breathe is not the kind that's made for me.

ÉDOUARD (*clearing his throat*): Think yourself lucky you don't suffer from ill health; you're not a sick man or an invalid.

BÉRENGER (*without paying attention to what* ÉDOUARD *is saying*): No. No. I've seen it, I thought I'd got somewhere... somewhere like a different universe. Yes, only beauty can make the spring flowers bloom eternally... everlasting flowers... but I'm sorry to say it was only a light that lied!... Once again everything fell into chaos... in a flash, in a flash! The same collapse, again and again... (*All this is said in a declamatory tone, halfway between sincerity and parody.*)

ÉDOUARD: You think only of yourself.

BÉRENGER (*with slight irritation*): That's not true! Not true. I don't just think of myself. It's not for myself... not only for myself that I'm suffering right now, that I refuse to accept things! There comes a time when they're too horrible, and you can't...

ÉDOUARD: But that's the way of the world. Think of me – I'm a sick man... I've come to terms...

BÉRENGER (*interrupting him*): It weighs on you, it weighs on you terribly, especially when you think you've seen... when you've thought you could hope... Oh!... then you can't go on... I'm tired... she's dead and they're dead and they'll all be killed... no one can stop it.

ÉDOUARD: But how did she die, this fiancée who perhaps wasn't? And who else is going to be killed, apart from the ones who usually get killed? What in fact are you talking about? Is it your dreams that are being killed? Generalities don't mean a thing.

BÉRENGER: I'm not talking through my hat...

ÉDOUARD: I'm sorry. I just can't understand you. I don't...

BÉRENGER: You're always wrapped up in your own little world. You never know anything. Where have you been living?

ÉDOUARD: Tell me about it then – give me some details.

BÉRENGER: It's absolutely incredible. There is in our town, though you're not aware of it, one beautiful district.

ÉDOUARD: Well?

BÉRENGER: Yes, there's one beautiful district. I've found it – I've just come from there. It's called the radiant city.

ÉDOUARD: Well, well!

BÉRENGER: In spite of its name, it's not a model neighbourhood, a happy or a perfect one. A criminal, an insatiable murderer, has turned it into hell.

ÉDOUARD (*coughing*): I'm sorry, I can't help coughing!

BÉRENGER: You heard what I said?

ÉDOUARD: Perfectly: a murderer's turned it into hell.

BÉRENGER: He terrorizes and kills everyone. The district's getting deserted. It'll soon cease to exist.

ÉDOUARD: Oh yes, of course. I know! It must be that beggar
who shows people a colonel's photo and while they're looking at it throws them in the water! It's a trick to catch a fool.
I thought you meant something else. If that's all it is...

BÉRENGER (*surprised*): You knew? Knew all about it?

ÉDOUARD: Of course – I've known for a long time. I thought you
were going to tell me something fresh – that there was another
beautiful district.

BÉRENGER: Why did you never tell me anything about it?

ÉDOUARD: I didn't think there was any point. The whole town
knows the story. I'm surprised, even, you didn't know about
it before – it's old news. Who doesn't know?... There didn't
seem any need to tell you.

BÉRENGER: What? You mean everyone knows?

ÉDOUARD: That's what I said. You see, even *I* knew. It's a known
fact, accepted and filed away. Even the schoolchildren know.

BÉRENGER: Even the schoolchildren?... Are you sure?

ÉDOUARD: Of course I am. (*He clears his throat.*)

BÉRENGER: How could schoolchildren have found out?...

ÉDOUARD: Must have heard their parents talking... or grandpar-
ents... the schoolmaster, too, when he teaches them to read and
write... Would you give me a little more rum?... Or perhaps
not – it's so bad for me... I'd better go without. (*Taking up
his explanation again:*) It's a pity, I agree.

BÉRENGER: A great pity! A terrible pity...

ÉDOUARD: What can we do about it?

BÉRENGER: Now it's my turn to say how very surprised *I* am to
see you taking the matter so calmly... I always thought you
were a sensitive, humane man.

ÉDOUARD: Perhaps I am.

BÉRENGER: But it's atrocious. Atrocious.

ÉDOUARD: I agree, I don't deny it.

BÉRENGER: Your indifference makes me sick! And I don't mind
saying it to your face.

ÉDOUARD: Well you know... I—

BÉRENGER (*louder*): Your indifference makes me sick!

ÉDOUARD: Don't forget... this is all new to you...

BÉRENGER: That's no excuse. You disappoint me, Édouard, frankly, you disappoint me...

(ÉDOUARD *has a violent bout of coughing; he spits into his hand-kerchief.* BÉRENGER *rushes up to* ÉDOUARD, *who nearly collapses.*)

You're really ill.

ÉDOUARD: A glass of water.

BÉRENGER: At once. I'll go and fetch one. (*Supporting him.*) Lie down here... on the couch...

ÉDOUARD (*between coughs*): My briefcase... (BÉRENGER *bends down to pick up* ÉDOUARD's *briefcase. In spite of his state of collapse,* ÉDOUARD *springs away from* BÉRENGER *to get hold of it himself.*) No... let me... (*He takes the briefcase from* BÉRENGER's *hand, then, still weak and supported by* BÉRENGER, *he reaches the couch, still clinging to the briefcase, and lies down with* BÉRENGER's *help, the briefcase at his side.*)

BÉRENGER: You're soaked in perspiration...

ÉDOUARD: And frozen stiff as well. Oh... this cough... it's awful...

BÉRENGER: You mustn't catch cold. Would you like a blanket?

ÉDOUARD (*shivering*): Don't worry. It's nothing... it'll pass...

BÉRENGER: Settle down and rest.

ÉDOUARD: A glass of water.

BÉRENGER: At once... I'll fetch one.

(*He hurries out to fetch a glass of water; you can hear the water running at the tap. Meanwhile* ÉDOUARD *raises himself on one elbow and stops coughing; with one anxious hand he checks the lock of his enormous black briefcase, and then, somewhat relieved, lies back again, still coughing, but not so loudly.* ÉDOUARD *must not give the impression he is trying to deceive* BÉRENGER: *he is really ill, and he has other worries – his briefcase, for example. He wipes his brow.* BÉRENGER *returns with the glass of water.*)

Feel better?

ÉDOUARD: Thanks… (*He takes a sip of the water and* BÉRENGER *takes the glass from him.*) I'm sorry, it's stupid of me. I'm all right now.

BÉRENGER: I'm the one to say I'm sorry. I should have realized… When you're ill – when you're a really sick man, like you, it's hard to get carried away by something else… I've not been fair to you. After all, these terrible crimes in the radiant city might be the cause of your illness. It must have affected you, consciously or otherwise. Yes, I'm sure it's that that's eating you away. I confess it's wrong to pass judgement too lightly. You can't know people's hearts…

ÉDOUARD (*getting up*): I'm freezing here…

BÉRENGER: Don't get up. I'll go and fetch a blanket.

ÉDOUARD: I'd rather we went for a little walk, for the fresh air. I waited for you too long in this cold. I'm sure it's warmer outside.

BÉRENGER: I'm so tired emotionally, so depressed. I'd rather have gone to bed… Still, if that's what you really want, I don't mind coming with you for a while!

ÉDOUARD: That's very charitable of you!

(ÉDOUARD *puts his black-ribboned felt hat on again, buttons his dark overcoat and dusts it down, while* BÉRENGER *also puts his hat on.* ÉDOUARD *picks up his heavy, bulging black briefcase.* BÉRENGER *walks in front of him, turning his back to* ÉDOUARD, *who, as he passes the table, lifts the briefcase over it. As he does so, the briefcase opens and some of the contents spill over the table: at first, large photographs.*)

My briefcase!

BÉRENGER (*turning round at the noise*): What the… ah!

(*They both make a quick movement to the briefcase at the same time.*)

ÉDOUARD: Leave it to me.

BÉRENGER: No, wait, I'll help you... (*He sees the photos.*) But... but... what have you got there?

(*He picks up one of the photos.* ÉDOUARD *tries, but without appearing too alarmed, to take it back from him, to hide the other photos falling from his briefcase with his hands, and push them back.* BÉRENGER, *who has held on to the photo, looks at it in spite of* ÉDOUARD'*s opposition.*)

What is it?

ÉDOUARD: I expect it's a photo... some photos...

BÉRENGER (*still holding the photo and inspecting it*): It's an army man, with a moustache and pips... a Colonel with decorations, the Military Cross... (*He picks up other photos.*) More photos! And always the same face.

ÉDOUARD (*also looking*): Yes... it is... it's a Colonel. (*He seems to be trying to lay his hands on the photos; meanwhile a lot of others keep on pouring over the table.*)

BÉRENGER (*with authority*): Let me see! (*He dives into the briefcase, pulls out more photos and looks at one:*) Quite a nice face. With the kind of expression that makes you feel sorry for him. (*He takes out more photos.* ÉDOUARD *mops his brow.*) What *is* all this? Why, it's the photo, the famous photo of the Colonel! You had it in there... you never told me!

ÉDOUARD: I'm not always looking inside my briefcase!

BÉRENGER: But it *is* your briefcase, all right – you're never without it.

ÉDOUARD: That's no reason...

BÉRENGER: Oh well... We'll take the opportunity, while we're at it, to have another look!

(BÉRENGER *sticks his hands into the huge black briefcase.* ÉDOUARD *does the same with his own too-white hand, whose twisted fingers are now very clearly visible.*)

More photos of the Colonel... and more... and more... (*To* ÉDOUARD, *who is now taking things out of the briefcase too, and looking astonished*:) What are these?

ÉDOUARD: You can see – they're artificial flowers.

BÉRENGER: There are masses of them!... And these... Look, dirty pictures... (*He inspects them while* ÉDOUARD *goes and looks over his shoulder*:) Nasty!

ÉDOUARD: Excuse me! (*He takes a step away.*)

BÉRENGER (*discarding the obscene photos and continuing his inventory*): Some sweets... money boxes... (*They both take from the briefcase a collection of miscellaneous articles.*) ...children's watches!... What are they doing here?

ÉDOUARD (*stammering*): I... I don't know... I tell you...

BÉRENGER: What do you make of it?

ÉDOUARD: Nothing. What *can* you make of it?

BÉRENGER (*still taking from the briefcase, which is like a conjuror's bottomless bag, an amazing quantity of all types of objects, which cover the whole surface of the table and even fall on the floor*): ...pins... and more pins... pen holders... and these... and these... what's that?

(*Much should be made of this scene: some of the objects can fly away on their own, others can be thrown by* BÉRENGER *to the four corners of the stage.*)

ÉDOUARD: That?... I don't know... I don't know at all... I know nothing about it.

BÉRENGER (*showing him a box*): What on earth's this?

ÉDOUARD (*taking it in his hand*): Looks to me like a box, isn't it?

BÉRENGER: It is. A cardboard box. What's inside?

ÉDOUARD: I don't know. I don't know. I couldn't tell you.

BÉRENGER: Open it, go on, open it.

ÉDOUARD (*almost indifferently*): If you like... (*He opens the box.*) Nothing there! Oh yes, another box... (*He takes the small box out.*)

BÉRENGER: And that box?

ÉDOUARD: See for yourself.

BÉRENGER (*taking a third box from the second box*): Another box. (*He looks into the third box.*) Inside there's another box. (*He takes it out.*) And another inside that… (*He looks into the fourth box.*) And another box inside that… and so on, ad infinitum! Let's look again…

ÉDOUARD: Oh, if you want… But it'll stop us going for a walk…

BÉRENGER (*taking boxes out*): Box… after box… after box… after box… after box!…

ÉDOUARD: Nothing but boxes…

BÉRENGER (*taking a handful of cigarettes from the briefcase*): Cigarettes!

ÉDOUARD: Those belong to me! (*He starts collecting them, then stops.*) Take one if you like…

BÉRENGER: Thanks, I don't smoke.

(ÉDOUARD *puts a handful of cigarettes into his pocket, while others scatter over the table and fall onto the floor.* BÉRENGER *stares at* ÉDOUARD:)

These things belong to that monster! You had them in here!

ÉDOUARD: I didn't know – I didn't know about it! (*He goes to take the briefcase back.*)

BÉRENGER: No, no. Empty it all! Go on!

ÉDOUARD: It makes me tired. You can do it yourself, but I don't see what use it is. (*He passes him the gaping briefcase.*)

BÉRENGER (*taking another box out*): It's only another box.

ÉDOUARD: I told you.

BÉRENGER (*looking inside the empty briefcase*): There's nothing else.

ÉDOUARD: Can I put the things back? (*He begins picking up the objects and putting them back in the briefcase, higgledy-piggledy.*)

BÉRENGER: The monster's things! Those are the monster's things. It's extraordinary…

ÉDOUARD (*as before*): Er… yes… there's no denying it… It's true.

67

BÉRENGER: How do they come to be in your briefcase?

ÉDOUARD: Really... I... What do you expect me to say?... You can't always explain everything... May I put them back?

BÉRENGER: I suppose so, yes, why not... What good could they be to us? (*He begins helping* ÉDOUARD *to fill the briefcase with the things he has taken out; then suddenly, as he is about to put back the last box – the one he did not examine – it opens and scatters over the table all kinds of documents, as well as several dozen visiting cards. All this is in the style of a conjuring trick.*) Look, visiting cards.

ÉDOUARD: Yes. Visiting cards. So they are, how amazing... well I never!

BÉRENGER (*inspecting the visiting cards*): That must be his name...

ÉDOUARD: Whose name?

BÉRENGER: The criminal's name, of course, the criminal's name!

ÉDOUARD: You think so?

BÉRENGER: It seems obvious to me.

ÉDOUARD: Really? Why?

BÉRENGER: You can see for yourself, can't you! All the visiting cards have the same name. Look and read! (*He offers* ÉDOUARD *a few of the cards.*)

ÉDOUARD (*reading the name written on the cards*): You're right... the same name... the same name on them all... It's quite true!

BÉRENGER: Ah... but... my dear Édouard, this is getting more and more peculiar – yes (*looking at him*), more and more peculiar!

ÉDOUARD: You don't think...

BÉRENGER (*taking the objects he mentions from the box*): And here's his address... (ÉDOUARD *gently clears his throat, appearing slightly worried.*) And his identity card... a photo of him!... It's him all right... His own photo clipped to the Colonel's. (*With growing excitement:*) An address book... with the names and addresses... of all his victims!... We'll catch him, Édouard, we'll catch him!

ÉDOUARD (*suddenly producing a neat little box; he could take it from his pocket or from one of his sleeves, like a conjuror, a folding box perhaps, which he flicks into shape as he shows it*): There's this too…

BÉRENGER (*excited*): Quick, show me! (*He opens the little box and takes out more documents, which he lays out on the table.*) A notebook… (*He turns the pages:*) "13th January: today I shall kill… 14th January: yesterday evening I pushed an old woman with gold-rimmed spectacles into the lake…" It's his private diary! (*He eagerly turns the pages, while* ÉDOUARD *appears very uneasy.*) "23rd January: nothing to kill today. 25th January: nothing to get my teeth into today, either…"

ÉDOUARD (*timidly*): Aren't we being indiscreet?

BÉRENGER (*continuing*): "26th January: yesterday evening, just when I'd given up hope and was getting bored stiff, I managed to persuade two people to look at the Colonel's photo near the pool… February: tomorrow I think I'll be able to persuade a young blonde girl I've been after for some time to look at the photo…" Ah, that must be Dany, my poor fiancée…

ÉDOUARD: Seems quite likely.

BÉRENGER (*still turning the pages*): Why look, Édouard, look – it's incredible…

ÉDOUARD (*reading over* BÉRENGER'*s shoulder*): Criminology. Does that mean something?

BÉRENGER: It means it's an essay on crime… Now we've got his profession of faith, his credo… Here it is, you see. Have a look…

ÉDOUARD (*as before: reading*): A detailed confession.

BÉRENGER: We've got him, the devil!

ÉDOUARD (*as before: reading*): Future projects. Plan of campaign.

BÉRENGER: Dany, dear Dany, you'll be revenged. (*To* ÉDOUARD:) That's all the proof you need. We can have him arrested. Do you realize?

ÉDOUARD (*stammering*): I didn't know… I didn't know…

BÉRENGER: So many human lives you could have saved.

ÉDOUARD (*as before*): Yes… I see now. I feel awful about it. I didn't know. I never know what I've got in my briefcase; I never look inside.

BÉRENGER: Carelessness like that is unforgivable.

ÉDOUARD: It's true – forgive me; I'm so sorry.

BÉRENGER: After all, you don't mean to say these things got here all by themselves! You must have found them or been given them.

ÉDOUARD (*coughing, mopping his brow and staggering*): I'm ashamed... I can't explain... I don't understand... I...

BÉRENGER: Don't blush. I'm really sorry for you, old chap. Don't you realize you're partly responsible for Dany's murder... and for so many others?

ÉDOUARD: I'm sorry... I didn't know.

BÉRENGER: Let's see what's to be done now. (*Heavy sigh.*) I'm afraid it's no good regretting the past. Feeling sorry won't help.

ÉDOUARD: You're right, you're right, you're right. (*Then, making an effort to remember:*) Ah yes, I remember now. It's funny – well, no, I suppose it isn't funny. The criminal sent me his private diary, his notes and index cards a very long time ago, asking me to publish them in a literary journal. That was before the murders were committed.

BÉRENGER: And yet he notes down what he's just done... in detail... It's like a logbook.

ÉDOUARD: No, no. Just then, they were only projects... imaginary projects. I'd forgotten the whole affair. I don't think he really intended to carry out all those crimes. His imagination carried him away. It's only later he must have thought of putting his plans into operation. *I* took them all for idle dreams of no importance...

BÉRENGER (*raising his arms to heaven*): You're so *innocent*!

ÉDOUARD (*continuing*): Something like a murder story, poetry or literature...

BÉRENGER: Literature can lead anywhere. Didn't you know that?

ÉDOUARD: We can't stop writers writing, or poets dreaming.

BÉRENGER: We ought to.

ÉDOUARD: I'm sorry I didn't give it more thought and see the connection between these documents and what's been happening...

(*While talking,* ÉDOUARD *and* BÉRENGER *start making an attempt to collect and restore to the briefcase the various objects scattered over the table, the floor and the other pieces of furniture.*)

BÉRENGER (*putting things back in the briefcase*): And yet the connection is simply between the intention and the act – no more, no less – it's clear as daylight...

ÉDOUARD (*taking a big envelope from his pocket*): There's still this!

BÉRENGER: What is it? (*They open the envelope.*) Ah, it's a map, a plan... Those crosses on it – what do they mean?

ÉDOUARD: I think... why, yes... they're the places where the murderer's meant to be...

BÉRENGER (*inspecting the map, which is spread right out on the table*): And this? Nine fifteen, thirteen twenty-seven, fifteen forty-five, eighteen oh three...

ÉDOUARD: Probably his timetable. Fixed in advance. Place by place, hour by hour, minute by minute.

BÉRENGER: ...Twenty-three hours, nine minutes, two seconds...

ÉDOUARD: Second by second. He doesn't waste time. (*He says this with a mixture of admiration and indifference.*)

BÉRENGER: Let's not waste ours either. It's easy. We notify the police. Then they just have to pick him up. But we must hurry – the offices of the Prefecture close before nightfall. Then there's no one there. Between now and tomorrow he might alter his plan. Let's go quickly and see the Architect, the Superintendent.

ÉDOUARD: You're becoming quite a man of action. I...

BÉRENGER (*continuing*): We'll show him the proof!

ÉDOUARD (*rather weakly*): I'll come if you like.

BÉRENGER (*excited*): Let's go, then. Not a moment to lose! We'll finish putting all this away.

(*They pile the objects as best they can into the huge briefcase, into their pockets and the lining of their hats.*)

Mustn't forget any of the documents... quick.

ÉDOUARD (*still more weakly*): Yes, all right.

BÉRENGER (*who has finished filling the briefcase, although there could still be several visiting cards and other objects on the floor and the table*): Quick, don't go to sleep, quick, quick… We need all the evidence… Now then, close it properly… lock it…

(ÉDOUARD, *who is rather harassed, tries in vain to lock the briefcase with a small key; he is interrupted by a fit of coughing.*)

Double lock it!… This is no time for coughing!

(ÉDOUARD *goes on trying, and struggles not to cough.*)

BÉRENGER: Oh God, how clumsy you are; you've no strength in your fingers. Put some life into it, come on!… Get a move on. Oh, give it to me! (*He takes the briefcase and the key from* ÉDOUARD.)

ÉDOUARD: I'm sorry, I'm not very good with my hands…

BÉRENGER: It's *your* briefcase, and you don't even know how to close it… Let me have the key, can't you.

(*He snatches the key quite roughly from* ÉDOUARD, *who had taken it back from him.*)

ÉDOUARD: Take it then, here you are, there.

BÉRENGER (*fastening the briefcase*): How do you think you can close it without a key? That's it. Keep it…

ÉDOUARD: Thank you.

BÉRENGER: Put it in your pocket or you'll lose it.

(ÉDOUARD *obeys.*)

That's the way. Let's go… (*He makes for the door, reluctantly followed by* ÉDOUARD, *and turns round to say:*) Don't leave the light on – switch it off, please.

(ÉDOUARD *turns back and goes to switch off. To do this he sets the briefcase down near the chair: he will leave it behind.*)

Come on… Come on… Hurry up… Hurry… (*They both go out quickly. You can hear the door opening and slamming shut, then their footsteps in the entrance. While the noises of the town become audible again, you can see the two in the street. In their haste they bump into the* CONCIERGE, *who can be seen in front of the window.* BÉRENGER *is pulling* ÉDOUARD *along by the hand.*)

CONCIERGE (*who has just been knocked into, while* BÉRENGER *and* ÉDOUARD *disappear*): Of all the!… (*She goes on muttering, incomprehensibly.*)

CURTAIN

Act Three

A wide avenue in an outlying part of town. At the back of the stage the view is masked by a raised pavement, a few yards wide, with a railing along the edge. Steps, also with a railing, leading up from street to pavement, in full view of the audience. This short flight of stone steps should be like those in some of the old streets of Paris, such as the Rue Jean de Beauvais.

Later, at the back, there is a setting sun, large and red, but without brilliance: the light does not come from there.

So at the back of the stage it is as though there were a kind of wall, four and a half or six feet high, according to the height of the stage. In the second half of the act this wall will have to open to reveal a long street in perspective with some buildings in the distance: the buildings of the Prefecture.

To the right of the stage, in the foreground, a small bench.

Before the curtain rises you can hear shouts of "Long live Mother Peep's geese! Long live Mother Peep's geese!"

The curtain goes up.

On the raised part of the stage, near the railing, is MOTHER PEEP – *a fat soul resembling the* CONCIERGE *of Act II. She is addressing a crowd, which is out of sight: all you can see are two or three flags, with the device of a goose in the middle. The white goose stands out against the green background of the flags.*

PEEP (*also carrying a green flag with a goose in the middle*):
People, listen to me. I'm Mother Peep, and I keep the public geese! I've a long experience of politics. Trust me with the chariot of state, drawn by my geese, so I can legislate. Vote for *me*. Give *me* your confidence. Me and my geese are asking for power.

(*Shouts from the crowd; the flags are waved:* "Long live Mother Peep! Long live Mother Peep's geese!" BÉRENGER *comes in from the right, followed by* ÉDOUARD, *who is out of breath.* BÉRENGER *drags him along, pulling him by the sleeve. In this way they cross the stage from right to left and from left to right. During the dialogue between* ÉDOUARD *and* BÉRENGER, MOTHER PEEP *cannot be heard speaking, but she will be seen gesticulating and opening her mouth wide. The acclamation of the hidden crowd forms no more than a quiet background sound.* MOTHER PEEP's *words and the sound of voices can, of course, be heard between the speeches of* ÉDOUARD *and* BÉRENGER.)

BÉRENGER: Come along, hurry up – do hurry up. Just one more effort. It's down there, right at the end. (*He points.*) Down there, the Prefecture buildings – we must arrive in time, before the offices close; in half an hour it'll be too late. The Architect – I mean the Superintendent – will have gone, and I've told you why we can't wait for tomorrow. Between now and then the killer might take off… or find some fresh victims! He must know I'm on his track.

ÉDOUARD (*breathless but polite*): Wait a minute, please, you've made me run too fast.

PEEP: Fellow citizens, citizenesses…

BÉRENGER: Come on, come on.

ÉDOUARD: Let me rest… I can't keep going.

BÉRENGER: We haven't got time!

PEEP: Fellow citizens, citizenesses…

ÉDOUARD: I can't go on. (*He sits down on the bench.*)

BÉRENGER: All right, then. For one second, not more. (*He remains standing, near the bench.*) I wonder what all that crowd's for.

ÉDOUARD: Election rally.

PEEP: Vote for us! Vote for us!

BÉRENGER: Looks like my concierge.

ÉDOUARD: You're seeing things. She's a politician – Mother Peep, a keeper of geese. A striking personality.

BÉRENGER: The name sounds familiar, but I've no time to listen.

ÉDOUARD (*to* BÉRENGER): Sit down for a moment – you're tired.

PEEP: People, you are mystified. You shall be demystified.

BÉRENGER (*to* ÉDOUARD): I haven't time to feel tired.

VOICE FROM THE CROWD: Down with mystification! Long live Mother Peep's geese!

ÉDOUARD (*to* BÉRENGER): I'm sorry. Just a second. You said a second.

PEEP: I've raised a whole flock of demystifiers for you. They'll demystify you. But to demystify, you must first mystify. We need a new mystification.

BÉRENGER: We haven't time, we haven't time!

VOICE FROM THE CROWD: Up with the mystification of the demystifiers!

BÉRENGER: We haven't a moment to lose! (*He sits down all the same, consulting his watch:*) Time's getting on.

VOICE FROM THE CROWD: Up with the new mystification!

BÉRENGER (*to* ÉDOUARD): Let's go.

ÉDOUARD (*to* BÉRENGER): Don't worry. You know perfectly well the time's the same as it was just now.

PEEP: I promise you I'll change everything. And changing everything means changing nothing. You can change the names, but the things remain the same. The old mystifications haven't stood up to psychological and sociological analysis. The new one will be foolproof and cause nothing but misunderstanding. We'll bring the lie to perfection.

BÉRENGER (*to* ÉDOUARD): Let's go!

ÉDOUARD: If you like.

BÉRENGER (*noticing that* ÉDOUARD, *who is painfully rising to his feet, no longer has his briefcase*): Where's your briefcase?

ÉDOUARD: My briefcase? What briefcase? Ah yes, my briefcase. It must be on the bench. (*He looks on the bench.*) No. It's not on the bench.

BÉRENGER: It's extraordinary! You always have it with you!

ÉDOUARD: Perhaps it's *under* the bench.

PEEP: We're going to disalienate mankind.

BÉRENGER (*to* ÉDOUARD): Look for it – why don't you look for it?

(*They start looking for the briefcase under the bench, then on the floor of the stage.*)

PEEP (*to the crowd*): To disalienate mankind, we must alienate each individual man... and there'll be soup kitchens for all!

VOICE FROM THE CROWD: Soup kitchens for all and Mother Peep's geese!

BÉRENGER (*to* ÉDOUARD): We must find it, hurry! Where could you have left it?

PEEP (*to the crowd, while* BÉRENGER *and* ÉDOUARD *look for the briefcase, the former frantically, the latter apathetically*): We won't persecute, but we'll punish, and deal out justice. We won't colonize, we'll occupy the countries we liberate. We won't exploit men, we'll make them productive. We'll call compulsory work voluntary. War shall change its name to Peace and everything will be altered, thanks to me and my geese.

BÉRENGER (*still searching*): It's incredible, unbelievable – where can it have got to? I hope it hasn't been stolen. That would be a catastrophe – a catastrophe!

VOICE FROM THE CROWD: Long live Mother Peep's geese! Long live soup for the people!

PEEP: When tyranny is restored we'll call it discipline and liberty. The misfortune of one is the happiness of all.

BÉRENGER (*to* ÉDOUARD): You don't realize... it's a disaster – we can't do a thing without proof, without the documents. They won't believe us.

ÉDOUARD (*to* BÉRENGER, *nonchalantly*): Don't worry, we'll find it again. Let's look for it quietly. The great thing is to keep calm.

(*They start searching again.*)

PEEP (*to the crowd*): Our political methods will be more than scientific. They'll be para-scientific. Our reason will be founded on anger. And there'll be soup kitchens for all.

VOICE FROM THE CROWD: Long live Mother Peep! Long live the geese! Long live the geese!

VOICE FROM THE CROWD: And we'll be disalienated, thanks to Mother Peep.

PEEP: Objectivity is subjective in the para-scientific age.

BÉRENGER (*wringing his hands, to* ÉDOUARD): It's one of the criminal's tricks!

ÉDOUARD (*to* BÉRENGER): It's interesting, what Mother Peep says!

VOICE FROM THE CROWD: Long live Mother Peep!

BÉRENGER (*to* ÉDOUARD): I tell you, it's one of the criminal's tricks!

ÉDOUARD (*to* BÉRENGER): You think so?

(*From the left a man appears in top hat and tails, dead drunk, holding a briefcase.*)

MAN: I am… (*hiccup*)… I am for… (*hiccup*)… the rehabilitation of the hero.

BÉRENGER (*noticing the man*): There it is! *He's* got it! (*He makes for the* MAN.)

ÉDOUARD: Long live Mother Peep!

BÉRENGER: Where did you find that briefcase? Give it back!

MAN: Don't you favour the rehabilitation of the hero?

PEEP (*to the crowd*): As for the intellectuals…

BÉRENGER (*trying to pull the briefcase away from the* MAN): Thief!… Let go of that briefcase!

PEEP (*to the crowd*): We'll make them do the goose-step! Long live the geese!

MAN (*between two hiccups, clinging on to the briefcase*): I didn't steal it. It's *my* briefcase.

VOICE FROM THE CROWD: Long live the geese!

BÉRENGER (*to the* MAN): Where did you get it from? Where did you buy it?

MAN (*hiccupping while being shaken by* BÉRENGER, *to* ÉDOUARD): Are you sure it's your briefcase?

ÉDOUARD: I think so... Looks like it.

BÉRENGER (*to the* MAN): Give it back to me, then!

MAN: I'm for the hero!

BÉRENGER (*to* ÉDOUARD): Help me! (BÉRENGER *tackles the* MAN.)

ÉDOUARD: Yes, of course. (*He goes up to the* MAN, *but lets* BÉRENGER *tackle him on his own. He is looking at* MOTHER PEEP.)

PEEP: While they're demystifying the mystifications demystified long ago, the intellectuals will give us a rest and leave *our* mystifications alone.

VOICE FROM THE CROWD: Long live Mother Peep!

MAN: I tell you, it's mine!

PEEP: They'll be stupid – that means intelligent. Cowardly – that means brave. Clear-sighted – that means blind.

ÉDOUARD & VOICE FROM THE CROWD: Long live Mother Peep!

BÉRENGER (*to* ÉDOUARD): This is no time to stand and gape. Leave Mother Peep alone.

ÉDOUARD (*to the* MAN, *coolly*): Give him the briefcase or else tell him where you bought it.

MAN (*hiccup*): We need a hero!

BÉRENGER (*to the* MAN, *having at last managed to get hold of the briefcase*): What's inside?

MAN: I don't know. Papers.

BÉRENGER (*opening the briefcase*): At last! Drunken sot.

ÉDOUARD: What do you mean by "a hero"?

PEEP: We'll march backwards and be in the forefront of history...

MAN (*while* BÉRENGER *digs into the briefcase, and* ÉDOUARD *has a look over his shoulder, absentmindedly*): A hero? A man who dares to think against history and react against his times. (*Loudly.*) Down with Mother Peep!

BÉRENGER (*to the* MAN): You're blind drunk!

MAN: A hero fights his own age and creates a different one.

BÉRENGER (*taking bottles of wine out of the* MAN*'s briefcase*): Bottles of wine!

MAN: Half empty! That's not a crime!

PEEP: ...for history has reason on its side...

MAN (*pushed by* BÉRENGER, *he staggers and falls on his behind, exclaiming*): ...when reason's lost its balance...

BÉRENGER: And are you reasonable to get drunk like this? (*To* ÉDOUARD:) Where the devil *is* your briefcase, then?

MAN: Didn't I tell you it was mine? Down with Mother Peep!

ÉDOUARD (*still indifferent and without moving*): How do I know? You can see I'm looking for it.

VOICE FROM THE CROWD: Up with Mother Peep! Up with Mother Peep's geese! She changes everything by changing nothing.

BÉRENGER (*to* ÉDOUARD): I shan't forgive you for this!

MAN (*stumbling to his feet*): Down with Mother Peep!

ÉDOUARD (*to* BÉRENGER, *snivelling*): Oh, don't go`on at me! I'm not well.

BÉRENGER (*to* ÉDOUARD): I can't help it, I'm sorry! Think of the state *I'm* in!

(*At this moment a little* OLD MAN, *with a pointed white beard, who looks shy and is poorly dressed, comes in from the right, holding in one hand an umbrella and in the other a huge black briefcase, identical with the one* ÉDOUARD *had in Act* II.)

MAN (*pointing to the* OLD MAN): There's your briefcase! That must be the one!

(BÉRENGER *makes a dive at the* OLD MAN.)

PEEP: If an ideology doesn't apply to real life, we'll say it does and it'll all be perfect. The intellectuals will back us up. They'll find us anti-myths to set against the old ones. We'll replace the myths...

BÉRENGER (*to the* OLD MAN): I beg pardon, Monsieur.

PEEP: ...with slogans... and the latest platitudes!...

OLD MAN (*raising his hat*): I beg pardon, Monsieur – can you tell me where the Danube is?

MAN (*to the* OLD MAN): Are you for the hero?

BÉRENGER (*to the* OLD MAN): Your briefcase looks just like my
   friend's. (*Pointing to him:*) Monsieur Édouard.
ÉDOUARD (*to the* OLD MAN): How do you do?
VOICE FROM THE CROWD: Up with Mother Peep!
OLD MAN (*to* ÉDOUARD): Danube Street, please?
BÉRENGER: Never mind about Danube Street.
OLD MAN: Not Danube *Street*. The Danube.
MAN: But this is Paris.
OLD MAN (*to the* MAN): I know. I *am* a Parisian.
BÉRENGER (*to the* OLD MAN): It's about the briefcase!
MAN (*to the* OLD MAN): He wants to see what you've got in your
   briefcase.
OLD MAN: That's nobody's business. I don't even ask myself. I'm
   not so inquisitive.
BÉRENGER: Of your own free will or by force you're going to
   show us...

(BÉRENGER, *the* MAN *and even* ÉDOUARD *try to take the briefcase
from the* OLD MAN, *who fights back, protesting.*)

OLD MAN (*struggling*): I won't let you!
PEEP: No more profiteers. It's me and my geese...

(*They are all round the* OLD MAN, *harrying him and trying to
take the briefcase from him: the* MAN *manages to get it away from
him first, then the* OLD MAN *snatches it back and* ÉDOUARD *lays
hands on it, only to lose it again to the* OLD MAN: *they also get
hold of the* MAN'*s briefcase again, realize their mistake when they
see the bottles and give it him back, etc.*)

BÉRENGER (*to* ÉDOUARD): Idiot!

(*He gets hold of the briefcase, the* OLD MAN *takes it back again
and the* MAN *takes it from him.*)

MAN (*offering it to* ÉDOUARD): Here it is!

(*The* OLD MAN *snatches it and tries to run away; the others catch him, etc. Meanwhile* MOTHER PEEP *is continuing her speech*:)

PEEP: …me and my geese who'll dole out public property. Fair shares for all. I'll keep the lion's share for myself and my geese…

VOICE FROM THE CROWD: Up with the geese!

PEEP: …to give my geese more strength to draw the carts of state.

VOICE FROM THE CROWD: The lion's share for the geese! The lion's share for the geese!

MAN (*shouting to* MOTHER PEEP): And we'll be free to criticize?

PEEP: Let's all do the goose-step!

VOICE FROM THE CROWD: The goose-step, the goose-step!

MAN: Free to criticize?

PEEP (*turning to the* MAN): Everyone will be free to say if the goose-step's not well done!

(*A kind of rhythmic marching is heard and the crowd shouting: "The goose-step, the goose-step!" Meanwhile the* OLD MAN *has managed to escape with his briefcase. He goes off left, followed by* BÉRENGER. ÉDOUARD, *who has made as if to follow* BÉRENGER *and the* OLD MAN, *turns back and goes to lie down on the bench, coughing. The* MAN *goes up to him.*)

MAN (*to* ÉDOUARD): Aren't you well? Have a swig! (*He tries to offer him a half-empty bottle of wine.*)

ÉDOUARD (*refusing*): No, thank you.

MAN: Yes, yes. It'll do you good. Cheer you up.

ÉDOUARD: I don't want to be cheered up.

(*The* MAN *makes the protesting* ÉDOUARD *drink; wine is spilt on the ground; the bottle too can fall and break. The* MAN *goes on making* ÉDOUARD *drink, while he speaks to* MOTHER PEEP:)

MAN (*very drunk*): Science and art have done far more to change thinking than politics have. The real revolution is taking place in the scientists' laboratories and in the artists' studios. Einstein, Oppenheimer, Breton, Kandinsky, Picasso, Pavlov – they're the ones who are really responsible. They're extending our field of knowledge, renewing our vision of the world, transforming us. Soon the means of production will give everyone a chance to live. The problem of economics will settle itself. Revolutions are a barbarous weapon, myths and grudges that go off in your face. (*He takes another bottle of wine from his briefcase and has a good swig.*) Penicillin and the fight against dypsomania are worth more than politics and a change of government.

PEEP (*to the* MAN): Bastard! Drunkard! Enemy of the people! Enemy of history! (*To the crowd*:) I denounce this man: the drunkard, the enemy of history.

VOICE FROM THE CROWD: Down with history's enemy! Let's kill the enemy of history!

ÉDOUARD (*painfully getting up*): We are all going to die. That's the only alienation that counts!

BÉRENGER (*comes in holding the* OLD MAN's *briefcase*): There's nothing in the briefcase.

OLD MAN (*following* BÉRENGER): Give it back to me, give it back!

MAN: I'm a hero! I'm a hero! (*He staggers quickly to the back of the stage and climbs up the stairs to* MOTHER PEEP.) I don't think like other people! I'm going to tell them!

BÉRENGER (*to the* OLD MAN): It's not Édouard's briefcase; here it is; I'm sorry.

ÉDOUARD: Don't go. It's heroism to think against your times, but madness to say so.

BÉRENGER: It's not *your* briefcase. So where the devil *is* yours?

(*Meanwhile the* MAN *has reached the top of the steps, next to* MOTHER PEEP.)

PEEP (*producing a huge briefcase, which has not been noticed up to now, and brandishing it*): Let's have a free discussion! (*She hits the* MAN *over the head with her briefcase.*) Rally round, my geese! Here's pasture for you!

(MOTHER PEEP *and the* MAN *fall struggling onto the raised pavement. During the following scene either* MOTHER PEEP*'s head, or the* MAN*'s, or both at once, will become visible, in the midst of a frightful hubbub of voices crying: "Up with Mother Peep! Down with the drunk!" Then, at the end of the following dialogue,* MOTHER PEEP*'s hideous face reappears, alone, for the last time. Before disappearing, she says: "My geese have liquidated him. But only physically." Punch and Judy style.*)

ÉDOUARD: The wise man says nothing. (*To the* OLD MAN:) Doesn't he, Monsieur?
BÉRENGER (*wringing his hands*): But where is it? We must have it.
OLD MAN: Where are the banks of the Danube? You can tell me *now*!

(*He straightens his clothes, shuts his briefcase and takes back his umbrella.* MOTHER PEEP*'s briefcase had opened as she hit the* MAN, *and rectangular cardboard boxes have fallen from it to the ground.*)

BÉRENGER: There's your briefcase, Édouard! It's Mother Peep's.
(*He notices the boxes.*) And there are the documents.
ÉDOUARD: You think so?
OLD MAN (*to* ÉDOUARD): Damn it, he's got a mania for running after briefcases! What's he looking for?

(BÉRENGER *bends down, picks up the boxes and then comes back to the front of the stage to* ÉDOUARD *and the* OLD MAN, *looking disappointed.*)

ÉDOUARD: It's my briefcase he wants to find!
BÉRENGER (*showing the boxes*): It's not the documents! It's only the goose game!
OLD MAN: I haven't played that for a long time.
BÉRENGER (*to* ÉDOUARD): It's no concern of yours! It's the briefcase we're after... the briefcase with the documents. (*To the* OLD MAN:) The evidence – to arrest the criminal!
OLD MAN: So that's it, you should have said so before.

(*It is at this moment that* MOTHER PEEP's *head appears for the last time to make the remark already mentioned. Immediately afterwards the noise of the engine of a truck is heard, which drowns out the voices of the crowd and the three characters on the stage, who go on talking and gesticulating without a word being heard. A* POLICE SERGEANT *appears, who should be unusually tall: with a white stick he taps the invisible people on the other side of the wall over the head.*)

POLICEMAN (*only visible from head to waist, wielding the stick in one hand and blowing his whistle with the other*): Come along now, move on there. (*The crowd cries: "The police, the police. Up with the police." The* POLICEMAN *continues moving them on in the same way, so that the noise of the crowd gradually dies and fades right away. A huge military truck coming from the left blocks half the upper part of the stage.*)
ÉDOUARD (*indifferently*): Look, an army truck!
BÉRENGER (*to* ÉDOUARD): Never mind about that.

(*Another military truck coming from the opposite side blocks the other half of the upper part of the stage, just leaving enough room for the* POLICEMAN *in between the two trucks.*)

OLD MAN (*to* BÉRENGER): You should have said you were looking for your friend's briefcase with the documents. I know where it is.
POLICEMAN (*above, blowing his whistle, between the trucks*): Move along there, move along.
OLD MAN (*to* BÉRENGER): Your friend must have left it at home in your hurry to leave.
BÉRENGER (*to the* OLD MAN): How did you know?
ÉDOUARD: He's right, I should have thought! Were you watching us?
OLD MAN: Not at all. It's a simple deduction.
BÉRENGER (*to* ÉDOUARD): Idiot!
ÉDOUARD: I'm sorry... we were in such a hurry!

(*A young* SOLDIER *gets out of the military truck, holding a bunch of red carnations. He uses it as a fan. He goes and sits on the top of the wall, the flowers in his hand, his legs dangling over the edge.*)

BÉRENGER (*to* ÉDOUARD): Go and fetch it – go and fetch it at once! You're impossible! I'll go and warn the Superintendent, so he'll wait for us. Hurry and join me as soon as you can. The Prefecture's right at the end. In an affair like this I don't like being alone on the road. It's not pleasant. You understand?

ÉDOUARD: Of course I do, I understand. (*To the* OLD MAN:) Thank you, Monsieur.

OLD MAN (*to* BÉRENGER): Could you tell me now where the Danube Embankment is?

BÉRENGER (*to* ÉDOUARD, *who hasn't moved*): Well, hurry up! Don't stand there! Come back quick.

ÉDOUARD: All right.

BÉRENGER (*to the* OLD MAN): I don't know, Monsieur, I'm sorry.

ÉDOUARD (*making off very slowly to the right, where he disappears, saying nonchalantly*): All right, then, I'll hurry. I'll hurry. Won't be long. Won't be long.

BÉRENGER (*to the* OLD MAN): You must ask – ask a policeman!

(*On his way out* ÉDOUARD *nearly knocks into the* 2ND POLICEMAN, *who appears, blowing his whistle and waving his white stick about too: he should be immensely tall – perhaps he could walk on stilts.*)

ÉDOUARD (*dodging the* POLICEMAN, *who doesn't look at him*): Oh, sorry! (*He disappears.*)

BÉRENGER (*to the* OLD MAN): There's one. You can find out.

OLD MAN: He's very busy. Do you think I dare?

BÉRENGER: Yes, of course – he's all right.

(BÉRENGER *goes to the back of the stage after crying one last time after* ÉDOUARD: "*Hurry up!*" *The* OLD MAN *very shyly and hesitantly approaches the* 2ND POLICEMAN.)

OLD MAN (*timidly, to the* 2ND POLICEMAN): I beg your pardon!
   I beg your pardon!

BÉRENGER (*he has gone right to the back of the stage and has
   one foot on the first step of the stairs*): I must hurry!

1ST POL. (*between two blasts, pointing his white stick down at
   BÉRENGER to make him move away*): Move on, move on there.

BÉRENGER: It's terrible. What a traffic jam! I'll never, never get
   there. (*Addressing first one, then the other policeman:*) It's
   a good thing we've got you here to keep the traffic moving.
   You've no idea what bad luck this hold-up is for me!

OLD MAN (*to the* 2ND POLICEMAN): Excuse me, please,
   Monsieur. (*Before addressing the* 2ND POLICEMAN *the*
   OLD MAN *has respectfully removed his hat and made a low
   bow; the* 2ND POLICEMAN *takes no notice; he is getting
   excited, making signals which are answered by the* 1ST
   POLICEMAN *the other side of the wall with his white stick,
   while he too energetically blows his whistle.* BÉRENGER
   goes frantically from one to the other.)

BÉRENGER (*to the* 1ST POLICEMAN): Oh, hurry up, I've got to
   get by. I've a very important mission. It's humanitarian.

1ST POL. (*who goes on blowing his whistle and urging* BÉRENGER
   on with his stick): Move along!

OLD MAN (*to the* 2ND POLICEMAN): Monsieur... (*To* BÉRENGER:)
   He won't answer. He's too busy.

BÉRENGER: Oh, these trucks are here for good. (*He looks at his
   watch.*) Luckily, it's still the same time. (*To the* OLD MAN:)
   Ask him – go on and ask him, he won't bite you.

OLD MAN (*to the* 2ND POLICEMAN, *who is still blowing his
   whistle*): Please, Monsieur.

2ND POL. (*to the* 1ST POLICEMAN): Get them to go back! (*Sound
   of the engines of the still stationary trucks.*) Make them go
   forwards! (*Same sound.*)

SOLDIER (*to* BÉRENGER): If I knew the city I'd tell him the way.
   But I'm not a local.

BÉRENGER (*to the* OLD MAN): The policeman's bound to give
   you satisfaction. That's his privilege. Speak louder.

(*The* SOLDIER *goes on fanning himself with his bunch of red flowers.*)

OLD MAN (*to the* 2ND POLICEMAN): I'm sorry, Monsieur, listen, Monsieur.

2ND POL. What?

OLD MAN: Monsieur, I'd like to ask you a simple question.

2ND POL. (*sharply*): One minute! (*To the* SOLDIER:) You – why have you left your truck, eh?

SOLDIER: I... I... but it's stopped!

BÉRENGER (*aside*): Good Heavens – that Policeman's got the Superintendent's voice! Could it be him? (*He goes to have a closer look.*) No. He wasn't so tall.

2ND POL. (*to the* OLD MAN *again, while the other policeman is still controlling the traffic*): What's that you wanted, you there?

BÉRENGER (*aside*): No, it's not him. His voice wasn't quite as hard as that.

OLD MAN (*to the* 2ND POLICEMAN): The Danube Embankment, please, Monsieur l'Agent, I'm sorry.

2ND POL. (*his reply is aimed at the* OLD MAN *as well as the* 1ST POLICEMAN *and the invisible drivers of the two trucks; it precipitates a scene of general chaos, which should be comic, involving everyone; even the two trucks move*): To the left! To the right! Straight on! Straight back! Forwards!

(*The* 2ND POLICEMAN, *the upper part of whom only is seen above, moves his head and white stick in obedience to his words;* BÉRENGER *makes parallel gestures, still standing on the same spot; the* SOLDIER *does the same with his bunch of flowers. The* OLD MAN *steps to the left, then to the right, then straight on, straight back and forwards.*)

BÉRENGER (*aside*): All the police have the same voice.

OLD MAN (*returning to the* 2ND POLICEMAN): Excuse me, Monsieur, excuse me, I'm rather hard of hearing. I didn't quite understand which way you told me to go... for the Danube Embankment, please...

2ND POL. (*to the* OLD MAN): You trying to get a rise out of me? Oh no, there are *times*...

BÉRENGER (*aside*): The Superintendent was much more pleasant...

2ND POL. (*to the* OLD MAN): Come on... Clear off... deaf or daft... bugger off! (*Blasts on the whistle from the* 2ND POLICEMAN, *who starts dashing about and knocks into the* OLD MAN, *who drops his walking stick.*)

SOLDIER (*on the steps*): Your stick, Monsieur.

OLD MAN (*picking up his stick, to the* 2ND POLICEMAN): Don't lose your temper, Monsieur l'Agent, don't lose your temper! (*He is very frightened.*)

2ND POL. (*still directing the traffic jam*): Left...

BÉRENGER (*to the* OLD MAN, *while the trucks move a little at the back of the stage, threatening for a moment to crush the* 1ST POLICEMAN): That policeman's behaviour is disgraceful!

1ST POL.: Look out, half-wits!

BÉRENGER (*to the* OLD MAN): After all, he has a duty to be polite to the public.

1ST POL. (*to the supposed drivers of the two trucks*): Left!

2ND POL. (*as above*): Right!

BÉRENGER (*to the* OLD MAN): It must be part of their regulations!... (*To the* SOLDIER:) Mustn't it?

1ST POL. (*as before*): Right!

SOLDIER (*like a child*): I don't know... (*Fanning himself with his flowers.*) *I've* got my flowers.

BÉRENGER (*aside*): When I see his boss, the Architect, I'll tell him about it.

2ND POL. (*as before*): Straight on!

OLD MAN: It doesn't matter, Monsieur l'Agent, I'm sorry... (*He goes out left.*)

2ND POL. (*as before*): To the left, left!

BÉRENGER (*while the* 2ND POLICEMAN *is saying faster and faster and more and more mechanically: "Straight on, left, right, straight on, forwards, backwards, etc....' and the*

1ST POLICEMAN *repeats his orders in the same way, turning his head from right to left, etc., like a puppet*): I think, Soldier, we're too polite, far too nervous, with the police. We've got them into bad habits – it's our fault!

SOLDIER (*offering the bunch of flowers to* BÉRENGER, *who has come close to him and climbed up one or two steps*): See how good they smell!

BÉRENGER: No thank you, I don't.

SOLDIER: Can't you see they're carnations?

BÉRENGER: Yes, but that's not the point. I've simply got to keep going. This hold-up's a disaster!

2ND POL. (*to* BÉRENGER, *then he goes towards the young* SOLDIER, *when* BÉRENGER *moves away from him*): Move on.

BÉRENGER (*moving away from the* POLICEMAN *who has just addressed this order to him*): You don't like these trucks either, Monsieur l'Agent. I can see that in your face. And how right you are!

2ND POL. (*to the* 1ST POLICEMAN): Go on blowing your whistle for a minute.

(*The* 1ST POLICEMAN *goes on as before.*)

1ST POL.: All right! Carry on!

BÉRENGER (*to the* 2ND POLICEMAN): The traffic's getting impossible. Especially when there are things… things that can't wait…

2ND POL. (*to the* SOLDIER, *pointing at the bunch of red carnations the latter is still holding and fanning himself with*): Haven't you got anything better to do than play with that?

SOLDIER (*politely*): I'm not doing any harm, Monsieur l'Agent; that's not stopping the trucks from moving.

2ND POL.: It puts a spanner in the works, wise guy! (*He slaps the* SOLDIER *across the face; the* SOLDIER *says nothing. The* POLICEMAN *is so tall that he does not need to climb the steps to reach the* SOLDIER.)

BÉRENGER (*aside, in the centre of the stage, indignantly*): Oh!

2ND POL. (*snatching the flowers from the* SOLDIER *and hurling them into the wings*): Lunatic! Aren't you ashamed of yourself? Get back in that truck with your mates.

SOLDIER: All right, Monsieur l'Agent.

2ND POL. (*to the* SOLDIER): Look alive there, stupid bastard!

BÉRENGER (*in the same position*): Going much too far!

SOLDIER (*climbing back into the truck with the help of the* 1ST POLICEMAN'*s fist and the* 2ND POLICEMAN'*s stick*): Yes, all right, I will! (*He disappears into the truck.*)

BÉRENGER (*in the same position*): Much too far!

2ND POL. (*to the other invisible soldiers who are supposed to be in the trucks and who could, perhaps, be represented by puppets or simply be painted sitting on painted benches in the trucks*): You're blocking the road! We're fed up with your damned trucks!

BÉRENGER (*aside, in same position*): In my view a country's done for if the police lays a hand... and its fingers on the army.

2ND POL. (*turning to* BÉRENGER): What's the matter with you? It's none of your business if—

BÉRENGER: But I didn't say anything, Monsieur l'Agent, not a thing...

2ND POL.: It's easy to guess what's going on in the minds of people of your type!

BÉRENGER: How do you know what I—

2ND POL.: Never you mind! You try and put your wrong thinking right.

BÉRENGER (*stammering*): But it's not that, Monsieur, not that at all – you're mistaken – I'm sorry, I'd not... I'd never... on the contrary, I'd even...

2ND POL.: What are you up to here, anyway? Where are your identification papers?

BÉRENGER (*looking in his pockets*): Oh well, if that's what you want, Monsieur l'Agent... You've a right to see them...

2ND POL. (*who is now in the centre of the stage, close to* BÉRENGER, *who naturally looks very small beside him*): Come on, quicker than that. I've no time to waste!

1ST POL. (*still above, between the two trucks*): Hey! You leaving me on my own to unscramble this traffic? (*He blows his whistle.*)

2ND POL. (*shouting to the* 1ST POLICEMAN): Just a minute, I'm busy. (*To* BÉRENGER:) Quicker than that. Well, aren't they coming, those papers?

BÉRENGER (*who has found his papers*): Here they are, Monsieur l'Agent.

2ND POL. (*examining the papers, then returning them to* BÉRENGER): Well... all in order!

(*The* 1ST POLICEMAN *blows his whistle and waves his white stick. The truck engines are heard.*)

1ST POL. (*to the* 2ND POLICEMAN): Doesn't matter. We'll get him yet – next time.

BÉRENGER (*to the* 2ND POLICEMAN, *taking his papers back*): Thanks very much, Monsieur l'Agent.

2ND POL.: You're welcome...

BÉRENGER (*to the* 2ND POLICEMAN, *who is about to move off*): Now you know who I am and all about my case, perhaps I can ask for your help and advice.

2ND POL.: I don't know about your case.

BÉRENGER: Yes, you do, Monsieur l'Agent. You must have realized I'm looking for the killer. What else could I be doing round here?

2ND POL.: Stopping me from controlling the traffic, perhaps.

BÉRENGER (*without hearing the last remark*): We can lay hands on him, I've all the evidence... I mean, Édouard has; he's bringing it along in his briefcase... Theoretically, I've got it... meanwhile I'm off to the Prefecture, and it's still a long way... Can you send someone with me?

2ND POL.: Hear that? He's got a nerve!

1ST POL. (*interrupting his mime, to the* 2ND POLICEMAN): Is he one of us? He an informer?

2ND POL. (*to the* 1ST POLICEMAN): He's not even that! Who does he think he is!

(*He blows his whistle for the traffic.*)

BÉRENGER: Listen to me, please – this is really serious. You've seen for yourself, I'm a respectable man.

2ND POL. (*to* BÉRENGER): What's it all got to do with you, eh?

BÉRENGER (*drawing himself up*): I beg your pardon, but I *am* a citizen – it matters to me – it concerns us all – we're all responsible for the crimes that... You see, I'm a really serious citizen.

2ND POL. (*to the* 1ST POLICEMAN): Hear that? Likes to hear himself talk.

BÉRENGER: I'm asking you once more, Monsieur l'Agent! (*To the* 1ST POLICEMAN:) I'm asking you, too!

1ST POL. (*still busy with the traffic*): That's enough, now.

BÉRENGER (*continuing, to* 2ND POLICEMAN): ...you, too: can you send someone with me to the Prefecture? I'm a friend of the Superintendent's – of the Architect's.

2ND POL.: That's not my department. I suppose even you can see I'm in "traffic control".

BÉRENGER (*plucking up more courage*): I'm a friend of the Superintendent's—

2ND POL. (*bending down to* BÉRENGER *and almost shouting in his ear*): I'm – in – traffic – control!

BÉRENGER (*recoiling slightly*): Yes, I see, but... all the same... in the public interest... public safety, you know!

2ND POL.: Public safety? *We* look after that. When we've the time. Traffic comes first!

1ST POL.: Who *is* this character? Reporter?

BÉRENGER: No, Messieurs, no, I'm *not* a reporter... just a citizen, that's all...

1ST POL. (*between two blasts on the whistle*): Has he got a camera?

BÉRENGER: No, Messieurs, I haven't, search me... (*He turns out his pockets.*) ...I'm *not* a reporter...

2ND POL. (*to* BÉRENGER): Lucky you hadn't got it on you, or I'd have smashed your face in!

BÉRENGER: I don't mind your threats. Public safety's more important than I am. He killed Dany, too.

2ND POL.: Who's this Dany?

BÉRENGER: He killed her.

1ST POL. (*between two blasts, signals and shouts of: "Right! Left!"*): It's his tart...

BÉRENGER: No, Monsieur, she's my fiancée. Or was to be.

2ND POL. (*to the* 1ST POLICEMAN): That's it all right. He wants revenge on account of his tart!

BÉRENGER: The criminal must pay for his crime!

1ST POL.: Phew! They can talk themselves silly, some of them!

2ND POL. (*louder, turning to* BÉRENGER *again*): It's not my business, get it? I don't give a good goddam for your story. If you're one of the boss's pals, go and see him and leave me in goddam peace.

BÉRENGER (*trying to argue*): Monsieur l'Agent... I... I...

2ND POL. (*as before, while the* 1ST POLICEMAN *laughs sardonically*): I keep the peace, so leave *me* in peace! You know the way... (*He points to the back of the stage, blocked by the trucks.*) So bugger off, the road's clear!

BÉRENGER: Right, Monsieur l'Agent, right, Monsieur l'Agent!

2ND POL. (*to the* 1ST POLICEMAN, *ironically*): Let the gentleman through!

(*As though by magic the trucks move back; the whole set at the back of the stage is movable, and so comes apart.*)

Let the gentleman through!

(*The* 1ST POLICEMAN *has disappeared with the back wall and the trucks; now, at the back of the stage, you can see a very long street or avenue with the Prefecture buildings in the far distance against the setting sun. A miniature tram crosses the stage far away.*)

Let the gentleman through!

1ST POL. (*whose face appears over the roof of one of the houses in the street that has just appeared*): Come on, get moving! (*He gestures to him to start moving and disappears.*)

BÉRENGER: That's just what I'm doing...

2ND POL. (*to* BÉRENGER): I hate you!

(*It is the* 2ND POLICEMAN*'s turn to make a sudden disappearance; the stage has got slightly darker.* BÉRENGER *is now alone.*)

BÉRENGER (*calling after the* 2ND POLICEMAN, *who has just disappeared*): I've more right to say that than you have! Just now I haven't got time... but you haven't heard the last of me! (*He shouts after the vanished policeman:*) You – haven't – heard – the – last – of – me!!

(*The* ECHO *answers: last – of – me...*

BÉRENGER *is now quite alone on the stage. The miniature tram is no longer visible at the back. It is up to the producer, the designer and the electrician to bring out* BÉRENGER*'s utter loneliness, the emptiness around him and the deserted avenue somewhere between town and country. A part of the mobile set could disappear completely to increase the area of the stage.* BÉRENGER *should appear to be walking for a long time in the ensuing scene; if there is no revolving stage he can make the steps without advancing. It might, in fact, be possible to have the walls back again to give the impression of a long, narrow passage, so that* BÉRENGER *seems to be walking into some ambush; the light does not change; it is twilight, with a red sun glowing at the back of the stage. Whether the stage is broad and open or reduced by flats to represent a long, narrow street, there is a still, timeless half-light.*

While he is walking, BÉRENGER *will grow more and more anxious; at the start, he sets off, or appears to, at a fast pace; then he takes to turning round more and more frequently until his walk has become hesitant; he looks to right and left, and then behind him again, so that in the end he appears to be on the point of flight, ready to turn back; but he controls himself with difficulty, and after a great effort decides to go forwards again; if the set is movable and can be changed without having to lower the curtain or the lights,* BÉRENGER *might just as well walk from one end of the stage to the other, and then come back, etc.*

Finally, he will advance cautiously, glancing all around; and yet, at the end of the act, when the last character in the play makes his appearance – or is first heard, or heard and seen at the same time – BÉRENGER *will be taken by surprise: so this character should appear just when* BÉRENGER *is looking the other way. The appearance of this character must, however, be prepared for by* BÉRENGER *himself:* BÉRENGER*'s mounting anguish should make the audience aware that the character is getting nearer and nearer.*)

BÉRENGER (*starting to walk, or appearing to, and at the same time turning his head in the direction of the policemen towards the wings on the right, and shaking his fist at them*): I can't do everything at once. Now for the murderer. It'll be your turn next. (*He walks in silence for a second or two, stepping it out.*) Outrageous attitude! I don't believe in reporting people, but I'll talk to the Chief Superintendent about it – you bet I will! (*He walks in silence.*) I hope I'm not too late! (*The noise of the wind; a dead leaf flutters down and* BÉRENGER *turns up his overcoat collar.*) And now, on top of everything else, the wind's got up. And the light's going. Will Édouard be able to catch up with me in time? Will he catch up with me in time? He's so slow! (*He walks on in silence while the set changes.*) Everything will have to be changed. First we must start by reforming the police force… All they're good for is teaching you manners, but when you really *need* them – when you want them to protect you – they couldn't care less… they let you down… (*He looks round.*) They and their trucks – they're a long way off already… Better hurry. (*He sets off again.*) I *must* get there before it's dark. It can't be too safe on the road. Still a long way… Not getting any nearer… I'm not making any progress. It's as though I wasn't moving at all. (*Silence.*) There's no end to this avenue and its tramlines. (*Silence.*) …There's the boundary, anyway, the start of the outer boulevards… (*He walks in silence.*) I'm shivering. Because of the cold wind. You'd think I was frightened, but I'm not. I'm used to being alone… (*He walks in silence.*) I've always been alone… And yet I love the human race, but at a distance.

What's that matter, when I'm interested in the fate of mankind? Fact is, I *am doing* something... (*He smiles.*) Doing... acting... acting, not play-acting, doing! Well, really I'm even running risks, you might say, for mankind... and for Dany, too. Risks? The Civil Service will protect me. Dear Dany, those policemen defiled your memory. I'll make them pay. (*He looks behind him, ahead, then behind again; he stops.*) I'm halfway there. Not quite. Nearly... (*He sets off again at a not very determined pace; while he walks he glances behind him:*) Édouard! That you, Édouard? (*The Echo answers: "ouard... ouard..."*) No... it's not Édouard... Once he's arrested, bound hand and foot, out of harm's way, the spring will come back for ever, and every city will be radiant... I shall have my reward. That's not what I'm after. To have done my duty, that's enough... So long as it's not too late – so long as it's not too late. (*Sound of the wind or the cry of an animal.* BÉRENGER *stops.*) Supposing I went back... to look for Édouard? We could go to the Prefecture tomorrow. Yes, I'll go tomorrow, with Édouard... (*He turns in his tracks and takes a step on the road back.*) No. Édouard's sure to catch me up in a moment or two. (*To himself:*) Think of Dany. I must have revenge for Dany. I must stop the rot. Yes, yes, I know I can. Besides, I've gone too far now; it's darker that way than the way I'm going. The road to the Prefecture is still the safest. (*He shouts again:*) Édouard! Édouard!

ECHO: É-dou-ard... ou... ard...

BÉRENGER: Can't see now whether he's coming or not. Perhaps he's quite near. Go on again. (*Setting off again with great caution.*) Doesn't seem like it, but I've covered some ground... Oh yes I have, no doubt about it... You wouldn't think so, but I *am* advancing... advancing... Ploughed fields on my right, and this deserted street... No risk of a traffic jam now, anyway; you can keep going. (*He laughs. The echo vaguely repeats the laugh.* BÉRENGER, *scared, looks round:*) What's that?... It's the echo... (*He resumes his walking.*) No one there, stupid... Over there, who's that? There, behind that tree! (*He rushes behind a leafless tree, which could be part of the moving scene.*)

Why, no, it's nobody... (*The leaf of an old newspaper falls from the tree.*) Aah!... Afraid of a newspaper now. What a fool I am! (*He bursts out laughing. The echo repeats: "...fool... I... am..." and distorts the laugh.*) I must get farther... I must go on! Advancing under cover of the Civil Service... advancing... I must... I must... (*Halt.*) No, no. It's not worth it; in any case, I'll arrive too late. Not my fault; it's the fault of the... fault of the... of the traffic – the hold-up made me late... And above all it's Édouard's fault... he forgets everything – every blessed thing... Perhaps the murderer will strike again tonight... (*With a start:*) I've simply got to stop him. I *must* go. I'm going. (*Another two or three paces in the direction of the supposed Prefecture.*) Come to think of it, it's all the same really, as it's too late. Another victim here or there – what's it matter in the state we're in... We'll go tomorrow, go tomorrow, Édouard and I, and much simpler that way; the offices will be closed this evening, perhaps they are already... What good would it do to... (*He shouts off right into the wings:*) Édouard! Édouard!

ECHO: É... ard... É... ard...

BÉRENGER: He won't come now. No point in thinking he will. It's too late. (*He looks at his watch.*) My watch has stopped... Never mind, there's no harm putting it off... I'll go tomorrow, with Édouard!... The Superintendent will arrest him tomorrow. (*He turns round.*) Where am I? I hope I can find my way home! It's in this direction! (*He turns round again quickly and suddenly sees the* KILLER *quite close to him.*) Ah!... (*The set has, of course, stopped changing. In fact there is practically no scenery. All there is is a wall and a bench. The empty waste of a plain and a slight glow on the horizon. The two characters are picked out in a pale light, while the rest is in semi-darkness. Derisive laugh from the* KILLER: *he is very small and puny, ill-shaven, with a torn hat on his head and a shabby old gabardine; he has only one eye, which shines with a steely glitter, and a set expression on his still face; his toes are peeping out of the holes in his old shoes. When the* KILLER *appears, laughing derisively, he should be standing on the bench, or perhaps somewhere on the wall: he calmly jumps down and approaches* BÉRENGER, *chuckling unpleasantly, and it is at this moment that one notices how small he is. Or possibly there is no Killer at all.* BÉRENGER *could be talking to himself, alone in the half-light.*) It's him, it's the killer! (*To the* KILLER:) So it's you, then!

(*The* KILLER *chuckles softly:* BÉRENGER *glances round, anxiously.*)

Nothing but the dark plain all around… You needn't tell me, I can see that as well as you.

(*He looks towards the distant Prefecture. Soft chuckle from the* KILLER.)

The Prefecture's too far away? That's what you just meant? I know.

(*Chuckle from the* KILLER.)

Or was that me talking?

(*Chuckle from the* KILLER.)

You're laughing at me! I'll call the police and have you arrested.

(*Chuckle from the* KILLER.)

It's no good, you mean; they wouldn't hear me? (*The* KILLER *gets down from the bench or the wall and approaches* BÉRENGER, *horribly detached and vaguely chuckling, both hands in his pockets. Aside:*) Those dirty coppers left me alone with him on purpose. They wanted to make me believe it was just a private feud. (*To the* KILLER, *almost shouting:*) Why? Just tell me why!

(*The* KILLER *chuckles and gives a slight shrug of the shoulders; he is quite close to* BÉRENGER, *who should appear not only bigger but also stronger than the almost dwarf-like* KILLER. BÉRENGER *lets out a burst of nervous laughter.*)

Oh, you really are rather puny, aren't you? Too puny to be a criminal! I'm not afraid of you! Look at me, look how much stronger I am. I could knock you down, knock you flying with a flick of my fingers. I could put you in my pocket. Do you realize? (*Same chuckle from the* KILLER.) I'm – not – afraid – of – you!

(*Chuckle from the* KILLER.)

I could squash you like a worm. But I won't. I want to understand. You're going to answer my questions. After all, you are a human being. You've got reasons, perhaps. You must explain, or else I don't know what... You're going to tell me why... Answer me!

(*The* KILLER *chuckles and gives a slight shrug of the shoulders.* BÉRENGER *should be pathetic and naive – rather ridiculous; his behaviour should seem sincere and grotesque at the same time, both pathetic and absurd. He speaks with an eloquence that should underline the tragically worthless and outdated commonplaces he is advancing.*)

Anyone who does what you do does it, perhaps, because... Listen... You've stopped me from being happy, and stopped a great many more... In that shining district of the town, which would surely have cast its radiance over the whole world... a new light radiating from France! If you've any feeling left for your country... it would have shone on you, would have moved you, too, as well as countless others, would have made you happy in yourself... a question of waiting, it was only a matter of patience... impatience, that's what spoils everything...

yes, you would have been happy – happiness would have come even to you, and it would have spread; perhaps you didn't know, perhaps you didn't believe it... You were wrong... Well, it's your own happiness you've destroyed, as well as mine and that of all the others...

(*Slight chuckle from the* KILLER.)

I suppose you don't believe in happiness. You think happiness is impossible in this world? You want to destroy the world because you think it's doomed. Don't you? That's it, isn't it? Answer me!

(*Chuckle from the* KILLER.)

I suppose you never thought for a single moment that you'd got it wrong. You were sure you were right. It's just your stupid pride. Before you finally make up your mind about this, at least let other people experiment for themselves. They're trying to realize a practical and technical ideal of happiness, here and now, on this earth of ours; and they'll succeed, perhaps – how can you tell? If they don't, then you can think again...

(*Chuckle from the* KILLER.)

You're a pessimist?

(*Chuckle from the* KILLER.)

You're a nihilist?

(*Chuckle from the* KILLER.)

An anarchist?

(*Chuckle from the* KILLER.)

Perhaps you don't like happiness? Perhaps happiness is different for you? Tell me your ideas about life. What's your philosophy? Your motives? Your aims? Answer me!

(*Chuckle from the* KILLER.)

Listen to me: you've hurt me personally in the worst possible way, destroying everything... all right, forget that... I'll not talk about myself. But you killed Dany! What had Dany done to you? She was a wonderful creature, with a few faults, of course – I suppose she was rather hot-tempered, liked her own way – but she had a kind heart, and beauty like that is an excuse for anything! If you killed every girl who liked her own way just because she liked her own way, or the neighbours because they make a noise and keep you awake, or someone for holding different opinions from you, it would be ridiculous, wouldn't it? Yet that's what you do! Don't you? Don't you?

(*Chuckle from the* KILLER.)

We won't talk about Dany any more. She was my fiancée, and you might believe it's all just a personal matter. But tell me this... what had that Officer in the Engineers done to you, that Staff Officer?

(*Chuckle from the* KILLER.)

All right, I know... I understand – there are some people who hate a uniform. Rightly or wrongly, they see it as the symbol of an abuse of power, of tyranny and of war, which destroys civilizations. Right: we won't raise the question – it might take us too far – but that woman...

(*Chuckle from the* KILLER.)

...you know the one I mean – that young redhead – what had she done to you? What had you got against her? Answer me!

(*Chuckle from the* KILLER.)

We'll suppose you hate women, then: perhaps they betrayed you, didn't love you, because you're not, let's face it, you're not much to look at... it's not fair, I agree, but there's more than just the sexual side to life – there are some religious people who've given that up for all time... you can find satisfaction of a different kind in life and overcome that feeling of resentment...

(*Chuckle from the* KILLER.)

But the child, that child, what had he done to you? Children can't be guilty of anything, can they? You know the one I mean: the little fellow you pushed into the pool with the woman and the officer, poor little chap... our hopes are in the children – no one should touch a child; everyone agrees about that.

(*Chuckle from the* KILLER.)

Perhaps you think the human race is rotten in itself. Answer me! You want to punish the human race even in a child, the least impure of all... We could debate the problem, if you like, publicly, defend and oppose the motion – what do you say?

(*Chuckle from the* KILLER, *who shrugs his shoulders.*)

Perhaps you kill all these people out of kindness! To save them from suffering! For you, life is just suffering! Perhaps you want to cure people of the haunting fear of death? You think, like others before you, that man is and always will be the sick animal, in spite of all social, technical or scientific progress, and I suppose you want to carry out a sort of universal mercy-killing? Well you're mistaken – you're wrong. Answer me!

(*Chuckle from the* KILLER.)

Anyway, if life's of little value, if it's too short, the suffering of mankind will be short too: whether men suffer thirty or forty years, ten years more or less, what's it matter to you? Let people suffer if that's what they want. Let them suffer, as long as they're willing to suffer... Besides, time goes by – a few years hardly count – they'll have a whole eternity of not suffering. Let them die in their own time, and it will all be over quite soon. Everything will flicker out and finish on its own. Don't hurry things up – there's no point.

(*Chuckle from the* KILLER.)

Why, you're putting yourself in an absurd position – if you think you're doing mankind a service by destroying it, you're wrong, that's stupid! Aren't you afraid of ridicule? Eh? Answer me that!

(*Chuckle from the* KILLER; *loud, nervous laugh from* BÉRENGER. *Then, after watching the* KILLER *for a while*:)

I see this doesn't interest you. I haven't laid my finger on the real problem, on the spot that really hurts. Tell me: do you hate mankind? Do you hate mankind?

(*Chuckle from the* KILLER.)

But why? Answer me!

(*Chuckle from the* KILLER.)

If that is the case, don't vent your spleen on men – that's no good – it only makes you suffer yourself; it hurts to hate; better despise them; yes, I'll allow you to despise them, isolate yourself from them, go and live in the mountains, become a shepherd – why not – and you'll live among sheep and dogs.

(*Chuckle from the* KILLER.)

You don't like animals either? You don't love anything that's alive? Not even the plants?... What about stones and stars, the sun and the blue sky?

(*Chuckle and shrug of the shoulders from the* KILLER.)

No. No, I'm being silly. One can't hate everything. Do you believe society's rotten, that it can't be improved, that revolutionaries are fools? Or do you believe the existence of the universe is a mistake?

(*The* KILLER *shrugs his shoulders.*)

Why can't you answer me... answer me! Oh! Argument's impossible with you! Listen, you'll make me angry, I warn you! No... no... I mustn't lose my self-control. I must understand you. Don't look at me like that with your glittering eye. I'm going to talk frankly. Just now I meant to have my revenge, for myself and the others. I wanted to have you arrested, sent to the guillotine. Vengeance is stupid. Punishment's not the answer. I was furious with you. I was after your blood... as soon as I saw you... not immediately, not that very moment, no, but a few seconds later, I... it sounds silly – you won't believe me, and yet I must tell you... yes... you're a human being: we're the same species; we've got to understand each other; it's our duty; a few seconds later, I loved you, or almost... because we're brothers, and if I hate you, I can't help hating myself...

(*Chuckle from the* KILLER.)

Don't laugh: it exists, fellow feeling, the brotherhood of man – I know it does; don't sneer...

(*Chuckle and shrug of the shoulders from the* KILLER.)

Ah... but you're a... you're nothing but a... now listen to this. We're the strongest – *I'm* stronger physically than you are – you're a helpless feeble little runt! What's more, I've the law on my side... the police!

(*Chuckle from the* KILLER.)

Justice, the whole force of law and order!

(*Chuckle from the* KILLER.)

I mustn't... I mustn't get carried away... I'm sorry...

(*Chuckle from the* KILLER; BÉRENGER *mops his brow.*)

You've got more self-control than I have... but I'll calm down, I'll calm down... no need to be afraid... You don't seem very frightened... I mean, don't hold it against me... but you're not even scared, are you?... No, it's not that – that's not what I mean... Ah yes, yes... perhaps you don't realize. (*Very loud:*) Christ died on the Cross for you; it was for you he suffered; he loves you... And you really need to be loved, though you think you don't!

(*Chuckle from the* KILLER.)

I swear to you that the blessed saints are pouring out tears for you, torrents and oceans of tears. You're soaked in their tears from head to foot; it's impossible for you not to feel a little wet!

(*Chuckle from the* KILLER.)

Stop sneering like that. You don't believe me, you don't believe me!... If Christ's not enough for you, I give you my solemn word I'll have an army of saviours climbing new Calvaries just for you, and have them crucified for love of you!... They must exist and I'll find them! Will that do?

(*Chuckle from the* KILLER.)

Do you want the whole world to destroy itself to give you a moment of happiness, to make you smile just once? That's possible too! I'm ready myself to embrace you, to be one of your comforters; I'll dress your wounds, because you *are* wounded, aren't you? You've suffered, haven't you? You're still suffering? I'll take pity on you – you know that now. Would you like me to wash your feet? Then perhaps you'd like some new shoes? You loathe sloppy sentimentality. Yes, I can see it's no good trying to touch your feelings. You don't want to be trapped by tenderness! You're afraid it'll make a fool of you. You've a tempera-ment that's diametrically opposed to mine. All men are brothers, of course – they're like each other, but they're not always alike. And they've one thing in common. There must be one thing in common: a common language... What is it? What is it?

(*Chuckle from the* KILLER.)

Ah, I know now, I know... You see, I'm right not to give up hope for you. We can speak the language of reason. It's the language that suits you best. You're a scientific man, aren't you – a man of the modern era – I've guessed it now, haven't I: a cerebral man? You deny love, you doubt charity, it doesn't enter into your calculations, and you think charity's a cheat, don't you, don't you?

(*Chuckle from the* KILLER.)

I'm not blaming you. I don't despise you for that. After all, it's a point of view, a possible point of view, but between ourselves, listen here: what do you get out of all this? What good does it do you? Kill people if you like, but in your mind... leave them alive in the flesh.

(Shrug of the shoulders and chuckle from the KILLER.*)*

Oh, yes, in your opinion that would be a comic contradiction. Idealism, you'd call it – you're for a practical philosophy, you're a man of action. Why not? But where's the action leading you? What's the final object? Have you asked yourself the question of ultimate ends?

(A more accentuated chuckle and shrug of the shoulders from the KILLER.*)*

It's an action that's utterly sterile in fact; it wears you out. It only brings trouble... Even if the police shut their eyes to it, which is what usually happens, what's the good of all the effort, the fatigue, the complicated preparations and exhausting nights on the watch... people's contempt for you? Perhaps you don't mind. You earn their fear, it's true, that's something. All right, but what do you do with it? It's not a form of capital. You don't even exploit it. Answer me!

(Chuckle from the KILLER.*)*

You're poor now, aren't you? Do you want some money? I can find you work, a decent job... No. You're not poor? Rich then?... Aaah, I see, neither rich nor poor!

(Chuckle from the KILLER.*)*

I see: you don't want to work; well, you shan't, then. I'll look after you, or, as I'm poor myself, I'd better say I'll arrange for me and my friends to club together; I'll talk to the Architect about it. And you'll lead a quiet life. We'll go to the cafés and the bars, and I'll introduce you to girls who aren't too difficult... Crime doesn't pay. So stop being a criminal and we'll pay you. It's only common sense.

(*Chuckle from the* KILLER.)

You agree? Answer, answer, can't you? You understand the language!... Listen, I'm going to make you a painful confession. Often, I have my doubts about everything, too. But don't tell anyone. I doubt the point of living, the meaning of life, doubt my own values and every kind of rational argument. I no longer know what to hang on to; perhaps there's no more truth or charity. But if that's the case, be philosophical; if all is vanity, if charity is vanity, crime's just vanity too... When you know everything's dust and ashes, you'd be a fool if you set any store by crime, for that would be setting store by life... That would mean you were taking things seriously... and then you'd be in complete contradiction with yourself. (*Gives nervous laugh.*) Eh? It's obvious. It's only logic; I caught you there. And then you'd be in a bad way – you'd be feeble-minded, a poor specimen. Logically, we'd have the right to make fun of you! Do you want us to make fun of you? Of course you don't! You must have your pride, respect your own intelligence. There's nothing worse than being stupid. It's much more compromising than being a criminal; even madness has a halo round it. But to be stupid? To be ignorant? Who can accept that?

(*Chuckle from the* KILLER.)

Everyone will point at you and laugh!

(*Chuckle from the* KILLER: BÉRENGER *is obviously more and more baffled.*)

There's the idiot going by, there's the idiot! Ha! Ha! Ha!

(*Chuckle from the* KILLER.)

He kills people, gives himself all that trouble – ha! ha! ha! – and doesn't get anything out of it, it's all for nothing – ha!

ha! Do you want to hear that said, be taken for an idiot, an idealist, a crank who "believes" in something, who "believes" in crime, the simpleton! Ha! Ha! Ha!

(*Chuckle from the* KILLER.)

…Who believes in crime for its own sake! Ha! Ha! (*His laugh suddenly freezes.*) Answer me! That's what they'll say, yes… if there's anyone left to say it… (*Wrings his hands, clasps them, kneels down and begs the* KILLER:) I don't know what else I can say to you. We must have done something to hurt you.

(*Chuckle from the* KILLER.)

Perhaps there's no wrong on our side.

(*Chuckle from the* KILLER.)

I don't know. It may be my fault, it may be yours. It may not be yours or mine. It may not be anyone's fault. What you're doing may be wrong or it may be right, or it may be neither right nor wrong. I don't know how to tell. It's possible that the survival of the human species is of no importance, so what does it matter if it disappears… perhaps the whole universe is no good and you're right to want to blast it all, or at least nibble at it, creature by creature, piece by piece… or perhaps that's wrong. I don't know any more, I just don't know. You may be mistaken; perhaps mistakes don't really exist; perhaps it's we who are mistaken to want to exist… say what you believe, can't you? *I* can't, *I* can't.

(*Chuckle from the* KILLER.)

Some think just being is a mistake, an aberration.

(*Chuckle from the* KILLER.)

Perhaps your pretended motives are only a mask for the real cause you unconsciously hide from yourself. Who knows. Let's sweep all these reasons away and forget the trouble you've already caused...

(*Chuckle from the* KILLER.)

Agreed? You kill without reason in that case, and I beg you, without reason I implore you, yes, please stop... There's no reason why you should, naturally, but please stop, just because there's no reason to kill or not to kill. You're killing people for nothing, save them for nothing. Leave people alone to live their stupid lives – leave them all alone, even the policemen... Promise me you'll stop, for at least a month... please do as I ask, for a week, for forty-eight hours, to give us a chance to breathe... You will do that, won't you?...

(*The* KILLER *chuckles softly; very slowly he takes from his pocket a knife with a large shining blade and plays with it.*)

You filthy, dirty, moronic imbecile! You're ugly as a monkey! Fierce as a tiger, stupid as a mule...

(*Slight chuckle from the* KILLER.)

I'm on my knees, yes... but it's not to beg for mercy...

(*Slight chuckle from the* KILLER.)

It's to take better aim... I'm going to finish you, and then I'll stamp on you and squash you to pulp, you stinking rotten carcass of a hyena! (*Takes two pistols from his pockets and aims them at the* KILLER, *who doesn't move a muscle.*) I'll kill you; you're going to pay for it; I'll shoot and shoot, and then I'll hang you; I'll chop you into a thousand pieces; I'll throw your ashes into hell with the excrement you came from, you vomit of Satan's mangy cur, criminal cretin...

(*The* KILLER *goes on playing with the blade of his knife; slight chuckle and shrug of the shoulders, but he does not move.*)

Don't look at me like that; I'm not afraid of you, you shame creation.

(BÉRENGER *aims without firing at the* KILLER, *who is two paces away, standing still, chuckling unpleasantly and quietly raising his knife.*)

Oh... how weak my strength is against your cold determination, your ruthlessness! And what good are bullets, even, against the resistance of an infinitely stubborn will! (*With a start*:) But I'll get you, I'll get you...

(*Then, still in front of the* KILLER, *whose knife is raised and who is chuckling and quite motionless,* BÉRENGER *slowly lowers his two old-fashioned pistols, lays them on the ground, bends his head and then, on his knees with his head down and his arms hanging at his side, he stammers*:)

Oh God! There's nothing we can do. What can we do... What can we do...

(*While the* KILLER *draws nearer, still chuckling, but very very softly.*)

CURTAIN

RHINOCEROS

*A Play in Three Acts
and Four Scenes*

*First produced in Paris by Jean-Louis Barrault at
the Théâtre de l'Odéon on 25th January 1960*

Characters

BÉRENGER

JEAN

DAISY

THE WAITRESS

THE GROCER

THE GROCER'S WIFE

THE OLD GENTLEMAN

THE LOGICIAN

THE HOUSEWIFE

THE CAFÉ PROPRIETOR

MR PAPILLON

DUDARD

BOTARD

MRS BOEUF

A FIREMAN

THE LITTLE OLD MAN

THE LITTLE OLD MAN'S WIFE

And a lot of Rhinoceros heads

Act One

The scene is a square in a small provincial town. Upstage a house composed of a ground floor and one storey. The ground floor is the window of a grocer's shop. The entrance is up two or three steps through a glass-paned door. The word ÉPICERIE* *is written in bold letters above the shop window. The two windows on the first floor are the living quarters of the grocer and his wife. The shop is upstage, but slightly to the left, not far from the wings. In the distance a church steeple is visible above the grocer's house. Between the shop and the left of the stage there is a little street in perspective. To the right, slightly at an angle, is the front of a café. Above the café, one floor with a window; in front, the café terrace; several chairs and tables reach almost to centre stage. A dusty tree stands near the terrace chairs. Blue sky; harsh light; very white walls. The time is almost midday on a Sunday in summertime.* JEAN *and* BÉRENGER *will sit at one of the terrace tables.*

The sound of church bells is heard, which stop a few moments before the curtain rises. When the curtain rises, a woman carrying a basket of provisions under one arm and a cat under the other crosses the stage in silence from right to left. As she does so, the GROCER'S WIFE *opens her shop door and watches her pass.*

GROCER'S WIFE: Oh that woman gets on my nerves! (*To her husband, who is in the shop:*) Too stuck-up to buy from us nowadays. (*The* GROCER'S WIFE *leaves; the stage is empty for a few moments.*)

(JEAN *enters right at the same time as* BÉRENGER *enters left.*

JEAN *is very fastidiously dressed: brown suit, red tie, stiff collar, brown hat. He has a reddish face. His shoes are yellow and well-polished.* BÉRENGER *is unshaven and hatless, with unkempt hair and creased clothes; everything about him indicates negligence. He seems weary, half-asleep; from time to time he yawns.*)

JEAN (*advancing from right*): Oh, so you managed to get here at last, Bérenger!

BÉRENGER (*advancing from left*): Morning, Jean!

JEAN: Late as usual, of course. (*He looks at his wristwatch.*) Our appointment was for 11.30. And now it's practically midday.

BÉRENGER: I'm sorry. Have you been waiting long?

JEAN: No, I've only just arrived myself, as you saw.

(*They go and sit at one of the tables on the café terrace.*)

BÉRENGER: In that case, I don't feel so bad, if you've only *just*—

JEAN: It's different with me. I don't like waiting – I've no time to waste. And as you're never on time; I come late on purpose – at a time when I presume you'll be there.

BÉRENGER: You're right... quite right, but—

JEAN: Now don't try to pretend you're ever on time!

BÉRENGER: No, of course not... I wouldn't say that.

(JEAN *and* BÉRENGER *have sat down.*)

JEAN: There you are, you see!

BÉRENGER: What are you drinking?

JEAN: You mean to say you've got a thirst even at this time in the morning?

BÉRENGER: It's so hot and dry.

JEAN: The more you drink the thirstier you get – popular science tells us that...

BÉRENGER: It would be less dry, and we'd be less thirsty, if they'd invent us some scientific clouds in the sky.

JEAN (*studying* BÉRENGER *closely*): That wouldn't help you any. You're not thirsty for water, Bérenger...

BÉRENGER: I don't understand what you mean.

JEAN: You know perfectly well what I mean. I'm talking about your parched throat. That's a territory that can't get enough!

BÉRENGER: To compare my throat to a piece of land seems—

JEAN (*interrupting him*): You're in a bad way, my friend.

BÉRENGER: In a bad way? You think so?

JEAN: I'm not blind, you know. You're dropping with fatigue. You've gone without sleep again, you yawn all the time, you're dead-tired...

BÉRENGER: There is something the matter with my hair...

JEAN: You reek of alcohol.

BÉRENGER: I have got a bit of a hangover, it's true!

JEAN: It's the same every Sunday morning – not to mention the other days of the week.

BÉRENGER: Oh no, it's less frequent during the week, because of the office...

JEAN: And what's happened to your tie? Lost it during your orgy, I suppose!

BÉRENGER (*putting his hand to his neck*): You're right. That's funny! Whatever could I have done with it?

JEAN (*taking a tie out of his coat pocket*): Here, put this one on.

BÉRENGER: Oh thank you, that is kind. (*He puts on the tie.*)

JEAN (*while* BÉRENGER *is unskilfully tying his tie*): Your hair's all over the place.

(BÉRENGER *runs his fingers through his hair.*)

Here, here's a comb! (*He takes a comb from his other pocket.*)

BÉRENGER (*taking the comb*): Thank you. (*He vaguely combs his hair.*)

JEAN: You haven't even shaved! Just take a look at yourself! (*He takes a mirror from his inside pocket and hands it to* BÉRENGER, *who looks at himself; as he does so, he examines his tongue.*)

BÉRENGER: My tongue's all coated.

JEAN (*taking the mirror and putting it back in his pocket*): I'm not surprised! (*He takes back the comb as well, which* BÉRENGER *offers to him, and puts it in his pocket.*) You're heading for cirrhosis, my friend.

BÉRENGER (*worried*): Do you think so?

JEAN (*to* BÉRENGER, *who makes to give him back his tie*): Keep the tie – I've got plenty more.

BÉRENGER (*admiringly*): You always look so immaculate.

JEAN (*continuing his inspection of* BÉRENGER): Your clothes are all crumpled, they're a disgrace! Your shirt is downright filthy, and your shoes... (BÉRENGER *tries to hide his feet under the table.*) Your shoes haven't been polished. What a mess you're in! And look at your shoulders...

BÉRENGER: What's the matter with my shoulders?

JEAN: Turn round! Come on, turn round! You've been leaning against some wall. (BÉRENGER *meekly holds out his hand to* JEAN.) No, I haven't got a brush with me; it would make my pockets bulge. (*Still meekly,* BÉRENGER *flicks his shoulders to get rid of the white dust;* JEAN *averts his head.*) Heavens! Where did you get all that from?

BÉRENGER: I don't remember.

JEAN: It's a positive disgrace! I feel ashamed to be your friend.

BÉRENGER: You're very hard on me...

JEAN: I've every reason to be.

BÉRENGER: Listen, Jean. There are so few distractions in this town – I get so bored. I'm not made for the work I'm doing... every day at the office, eight hours a day – and only three weeks' holiday a year! When Saturday night comes round I feel exhausted and so – you know how it is – just to relax...

JEAN: My dear man, everybody has to work. I spend eight hours a day in the office – the same as everyone else. And I only get three weeks off a year, but even so, you don't catch me... Will-power, my good man!

BÉRENGER: But not everybody has as much will-power as you have. I can't get used to it. I just can't get used to life.

JEAN: Everybody has to get used to it. Or do you consider yourself to be some superior being?

BÉRENGER: I don't pretend to be—

JEAN (*interrupting him*): I'm just as good as you are; I think, with all due modesty, I may say I'm better. The superior man is the man who fulfils his duty.

BÉRENGER: What duty?

JEAN: His duty... his duty as an employee, for example.

BÉRENGER: Oh yes, his duty as an employee...

JEAN: Where did your debauchery take place last night? If you can remember!

BÉRENGER: We were celebrating Auguste's birthday, our friend Auguste...

JEAN: Our friend Auguste? Nobody invited me to our friend Auguste's birthday...

(*At this moment a noise is heard, far off, but swiftly approaching, of a beast panting in its headlong course, and of a long trumpeting.*)

BÉRENGER: I couldn't refuse. It wouldn't have been nice...

JEAN: Did I go there?

BÉRENGER: Well, perhaps it was because you weren't invited.

WAITRESS (*coming out of café*): Good morning, gentlemen. Can I get you something to drink?

(*The noise becomes very loud.*)

JEAN (*to Bérenger, almost shouting to make himself heard above the noise which he has not become conscious of*): True – I was not invited. That honour was denied me. But, in any case, I can assure you that, even if I had been invited, I would not have gone, because... (*The noise has become intense.*) What's going on? (*The noise of a powerful, heavy animal, galloping at great speed, is heard very close; the sound of panting.*) Whatever is it?

WAITRESS: Whatever is it?

(*Bérenger, still listless, without appearing to hear anything at all, replies tranquilly to* JEAN *about the invitation; his lips move, but one doesn't hear what he says;* JEAN *bounds to his feet, knocking his chair as he does so, looks off left, pointing, whilst* BÉRENGER, *still a little dopey, remains seated.*)

JEAN: Oh, a rhinoceros!

(*The noise made by the animal dies away swiftly, and one can already hear the following words. The whole of this scene must be played very fast, each repeating in swift succession: "Oh, a rhinoceros!"*)

WAITRESS: Oh, a rhinoceros!
GROCER'S WIFE (*sticks her head out of her shop doorway*): Oh, a rhinoceros! (*To her husband, still inside the shop:*) Quick, come and look – it's a rhinoceros!

(*They are all looking off left after the animal.*)

JEAN: It's rushing straight ahead, brushing up against the shop windows.
GROCER (*in his shop*): Whereabouts?
WAITRESS (*putting her hands on her hips*): Well!
GROCER'S WIFE (*to her husband, who is still in the shop*): Come and look!

(*At this moment the* GROCER *puts his head out.*)

GROCER: Oh, a rhinoceros!
LOGICIAN (*entering quickly left*): A rhinoceros going full-tilt on the opposite pavement!

(*All these speeches from the time when* JEAN *says "Oh, a rhinoceros!" are practically simultaneous. A woman is heard crying*

"Ah!". She appears. She runs to the centre stage; it is a housewife with a basket on her arm; once arrived centre stage she drops her basket; the contents scatter all over the stage, a bottle breaks, but she does not drop her cat.)

HOUSEWIFE: Ah! Oh!

(*An elegant old gentleman comes from left stage, after the* HOUSE-WIFE, *rushes into the* GROCER's *shop, knocks into the* GROCER *and his* WIFE, *whilst the* LOGICIAN *installs himself against the back wall on the left of the grocery entrance.* JEAN *and the* WAITRESS, *standing, and* BÉRENGER, *still apathetically seated, together form another group. At the same time, coming from the left, cries of "Oh" and "Ah" and the noise of people running can be heard. The dust raised by the animals spreads over the stage.*)

PROPRIETOR (*sticking his head out of the first-floor window*): What's going on?
OLD GENTLEMAN (*disappearing behind the* GROCER *and his* WIFE): Excuse me, please!

(*The* OLD GENTLEMAN *is elegantly dressed, with white spats, a soft hat and an ivory-handled cane; the* LOGICIAN, *propped up against the wall, has a little grey moustache and an eyeglass, and is wearing a straw hat.*)

GROCER's WIFE (*jostled by, and jostling her husband; to the* OLD GENTLEMAN): Watch out with that stick!
GROCER: Look where you're going, can't you!

(*The head of the* OLD GENTLEMAN *is seen behind the* GROCER *and his* WIFE.)

WAITRESS (*to the* PROPRIETOR): A rhinoceros!
PROPRIETOR (*to the* WAITRESS *from his window*): You're seeing things. (*He sees the rhinoceros:*) Well, I'll be!...

HOUSEWIFE: Ah!

(*The "Ohs" and "Ahs" from offstage form a background accompaniment to her "Ah". She has dropped her basket, her provisions and the bottle, but has nevertheless kept tight hold of her cat, which she carries under the other arm.*)

There, they frightened the poor pussy!

PROPRIETOR (*still looking off left, following the distant course of the animal as the noises fade; hooves, trumpeting, etc.* BÉRENGER *sleepily averts his head a little on account of the dust, but says nothing; he simply makes a grimace*): Well, of all things!

JEAN (*also averting his head a little, but very much awake*): Well, of all things! (*He sneezes.*)

HOUSEWIFE (*she is centre stage but turned towards the left, her provisions scattered on the ground round her*): Well, of all things! (*She sneezes.*)

(*The* OLD GENTLEMAN, *the* GROCER'S WIFE *and the* GROCER *upstage re-opening the glass door of the* GROCER's *shop that the* OLD GENTLEMAN *has closed behind him.*)

ALL THREE: Well, of all things!

JEAN: Well, of all things! (*To* BÉRENGER:) Did you see that?

(*The noise of the rhinoceros and its trumpeting are now far away; the people are still staring after the animal – all except for* BÉRENGER, *who is still apathetically seated.*)

ALL (*except* BÉRENGER): Well, of all things!

BÉRENGER (*to* JEAN): It certainly looked as if it was a rhinoceros. It made plenty of dust. (*He takes out a handkerchief and blows his nose.*)

HOUSEWIFE: Well, of all things! Gave me such a scare.

GROCER (*to the* HOUSEWIFE): Your basket... and all your things...

(*The* OLD GENTLEMAN *approaches the lady and bends to pick up her things, which are scattered about the stage. He greets her gallantly, raising his hat.*)

PROPRIETOR: Really, these days, you never know...

WAITRESS: Fancy that!

OLD GENTLEMAN (*to the* HOUSEWIFE): May I help you pick up your things?

HOUSEWIFE (*to the* OLD GENTLEMAN): Thank you – how very kind! Do put on your hat. Oh, it gave me such a scare!

LOGICIAN: Fear is an irrational thing. It must yield to reason.

WAITRESS: It's already out of sight.

OLD GENTLEMAN (*to the* HOUSEWIFE *and indicating the* LOGICIAN): My friend is a logician.

JEAN (*to* BÉRENGER): Well, what did you think of that?

WAITRESS: Those animals can certainly travel!

HOUSEWIFE (*to the* LOGICIAN): Very happy to meet you!

GROCER'S WIFE (*to the* GROCER): That'll teach her to buy her things from somebody else!

JEAN (*to the* PROPRIETOR *and the* WAITRESS): What did you think of that?

HOUSEWIFE: I still didn't let my cat go.

PROPRIETOR (*shrugging his shoulders, at the window*): You don't often see that!

HOUSEWIFE (*to the* LOGICIAN *and the* OLD GENTLEMAN, *who is picking up her provisions*): Would you hold him a moment!

WAITRESS (*to* JEAN): First time I've seen that!

LOGICIAN (*to the* HOUSEWIFE, *taking the cat in his arms*): It's not spiteful, is it?

PROPRIETOR (*to* JEAN): Went past like a comet!

HOUSEWIFE (*to the* LOGICIAN): He wouldn't hurt a fly. (*To the others:*) What happened to my wine?

GROCER (*to the* HOUSEWIFE): I've got plenty more.

JEAN (*to* BÉRENGER): Well, what did you think of that?

GROCER (*to the* HOUSEWIFE): And good stuff, too!

PROPRIETOR (*to the* WAITRESS): Don't hang about! Look after these gentlemen! (*He indicates* BÉRENGER *and* JEAN. *He withdraws.*)

BÉRENGER (*to* JEAN): What did I think of what?

GROCER'S WIFE (*to the* GROCER): Go and get her another bottle!

JEAN (*to* BÉRENGER): Of the rhinoceros, of course! What did you think I meant?

GROCER (*to the* HOUSEWIFE): I've got some first-class wine in unbreakable bottles! (*He disappears into his shop.*)

LOGICIAN (*stroking the cat in his arms*): Puss, puss, puss.

WAITRESS (*to* BÉRENGER *and* JEAN): What are you drinking?

BÉRENGER: Two pastis.

WAITRESS: Two pastis – right! (*She walks to the café entrance.*)

HOUSEWIFE (*picking up her things with the help of the* OLD GENTLEMAN): Very kind of you, I'm sure.

WAITRESS: Two pastis! (*She goes into the café.*)

OLD GENTLEMAN (*to the* HOUSEWIFE): Oh, please don't mention it – it's a pleasure.

(*The* GROCER'S WIFE *goes into the shop.*)

LOGICIAN (*to the* OLD GENTLEMAN *and the* HOUSEWIFE, *who are picking up the provisions*): Replace them in an orderly fashion.

JEAN (*to* BÉRENGER): Well, what did you think about it?

BÉRENGER (*to* JEAN, *not knowing what to say*): Well… nothing… it made a lot of dust…

GROCER (*coming out of shop with a bottle of wine; to the* HOUSEWIFE): I've some good leeks as well.

LOGICIAN (*still stroking the cat*): Puss, puss, puss.

GROCER (*to the* HOUSEWIFE): It's a hundred francs a litre.

HOUSEWIFE (*paying the* GROCER, *then to the* OLD GENTLEMAN, *who has managed to put everything back in the basket*): Oh, you are kind! Such a pleasure to come across the old French courtesy. Not like the young people today!

GROCER (*taking money*): You should buy from me. You wouldn't even have to cross the street, and you wouldn't run the risk of these accidents. (*He goes back into his shop.*)

JEAN (*who has sat down and is still thinking of the rhinoceros*): But you must admit, it's extraordinary.

OLD GENTLEMAN (*taking off his hat and kissing the* HOUSEWIFE's *hand*): It was a great pleasure to meet you!

HOUSEWIFE (*to the* LOGICIAN): Thank you very much for holding my cat.

(*The* LOGICIAN *gives the* HOUSEWIFE *back her cat. The* WAITRESS *comes back with drinks.*)

WAITRESS: Two pastis!

JEAN (*to* BÉRENGER): You're incorrigible!

OLD GENTLEMAN (*to the* HOUSEWIFE): May I accompany you part of the way?

BÉRENGER (*to* JEAN, *and pointing to the* WAITRESS, *who goes back into the café*): I asked for mineral water. She's made a mistake.

(JEAN, *scornful and disbelieving, shrugs his shoulders.*)

HOUSEWIFE (*to the* OLD GENTLEMAN): My husband's waiting for me, thank you. Perhaps some other time...

OLD GENTLEMAN (*to the* HOUSEWIFE): I sincerely hope so, Madame.

HOUSEWIFE (*to the* OLD GENTLEMAN): So do I! (*She gives him a sweet look as she leaves left.*)

BÉRENGER: The dust's settled... (JEAN *shrugs his shoulders again.*)

OLD GENTLEMAN (*to the* LOGICIAN, *and looking after the* HOUSEWIFE): Delightful creature!

JEAN (*to* BÉRENGER): A rhinoceros! I can't get over it!

(*The* OLD GENTLEMAN *and the* LOGICIAN *move slowly right and off. They chat amiably:*)

OLD GENTLEMAN (*to the* LOGICIAN, *after casting a last fond look after the* HOUSEWIFE): Charming, isn't she?

LOGICIAN (*to the* OLD GENTLEMAN): I'm going to explain to you what a syllogism is.

OLD GENTLEMAN: Ah yes, a syllogism.

JEAN (*to* BÉRENGER): I can't get over it! It's unthinkable!

(BÉRENGER *yawns.*)

LOGICIAN: A syllogism consists of a main proposition, a secondary one, and a conclusion.

OLD GENTLEMAN: What conclusion?

(*The* LOGICIAN *and the* OLD GENTLEMAN *go out.*)

JEAN: I just can't get over it.

BÉRENGER: Yes – I can see you can't. Well, it was a rhinoceros – all right, so it was a rhinoceros! It's miles away by now... miles away...

JEAN: But you must see it's fantastic! A rhinoceros loose in the town, and you don't bat an eyelid! It shouldn't be allowed!

(BÉRENGER *yawns.*)

Put your hand in front of your mouth!

BÉRENGER: Yais... yais... It shouldn't be allowed. It's dangerous. I hadn't realized. But don't worry about it, it won't get us here.

JEAN: We ought to protest to the Town Council! What's the Council there for?

BÉRENGER (*yawning, then quickly putting his hand to his mouth*): Oh, excuse me... perhaps the rhinoceros escaped from the zoo.

JEAN: You're daydreaming.

BÉRENGER: But I'm wide awake.

JEAN: Awake or asleep, it's the same thing.

BÉRENGER: But there is some difference.

JEAN: That's not the point.

BÉRENGER: But you just said being awake and being asleep were the same thing...

JEAN: You didn't understand. There's no difference between dreaming awake and dreaming asleep.

BÉRENGER: I do dream. Life is a dream.

JEAN: You're certainly dreaming when you say the rhinoceros escaped from the zoo—

BÉRENGER: I only said "perhaps".

JEAN: —because there's been no zoo in our town since the animals were destroyed in the plague... ages ago...

BÉRENGER (*with the same indifference*): Then perhaps it came from a circus.

JEAN: What circus are you talking about?

BÉRENGER: I don't know... some travelling circus.

JEAN: You know perfectly well that the Council banned all travelling performers from the district... There haven't been any since we were children.

BÉRENGER (*trying unsuccessfully to stop yawning*): In that case, maybe it's been hiding ever since in the surrounding swamps?

JEAN: The surrounding swamps! The surrounding swamps! My poor friend, you live in a thick haze of alcohol.

BÉRENGER (*naively*): That's very true... it seems to mount from my stomach...

JEAN: It's clouding your brain! Where do you think these surrounding swamps are? Our district is known as "little Castille" because the land is so arid.

BÉRENGER (*surfeited and pretty weary*): How do I know, then? Perhaps it's been hiding under a stone?... Or maybe it's been nesting on some withered branch?

JEAN: If you think you're being witty, you're very much mistaken! You're just being a bore with... with your stupid paradoxes. You're incapable of talking seriously!

BÉRENGER: Today, yes, only today... because of... because of... (*He indicates his head with a vague gesture.*)

JEAN: Today – the same as any other day!

BÉRENGER: Oh, not quite as much.

JEAN: Your witticisms are not very inspired.

BÉRENGER: I wasn't trying to be...

JEAN (*interrupting him*): I can't bear people to try and make fun of me!

BÉRENGER (*hand on his heart*): But, my dear Jean, I'd never allow myself to—

JEAN (*interrupting him*): My dear Bérenger, you are allowing yourself—

BÉRENGER: Oh no, never. I'd never allow myself to.

JEAN: Yes, you would; you've just done so.

BÉRENGER: But how could you possibly think—

JEAN (*interrupting him*): I think what is true!

BÉRENGER: But I assure you—

JEAN (*interrupting him*): —that you were making fun of me!

BÉRENGER: You really are obstinate, sometimes.

JEAN: And now you're calling me a mule into the bargain. Even you must see how insulting you're being.

BÉRENGER: It would never have entered my mind.

JEAN: You have no mind!

BÉRENGER: All the more reason why it would never enter it.

JEAN: There are certain things which enter the minds of even people without one.

BÉRENGER: That's impossible.

JEAN: And why, pray, is it impossible?

BÉRENGER: Because it's impossible.

JEAN: Then kindly explain to me why it's impossible, as you seem to imagine you can explain everything.

BÉRENGER: I don't imagine anything of the kind.

JEAN: Then why do you act as if you do? And, I repeat, why are you being so insulting to me?

BÉRENGER: I'm not insulting you. Far from it. You know what tremendous respect I have for you.

JEAN: In that case, why do you contradict me, making out that it's not dangerous to let a rhinoceros go racing about in the middle of the town – particularly on a Sunday morning when the streets are full of children... and adults, too...

BÉRENGER: A lot of them are in church. They don't run any risk...

JEAN (*interrupting him*): If you will allow me to finish... and at market time, too.

BÉRENGER: I never said it wasn't dangerous to let a rhinoceros go racing about the town. I simply said I'd personally never considered the danger. It had never crossed my mind.

JEAN: You never consider anything.

BÉRENGER: All right, I agree. A rhinoceros roaming about is not a good thing.

JEAN: It shouldn't be allowed.

BÉRENGER: I agree. It shouldn't be allowed. It's a ridiculous thing, all right! But it's no reason for you and me to quarrel. Why go on at me just because some wretched perissodactyl happens to pass by. A stupid quadruped not worth talking about. And ferocious into the bargain. And which has already disappeared, doesn't exist any longer. We're not going to bother about some animal that doesn't exist. Let's talk about something else, Jean, please (*he yawns*); there are plenty of other subjects for conversation. (*He takes his glass.*) To you!

(*At this moment the* LOGICIAN *and the* OLD GENTLEMAN *come back onstage from the left; they walk over, talking as they go, to one of the tables on the café terrace, some distance from* BÉRENGER *and* JEAN, *behind and to the right of them.*)

JEAN: Put that glass back on the table! You're not to drink it.

(JEAN *takes a large swallow from his own pastis and puts back the glass, half-empty, on the table.* BÉRENGER *continues to hold his glass, without putting it down, and without daring to drink from it either.*)

BÉRENGER (*timidly*): There's no point in leaving it for the proprietor. (*He makes as if to drink.*)

JEAN: Put it down, I tell you!

BÉRENGER: Very well.

(*He is putting the glass back on the table when* DAISY *passes. She is a young blonde typist and she crosses the stage from right to left.*

When he sees her, BÉRENGER *rises abruptly, and in doing so makes an awkward movement; the glass falls and splashes* JEAN's *trousers.)*

Oh, there's Daisy!

JEAN: Look out! How clumsy you are!

BÉRENGER: That's Daisy... I'm so sorry... (*He hides himself out of sight of* DAISY.) I don't want her to see me in this state.

JEAN: Your behaviour's unforgivable, absolutely unforgivable! (*He looks in the direction of* DAISY, *who is just disappearing.*) Why are you afraid of that young girl?

BÉRENGER: Oh, be quiet, please be quiet!

JEAN: She doesn't look an unpleasant person!

BÉRENGER (*coming back to* JEAN, *now that* DAISY *has gone*): I must apologize once more for—

JEAN: You see what comes of drinking? You can no longer control your movements, you've no strength left in your hands, you're besotted and fagged out. You're digging your own grave, my friend, you're destroying yourself.

BÉRENGER: I don't like the taste of alcohol much. And yet if I don't drink, I'm done for; it's as if I'm frightened, and so I drink not to be frightened any longer.

JEAN: Frightened of what?

BÉRENGER: I don't know exactly. It's a sort of anguish difficult to describe. I feel out of place in life, among people, and so I take to drink. That calms me down and relaxes me so I can forget.

JEAN: You try to escape from yourself!

BÉRENGER: I'm so tired – I've been tired for years. It's exhausting to drag the weight of my own body about...

JEAN: That's alcoholic neurasthenia, drinker's gloom...

BÉRENGER (*continuing*): I'm conscious of my body all the time, as if it were made of lead, or as if I were carrying another man around on my back. I can't seem to get used to myself. I don't even know if I *am* me. Then as soon as I have a drink, the lead slips away and I recognize myself – I become me again.

JEAN: That's just being fanciful. Look at me, Bérenger; I weigh more than you do. And yet I feel light – light as a feather!

(*He flaps his arms as if about to fly. The* OLD GENTLEMAN *and the* LOGICIAN *have come back and have taken a few steps onstage deep in talk. At this moment they are passing by* JEAN *and* BÉRENGER. JEAN'S *arm deals the* OLD GENTLEMAN *a sharp knock, which propels him into the arms of the* LOGICIAN.)

LOGICIAN: An example of a syllogism... (*He is knocked.*) Oh!

OLD GENTLEMAN (*to* JEAN): Look out! (*To the* LOGICIAN:) I'm so sorry.

JEAN (*to the* OLD GENTLEMAN): I'm so sorry.

LOGICIAN (*to the* OLD GENTLEMAN): No harm done.

OLD GENTLEMAN (*to* JEAN): No harm done.

(*The* OLD GENTLEMAN *and the* LOGICIAN *go and sit at one of the terrace tables a little to the right and behind* JEAN *and* BÉRENGER.)

BÉRENGER (*to* JEAN): You certainly are strong.

JEAN: Yes, I'm strong. I'm strong for several reasons. In the first place, I'm strong because I'm naturally strong, and secondly, I'm strong because I have moral strength. I'm also strong because I'm not riddled with alcohol. I don't wish to offend you, my dear Bérenger, but I feel I must tell you that it's alcohol which weighs so heavy on you.

LOGICIAN (*to the* OLD GENTLEMAN): Here is an example of a syllogism. The cat has four paws. Isidore and Fricot both have four paws. Therefore Isidore and Fricot are cats.

OLD GENTLEMAN (*to the* LOGICIAN): My dog has got four paws.

LOGICIAN (*to the* OLD GENTLEMAN): Then it's a cat.

BÉRENGER (*to* JEAN): I've barely got the strength to go on living. Maybe I don't even want to.

OLD GENTLEMAN (*to the* LOGICIAN, *after deep reflection*): So, then, logically speaking, my dog must be a cat?

LOGICIAN (*to the* OLD GENTLEMAN): Logically, yes. But the contrary is also true.

BÉRENGER (*to* JEAN): Solitude seems to oppress me. And so does the company of other people.

JEAN (*to* BÉRENGER): You contradict yourself. What oppresses you – solitude, or the company of others? You consider yourself a thinker, yet you're devoid of logic.

OLD GENTLEMAN (*to the* LOGICIAN): Logic is a very beautiful thing.

LOGICIAN (*to the* OLD GENTLEMAN): As long as it is not abused.

BÉRENGER (*to* JEAN): Life is an abnormal business.

JEAN: On the contrary. Nothing could be more natural, and the proof is that people go on living.

BÉRENGER: There are more dead people than living. And their numbers are increasing. The living are getting rarer.

JEAN: The dead don't exist – there's no getting away from that!… Ah! Ah!… (*He lets out a huge laugh.*) Yet you're oppressed by them, too? How can you be oppressed by something that doesn't exist?

BÉRENGER: I sometimes wonder if I exist myself.

JEAN: You don't exist, my dear Bérenger, because you don't think. Start thinking, then you will.

LOGICIAN (*to the* OLD GENTLEMAN): Another syllogism. All cats die. Socrates is dead. Therefore Socrates is a cat.

OLD GENTLEMAN: And he's got four paws. That's true. I've got a cat named Socrates.

LOGICIAN: There you are, you see…

JEAN (*to* BÉRENGER): Fundamentally you're just a bluffer. And a liar. You say that life doesn't interest you. And yet there's somebody who does.

BÉRENGER: Who?

JEAN: Your little friend from the office who just went past. You're very fond of her!

OLD GENTLEMAN (*to the* LOGICIAN): So Socrates was a cat, was he?

LOGICIAN: Logic has just revealed the fact to us.

JEAN (*to* BÉRENGER): You didn't want her to see you in your present state. (BÉRENGER *makes a gesture.*) That proves you're not indifferent to everything. But how can you expect Daisy to be attracted to a drunkard?

LOGICIAN (*to the* OLD GENTLEMAN): Let's get back to our cats.

OLD GENTLEMAN (*to the* LOGICIAN): I'm all ears.

BÉRENGER (*to* JEAN): In any case, I think she's already got her eye on someone.

JEAN: Oh, who?

BÉRENGER: Dudard. An office colleague, qualified in law, with a big future in the firm – and in Daisy's affections. I can't hope to compete with him.

LOGICIAN (*to the* OLD GENTLEMAN): The cat Isidore has four paws.

OLD GENTLEMAN: How do you know?

LOGICIAN: It's stated in the hypothesis.

BÉRENGER (*to* JEAN): The Chief thinks a lot of him. Whereas I've no future, I've no qualifications. I don't stand a chance.

OLD GENTLEMAN (*to the* LOGICIAN): Ah! In the hypothesis.

JEAN (*to* BÉRENGER): So you're giving up, just like that?...

BÉRENGER: What else can I do?

LOGICIAN (*to the* OLD GENTLEMAN): Fricot also has four paws. So how many paws have Fricot and Isidore?

OLD GENTLEMAN: Separately, or together?

JEAN (*to* BÉRENGER): Life is a struggle – it's cowardly not to put up a fight!

LOGICIAN (*to the* OLD GENTLEMAN): Separately or together, it all depends.

BÉRENGER (*to* JEAN): What can I do? I've nothing to put up a fight with.

JEAN: Then find yourself some weapons, my friend.

OLD GENTLEMAN (*to the* LOGICIAN, *after painful reflection*): Eight... eight paws.

LOGICIAN: Logic involves mental arithmetic, you see.

OLD GENTLEMAN: It certainly has many aspects!

BÉRENGER (*to* JEAN): Where can I find the weapons?

LOGICIAN (*to the* OLD GENTLEMAN): There are no limits to logic.

JEAN: Within yourself. Through your own will.

BÉRENGER: What weapons?

LOGICIAN (*to the* OLD GENTLEMAN): I'm going to show you...

JEAN (*to* BÉRENGER): The weapons of patience and culture, the weapons of the mind. (BÉRENGER *yawns.*) Turn yourself into a keen and brilliant intellect. Get yourself up to the mark!

BÉRENGER: How do I get myself up to the mark?

LOGICIAN (*to the* OLD GENTLEMAN): If I take two paws away from these cats, how many does each have left?

OLD GENTLEMAN: That's not so easy.

BÉRENGER (*to* JEAN): That's not so easy.

LOGICIAN (*to the* OLD GENTLEMAN): On the contrary, it's simple.

OLD GENTLEMAN (*to the* LOGICIAN): It may be simple for you, but not for me.

BÉRENGER (*to* JEAN): It may be simple for you, but not for me.

LOGICIAN (*to the* OLD GENTLEMAN): Come on, exercise your mind. Concentrate!

JEAN (*to* BÉRENGER): Come on, exercise your will. Concentrate!

OLD GENTLEMAN (*to the* LOGICIAN): I don't see how.

BÉRENGER (*to* JEAN): I really don't see how.

LOGICIAN (*to the* OLD GENTLEMAN): You have to be told everything.

JEAN (*to* BÉRENGER): You have to be told everything.

LOGICIAN (*to the* OLD GENTLEMAN): Take a sheet of paper and calculate. If you take six paws from the two cats, how many paws are left to each cat?

OLD GENTLEMAN: Just a moment... (*He calculates on a sheet of paper which he takes from his pocket.*)

JEAN: This is what you must do: dress yourself properly, shave every day, put on a clean shirt.

BÉRENGER: The laundry's so expensive...

JEAN: Cut down on your drinking. This is the way to come out: wear a hat, a tie like this, a well-cut suit, shoes well polished.

(*As he mentions the various items of clothing he points self-contentedly to his own hat, tie and shoes.*)

OLD GENTLEMAN (*to the* LOGICIAN): There are several possible solutions.

LOGICIAN (*to the* OLD GENTLEMAN): Tell me.

BÉRENGER (*to* JEAN): Then what do I do? Tell me…

LOGICIAN (*to the* OLD GENTLEMAN): I'm listening.

BÉRENGER (*to* JEAN): I'm listening.

JEAN: You're a timid creature, but not without talent.

BÉRENGER: I've got talent – me?

JEAN: So use it. Put yourself in the picture. Keep abreast of the cultural and literary events of the time.

OLD GENTLEMAN (*to the* LOGICIAN): One possibility is: one cat could have four paws and the other two.

BÉRENGER (*to* JEAN): I get so little spare time!

LOGICIAN (*to the* OLD GENTLEMAN): You're not without talent. You just needed to exercise it.

JEAN: Take advantage of what free time you *do* have. Don't just let yourself drift.

OLD GENTLEMAN: I've never had the time. I was an official, you know.

LOGICIAN: One can always find time to learn.

JEAN (*to* BÉRENGER): One can always find time.

BÉRENGER (*to* JEAN): It's too late now.

OLD GENTLEMAN (*to the* LOGICIAN): It's a bit late in the day for me.

JEAN (*to* BÉRENGER): It's never too late.

LOGICIAN (*to the* OLD GENTLEMAN): It's never too late.

JEAN (*to* BÉRENGER): You work eight hours a day, like me and everybody else, but not on Sundays, nor in the evening, nor for three weeks in the summer. That's quite sufficient, with a little method.

LOGICIAN (*to the* OLD GENTLEMAN): Well, what about the other solutions? Use a little method, a little method!

(*The* OLD GENTLEMAN *starts to calculate anew.*)

JEAN (*to* BÉRENGER): Look, instead of drinking and feeling sick, isn't it better to be fresh and eager, even at work? And you can spend your free time constructively.

BÉRENGER: How do you mean?

JEAN: By visiting museums, reading literary periodicals, going to lectures. That'll solve your troubles – it will develop your mind. In four weeks you'll be a cultured man.

BÉRENGER: You're right!

OLD GENTLEMAN (*to the* LOGICIAN): There could be one cat with five paws...

JEAN (*to* BÉRENGER): You see, you even think so yourself!

OLD GENTLEMAN (*to the* LOGICIAN): ...and one cat with one paw. But would they still be cats, then?

LOGICIAN (*to the* OLD GENTLEMAN): Why not?

JEAN (*to* BÉRENGER): Instead of squandering all your spare money on drink, isn't it better to buy a ticket for an interesting play? Do you know anything about the avant-garde theatre there's so much talk about? Have you seen Ionesco's plays?

BÉRENGER (*to* JEAN): Unfortunately, no. I've only heard people talk about them.

OLD GENTLEMAN (*to the* LOGICIAN): By taking two of the eight paws away from the two cats...

JEAN (*to* BÉRENGER): There's one playing now. Take advantage of it.

OLD GENTLEMAN (*to the* LOGICIAN): ...we could have one cat with six paws...

BÉRENGER: It would be an excellent initiation into the artistic life of our times.

OLD GENTLEMAN (*to the* LOGICIAN): We could have one cat with no paws at all.

BÉRENGER: You're right, perfectly right. I'm going to put myself into the picture, like you said.

LOGICIAN (*to the* OLD GENTLEMAN): In that case, one cat would be specially privileged.

BÉRENGER (*to* JEAN): I will, I promise you.

JEAN: You promise yourself, that's the main thing.

OLD GENTLEMAN: And one under-privileged cat deprived of all paws.

BÉRENGER: I make myself a solemn promise; I'll keep my word to myself.

LOGICIAN: That would be unjust, and therefore not logical.

BÉRENGER: Instead of drinking, I'll develop my mind. I feel better already. My head already feels clearer.

JEAN: You see!

OLD GENTLEMAN (*to the* LOGICIAN): Not logical?

BÉRENGER: This afternoon I'll go to the museum. And I'll book two seats for the theatre this evening. Will you come with me?

LOGICIAN (*to the* OLD GENTLEMAN): Because Logic means Justice.

JEAN (*to* BÉRENGER): You must persevere. Keep up your good resolutions.

OLD GENTLEMAN (*to the* LOGICIAN): I get it. Justice...

BÉRENGER (*to* JEAN): I promise you, and I promise myself. Will you come to the museum with me this afternoon?

JEAN (*to* BÉRENGER): I have to have a rest this afternoon; it's in my programme for the day.

OLD GENTLEMAN: Justice is one more aspect of Logic.

BÉRENGER (*to* JEAN): But you will come with me to the theatre this evening?

JEAN: No, not this evening.

LOGICIAN (*to the* OLD GENTLEMAN): Your mind is getting clearer!

JEAN (*to* BÉRENGER): I sincerely hope you'll keep up your good resolutions. But this evening I have to meet some friends for a drink.

BÉRENGER: For a drink?

OLD GENTLEMAN (*to the* LOGICIAN): What's more, a cat with no paws at all...

JEAN (*to* BÉRENGER): I've promised to go. I always keep my word.

OLD GENTLEMAN (*to the* LOGICIAN): ...wouldn't be able to run fast enough to catch mice.

BÉRENGER (*to* JEAN): Ah, now it's you that's setting me a bad example! You're going out drinking.

LOGICIAN (*to the* OLD GENTLEMAN): You're already making progress in logic.

(*A sound of rapid galloping is heard approaching again, trumpeting and the sound of rhinoceros hooves and panting; this time the sound comes from the opposite direction, approaching from backstage to front, in the left wings.*)

JEAN (*furiously to* BÉRENGER): It's not a habit with me, you know. It's not the same as with you. With you... you're... it's not the same thing at all...

BÉRENGER: Why isn't it the same thing?

JEAN (*shouting over the noise coming from the café*): I'm no drunkard, not me!

LOGICIAN (*shouting to the* OLD GENTLEMAN): Even with no paws, a cat must catch mice. That's in its nature.

BÉRENGER (*shouting very loudly*): I didn't mean you were a drunkard. But why would it make me one any more than you, in a case like that?

OLD GENTLEMAN (*shouting to the* LOGICIAN): What's in the cat's nature?

JEAN (*to* BÉRENGER): Because there's moderation in all things. I'm a moderate person, not like you!

LOGICIAN (*to the* OLD GENTLEMAN, *cupping his hands to his ears*): What did you say? (*Deafening sounds drown out the words of the four characters.*)

BÉRENGER (*to* JEAN, *cupping his hands to his ears*): What about me, what? What did you say?

JEAN (*roaring*): I said that...

OLD GENTLEMAN (*roaring*): I said that...

JEAN (*suddenly aware of the noises, which are now very near*): Whatever's happening?

LOGICIAN: What is going on?

JEAN (*rises, knocking his chair over as he does so; looks towards left wings, where the noises of the passing rhinoceros are coming from*): Oh, a rhinoceros!

LOGICIAN (*rising, knocking over his chair*): Oh, a rhinoceros!

OLD GENTLEMAN (*doing the same*): Oh, a rhinoceros!

BÉRENGER (*still seated, but this time, taking more notice*): Rhinoceros! In the opposite direction!

WAITRESS (*emerging with a tray and glasses*): What is it? Oh, a rhinoceros! (*She drops the tray, breaking the glasses.*)

PROPRIETOR (*coming out of the café*): What's going on?

WAITRESS (*to the* PROPRIETOR): A rhinoceros!

LOGICIAN: A rhinoceros, going full-tilt on the opposite pavement!

GROCER (*coming out of his shop*): Oh, a rhinoceros!

JEAN: Oh, a rhinoceros!

GROCER'S WIFE (*sticking her head through the upstairs window of shop*): Oh, a rhinoceros!

PROPRIETOR: It's no reason to break the glasses.

JEAN: It's rushing straight ahead, brushing up against the shop windows.

DAISY (*entering left*): Oh, a rhinoceros!

BÉRENGER (*noticing* DAISY): Oh, Daisy!

(*Noise of people fleeing, the same "Ohs" and "Ahs" as before.*)

WAITRESS: Well, of all things!

PROPRIETOR (*to the* WAITRESS): You'll be charged up for those!

(BÉRENGER *tries to make himself scarce, not to be seen by* DAISY. *The* OLD GENTLEMAN, *the* LOGICIAN, *the* GROCER *and his* WIFE *move to centre stage and say together*:)

ALL: Well, of all things!

JEAN and BÉRENGER: Well, of all things!

(*A piteous mewing is heard, then an equally piteous cry of a woman.*)

ALL: Oh!

(*Almost at the same time, and as the noises are rapidly dying away, the* HOUSEWIFE *appears without her basket, but holding the blood-stained corpse of her cat in her arms.*)

HOUSEWIFE (*wailing*): It ran over my cat, it ran over my cat!
WAITRESS: It ran over her cat!

(*The* GROCER, *his* WIFE, *at the window, the* OLD GENTLEMAN, DAISY *and the* LOGICIAN *crowd round the* HOUSEWIFE, *saying:*)

ALL: What a tragedy, poor little thing!
OLD GENTLEMAN: Poor little thing!
DAISY and WAITRESS: Poor little thing!
GROCER'S WIFE (*at the window*): ⎫
OLD GENTLEMAN: ⎬ Poor little thing!
LOGICIAN: ⎭
PROPRIETOR (*to the* WAITRESS, *pointing to the broken glasses and the upturned chairs*): Don't just stand there! Clear up the mess! (JEAN *and* BÉRENGER *also rush over to the* HOUSEWIFE, *who continues to lament, her dead cat in her arms.*)
WAITRESS (*moving to the café terrace to pick up the broken glasses and the chairs, and looking over her shoulder at the* HOUSEWIFE): Oh, poor little thing!
PROPRIETOR (*pointing, for the* WAITRESS's *benefit, to the debris*): Over there, over there!
OLD GENTLEMAN (*to the* GROCER): Well, what do you think of that?
BÉRENGER (*to the* HOUSEWIFE): You mustn't cry like that, it's too heartbreaking!
DAISY (*to* BÉRENGER): Were you there, Mr Bérenger? Did you see it?
BÉRENGER (*to* DAISY): Good morning, Miss Daisy; you must excuse me – I haven't had a chance to shave...
PROPRIETOR (*supervising the clearing up of the debris, then glancing towards the* HOUSEWIFE): Poor little thing!
WAITRESS (*clearing up the mess, her back to the* HOUSEWIFE): Poor little thing!

(*These remarks must obviously be made very rapidly – almost simultaneously.*)

GROCER'S WIFE (*at the window*): That's going too far!

JEAN: That's going too far!

HOUSEWIFE (*lamenting, and cradling the dead cat in her arms*):
My poor little pussy, my poor little cat.

OLD GENTLEMAN (*to the* HOUSEWIFE): What can you do, dear
lady? Cats are only mortal.

LOGICIAN: What do you expect, Madam? All cats are mortal! One
must accept that.

HOUSEWIFE (*lamenting*): My little cat, my poor little cat.

PROPRIETOR (*to the* WAITRESS, *whose apron is full of broken
glass*): Throw that in the dustbin! (*He has picked up the chairs.*)
You owe me a thousand francs.

WAITRESS (*moving into the café*): All you think of is money!

GROCER'S WIFE (*to the* HOUSEWIFE; *from the window*): Don't
upset yourself!

OLD GENTLEMAN (*to the* HOUSEWIFE): Don't upset yourself,
dear lady!

GROCER'S WIFE (*from the window*): It's very upsetting, a thing
like that!

HOUSEWIFE: My little cat, my little cat!

DAISY: Yes, it's very upsetting, a thing like that.

OLD GENTLEMAN (*supporting the* HOUSEWIFE *and guiding her to
a table on the terrace, followed by the others*): Sit down here,
dear lady.

JEAN (*to the* OLD GENTLEMAN): Well, what do you think of that?

GROCER (*to the* LOGICIAN): Well, what do you think of that?

GROCER'S WIFE (*to* DAISY, *from the window*): Well, what do you
think of that?

PROPRIETOR (*to the* WAITRESS, *who comes back while they
are installing the weeping* HOUSEWIFE *at one of the terrace tables, still cradling her dead cat*): A glass of water
for the lady.

OLD GENTLEMAN (*to the* HOUSEWIFE): Sit down, dear lady!

JEAN: Poor woman!

GROCER'S WIFE (*from the window*): Poor cat!

BÉRENGER (*to the* WAITRESS): Better give her a brandy.

PROPRIETOR (*to the* WAITRESS): A brandy! (*Pointing to* BÉRENGER:) This gentleman is paying!

WAITRESS (*going into the café*): One brandy, right away!

HOUSEWIFE (*sobbing*): I don't want any, I don't want any!

GROCER: It went past my shop a little while ago.

JEAN (*to the* GROCER): It wasn't the same one!

GROCER (*to* JEAN): But I could have—

GROCER'S WIFE: Yes it was, it was the same one.

DAISY: Did it go past twice, then?

PROPRIETOR: I think it was the same one.

JEAN: No, it was not the same rhinoceros. The one that went by first had two horns on its nose – it was an Asian rhinoceros – this only had one – it was an African rhinoceros!*

(*The* WAITRESS *appears with a glass of brandy and takes it to the* HOUSEWIFE.)

OLD GENTLEMAN: Here's a drop of brandy to help you pull yourself together.

HOUSEWIFE (*in tears*): No...o...o...

BÉRENGER (*suddenly unnerved, to* JEAN): You're talking nonsense... How could you possibly tell about the horns? The animal flashed past at such speed we hardly even saw it...

DAISY (*to the* HOUSEWIFE): Go on – it will do you good!

OLD GENTLEMAN (*to* BÉRENGER): Very true. It did go fast.

PROPRIETOR (*to the* HOUSEWIFE): Just have a taste, it's good.

BÉRENGER (*to* JEAN): You had no time to count its horns...

GROCER'S WIFE (*to the* WAITRESS, *from the window*): Make her drink it.

BÉRENGER (*to* JEAN): What's more, it was travelling in a cloud of dust.

DAISY (*to the* HOUSEWIFE): Drink it up.

OLD GENTLEMAN (*to the* HOUSEWIFE): Just a sip, dear little lady... be brave...

(*The* WAITRESS *forces her to drink it by putting the glass to her lips; the* HOUSEWIFE *feigns refusal, but drinks all the same.*)

WAITRESS: There, you see!

GROCER'S WIFE (*from her window*): and DAISY: There, you see!

JEAN (*to* BÉRENGER): I don't have to grope my way through a fog. I can calculate quickly – my mind is clear!

OLD GENTLEMAN (*to the* HOUSEWIFE): Better now?

BÉRENGER (*to* JEAN): But it had its head thrust down.

PROPRIETOR (*to the* HOUSEWIFE): Now wasn't that good?

JEAN (*to* BÉRENGER): Precisely – one could see all the better.

HOUSEWIFE (*after having drunk*): My little cat!

BÉRENGER (*irritated*): Utter nonsense!

GROCER'S WIFE (*to the* HOUSEWIFE, *from the window*): I've got another cat you can have.

JEAN (*to* BÉRENGER): What, me? You dare to accuse me of talking nonsense?

HOUSEWIFE (*to the* GROCER'S WIFE): I'll never have another! (*She weeps, cradling her cat.*)

BÉRENGER (*to* JEAN): Yes – absolute, blithering nonsense!

PROPRIETOR (*to the* HOUSEWIFE): You have to accept these things!

JEAN (*to* BÉRENGER): I've never talked nonsense in my life!

OLD GENTLEMAN (*to the* HOUSEWIFE): Try and be philosophic about it!

BÉRENGER (*to* JEAN): You're just a pretentious *show-off* (*raising his voice*) – a pedant!

PROPRIETOR (*to* JEAN *and* BÉRENGER): Now, gentlemen!

BÉRENGER (*to* JEAN, *continuing*): And what's more, a pedant who's not certain of his facts because, in the first place, it's the Asian rhinoceros with only one horn on its nose, and it's the African with two...

(*The other characters leave the* HOUSEWIFE *and crowd round* JEAN *and* BÉRENGER, *who argue at the top of their voices.*)

JEAN (*to* BÉRENGER): You're wrong – it's the other way about!

HOUSEWIFE (*left alone*): He was so sweet!

BÉRENGER: You want to bet?

WAITRESS: They want to make a bet!

DAISY (*to* BÉRENGER): Don't excite yourself, Mr Bérenger.

JEAN (*to* BÉRENGER): I'm not betting with you. If anybody's got two horns, it's you! You Asian Mongol!

WAITRESS: Oh!

GROCER'S WIFE (*from the window to her husband*): They're going to have a fight!

GROCER (*to his* WIFE): Nonsense, it's just a bet!

PROPRIETOR (*to* JEAN *and* BÉRENGER): We don't want any scenes here!

OLD GENTLEMAN: Now look... What kind of rhinoceros has one horn on its nose? (*To the* GROCER:) You're a tradesman – you should know.

GROCER'S WIFE (*to her husband*): Yes, you should know!

BÉRENGER (*to* JEAN): I've got no horns. And I never will have.

GROCER (*to the* OLD GENTLEMAN): Tradesmen can't be expected to know everything.

JEAN (*to* BÉRENGER): Oh yes, you have!

BÉRENGER (*to* JEAN): I'm not Asian either. And in any case, Asians are people, the same as everyone else...

WAITRESS: Yes, Asians are people, the same as we are...

OLD GENTLEMAN (*to the* PROPRIETOR): That's true!

PROPRIETOR (*to the* WAITRESS): Nobody's asking for your opinion!

DAISY (*to the* PROPRIETOR): She's right. They're people, the same as we are.

(*The* HOUSEWIFE *continues to lament throughout this discussion.*)

HOUSEWIFE: He was so gentle, just like one of us.

JEAN (*beside himself*): They're yellow!

(*The* LOGICIAN, *a little to one side between the* HOUSEWIFE *and the group which has formed round* JEAN *and* BÉRENGER, *follows the controversy attentively, without taking part.*)

Goodbye gentlemen! (*To* BÉRENGER:) You, I will not deign
to include!

HOUSEWIFE: He was devoted to us! (*She sobs.*)

DAISY: Now listen a moment, Mr Bérenger, and you, too, Mr Jean...

OLD GENTLEMAN: I once had some friends who were Asians! But
perhaps they weren't real ones...

PROPRIETOR: I've known some real ones.

WAITRESS (*to the* GROCER'S WIFE): I had an Asian friend once.

HOUSEWIFE (*still sobbing*): I had him when he was a little kitten.

JEAN (*still quite beside himself*): They're yellow, I tell you, bright
yellow!

BÉRENGER (*to* JEAN): Whatever they are, you're bright red!

GROCER'S WIFE (*from the window*): and WAITRESS: Oh!

PROPRIETOR: This is getting serious!

HOUSEWIFE: He was so clean. He always used his tray.

JEAN (*to* BÉRENGER): If that's how you feel, it's the last time
you'll see me. I'm not wasting my time with a fool like you.

HOUSEWIFE: He always made himself understood.

(JEAN *goes off right, very fast and furious... but doubles back before
making his final exit.*)

OLD GENTLEMAN (*to the* GROCER): There are white Asians as
well, and black and blue, and even some like us.

JEAN (*to* BÉRENGER): You drunkard! (*Everybody looks at him in
consternation.*)

BÉRENGER (*to* JEAN): I'm not going to stand for that!

ALL (*looking in* JEAN's *direction*): Oh!

HOUSEWIFE: He could almost talk – in fact, he did.

DAISY (*to* BÉRENGER): You shouldn't have made him angry.

BÉRENGER (*to* DAISY): It wasn't my fault.

PROPRIETOR (*to the* WAITRESS): Go and get a little coffin for the
poor thing...

OLD GENTLEMAN (*to* BÉRENGER): I think you're right. It's the
Asian rhinoceros with two horns and the African with one...

GROCER: But he was saying the opposite.

DAISY (*to* BÉRENGER): You were both wrong!

OLD GENTLEMAN (*to* BÉRENGER): Even so, you were right.

WAITRESS (*to the* HOUSEWIFE): Come with me – we're going to put him in a little box.

HOUSEWIFE (*sobbing desperately*): No, never!

GROCER: If you don't mind my saying so, I think Mr Jean was right.

DAISY (*turning to the* HOUSEWIFE): Now, you must be reasonable!

(DAISY *and the* WAITRESS *lead the* HOUSEWIFE, *with her dead cat, towards the café entrance.*)

OLD GENTLEMAN (*to* DAISY *and the* WAITRESS): Would you like me to come with you?

GROCER: The Asian rhinoceros has one horn and the African rhinoceros has two. And vice versa.

DAISY (*to the* OLD GENTLEMAN): No, don't worry.

(DAISY *and the* WAITRESS *enter the café leading the inconsolable* HOUSEWIFE.)

GROCER'S WIFE (*to the* GROCER, *from the window*): Oh, you always have to be different from everybody else!

BÉRENGER (*aside, whilst the others continue to discuss the horns of the rhinoceros*): Daisy was right – I should never have contradicted him.

PROPRIETOR (*to the* GROCER'S WIFE): Your husband's right: the Asian rhinoceros has two horns and the African one must have two, and vice versa.

BÉRENGER (*aside*): He can't stand being contradicted. The slightest disagreement makes him fume.

OLD GENTLEMAN (*to the* PROPRIETOR): You're mistaken, my friend.

PROPRIETOR (*to the* OLD GENTLEMAN): I'm very sorry, I'm sure.

PROPRIETOR (*aside*): His temper's his only fault.

GROCER'S WIFE (*from the window, to the* OLD GENTLEMAN, *the* PROPRIETOR *and the* GROCER): Maybe they're both the same.

BÉRENGER (*aside*): Deep down, he's got a heart of gold; he's done me many a good turn.

PROPRIETOR (*to the* GROCER'S WIFE): If the one has two horns, then the other must have one.

OLD GENTLEMAN: Perhaps it's the other with two and the one with one.

BÉRENGER (*aside*): I'm sorry I wasn't more accommodating. But why is he so obstinate? I didn't want to exasperate him. (*To the others*:) He's always making fantastic statements! Always trying to dazzle people with his knowledge. He will never admit he's wrong.

OLD GENTLEMAN (*to* BÉRENGER): Have you any proof?

BÉRENGER: Proof of what?

OLD GENTLEMAN: Of the statement you made just now which started the unfortunate row with your friend.

GROCER (*to* BÉRENGER): Yes – have you any proof?

OLD GENTLEMAN (*to* BÉRENGER): How do you know that one of the two rhinoceroses has one horn and the other two? And which is which?

GROCER'S WIFE: He doesn't know any more than we do.

BÉRENGER: In the first place, we don't know that there were two. I myself believe there was only one.

PROPRIETOR: Well, let's say there were two. Does the single-horned one come from Asia?

OLD GENTLEMAN: No. It's the one from Africa with two, I think.

PROPRIETOR: Which is two-horned?

GROCER: It's not the one from Africa.

GROCER'S WIFE: It's not easy to agree on this.

OLD GENTLEMAN: But the problem must be cleared up.

LOGICIAN (*emerging from his isolation*): Excuse me, gentlemen, for interrupting. But that is not the question. Allow me to introduce myself...

HOUSEWIFE (*in tears*): He's a logician.

PROPRIETOR: Oh! A logician, is he?

OLD GENTLEMAN (*introducing the* LOGICIAN *to* BÉRENGER): My friend, the Logician.

BÉRENGER: Very happy to meet you.

LOGICIAN (*continuing*): Professional Logician; my card. (*He shows his card.*)

BÉRENGER: It's a great honour.

GROCER: A great honour for all of us.

PROPRIETOR: Would you mind telling us then, sir, if the African rhinoceros is single-horned...

OLD GENTLEMAN: Or bicorned...

GROCER'S WIFE: And is the Asian rhinoceros bicorned...

GROCER: Or unicorned.

LOGICIAN: Exactly; that is not the question. Let me make myself clear.

GROCER: But it's still what we want to find out.

LOGICIAN: Kindly allow me to speak, gentlemen.

OLD GENTLEMAN: Let him speak!

GROCER'S WIFE (*to the* GROCER, *from the window*): Give him a chance to speak.

PROPRIETOR: We're listening, sir.

LOGICIAN (*to* BÉRENGER): I'm addressing you in particular. And all the others present as well.

GROCER: Us as well...

LOGICIAN: You see, you have got away from the problem which instigated the debate. In the first place you were deliberating whether or not the rhinoceros which passed by just now was the same one that passed by earlier, or whether it was another. That is the question to decide.

BÉRENGER: Yes, but how?

LOGICIAN: Thus: you may have seen on two occasions a single rhinoceros bearing a single horn...

GROCER (*repeating the words, as if to understand better*): On two occasions a single rhinoceros...

PROPRIETOR (*doing the same*): Bearing a single horn...

LOGICIAN: ...or you may have seen on two occasions a single rhinoceros with two horns.

OLD GENTLEMAN (*repeating the words*): A single rhinoceros with two horns on two occasions…

LOGICIAN: Exactly. Or again, you may have seen one rhinoceros with one horn, and then another also with a single horn.

GROCER'S WIFE (*from the window*): Ha, ha…

LOGICIAN: Or again, an initial rhinoceros with two horns, followed by a second with two horns…

PROPRIETOR: That's true.

LOGICIAN: Now, if you had seen…

GROCER: If we'd seen…

OLD GENTLEMAN: Yes, if we'd seen…

LOGICIAN: If on the first occasion you had seen a rhinoceros with two horns…

PROPRIETOR: With two horns…

LOGICIAN: And on the second occasion, a rhinoceros with one horn…

GROCER: With one horn…

LOGICIAN: That wouldn't be conclusive either.

OLD GENTLEMAN: Even that wouldn't be conclusive.

PROPRIETOR: Why not?

GROCER'S WIFE: Oh, I don't get it at all.

GROCER: Shoo! Shoo!

(*The* GROCER'S WIFE *shrugs her shoulders and withdraws from her window.*)

LOGICIAN: For it is possible that, since its first appearance, the rhinoceros may have lost one of its horns, and that the first and second transit were still made by a single beast.

BÉRENGER: I see, but—

OLD GENTLEMAN (*interrupting* BÉRENGER): Don't interrupt!

LOGICIAN: It may also be that two rhinoceroses, both with two horns, may each have lost a horn.

OLD GENTLEMAN: That is possible.

PROPRIETOR: Yes, that's possible.

GROCER: Why not?

BÉRENGER: Yes, but in any case—

OLD GENTLEMAN (*to* BÉRENGER): Don't interrupt.

LOGICIAN: If you could prove that on the first occasion you saw a rhinoceros with one horn, either Asian or African…

OLD GENTLEMAN: Asian or African…

LOGICIAN: And on the second occasion a rhinoceros with two horns…

GROCER: One with two…

LOGICIAN: No matter whether African or Asian…

OLD GENTLEMAN: African or Asian…

LOGICIAN: …we could then conclude that we were dealing with two different rhinoceroses, for it is hardly likely that a second horn could grow sufficiently in a space of a few minutes to be visible on the nose of a rhinoceros.

OLD GENTLEMAN: It's hardly likely.

LOGICIAN (*enchanted with his discourse*): That would imply one rhinoceros, either Asian or African…

OLD GENTLEMAN: Asian or African…

LOGICIAN: …and one rhinoceros, either African or Asian.

PROPRIETOR: African or Asian.

GROCER: Er… yais.

LOGICIAN: For good logic cannot entertain the possibility that the same creature be born in two places at the same time…

OLD GENTLEMAN: …or even successively.

LOGICIAN (*to* OLD GENTLEMAN): Which was to be proved.

BÉRENGER (*to* LOGICIAN): That seems clear enough, but it doesn't answer the question.

LOGICIAN (*to* BÉRENGER, *with a knowledgeable smile*): Obviously, my dear sir, but now the problem is correctly posed.

OLD GENTLEMAN: It's quite logical. Quite logical.

LOGICIAN (*raising his hat*): Goodbye, gentlemen.

(*He retires, going out left, followed by the* OLD GENTLEMAN:)

OLD GENTLEMAN: Goodbye, gentlemen. (*He raises his hat and follows the* LOGICIAN *out.*)

GROCER: Well, it may be logical…

(*At this moment the* HOUSEWIFE *comes out of the café in deep mourning, and carrying a box; she is followed by* DAISY *and the* WAITRESS, *as if for a funeral. The cortège moves towards the right exit.*)

…it may be logical, but are we going to stand for our cats being run down under our very eyes by one-horned rhinoceroses, or two, whether they're Asian or African? (*He indicates with a theatrical gesture the cortège, which is just leaving.*)

PROPRIETOR: He's absolutely right! We're not standing for our cats being run down by rhinoceroses or anything else!

GROCER: We're not going to stand for it!

GROCER'S WIFE (*sticking her head round the shop door, to her husband*): Are you coming in? The customers will be here any minute.

GROCER (*moving to the shop*): No, we're not standing for it.

BÉRENGER: I should never have quarrelled with Jean! (*To the* PROPRIETOR:) Get me a brandy! A double!

PROPRIETOR: Coming up! (*He goes into the café for the brandy.*)

BÉRENGER (*alone*): I never should have quarrelled with Jean. I shouldn't have got into such a rage!

(*The* PROPRIETOR *comes out, carrying a large glass of brandy.*)

I feel too upset to go to the museum. I'll cultivate my mind some other time. (*He takes the glass of brandy and drinks it.*)

CURTAIN

Act Two

SCENE ONE

A government office, or the office of a private concern – such as a large firm of law publications. Upstage centre, a large double door, above which a notice reads: "Chef du Service". Upstage left, near the Head of the Department's door, stands DAISY's *little table with a typewriter. By the left wall, between a door which leads to the staircase and* DAISY's *table, stands another table, on which the time sheets are placed, which the employees sign on arrival. The door leading to the staircase is downstage left. The top steps of the staircase can be seen, as can the top of a stair-rail and a small landing. In the foreground, a table with two chairs. On the table: printing proofs, an inkwell, pens; this is the table where* BOTARD *and* BÉRENGER *work;* BÉRENGER *will sit on the left chair,* BOTARD *on the right. Near the right wall, another bigger, rectangular table, also covered with papers, proofs, etc.*

Two more chairs stand at each end of this table – more elegant and imposing chairs. This is the table of DUDARD *and* MR BOEUF. DUDARD *will sit on the chair next to the wall, the other employees facing him. He acts as Deputy Head. Between the upstage door and the right wall there is a window. If the theatre has an orchestra pit, it would be preferable to have simply a window frame in front of the stage, facing the auditorium. In the right-hand corner, upstage, a coat-stand, on which grey smocks or old coats are hung. The coat-stand could also be placed downstage, near the right wall.*

On the walls are rows of books and dusty documents. On the back wall, left, above the shelves, there are signs: "Jurisprudence", "Codes"; on the right-hand wall, which can be slightly on an angle, the signs read: "Le Journal officiel", "Lois fiscales". Above the Head of the Department's door a clock registers three minutes past nine.

When the curtain rises, DUDARD *is standing near his chair, his right profile to the auditorium; on the other side of the desk, left profile to the auditorium, is* BOTARD; *between them, also near the desk, facing the auditorium, stands the Head of the Department;* DAISY *is near the Chief, a little upstage of him. She holds some sheets of typing paper. On the table round which the three characters stand, a large open newspaper lies on the printing proofs.*

When the curtain rises, the characters remain fixed for a few seconds in position for the first line of dialogue. They make a tableau vivant. The same effect marks the beginning of the first act.

The Head of the Department is about forty, very correctly dressed: dark-blue suit, a rosette of the Legion of Honour, starched collar, black tie, large brown moustache. He is MR PAPILLON.

DUDARD, *thirty-five years old, grey suit; he wears black lustrine sleeves to protect his coat. He may wear spectacles. He is quite tall, a young employee with a future. If the Department Head became the Assistant Director he would take his place:* BOTARD *does not like him.*

BOTARD: *former schoolteacher; short; he has a proud air, and wears a little white moustache; a brisk sixty year-old: he knows everything, understands everything, judges everything. He wears a Basque beret, and wears a long grey smock during working hours, spectacles on a longish nose, a pencil behind his ear; he also wears protective sleeves at work.*

DAISY: *young blonde.*

Later, MRS BOEUF: *a large woman of some forty to fifty years old, tearful and breathless.*

As the curtain rises, the characters are standing motionless around the table, right; the Chief with index finger pointing to the newspaper; DUDARD, *with his hand extended in* BOTARD's *direction, seems to be saying: "So you see!"* BOTARD, *hands in the pockets of his smock, wears an incredulous smile and seems to say: "You won't take me in."* DAISY, *with her typing paper in her hand seems, from her look, to be supporting* DUDARD.

After a few brief seconds, BOTARD *starts the attack.*

BOTARD: It's all a lot of made-up nonsense.

DAISY: But I saw it – I saw the rhinoceros!

DUDARD: It's in the paper, in black and white – you can't deny that.

BOTARD (*with an air of the greatest scorn*): Pfff!

DUDARD: It's all here; it's down here in the dead-cats column! Read it for yourself, Chief.

PAPILLON: "Yesterday, just before lunch time, in the church square of our town, a cat was trampled to death by a pachyderm."

DAISY: It wasn't exactly in the church square.

PAPILLON: That's all it says. No other details.

BOTARD: Pfff!

DUDARD: Well, that's clear enough.

BOTARD: I never believe journalists. They're all liars. I don't need them to tell me what to think; I believe what I see with my own eyes. Speaking as a former teacher, I like things to be precise, scientifically valid; I've got a methodical mind.

DUDARD: What's a methodical mind got to do with it?

DAISY (*to* BOTARD): I think it's stated very precisely, Mr Botard.

BOTARD: You call that precise? And what, pray, does it mean by "a pachyderm"? What does the editor of a dead-cats column understand by "a pachyderm"? He doesn't say. And what does he mean by "a cat"?

DUDARD: Everybody knows what a cat is.

BOTARD: Does it concern a male cat or a female? What breed was it? And what colour? The colour bar* is something I feel strongly about. I hate it.

PAPILLON: What has the colour bar to do with it, Mr Botard? It's quite beside the point.

BOTARD: Please forgive me, Mr Papillon. But you can't deny that the colour problem is one of the great stumbling blocks of our time.

DUDARD: I know that, we all know that, but it has nothing to do with—

BOTARD: It's not an issue to be dismissed lightly, Mr Dudard. The course of history has shown that racial prejudice—

DUDARD: I tell you, it doesn't enter into it!

BOTARD: I'm not so sure.

PAPILLON: The colour bar is not the issue at stake.

BOTARD: One should never miss an occasion to denounce it.

DAISY: But we told you that none of us is in favour of the colour bar. You're obscuring the issue; it's simply a question of a cat being run over by a pachyderm – in this case, a rhinoceros.

BOTARD: I'm a Northerner myself. Southerners have got too much imagination. Perhaps it was merely a flea run over by a mouse. People make mountains out of molehills.

PAPILLON (*to* DUDARD): Let us try and get things clear. Did you yourself, with your own eyes, see a rhinoceros strolling through the streets of the town?

DAISY: It didn't stroll, it ran.

DUDARD: No, I didn't see it personally. But a lot of very reliable people!—

BOTARD (*interrupting him*): It's obvious they were just making it up. You put too much trust in these journalists; they don't care what they invent to sell their wretched newspapers and please the bosses they serve! And you mean to tell me they've taken you in – you, a qualified man of law! Forgive me for laughing! Ha! Ha! Ha!

DAISY: But I saw it – I saw the rhinoceros. I'd take my oath on it.

BOTARD: Get away with you! And I thought you were a sensible girl!

DAISY: Mr Botard, I can see straight! And I wasn't the only one; there were plenty of other people watching.

BOTARD: Pfff! They were probably watching something else! A few idlers with nothing to do – work-shy loafers!

DUDARD: It happened yesterday, Sunday.

BOTARD: I work on Sundays as well. I've no time for priests who do their utmost to get you to church, just to prevent you from working and earning your daily bread by the sweat of your brow.

PAPILLON (*indignant*): Oh!

BOTARD: I'm sorry, I didn't mean to offend you. The fact that I despise religion doesn't mean I don't esteem it highly. (*To* DAISY:) In any case, do you know what a rhinoceros looks like?

DAISY: It's a… it's a very big, ugly animal.

BOTARD: And you pride yourself on your precise thinking! The rhinoceros, my dear young lady—

PAPILLON: There's no need to start a lecture on the rhinoceros here. We're not in school.

BOTARD: That's a pity.

(*During these last speeches* BÉRENGER *is seen climbing the last steps of the staircase; he opens the office door cautiously; as he does so one can read the notice on it: "Éditions de Droit".*)

PAPILLON: Well! It's gone nine, Miss Daisy; put the time sheets away. Too bad about the latecomers.

(DAISY *goes to the little table, left, on which the time sheets are placed, at the same moment as* BÉRENGER *enters.*)

BÉRENGER (*entering, whilst the others continue their discussion, to* DAISY): Good morning, Miss Daisy. I'm not late, am I?

BOTARD (*to* DUDARD *and* PAPILLON): I campaign against ignorance wherever I find it!…

DAISY (*to* BÉRENGER): Hurry up, Mr Bérenger.

BOTARD: …in palace or humble hut!

DAISY (*to* BÉRENGER): Quick! Sign the time sheet!

BÉRENGER: Oh thank you! Has the boss arrived?

DAISY (*a finger on her lips*): Shh! Yes, he's here.

BÉRENGER: Here already? (*He hurries to sign the time sheet.*)

BOTARD (*continuing*): No matter where! Even in printing offices.

PAPILLON (*to* BOTARD): Mr Botard, I consider…

BÉRENGER (*signing the sheet, to* DAISY): But it's not ten past…

PAPILLON (*to* BOTARD): I consider you have gone too far.

DUDARD (*to* PAPILLON): I think so too, sir.

PAPILLON (*to* BOTARD): Are you suggesting that Mr Dudard, my colleague and yours, a law graduate and a first-class employee, is ignorant?

BOTARD: I wouldn't go so far as to say that, but the teaching you get at university isn't up to what you get at ordinary schools.

PAPILLON (*to* DAISY): What about that time sheet?

DAISY (*to* PAPILLON): Here it is, sir. (*She hands it to him.*)

BOTARD (*to* DUDARD): There's no clear thinking at universities, no encouragement for practical observation.

DUDARD (*to* BOTARD): Oh come now!

BÉRENGER (*to* PAPILLON): Good morning, Mr Papillon. (*He has been making his way to the coat-rack behind the Chief's back and around the group formed by the three characters; there he takes down his working overall or his well-worn coat, and hangs up his street coat in its place; he changes his coat by the coat-rack, then makes his way to his desk, from the drawer of which he takes out his black protective sleeves, etc.*) Morning, Mr Papillon! Sorry I was almost late. Morning Dudard! Morning, Mr Botard.

PAPILLON: Well, BÉRENGER, did you see the rhinoceros by any chance?

BOTARD (*to* DUDARD): All you get at universities are effete intellectuals with no practical knowledge of life.

DUDARD (*to* BOTARD): Rubbish!

BÉRENGER (*continuing to arrange his working equipment with excessive zeal, as if to make up for his late arrival; in a natural tone to* PAPILLON): Oh yes, I saw it all right.

BOTARD (*turning round*): Pfff!

DAISY: So you see, I'm not mad after all.

BOTARD (*ironic*): Oh, Mr Bérenger says that out of chivalry – he's a very chivalrous man, even if he doesn't look it.

DUDARD: What's chivalrous about saying you've seen a rhinoceros?

BOTARD: A lot, when it's said to bolster up a fantastic statement by Miss Daisy. Everybody is chivalrous to Miss Daisy – it's very understandable.

PAPILLON: Don't twist the facts, Mr Botard. Mr Bérenger took no part in the argument. He's only just arrived.

BÉRENGER (*to* DAISY): But you did see it, didn't you? We both did.

BOTARD: Pfff! It's possible that Mr Bérenger thought he saw a rhinoceros. (*He makes a sign behind* BÉRENGER's *back to indicate he drinks.*) He's got such a vivid imagination! Anything's possible with him!

BÉRENGER: I wasn't alone when I saw the rhinoceros! Or perhaps there were two rhinoceroses.

BOTARD: He doesn't even know how many he saw.

BÉRENGER: I was with my friend Jean! And other people were there, too.

BOTARD (*to* BÉRENGER): I don't think you know what you're talking about.

DAISY: It was a unicorned rhinoceros.

BOTARD: Pff! They're in league, the two of them, to have us on.

DUDARD (*to* DAISY): I rather think it had two horns, from what I've heard!

BOTARD: You'd better make up your minds.

PAPILLON (*looking at the time*): That will do, gentlemen; time's getting on.

BOTARD: Did you see one rhinoceros, Mr Bérenger, or two rhinoceroses?

BÉRENGER: Well, it's hard to say!

BOTARD: You don't know. Miss Daisy saw *one* unicorned rhinoceros. What about your rhinoceros, Mr Bérenger – if indeed there was one – did it have one horn or two?

BÉRENGER: Exactly, that's the whole problem.

BOTARD: And it's all very dubious.

DAISY: Oh!

BOTARD: I don't mean to be offensive. But I don't believe a word of it. No rhinoceros has ever been seen in this country!

DAISY: There's a first time for everything.

BOTARD: It has never been seen! Except in school-book illustrations. Your rhinoceroses are a flower of some washerwoman's imagination.

BÉRENGER: The word "flower" applied to a rhinoceros seems a bit out of place.

DUDARD: Very true.

BOTARD (*continuing*): Your rhinoceros is a myth!

DAISY: A myth?

PAPILLON: Gentlemen, I think it is high time we started work.

BOTARD (*to* DAISY): A myth – like flying saucers.

DUDARD: But, nevertheless, a cat was trampled to death – that you can't deny.

BÉRENGER: I was a witness to that.

DUDARD (*pointing to* BÉRENGER): In front of witnesses.

BOTARD: Yes, and what a witness!

PAPILLON: Gentlemen, gentlemen!

BOTARD (*to* DUDARD): An example of collective psychosis, Mr Dudard. Just like religion – the opiate of the people!

DAISY: Well, I believe flying saucers exist!

BOTARD: Pfff!

PAPILLON (*firmly*): That's quite enough. There's been enough gossip! Rhinoceros or no rhinoceros, saucers or no saucers, work must go on! You're not paid to waste your time arguing about real or imaginary animals.

BOTARD: Imaginary!

DUDARD: Real!

DAISY: Very real!

PAPILLON: Gentlemen, I remind you once again that we are in working hours. I am putting an end to this futile discussion.

BOTARD (*wounded and ironic*): Very well, Mr Papillon. You are the chief. Your wishes are our commands.

PAPILLON: Get on, gentlemen. I don't want to be forced to make a deduction from your salaries! Mr Dudard, how is your report on the alcoholic-repression law coming along?

DUDARD: I'm just finishing it off, sir.

PAPILLON: Then do so. It's very urgent. Mr Bérenger and Mr Botard, have you finished correcting the proofs for the wine-trade control regulations?

BÉRENGER: Not yet, Mr Papillon. But they're well on the way.

PAPILLON: Then finish off the corrections together. The printers are waiting. And Miss Daisy, bring the letters to my office for signature. Hurry up and get them typed.

DAISY: Very good, Mr Papillon.

(DAISY *goes and types at her little desk.* DUDARD *sits at his desk and starts to work.* BÉRENGER *and* BOTARD *sit at their little tables in profile to the auditorium.* BOTARD, *his back to the staircase, seems in a bad temper.* BÉRENGER *is passive and limp; he spreads the proofs on the table, passes the manuscript to* BOTARD; BOTARD *sits down, grumbling, whilst* PAPILLON *exits, banging the door loudly.*)

PAPILLON: I shall see you shortly, gentlemen. (*Goes out.*)

BÉRENGER (*reading and correcting whilst* BOTARD *checks the manuscript with a pencil*): Laws relating to the control of proprietary wine produce... (*he corrects*) control with one L... (*he corrects*) proprietary... one P, proprietary... The controlled wines of the Bordeaux region, the lower sections of the upper slopes—

BOTARD: I haven't got that! You've skipped a line.

BÉRENGER: I'll start again. The Wine Control!

DUDARD (*to* BÉRENGER *and* BOTARD): Please don't read so loud. I can't concentrate with you shouting at the tops of your voices.

BOTARD (*to* DUDARD, *over* BÉRENGER's *head, resuming the recent discussion, whilst* BÉRENGER *continues the corrections on his own for a few moments; he moves his lips noiselessly as he reads*): It's all a hoax.

DUDARD: What's all a hoax?

BOTARD: Your rhinoceros business, of course. You've been making up all this propaganda to get these rumours started!

DUDARD (*interrupting his work*): What propaganda?

BÉRENGER (*breaking in*): No question of any propaganda.

DAISY (*interrupting her typing*): Do I have to tell you again? I saw it... I actually saw it, and others did, too.

DUDARD (*to* BOTARD): You make me laugh! Propaganda! Propaganda for what?

BOTARD (*to* DUDARD): Oh, you know more about that than I do. Don't make out you're so innocent.

DUDARD (*getting angry*): At any rate, Mr Botard, I'm not in the pay of any furtive underground organization.

BOTARD: That's an insult – I'm not standing for that… (*Rises.*)
BÉRENGER (*pleading*): Now, now, Mr Botard…
DAISY (*to* DUDARD, *who has also risen*): Now, now, Mr Dudard…
BOTARD: I tell you, it's an insult.

(MR PAPILLON's *door suddenly opens.* BOTARD *and* DUDARD *sit down again quickly;* MR PAPILLON *is holding the time sheet in his hand; there is silence at his appearance.*)

PAPILLON: Is Mr Boeuf not in today?
BÉRENGER (*looking around*): No, he isn't. He must be absent.
PAPILLON: Just when I needed him. (*To* DAISY:) Did he let anyone know he was ill or couldn't come in?
DAISY: He didn't say anything to me.
PAPILLON (*opening his door wide and coming in*): If this goes on I shall fire him. It's not the first time he's played this trick. Up to now I haven't said anything, but it's not going on like this. Has anyone got the key to his desk?

(*At this moment* MRS BOEUF *enters. She has been seen during the last speech coming up the stairs. She bursts through the door, out of breath, apprehensive.*)

BÉRENGER: Oh, here's Mrs Boeuf.
DAISY: Morning, Mrs Boeuf.
MRS BOEUF: Morning, Mr Papillon. Good morning, everyone.
PAPILLON: Well, where's your husband? What's happened to him? Is it too much trouble for him to come any more?
MRS BOEUF (*breathless*): Please excuse him, my husband, I mean… he went to visit his family for the weekend. He's got a touch of flu.
PAPILLON: So he's got a touch of flu, has he?
MRS BOEUF (*handing a paper to* PAPILLON): He says so in the telegram. He hopes to be back on Wednesday… (*Almost fainting.*) Could I have a glass of water… and sit down a moment…

(BÉRENGER *takes his own chair centre stage, on which she flops.*)

PAPILLON (*to* DAISY): Give her a glass of water.

DAISY: Yes, straight away! (*She goes to get her a glass of water, and gives it to her during the following speeches.*)

DUDARD (*to* PAPILLON): She must have a weak heart.

PAPILLON: It's a great nuisance that Mr Boeuf can't come. But that's no reason for you to go to pieces.

MRS BOEUF (*with difficulty*): It's not... it's... well, I was chased here all the way from the house by a rhinoceros...

BÉRENGER: How many horns did it have?

BOTARD (*guffawing*): Don't make me laugh!

DUDARD (*indignant*): Give her a chance to speak!

MRS BOEUF (*making a great effort to be exact, and pointing in the direction of the staircase*): It's down there, by the entrance. It seemed to want to come upstairs.

(*At this moment a noise is heard. The staircase steps are seen to crumble under an obviously formidable weight. From below an anguished trumpeting is heard. As the dust clears after the collapse of the staircase, the landing is seen to be hanging in space.*)

DAISY: My God!

MRS BOEUF (*seated, her hand on her heart*): Oh! Ah!

(BÉRENGER *runs to administer to* MRS BOEUF, *patting her cheeks and making her drink.*)

BÉRENGER: Keep calm!

(*Meanwhile,* PAPILLON, DUDARD *and* BOTARD *rush left, jostling each other in their efforts to open the door, and stand covered in dust on the landing; the trumpeting continues to be heard.*)

DAISY (*to* MRS BOEUF): Are you feeling better now, Mrs Boeuf?

PAPILLON (*on the landing*): There it is! Down there! It is one!

BOTARD: I can't see a thing. It's an illusion.

DUDARD: Of course it's one, down there, turning round and round.

DUDARD: It can't get up here. There's no staircase any longer.

BOTARD: It's most strange. What can it mean?

DUDARD (*turning towards* BÉRENGER): Come and look. Come and have a look at your rhinoceros.

BÉRENGER: I'm coming.

(BÉRENGER *rushes to the landing, followed by* DAISY, *who abandons* MRS BOEUF.)

PAPILLON (*to* BÉRENGER): You're the rhinoceros expert – take a good look.

BÉRENGER: I'm no rhinoceros expert...

DAISY: Oh, look at the way it's going round and round. It looks as if it was in pain... what can it want?

DUDARD: It seems to be looking for someone. (*To* BOTARD:) Can you see it now?

BOTARD (*vexed*): Yes, yes, I can see it.

DAISY (*to* PAPILLON): Perhaps we're all seeing things. You as well...

BOTARD: I never see things. Something is definitely down there.

DUDARD (*to* BOTARD): What do you mean, something?

PAPILLON (*to* BÉRENGER): It's obviously a rhinoceros. That's what you saw before, isn't it? (*To* DAISY:) And you, too?

DAISY: Definitely.

BÉRENGER: It's got two horns. It's an African rhinoceros, or Asian, rather. Oh! I don't know whether the African rhinoceros has one horn or two.

PAPILLON: It's demolished the staircase – and a good thing, too! When you think how long I've been asking the management to install stone steps in place of that worm-eaten old staircase.

DUDARD: I sent a report a week ago, Chief.

PAPILLON: It was bound to happen – I knew that. I could see it coming, and I was right.

DAISY (*to* PAPILLON, *ironically*): As always.

BÉRENGER (*to* DUDARD *and* PAPILLON): Now look, are two horns a characteristic of the Asian rhinoceros or the African?

And is one horn a characteristic of the African or the Asian one?...

DAISY: Poor thing, it keeps on trumpeting and going round and round. What does it want? Oh, it's looking at us! (*To the rhinoceros.*) Puss, puss, puss...

DUDARD: I shouldn't try to stroke it – it's probably not tame...

PAPILLON: In any case, it's out of reach.

(*The rhinoceros gives a horrible trumpeting.*)

DAISY: Poor thing!

BÉRENGER (*to* BOTARD, *still insisting*): You're very well informed; don't you think that the ones with two horns are—

PAPILLON: What are you rambling on about, Bérenger? You're still a bit under the weather; Mr Botard was right.

BOTARD: How can it be possible in a civilized country?...

DAISY (*to* BOTARD): All right. But does it exist or not?

BOTARD: It's all an infamous plot! (*With apolitical orator's gesture he points to* DUDARD, *quelling him with a look.*) It's all your fault!

DUDARD: Why mine, rather than yours?

BOTARD (*furious*): Mine? It's always the little people who get the blame. If I had my way...

PAPILLON: We're in a fine mess with no staircase.

DAISY (*to* BOTARD *and* DUDARD): Calm down, this is no time to quarrel!

PAPILLON: It's all the management's fault.

DAISY: Maybe. But how are we going to get down?

PAPILLON (*joking amorously and caressing* DAISY's *cheek*): I'll take you in my arms and we'll float down together.

DAISY (*rejecting* PAPILLON's *advances*): You keep your horny hands off my face, you old pachyderm!

PAPILLON: I was only joking!

(*Meanwhile, the rhinoceros has continued its trumpeting. MRS BOEUF has risen and joined the group. For a few moments she stares fixedly at the rhinoceros turning round and round below; suddenly she lets out a terrible cry.)*

MRS BOEUF: My God! It can't be true!

BÉRENGER (*to* MRS BOEUF): What's the matter?

MRS BOEUF: It's my husband. Oh Boeuf, my poor Boeuf, what's happened to you?

DAISY (*to* MRS BOEUF): Are you positive?

MRS BOEUF: I recognize him, I recognize him!

(*The rhinoceros replies with a violent but tender trumpeting.*)

PAPILLON: Well! That's the last straw. This time he's fired for good!

DUDARD: Is he insured?

BOTARD (*aside*): I understand it all now...

DAISY: How can you collect insurance in a case like this?

MRS BOEUF (*fainting into* BÉRENGER's *arms*): Oh! My God!

BÉRENGER: Oh!

DAISY: Carry her over here!

(BÉRENGER, *helped by* DUDARD *and* DAISY, *install* MRS BOEUF *in a chair.*)

DUDARD (*while they are carrying her*): Don't upset yourself, Mrs Boeuf.

MRS BOEUF: Ah! Oh!

DAISY: Maybe it can all be put right...

PAPILLON (*to* DUDARD): Legally, what can be done?

DUDARD: You need to get a solicitor's advice.

BOTARD (*following the procession, raising his hands to heaven*): It's the sheerest madness! What a society!

(*They crowd round* MRS BOEUF, *pinching her cheeks; she opens her eyes, emits an "Ah" and closes them again; they continue to pinch her cheeks as* BOTARD *speaks:*)

You can be certain of one thing: I shall report this to my union. I don't desert a colleague in the hour of need. It won't be hushed up.

MRS BOEUF (*coming to*): My poor darling! I can't leave him like that, my poor darling. (*A trumpeting is heard.*) He's calling me. (*Tenderly:*) He's calling me.

DAISY: Feeling better now, Mrs Boeuf?

DUDARD: She's picking up a bit.

BOTARD (*to* MRS BOEUF): You can count on the union's support. Would you like to become a member of the committee?

PAPILLON: Work's going to be delayed again. What about the post, Miss Daisy?

DAISY: I want to know first how we're going to get out of here.

PAPILLON: It is a problem. Through the window.

(*They all go to the window, with the exception of* MRS BOEUF, *slumped in her chair, and* BOTARD *who stays centre stage.*)

BOTARD: I know where it came from.

DAISY (*at the window*): It's too high.

BÉRENGER: Perhaps we ought to call the firemen, and get them to bring ladders!

PAPILLON: Miss Daisy, go to my office and telephone the fire brigade. (*He makes as if to follow her.*)

(DAISY *goes out upstage and one hears her voice on the telephone say: "Hello, hello, is that the Fire Brigade?" followed by a vague sound of telephone conversation.*)

MRS BOEUF (*rising suddenly*): I can't desert him, I can't desert him now!

PAPILLON: If you want to divorce him... you'd be perfectly justified.

DUDARD: You'd be the injured party.

MRS BOEUF: No! Poor thing! This is not the moment for that. I won't abandon my husband in such a state.

BOTARD: You're a good woman.

DUDARD (*to* MRS BOEUF): But what are you going to do?

(*She runs left towards the landing.*)

BÉRENGER: Watch out!
MRS BOEUF: I can't leave him, I can't leave him now!
DUDARD: Hold her back!
MRS BOEUF: I'm taking him home!
PAPILLON: What's she trying to do?
MRS BOEUF (*preparing to jump; on the edge of the landing*): I'm coming, my darling, I'm coming!
BÉRENGER: She's going to jump.
BOTARD: It's no more than her duty.
DUDARD: She can't do that.

(*Everyone, with the exception of* DAISY, *who is still telephoning, is near* MRS BOEUF *on the landing; she jumps;* BÉRENGER, *who tries to restrain her, is left with her skirt in his hand.*)

BÉRENGER: I couldn't hold her back.

(*The rhinoceros is heard from below, tenderly trumpeting.*)

VOICE OF MRS BOEUF: Here I am, my sweet, I'm here now.
DUDARD: She landed on his back in the saddle.
BOTARD: She's a good rider.
VOICE OF MRS BOEUF: Home now, dear, let's go home.
DUDARD: They're off at a gallop.

(DUDARD, BOTARD, BÉRENGER, PAPILLON *come back onstage and go to the window.*)

BÉRENGER: They're moving fast.
DUDARD (*to* PAPILLON): Ever done any riding?
PAPILLON: A bit... a long time ago... (*Turning to the upstage door, to* DUDARD:) Is she still on the telephone?

BÉRENGER (*following the course of the rhinoceros*): They're already a long way off. They're out of sight.

DAISY (*coming onstage*): I had trouble getting the firemen.

BOTARD (*as if concluding an interior monologue*): A fine state of affairs!

DAISY: ...I had trouble getting the firemen!

PAPILLON: Are there fires all over the place, then?

BÉRENGER: I agree with Mr Botard. Mrs Boeuf's attitude is very moving; she's a woman of feeling.

PAPILLON: It means I'm an employee down; he has to be replaced.

BÉRENGER: Do you really think he's no use to us any more?

DAISY: No, there aren't any fires – the firemen have been called out for other rhinoceroses.

BÉRENGER: For other rhinoceroses?

DAISY: Yes, other rhinoceroses. They've been reported all over the town. This morning there were seven, now there are seventeen.

BOTARD: What did I tell you?

DAISY: As many as thirty-two have been reported. They're not official yet, but they're bound to be confirmed soon.

BOTARD (*less certain*): Pff!! They always exaggerate.

PAPILLON: Are they coming to get us out of here?

BÉRENGER: I'm hungry!...

DAISY: Yes, they're coming; the firemen are on the way.

PAPILLON: What about work?

DUDARD: It looks as if it's out of our hands.

PAPILLON: We'll have to make up the lost time.

DUDARD: Well, Mr Botard, do you still deny all rhinocerotic evidence?

BOTARD: Our union is against your dismissing Mr Boeuf without notice.

PAPILLON: It's not up to me; we shall see what conclusions they reach at the inquiry.

BOTARD (*to* DUDARD): No, Mr Dudard, I do not deny the rhinocerotic evidence. I never have.

DUDARD: That's not true.

DAISY: Oh no, that's not true.

BOTARD: I repeat: I have never denied it. I just wanted to find out exactly where it was all leading. Because I know my own mind. I'm not content to simply state that a phenomenon exists. I make it my business to understand and explain it. At least, I could explain it if—

DUDARD: Then explain it to us.

DAISY: Yes, explain it, Mr Botard.

PAPILLON: Explain it when your colleagues ask you.

BOTARD: I will explain it...

DUDARD: We're all listening.

DAISY: I'm most curious.

BOTARD: I will explain it... one day...

DUDARD: Why not now?

BOTARD (*menacingly, to* MR PAPILLON): We'll go into the explanation later, in private. (*To everyone:*) I know the whys and the wherefores of this whole business...

DAISY: What whys?

BÉRENGER: What wherefores?

DUDARD: I'd give a lot to know these whys and wherefores...

BOTARD (*continuing; with a terrible air*): And I also know the names of those responsible. The names of the traitors. You can't fool me. I'll let you know the purpose and the meaning of this whole plot! I'll unmask the perpetrators!

BÉRENGER: But who'd want to...

DUDARD (*to* BOTARD): You're evading the question, Mr Botard.

PAPILLON: Let's have no evasions.

BOTARD: Evading? What, me?

DAISY: Just now you accused us of suffering from hallucinations.

BOTARD: Just now, yes. Now the hallucination has become a provocation.

DUDARD: And how do you consider this change came about?

BOTARD: It's an open secret, gentlemen. Even the man in the street knows about it. Only hypocrites pretend not to understand.

(*The noise and hooting of a fire engine is heard. The brakes are abruptly applied just under the window.*)

DAISY: That's the firemen!

BOTARD: There're going to be some big changes made; they won't get away with it as easily as that.

DUDARD: That doesn't mean anything, Mr Botard. The rhinoceroses exist, and that's that. That's all there is to it.

DAISY (*at the window, looking down*): Up here, firemen! (*A bustling is heard below, commotion, engine noises.*)

VOICE OF FIREMAN: Put up the ladder!

BOTARD (*to* DUDARD): I hold the key to all these happenings, an infallible system of interpretation.

PAPILLON: I want you all back in the office this afternoon.

(*The firemen's ladder is placed against the window.*)

BOTARD: Too bad about the office, Mr Papillon.

PAPILLON: I don't know what the management will say!

DUDARD: These are exceptional circumstances.

BOTARD (*pointing to the window*): They can't force us to come back this way. We'll have to wait till the staircase is repaired.

DUDARD: If anyone breaks a leg, it'll be the management's responsibility.

PAPILLON: That's true.

(*A fireman's helmet is seen, followed by the fireman.*)

BÉRENGER (*to* DAISY, *pointing to the window*): After you, Miss Daisy.

FIREMAN: Come on, Miss.

(*The fireman takes* DAISY *in his arms; she steps astride the window and disappears with him.*)

DUDARD: Goodbye, Miss Daisy. See you soon.

DAISY (*disappearing*): See you soon, goodbye!

PAPILLON (*at the window*): Telephone me tomorrow morning, Miss Daisy. You can come and type the letters at my house. (*To* BÉRENGER:) Mr Bérenger, I draw your attention to the fact that we are not on holiday, and that work will resume as soon as possible. (*To the other two:*) You hear what I say, gentlemen?

DUDARD: Of course, Mr Papillon.

BOTARD: They'll go on exploiting us till we drop, of course.

FIREMAN (*reappearing at the window*): Who's next?

PAPILLON (*to all three of them*): Go on!

DUDARD: After you, Mr Papillon.

BÉRENGER: After you, Chief.

BOTARD: You first, of course.

PAPILLON (*to* BÉRENGER): Bring me Miss Daisy's letters. There, on the table.

(BÉRENGER *goes and gets the letters, brings them to* PAPILLON.)

FIREMAN: Come on, hurry up. We've not got all day. We've got other calls to make.

BOTARD: What did I tell you?

(PAPILLON, *the letters under his arm, steps astride the window.*)

PAPILLON (*to the* FIREMAN): Careful of the documents! (*Turning to the others:*) Goodbye, gentlemen.

DUDARD: Goodbye, Mr Papillon.

BÉRENGER: Goodbye, Mr Papillon.

PAPILLON (*he has disappeared; one hears him say*): Careful of my papers. Dudard! Lock up the offices!

DUDARD (*shouting*): Don't you worry, Mr Papillon. (*To* BOTARD:) After you, Mr Botard.

BOTARD: I am about to descend, gentlemen. And I am going to take this matter up immediately with the proper authorities. I'll get to the bottom of this so-called mystery. (*He moves to the window.*)

DUDARD (*to* BOTARD): I thought it was all perfectly clear to you!

BOTARD (*astride the window*): Your irony doesn't affect me. What I'm after are the proofs and the documents – yes, proof positive of your treason.

DUDARD: That's absurd…

BOTARD: Your insults—

DUDARD (*interrupting him*): It's you who are insulting me…

BOTARD (*disappearing*): I don't insult. I merely prove.

VOICE OF FIREMAN: Come on, there!

DUDARD (*to* BÉRENGER): What are you doing this afternoon? Shall we meet for a drink?

BÉRENGER: Sorry, I can't. I'm taking advantage of this afternoon off to go and see my friend Jean. I do want to make up with him, after all. We got carried away. It was all my fault.

(*The* FIREMAN*'s head reappears at the window.*)

FIREMAN: Come along, there!

BÉRENGER (*pointing to the window*): After you.

DUDARD: After you.

BÉRENGER: Oh no, after you,

DUDARD: No, I insist, after you.

BÉRENGER: No, please, after you, after you.

FIREMAN: Hurry up!

DUDARD: After you, after you.

BÉRENGER: No, after you, after you.

(*They climb through the window together. The* FIREMAN *helps them down, as the curtain falls.*)

CURTAIN

Act Two

SCENE TWO

JEAN's house. The layout is roughly the same as Act II, Scene One. That is to say, the stage is divided into two. To the right, occupying three-quarters or four-fifths of the stage, according to size, is JEAN's bedroom. Upstage, a chair or an armchair, on which BÉRENGER will sit. Right centre, a door leading to JEAN's bathroom. When JEAN goes in to wash, the noise of a tap is heard, and that of the shower. To the left of the room, a partition divides the stage in two. Centre stage, the door leading to the stairs. If a less realistic, more stylized decor is preferred, the door may be placed without a partition. To the left is the staircase; the top steps are visible, leading to JEAN's flat, the banister and the landing. At the back, on the landing level, is the door to the neighbour's flat. Lower down, at the back, there is a glass door, over which is written: CONCIERGE.

When the curtain rises, JEAN is in bed, lying under the blanket, his back to the audience. One hears him cough. After a few moments BÉRENGER is seen, climbing the top steps of the staircase. He knocks at the door; JEAN does not answer. BÉRENGER knocks again.

BÉRENGER: Jean! (*He knocks again.*) Jean!

(*The door at the end of the landing opens slightly, and a little old man with a white goatee appears.*)

OLD MAN: What is it?
BÉRENGER: I want to see Jean. I am a friend of his.

OLD MAN: I thought it was me you wanted. My name's Jean as well, but it's the other one you want.

VOICE OF OLD MAN'S WIFE (*from within the room*): Is it for us?

OLD MAN (*turning to his wife who is not seen*): No, for the other one.

BÉRENGER (*knocking*): Jean!

OLD MAN: I didn't see him go out. But I saw him last night. He looked in a bad temper.

BÉRENGER: Yes, I know why; it was my fault.

OLD MAN: Perhaps he doesn't feel like opening the door to you. Try again.

VOICE OF OLD MAN'S WIFE: Jean, don't stand gossiping, Jean!

BÉRENGER (*knocking*): Jean!

OLD MAN (*to his wife*): Just a moment. Oh dear, dear... (*He closes the door and disappears.*)

JEAN (*still lying down, his back to the audience, in a hoarse voice*): What is it?

BÉRENGER: I've dropped by to see you, Jean.

JEAN: Who is it?

BÉRENGER: It's me, Bérenger. I hope I'm not disturbing you.

JEAN: Oh it's you, is it? Come in!

BÉRENGER (*trying to open the door*): The door's locked.

JEAN: Just a moment. Oh dear, dear... (JEAN *gets up in a pretty bad temper. He is wearing green pyjamas, his hair is tousled.*) Just a moment. (*He unlocks the door.*) Just a moment. (*He goes back to bed, gets under the blanket.*) Come in!

BÉRENGER (*coming in*): Hello Jean!

JEAN (*in bed*): What time is it? Aren't you at the office?

BÉRENGER: You're still in bed; you're not at the office, then? Sorry if I'm disturbing you.

JEAN (*still with his back turned*): Funny, I didn't recognize your voice.

BÉRENGER: I didn't recognize yours either.

JEAN (*still with his back turned*): Sit down!

BÉRENGER: Aren't you feeling well? (JEAN *replies with a grunt.*) You know, Jean, it was stupid of me to get so upset yesterday over a thing like that.

JEAN: A thing like what?

BÉRENGER: Yesterday...

JEAN: When yesterday? Where yesterday?

BÉRENGER: Don't you remember? It was about that wretched rhinoceros.

JEAN: What rhinoceros?

BÉRENGER: The rhinoceros; or rather, the two wretched rhinoceroses we saw.

JEAN: Oh yes, I remember... How do you know they were wretched?

BÉRENGER: Oh, I just said that.

JEAN: Oh. Well let's not talk any more about it.

BÉRENGER: That's very nice of you.

JEAN: Then that's that.

BÉRENGER: But I would like to say how sorry I am for being so insistent... and so obstinate... and getting so angry... in fact... I acted stupidly.

JEAN: That's not surprising with you.

BÉRENGER: I'm very sorry.

JEAN: I don't feel very well. (*He coughs.*)

BÉRENGER: That's probably why you're in bed. (*With a change of tone:*) You know, Jean, as it turned out, we were both right.

JEAN: What about?

BÉRENGER: About... well, you know, the same thing. Sorry to bring it up again, but I'll only mention it briefly. I just wanted you to know that in our different ways we were both right. It's been proved now. There are some rhinoceroses in the town with two horns and some with one.

JEAN: That's what I told you! Well, that's just too bad.

BÉRENGER: Yes, too bad.

JEAN: Or maybe it's all to the good; it depends.

BÉRENGER (*continuing*): In the final analysis it doesn't much matter which comes from where. The important thing, as I see it, is the fact that they're there at all, because—

JEAN (*turning and sitting on his unmade bed, facing* BÉRENGER): I don't feel well – I don't feel well at all!

BÉRENGER: Oh I am sorry! What do you think it is?

JEAN: I don't know exactly, there's something wrong somewhere...

BÉRENGER: Do you feel weak?

JEAN: Not at all. On the contrary – I feel full of beans.

BÉRENGER: I meant just a passing weakness. It happens to everybody.

JEAN: It never happens to me.

BÉRENGER: Perhaps you're too healthy, then. Too much energy can be a bad thing. It unsettles the nervous system.

JEAN: My nervous system is in perfect order. (*His voice has become more and more hoarse.*) I'm sound in mind and limb. I come from a long line of—

BÉRENGER: I know you do. Perhaps you've just caught a chill. Have you got a temperature?

JEAN: I don't know. Yes, probably I have a touch of fever. My head aches.

BÉRENGER: Just a slight migraine. Would you like me to leave you alone?

JEAN: No, stay. You don't worry me.

BÉRENGER: Your voice is hoarse, too.

JEAN: Hoarse?

BÉRENGER: A bit hoarse, yes. That's why I didn't recognize it.

JEAN: Why should I be hoarse? My voice hasn't changed; it's yours that's changed!

BÉRENGER: Mine?

JEAN: Why not?

BÉRENGER: It's possible. I hadn't noticed. I sometimes wonder if you're capable of noticing anything. (*Putting his hand to his forehead.*) Actually, it's my forehead that hurts. I must have given it a knock. (*His voice is even hoarser.*)

BÉRENGER: When did you do that?

JEAN: I don't know. I don't remember it happening.

BÉRENGER: But it must have hurt you.

JEAN: I must have done it while I was asleep.

BÉRENGER: The shock would have wakened you up. You must have just dreamt you knocked yourself.

JEAN: I never dream…

BÉRENGER (*continuing*): Your headache must have come on while you were asleep. You've forgotten you dreamt, or rather, you only remember subconsciously.

JEAN: Subconsciously, me? I'm master of my own thoughts – my mind doesn't wander. I think straight – I always think straight.

BÉRENGER: I know that. I haven't made myself clear.

JEAN: Then make yourself clearer. And you needn't bother to make any of your unpleasant observations to me.

BÉRENGER: One often has the impression that one has knocked oneself when one has a headache. (*Coming closer to* JEAN:) If you'd really knocked yourself, you'd have a bump. (*Looking at* JEAN:) Oh, you've got one – you do have a bump, in fact.

JEAN: A bump?

BÉRENGER: Just a tiny one…

JEAN: Where?

BÉRENGER (*pointing to* JEAN's *forehead*): There – it starts just above your nose.

JEAN: I've no bump. We've never had bumps in my family.

BÉRENGER: Have you got a mirror?

JEAN: That's the limit! (*Touching his forehead.*) I can feel something. I'm going to have a look, in the bathroom. (*He gets up abruptly and goes to the bathroom.* BÉRENGER *watches him as he goes. Then, from the bathroom:*) It's true, I have got a bump. (*He comes back; his skin has become greener.*) So you see, I did knock myself.

BÉRENGER: You don't look well – your skin is quite green.

JEAN: You seem to delight in saying disagreeable things to me. Have you taken a look at yourself lately?

BÉRENGER: Forgive me. I didn't mean to upset you.

JEAN (*very hoarse*): That's hard to believe.

BÉRENGER: Your breathing's very heavy. Does your throat hurt? (JEAN *goes and sits on his bed again.*) If your throat hurts, perhaps it's a touch of quinsy.

JEAN: Why should I have a touch of quinsy?

BÉRENGER: It's nothing to be ashamed of – I sometimes get it. Let me feel your pulse. (*He rises and takes* JEAN's *pulse.*)

JEAN (*in an even hoarser voice*): Oh, it'll pass.

BÉRENGER: Your pulse is normal. You needn't be alarmed.

JEAN: I'm not alarmed in the slightest – why should I be?

BÉRENGER: You're right. A few days' rest will put you right.

JEAN: I've no time to rest. I must go and buy some food.

BÉRENGER: There's not much the matter with you, if you're hungry. But even so, you ought to take a few days rest. It's wise to take care. Has the Doctor been to see you?

JEAN: I don't need a doctor.

BÉRENGER: Oh, but you ought to get the Doctor.

JEAN: You're not going to get the Doctor because I don't want the Doctor. I can look after myself.

BÉRENGER: You shouldn't reject medical advice.

JEAN: Doctors invent illnesses that don't exist.

BÉRENGER: They do it in good faith – just for the pleasure of looking after people.

JEAN: They invent illnesses – they invent them, I tell you.

BÉRENGER: Perhaps they do – but after they invent them, they cure them.

JEAN: I only have confidence in veterinary surgeons. There!

BÉRENGER (*who has released* JEAN's *wrist, now takes it up again*): Your veins look swollen. They're jutting out.

JEAN: It's a sign of virility.

BÉRENGER: Of course, it's a sign of health and strength. But... (*He examines* JEAN's *forearm more closely, until* JEAN *violently withdraws it.*)

JEAN: What do you think you're doing – scrutinizing me as if I was some strange animal?

BÉRENGER: It's your skin...

JEAN: What's my skin got to do with you? I don't go on about your skin, do I?

BÉRENGER: It's just that… it seems to be changing colour all the time. It's going green. (*He tries to take* JEAN's *hand.*) It's hardening as well.

JEAN (*withdrawing his hand again*): Stop mauling me about! What's the matter with you? You're getting on my nerves.

BÉRENGER (*to himself*): Perhaps it's more serious than I thought. (*To* JEAN:) We must get the Doctor. (*He goes to the telephone.*)

JEAN: Leave that thing alone. (*He darts over to* BÉRENGER *and pushes him.* BÉRENGER *staggers.*) You mind your own business.

BÉRENGER: All right. It was for your own good.

JEAN (*coughing and breathing noisily*): I know better than you what's good for me.

BÉRENGER: You're breathing very hard.

JEAN: One breathes as best one can. You don't like the way I breathe, and I don't like the way you breathe. Your breathing's too feeble – you can't even hear it; it's as if you were going to drop dead any moment.

BÉRENGER: I know I'm not as strong as you.

JEAN: I don't keep trying to get you to the Doctor, do I? Leave people to do as they please.

BÉRENGER: Don't get angry with me. You know very well I'm your friend.

JEAN: There's no such thing as friendship. I don't believe in your friendship.

BÉRENGER: That's a very hurtful thing to say.

JEAN: There's nothing for you to be hurt about.

BÉRENGER: My dear Jean—

JEAN: I'm not your dear Jean.

BÉRENGER: You're certainly in a very misanthropic mood today.

JEAN: Yes, I am misanthropic – very misanthropic indeed. I like being misanthropic.

BÉRENGER: You're probably still angry with me over our silly quarrel yesterday. I admit it was my fault. That's why I came to say I was sorry…

JEAN: What quarrel are you talking about?

BÉRENGER: I told you just now. You know, about the rhinoceros.

JEAN (*not listening to* BÉRENGER): It's not that I hate people. I'm just indifferent to them – or rather, they disgust me; and they'd better keep out of my way, or I'll run them down.

BÉRENGER: You know very well that I shall never stand in your way.

JEAN: I've got one aim in life. And I'm making straight for it.

BÉRENGER: I'm sure you're right. But I feel you're passing through a moral crisis. (JEAN *has been pacing the room like a wild beast in a cage, from one wall to the other.* BÉRENGER *watches him, occasionally stepping aside to avoid him.* JEAN's *voice has become more and more hoarse.*) You mustn't excite yourself – it's bad for you.

JEAN: I felt uncomfortable in my clothes; now my pyjamas irritate me as well. (*He undoes his pyjama jacket and does it up again.*)

BÉRENGER: But whatever's the matter with your skin?

JEAN: Can't you leave my skin alone? I certainly wouldn't want to change it for yours.

BÉRENGER: It's gone like leather.

JEAN: That makes it more solid. It's weatherproof.

BÉRENGER: You're getting greener and greener.

JEAN: You've got colour mania today. You're seeing things – you've been drinking again.

BÉRENGER: I did yesterday, but not today.

JEAN: It's the result of all your past debauchery.

BÉRENGER: I promised you I'd turn over a new leaf. I take notice when friends like you give me advice. And I never feel humiliated – on the contrary!

JEAN: I don't care what you feel. Brrr...

BÉRENGER: What did you say?

JEAN: I didn't say anything. I just went Brrrr... because I felt like it.

BÉRENGER (*looking fixedly at* JEAN): Do you know what happened to Boeuf? He turned into a rhinoceros.

JEAN: What happened to Boeuf?

BÉRENGER: He turned into a rhinoceros.

JEAN (*fanning himself with the flaps of his jacket*): Brrr...

BÉRENGER: Come on now – stop joking.

JEAN: I can puff if I want to, can't I? I've every right... I'm in my own house.

BÉRENGER: I didn't say you couldn't.

JEAN: And I shouldn't, if I were you. I feel hot, I feel hot. Brrr... Just a moment. I must cool myself down.

BÉRENGER (*whilst* JEAN *darts to the bathroom*): He must have a fever. (JEAN *is in the bathroom; one hears him puffing, and also the sound of a running tap.*)

JEAN (*off*): Brrr...

BÉRENGER: He's got the shivers. I'm jolly well going to phone the Doctor. (*He goes to the telephone again, then comes back quickly when he hears* JEAN's *voice.*)

JEAN (*off*): So old Boeuf turned into a rhinoceros, did he? Ah, ah, ah!... He was just having you on, he'd disguised himself. (*He pokes his head round the bathroom door. He is very green. The bump over his nose is slightly larger.*) He was just disguised.

BÉRENGER (*walking about the room, without seeing* JEAN): He looked very serious about it, I assure you.

JEAN: Oh well, that's his business.

BÉRENGER (*turning to* JEAN, *who disappears again into the bathroom*): I'm sure he didn't do it on purpose. He didn't want to change.

JEAN (*off*): How do you know?

BÉRENGER: Well, everything led one to suppose so.

JEAN: And what if he did do it on purpose? Eh? What if he did it on purpose?

BÉRENGER: I'd be very surprised. At any rate, Mrs Boeuf didn't seem to know about it...

JEAN (*in a very hoarse voice*): Ah, ah, ah! Fat old Mrs Boeuf. She's just a fool!

BÉRENGER: Well fool or no fool...

JEAN (*he enters swiftly, takes off his jacket, and throws it on the bed.* BÉRENGER *discreetly averts his gaze.* JEAN, *whose back and chest are now green, goes back into the bathroom. As he walks in and out*): Boeuf never let his wife know what he was up to...

BÉRENGER: You're wrong there, Jean – it was a very united family.

JEAN: Very united, was it? Are you sure? Hum, hum, Brr...

BÉRENGER (*moving to the bathroom, where* JEAN *slams the door in his face*): Very united. And the proof is that—

JEAN (*from within*): Boeuf led his own private life. He had a secret side to him, deep down, which he kept to himself.

BÉRENGER: I shouldn't make you talk – it seems to upset you.

JEAN: On the contrary – it relaxes me.

BÉRENGER: Even so, let me call the Doctor, I beg you.

JEAN: I absolutely forbid it. I can't stand obstinate people.

(JEAN *comes back into the bedroom.* BÉRENGER *backs away, a little scared, for* JEAN *is greener than ever and speaks only with difficulty. His voice is unrecognizable.*)

Well, whether he changes into a rhinoceros on purpose or against his will, he's probably all the better for it.

BÉRENGER: How can you say a thing like that? Surely you don't think—

JEAN: You always see the black side of everything. It obviously gave him great pleasure to turn into a rhinoceros. There's nothing extraordinary in that.

BÉRENGER: There's nothing extraordinary in it, but I doubt if it gave him much pleasure.

JEAN: And why not, pray?

BÉRENGER: It's hard to say exactly why; it's just something you feel.

JEAN: I tell you, it's not as bad as all that. After all, rhinoceroses are living creatures the same as us; they've got as much right to life as we have!

BÉRENGER: As long as they don't destroy ours in the process. You must admit the difference in mentality.

JEAN (*pacing up and down the room, and in and out of the bathroom*): Are you under the impression that our way of life is superior?

BÉRENGER: Well, at any rate, we have our own moral standards, which I consider incompatible with the standards of these animals.

JEAN: Moral standards! I'm sick of moral standards! We need to go beyond moral standards!

BÉRENGER: What would you put in their place?

JEAN (*still pacing*): Nature!

BÉRENGER: Nature?

JEAN: Nature has its own laws. Morality's against Nature.

BÉRENGER: Are you suggesting we replace our moral laws with the law of the jungle?

JEAN: It would suit me – suit me fine.

BÉRENGER: You say that. But deep down, no one...

JEAN (*interrupting him, pacing up and down*): We've got to build our life on new foundations. We must get back to primeval integrity.

BÉRENGER: I don't agree with you at all.

JEAN (*breathing noisily*): I can't breathe.

BÉRENGER: Just think a moment. You must admit that we have a philosophy that animals don't share, and an irreplaceable set of values, which it's taken centuries of human civilization to build up...

JEAN (*in the bathroom*): When we've demolished all that, we'll be better off!

BÉRENGER: I know you don't mean that seriously. You're joking! It's just a poetic fancy.

JEAN: Brrr. (*He almost trumpets.*)

BÉRENGER: I'd never realized you were a *poet*.

JEAN (*comes out of the bathroom*): Brrr. (*He trumpets again.*)

BÉRENGER: That's not what you believe fundamentally – I know you too well. You know as well as I do that mankind—

JEAN (*interrupting him*): Don't talk to me about mankind!

BÉRENGER: I mean the human individual, humanism—

JEAN: Humanism is all washed up! You're a ridiculous old sentimentalist. (*He goes into the bathroom.*)

BÉRENGER: But you must admit that the mind—

JEAN (*from the bathroom*): Just clichés! You're talking rubbish!

BÉRENGER: Rubbish!

JEAN (*from the bathroom in a very hoarse voice, difficult to understand*): Utter rubbish!

BÉRENGER: I'm amazed to hear you say that, Jean, really! You must be out of your mind. You wouldn't like to be a rhinoceros yourself, now, would you?

JEAN: Why not? I'm not a victim of prejudice like you.

BÉRENGER: Can you speak more clearly? I didn't catch what you said. You swallowed the words.

JEAN (*still in the bathroom*): Then keep your ears open.

BÉRENGER: What?

JEAN: Keep your ears open! I said what's wrong with being a rhinoceros? I'm all for change.

BÉRENGER: It's not like you to say a thing like that... (BÉRENGER *stops short, for* JEAN*'s appearance is truly alarming.* JEAN *has become, in fact, completely green. The bump on his forehead is practically a rhinoceros horn.*) Oh! You really must be out of your mind!

(JEAN *dashes to his bed, throws the covers on the floor, talking in a fast and furious gabble, and making very weird sounds.*)

You mustn't get into such a state – calm down! I hardly recognize you any more.

JEAN (*hardly distinguishable*): Hot... far too hot! Demolish the lot – clothes itch, they itch! (*He drops his pyjama trousers.*)

BÉRENGER: What are you doing? You're not yourself! You're generally so modest!

JEAN: The swamps! The swamps!

BÉRENGER: Look at me! Can't you see me any longer? Can't you hear me?

JEAN: I can hear you perfectly well! I can see you perfectly well!

(*He lunges towards* BÉRENGER, *head down,* BÉRENGER *gets out of the way.*)

BÉRENGER: Watch out!

JEAN (*puffing noisily*): Sorry! (*He darts at great speed into the bathroom.*)

BÉRENGER (*makes as if to escape by the door left, then comes back and goes into the bathroom after* JEAN, *saying*): I really can't leave him like that – after all, he is a friend. (*From the bathroom:*) I'm going to get the Doctor! It's absolutely necessary, believe me!

JEAN (*from the bathroom*): No!

BÉRENGER (*from the bathroom*): Calm down, Jean, you're being ridiculous! Oh, your horn's getting longer and longer – you're a rhinoceros!

JEAN (*from the bathroom*): I'll trample you – I'll trample you down!

(*A lot of noise comes from the bathroom – trumpeting, objects falling, the sound of a shattered mirror – then* BÉRENGER *reappears, very frightened; he closes the bathroom door with difficulty against the resistance that is being made from inside.*)

BÉRENGER (*pushing against the door*): He's a rhinoceros, he's a rhinoceros!

(BÉRENGER *manages to close the door. As he does so, his coat is pierced by a rhinoceros horn. The door shakes under the animal's constant pressure and the din continues in the bathroom; trumpeting is heard, interspersed with indistinct phrases such as: "I'm furious! The swine!", etc.* BÉRENGER *rushes to the door right.*)

I never would have thought it of him – never!

(*He opens the staircase door and goes and knocks at the landing door; he bangs repeatedly on it with his fist.*)

There's a rhinoceros in the building! Get the police!

OLD MAN (*poking his head out*): What's the matter?

BÉRENGER: Get the police! There's a rhinoceros in the house!

VOICE OF OLD MAN'S WIFE: What are you up to, Jean? Why are you making all that noise?

OLD MAN (*to his wife*): I don't know what he's talking about. He's seen a rhinoceros.

BÉRENGER: Yes, here in the house. Get the police!

OLD MAN: What do you think you're up to, disturbing people like that? What a way to behave! (*He shuts the door in his face.*)

BÉRENGER (*rushing to the stairs*): Porter, porter, there's a rhinoceros in the house! Get the police! Porter!

(*The upper part of the porter's lodge is seen to open; the head of a rhinoceros appears.*)

Another!

(BÉRENGER *rushes upstairs again. He wants to go back into* JEAN's *room, hesitates, then makes for the door of the* OLD MAN *again. At this moment the door of the room opens to reveal two rhinoceros heads.*)

Oh, my God!

(BÉRENGER *goes back into* JEAN's *room, where the bathroom door is still shaking. He goes to the window, which is represented simply by the frame, facing the audience. He is exhausted, almost fainting; he murmurs.*)

My God! Oh my God!

(*He makes a gigantic effort, and manages to get astride the window (that is, towards the audience) but gets back again quickly, for at the same time, crossing the orchestra pit at great speed, move a large number of rhinoceros heads in line.* BÉRENGER *gets back with all speed, looks out of the window for a moment.*)

There's a whole herd of them in the street now! An army of rhinoceroses, surging up the avenue!... (*He looks all around.*) Where can I get out? Where can I get out? If only they'd keep to the middle of the road! They're all over the pavement as well. Where can I get out? Where can I get out?

(*Distracted, he goes from door to door and to the window, whilst the bathroom door continues to shake and* JEAN *continues to trumpet and hurl incomprehensible insults. This continues for some moments; whenever* BÉRENGER, *in his disordered attempts to escape, reaches the door of the Old People's flat or the stairway, he is greeted by rhinoceros heads, which trumpet and cause him to beat a hasty retreat. He goes to the window for the last time and looks out.*)

A whole herd of them! And they always said the rhinoceros was a solitary animal! That's not true – that's a conception they'll have to revise! They've smashed up all the public benches. (*He wrings his hands.*) What's to be done?

(*He goes once more to the various exits, but the spectacle of the rhinoceros halts him. When he gets back to the bathroom door it seems about to give way.* BÉRENGER *throws himself against the back wall, which yields; the street is visible in the background; he flees, shouting:*)

Rhinoceros! Rhinoceros!

(*Noises. The bathroom door is on the point of yielding.*)

CURTAIN

Act Three

The arrangement is roughly the same as in the previous scene.

It is BÉRENGER's *room, which bears a striking resemblance to that of* JEAN's. *Only certain details, one or two extra pieces of furniture, reveal that it is a different room. Staircase to the left, and landing. Door at the end of the landing. There is no porter's lodge. Upstage is a divan.*

An armchair, and a little table with a telephone. Perhaps an extra telephone, and a chair. Window upstage, open. A window frame in the foreground.

BÉRENGER *is lying on his divan, his back to the audience.* BÉRENGER *is lying fully dressed. His head is bandaged. He seems to be having a bad dream, and writhes in his sleep.*

BÉRENGER: No! (*Pause.*) Watch out for the horns! (*Pause.*)

(*The noise of a considerable number of rhinoceroses is heard passing under the upstage window.*)

No! (*He falls to the floor, still fighting with what he has seen in his dream, and wakes up. He puts his hand to his head with an apprehensive air, then moves to the mirror and lifts his bandage, as the noises fade away. He heaves a sigh of relief when he sees he has no bump. He hesitates, goes to the divan, lies down, and instantly gets up again. He goes to the table, where he takes up a bottle of brandy and a glass, and is about to pour himself a drink. Then, after a short internal struggle, he replaces the bottle and glass.*) Now, now, where's your will-power! (*He wants to go back to his divan, but the rhinoceroses are heard again under the upstage window. The noises stop; he goes to the little table, hesitates a moment, then, with a gesture of "Oh what's it matter!", he pours himself a glass of brandy, which he downs at one go. He puts the bottle and glass back in place. He coughs. His cough seems to worry him; he coughs again and listens hard to the sound. He looks at himself again in the mirror, coughing, then opens the window; the panting of the animals becomes louder; he coughs again.*) No, it's not the same! (*He calms down, shuts the window, feels his bandaged forehead, goes to his divan and seems to fall asleep.*)

(DUDARD *is seen mounting the top stairs; he gets to the landing and knocks on* BÉRENGER'*s door.*)

BÉRENGER (*starting up*): What is it?

DUDARD: I've dropped by to see you, Bérenger.

BÉRENGER: Who is it?

DUDARD: It's me.

BÉRENGER: Who's me?

DUDARD: Me, Dudard.

BÉRENGER: Ah, it's you, come in!

DUDARD: I hope I'm not disturbing you. (*He tries to open the door.*) The door's locked.

BÉRENGER: Just a moment. Oh dear, dear! (*He opens the door. DUDARD enters.*)

DUDARD: Hello Bérenger.

BÉRENGER: Hello Dudard, what time is it?

DUDARD: So, you're still barricaded in your room! Feeling any better, old man?

BÉRENGER: Forgive me – I didn't recognize your voice. (*Goes to open the window.*) Yes, yes, I think I'm a bit better.

DUDARD: My voice hasn't changed. I recognized yours easily enough.

BÉRENGER: I'm sorry, I thought that... you're right, your voice is quite normal. Mine hasn't changed either, has it?

DUDARD: Why should it have changed?

BÉRENGER: I'm not a bit... a bit hoarse, am I?

DUDARD: Not that I notice.

BÉRENGER: That's good. That's very reassuring.

DUDARD: Why, what's the matter with you?

BÉRENGER: I don't know – does one ever know? Voices can suddenly change – they do change, alas!

DUDARD: Have you caught cold as well?

BÉRENGER: I hope not... I sincerely hope not. But do sit down, Dudard, take a seat. Sit in the armchair.

DUDARD (*sitting in the armchair*): Are you still feeling a bit off colour? Is your head still bad? (*He points to* BÉRENGER'*s bandage.*)

BÉRENGER: Oh yes, I've still got a headache. But there's no bump I haven't knocked myself... have I? (*He lifts the bandage, shows his forehead to* DUDARD.)

DUDARD: No – there's no bump as far as I can see.

BÉRENGER: I hope there never will be. Never.

DUDARD: If you don't knock yourself, why should there be?

BÉRENGER: If you really don't want to knock yourself, you don't.

DUDARD: Obviously. One just has to take care. But what's the matter with you? You're all nervous and agitated. It must be your migraine. You just stay quiet and you'll feel better.

BÉRENGER: Migraine! Don't talk to me about migraines! Don't talk about them!

DUDARD: It's understandable that you've got a migraine after all that emotion.

BÉRENGER: I can't seem to get over it!

DUDARD: Then it's not surprising you've got a headache.

BÉRENGER (*darting to the mirror, lifting the bandage*): Nothing there... You know, it can all start from something like that.

DUDARD: What can all start?

BÉRENGER: I'm frightened of becoming someone else.

DUDARD: Calm yourself, now, and sit down. Dashing up and down the room like that can only make you more nervous.

BÉRENGER: You're right, I must keep calm. (*He goes and sits down.*) I just can't get over it, you know.

DUDARD: About Jean, you mean? I know.

BÉRENGER: Yes, Jean, of course – and the others, too.

DUDARD: I realize it must have been a shock to you.

BÉRENGER: Well, that's not surprising, you must admit.

DUDARD: I suppose so, but you mustn't dramatize the situation; it's no reason for you to—

BÉRENGER: I wonder how you'd have felt. Jean was my best friend. Then to watch him change before my eyes, and the way he got so furious!

DUDARD: I know. You felt let down; I understand. Try and not think about it.

BÉRENGER: How can I help thinking about it? He was such a warm-hearted person, always so human! Who'd have thought it of him! We'd known each other for... for donkey's years. He was the last person I'd have expected to change like that. I felt more sure of him than of myself! And then to do that to me!

DUDARD: I'm sure he didn't do it specially to annoy you!

BÉRENGER: It seemed as if he did. If you'd seen the state he was in... the expression on his face...

DUDARD: It's just that you happened to be with him at the time. It would have been the same no matter who was there.

BÉRENGER: But after all our years together, he might have controlled himself in front of me.

DUDARD: You think everything revolves round you; you think that everything that happens concerns you personally; you're not the centre of the universe, you know.

BÉRENGER: Perhaps you're right. I must try to re-adjust myself, but the phenomenon in itself is so disturbing. To tell the truth, it absolutely shatters me. What can be the explanation?

DUDARD: For the moment I haven't found a satisfactory explanation. I observe the facts, and I take them in. They exist, so they must have an explanation. A freak of Nature, perhaps, some bizarre caprice, an extravagant joke, a game – who knows?

BÉRENGER: Jean was very proud, of course. I'm not ambitious at all. I'm content to be what I am.

DUDARD: Perhaps he felt an urge for some fresh air, the country, the wide-open spaces... perhaps he felt the need to relax. I'm not saying that's any excuse...

BÉRENGER: I understand what you mean – at least, I'm trying to. But you know, if someone accused me of being a bad sport, or hopelessly middle class, or completely out of touch with life, I'd still want to stay as I am.

DUDARD: We'll all stay as we are, don't worry. So why get upset over a few cases of rhinoceritis? Perhaps it's just another disease.

BÉRENGER: Exactly! And I'm frightened of catching it.

DUDARD: Oh stop thinking about it. Really, you attach too much importance to the whole business. Jean's case isn't symptomatic – he's not a typical case – you said yourself he was proud. In my opinion – if you'll excuse me saying this about your friend – he was far too excitable, a bit wild, an eccentric. You mustn't base your judgements on exceptions. It's the average case you must consider.

BÉRENGER: I'm beginning to see daylight. You see, you couldn't explain this phenomenon to me. And yet you just provided me with a plausible explanation. Yes, of course – he must have been in a critical condition to have got himself into that state. He must have been temporarily unbalanced. And yet he gave his reasons for it; he'd obviously given it a lot of thought, and weighed the pros and cons... And what about Boeuf, then – was he mad, too?... And what about all the others?...

DUDARD: There's still the epidemic theory. It's like influenza. It's not the first time there's been an epidemic.

BÉRENGER: There's never been one like this. And what if it's come from the colonies?

DUDARD: In any case, you can be sure that Boeuf and the others didn't do what they did – become what they became – just to annoy you. They wouldn't have gone to all that trouble.

BÉRENGER: That's true – that makes sense – it's a reassuring thought... or, on the other hand, perhaps that makes it worse?

(*Rhinoceroses are heard, galloping under the upstage window.*)

There, you hear that? (*He darts to the window.*)

DUDARD: Oh, why can't you leave them alone!

(BÉRENGER *closes the window again.*)

> They're not doing you any harm. Really, you're obsessed by them! It's not good for you. You're wearing yourself out. You've had one shock – why look for more? You just concentrate on getting back to normal.

BÉRENGER: I wonder if I'm immune.

DUDARD: In any case, it's not fatal. Certain illnesses are good for you. I'm convinced this is something you can recover from if you want to. They'll get over it – you'll see.

BÉRENGER: But it's bound to have certain after-effects! An organic upheaval like that can't help but leave—

DUDARD: It's only temporary, don't you worry.

BÉRENGER: Are you absolutely certain?

DUDARD: I think so, yes... I suppose so.

BÉRENGER: But if one really doesn't want to – really doesn't want to – catch this thing, which, after all, is a nervous disease, then you don't catch it – you simply don't catch it! Do you feel like a brandy? (*He goes to the table, where the bottle stands.*)

DUDARD: Not for me, thank you – I never touch it. But don't mind me if you want some – you go ahead, don't worry about me. But watch out it doesn't make your headache worse.

BÉRENGER: Alcohol is good for epidemics. It immunizes you. It kills influenza microbes, for instance.

DUDARD: Perhaps it doesn't kill all microbes. They don't know about rhinoceritis yet.

BÉRENGER: Jean never touched alcohol. He just pretended to. Maybe that's why he... perhaps that explains his attitude. (*He offers a full glass to* DUDARD:) You're sure you won't?

DUDARD: No, no, never before lunch, thank you.

(BÉRENGER *empties his glass, continues to hold it, together with the bottle, in his hands; he coughs.*)

> You see, you can't take it. It makes you cough.

BÉRENGER (*worried*): Yes, it did make me cough. How did I cough?

DUDARD: Like everyone coughs when they drink something a bit strong.

BÉRENGER (*moving to put the glass and bottle back on the table*): There wasn't anything odd about it, was there? It *was* a real human cough?

DUDARD: What are you getting at? It was an ordinary human cough. What other sort of cough could it have been?

BÉRENGER: I don't know... Perhaps an animal's cough... Do rhinoceroses cough?

DUDARD: Look, Bérenger, you're being ridiculous – you invent difficulties for yourself, you ask yourself the weirdest questions... I remember you said yourself that the best protection against the thing was will-power.

BÉRENGER: Yes, I did.

DUDARD: Well then, prove you've got some.

BÉRENGER: I have, I assure you—

DUDARD: Prove it to yourself – now, don't drink any more brandy. You'll feel more sure of yourself then.

BÉRENGER: You deliberately misunderstand me. I told you the only reason I drink it is because it keeps the worst at bay; I'm doing it quite deliberately. When the epidemic's over, then I shall stop drinking. I'd already decided that before the whole business began. I'm just putting it off for the time being!

DUDARD: You're inventing excuses for yourself.

BÉRENGER: Do you think I am?... In any case, that's got nothing to do with what's happening now.

DUDARD: How do we know?

BÉRENGER (*alarmed*): Do you really think so? You think that's how the rot sets in? I'm not an alcoholic. (*He goes to the mirror and examines himself.*) Do you think, by any chance... (*He touches his face, pats his bandaged forehead.*) Nothing's changed; it hasn't done any harm, so it must have done good... or it's harmless, at any rate.

DUDARD: I was only joking. I was just teasing you. You see the black side of everything – watch out, or you'll become a neurotic. When you've got over your shock completely and you can get out for a breath of fresh air, you'll feel better – you'll see! All these morbid ideas will vanish.

BÉRENGER: Go out? I suppose I'll have to. I'm dreading the moment. I'll be bound to meet some of them...

DUDARD: What if you do? You only have to keep out of their way. And there aren't as many as all that.

BÉRENGER: I see them all over the place. You'll probably say that's being morbid, too.

DUDARD: They don't attack you. If you leave them alone, they just ignore you. You can't say they're spiteful. They've even got a certain natural innocence, a sort of frankness. Besides, I walked right along the avenue to get to you today. I got here safe and sound, didn't I? No trouble at all.

BÉRENGER: Just the sight of them upsets me. It's a nervous thing. I don't get angry – no, it doesn't pay to get angry – you never know where it'll lead to – I watch out for that. But it does something to me here! (*He points to his heart.*) I get a tight feeling inside.

DUDARD: I think you're right, to a certain extent, to have some reaction. But you go too far. You've no sense of humour, that's your trouble, none at all. You must learn to be more detached, and try and see the funny side of things.

BÉRENGER: I feel responsible for everything that happens. I feel involved; I can't just be indifferent.

DUDARD: Judge not lest ye be judged.* If you start worrying about everything that happens you'll never be able to go on living.

BÉRENGER: If only it had happened somewhere else, in some other country, and we'd just read about it in the papers – one could discuss it quietly, examine the question from all points of view and come to an objective conclusion. We could organize debates with professors and writers and lawyers, and bluestockings and artists and people. And the ordinary man in the street, as well – it would be very interesting and instructive. But when you're involved yourself, when you suddenly find yourself up against the brutal facts, you can't help feeling directly concerned – the shock is too violent for you to stay cool and detached. I'm frankly surprised – I'm very, very surprised. I can't get over it.

DUDARD: Well, I'm surprised too. Or rather, I was. Now I'm starting to get used to it.

BÉRENGER: Your nervous system is better balanced than mine. You're lucky. But don't you agree, it's all very unfortunate…

DUDARD (*interrupting him*): I don't say it's a good thing. And don't get the idea that I'm on the rhinoceroses' side…

(*More sounds of rhinoceroses passing, this time under the downstage window frame.*)

BÉRENGER (*with a start*): There they are – there they are again! Oh, it's no use, I just can't get used to them. Maybe it's wrong of me, but they obsess me so much, in spite of myself, I just can't sleep at night. I get insomnia. I doze a bit in the daytime out of sheer exhaustion.

DUDARD: Take some sleeping tablets.

BÉRENGER: That's not the answer. If I sleep, it's worse. I dream about them, I get nightmares.

DUDARD: That's what comes of taking things too seriously. You get a kick out of torturing yourself – admit it!

BÉRENGER: I'm no masochist, I assure you.

DUDARD: Then face the facts and get over it. This is the situation, and there's nothing you can do about it.

BÉRENGER: That's fatalism.

DUDARD: It's common sense. When a thing like this happens, there's bound to be a reason for it. That's what we must find out.

BÉRENGER (*getting up*): Well, I don't want to accept the situation.

DUDARD: What else can you do? What are your plans?

BÉRENGER: I don't know for the moment. I must think it over. I shall write to the papers; I'll draw up manifestos; I shall apply for an audience with the Mayor – or his deputy, if the Mayor's too busy.

DUDARD: You leave the authorities to act as they think best! I'm not sure if morally you have the right to butt in. In any case, I still think it's not all that serious. I consider it silly to get worked up because a few people decide to change their skins. They just didn't feel happy in the ones they had. They're free to do as they like.

BÉRENGER: We must attack the evil at its root.

DUDARD: The evil! That's just a phrase! Who knows what is evil and what is good? It's just a question of personal preference. You're worried about your own skin – that's the truth of the matter. But you'll never become a rhinoceros – really, you won't... you haven't got the vocation!

BÉRENGER: There you are, you see! If our leaders and fellow citizens all think like you, they'll never take any action.

DUDARD: You wouldn't want to ask for help from abroad, surely? This is an internal affair – it only concerns our country.

BÉRENGER: I believe in international solidarity...

DUDARD: You're a Don Quixote.* Oh, I don't mean that nastily, don't be offended! I'm only saying it for your own good, because you really need to calm down.

BÉRENGER: You're right, I know – forgive me. I get too worked up. But I'll change, I will change. I'm sorry to keep you all this time listening to my ramblings. You must have work to do. Did you get my application for sick leave?

DUDARD: Don't worry about that. It's all in order. In any case, the office hasn't resumed work.

BÉRENGER: Haven't they repaired the staircase yet? What negligence! That's why everything goes so badly.

DUDARD: They're repairing it now. But it's slow work. It's not easy to find the workmen. They sign on and work for a couple of days, then don't turn up any more. You never see them again. Then you have to look for others.

BÉRENGER: And they talk about unemployment! I hope, at least, we're getting a stone staircase.

DUDARD: No, it's wood again, but new wood this time.

BÉRENGER: Oh! The way these organizations stick to the old routine. They chuck money down the drain, but when it's needed for something really useful they pretend they can't afford it. I bet Mr Papillon's none too pleased. He was dead set on having a stone staircase. What's he say about it?

DUDARD: We haven't got a Chief any more. Mr Papillon's resigned.

BÉRENGER: It's not possible!

DUDARD: It's true, I assure you.

BÉRENGER: Well, I'm amazed... Was it on account of the staircase?

DUDARD: I don't think so. Anyway, that wasn't the reason he gave.

BÉRENGER: Why was it then? What got into him?

DUDARD: He's retiring to the country.

BÉRENGER: Retiring? He's not the age. He might still have become the Director.

DUDARD: He's given it all up! Said he needed a rest.

BÉRENGER: I bet the management's pretty upset to see him go; they'll have to replace him. All your diplomas should come in useful – you stand a good chance.

DUDARD: I suppose I might as well tell you – it's really rather funny – the fact is, he turned into a rhinoceros.

(*Distant rhinoceros noises.*)

BÉRENGER: A rhinoceros! Mr Papillon, a rhinoceros! I can't believe it! I don't think it's funny at all! Why didn't you tell me before?

DUDARD: Well, you know you've no sense of humour. I didn't want to tell you... I didn't want to tell you because I knew very well you wouldn't see the funny side, and it would upset you. You know how impressionable you are!

BÉRENGER (*raising his arms to heaven*): Oh, that's awful... Mr Papillon! And he had such a good job.

DUDARD: That proves his metamorphosis was sincere.

BÉRENGER: He couldn't have done it on purpose. I'm certain it must have been involuntary.

DUDARD: How can we tell? It's hard to know the real reasons for people's decisions.

BÉRENGER: He must have made a mistake. He'd got some hidden complexes. He should have been psychoanalysed.

DUDARD: Even if it's a case of dissociation it's still very revealing. It was his way of sublimating himself.

BÉRENGER: He let himself be talked into it, I feel sure.

DUDARD: That could happen to anybody!

BÉRENGER (*alarmed*): To anybody? Oh no – not to you, it couldn't – could it? And not to me!

DUDARD: We must hope not.

BÉRENGER: Because we don't want to... that's so, isn't it? Tell me, that *is* so, isn't it?

DUDARD: Yes, yes, of course...

BÉRENGER (*a little calmer*): I still would have thought Mr Papillon would have had the strength to resist. I thought he had a bit more character! Particularly as I fail to see where his interest lay – what possible material or moral interest...

DUDARD: It was obviously a disinterested gesture on his part.

BÉRENGER: Obviously. There were extenuating circumstances... or were they aggravating? Aggravating, I should think, because if he did it from choice... You know, I feel sure that Botard must have taken a very poor view of it – what did he think of his Chief's behaviour?

DUDARD: Oh, poor old Botard was quite indignant – absolutely outraged. I've rarely seen anyone so incensed.

BÉRENGER: Well for once I'm on his side. He's a good man, after all. A man of sound common sense. And to think I misjudged him.

DUDARD: He misjudged you, too.

BÉRENGER: That proves how objective I'm being now. Besides, you had a pretty bad opinion of him yourself.

DUDARD: I wouldn't say I had a bad opinion. I admit I didn't often agree with him. I never liked his scepticism, the way he was always so incredulous and suspicious. Even in this instance I didn't approve of him entirely.

BÉRENGER: This time for the opposite reasons.

DUDARD: No, not exactly – my own reasoning and my judgement are a bit more complex than you seem to think. It was because there was nothing precise or objective about the way Botard argued. I don't approve of the rhinoceroses myself, as you know – not at all, don't go thinking that! But Botard's attitude was too passionate, as usual, and therefore over-simplified. His stand seems to me entirely dictated by hatred of his superiors. That's where he gets his inferiority complex and his resentment. What's more, he talks in clichés, and commonplace arguments leave me cold.

BÉRENGER: Well, forgive me, but this time I'm in complete agreement with Botard. He's somebody worthwhile.

DUDARD: I don't deny it, but that doesn't mean anything.

BÉRENGER: He's a very worthwhile person – and they're not easy to find these days. He's down-to-earth, with four feet planted firmly on the ground – I mean, both feet. I'm in complete agreement with him, and I'm proud of it. I shall congratulate him when I see him. I deplore Mr Papillon's action; it was his duty not to succumb.

DUDARD: How intolerant you are! Maybe Papillon felt the need for a bit of relaxation after all these years of office life.

BÉRENGER (*ironically*): And you're too tolerant – far too broad-minded!

DUDARD: My dear Bérenger, one must always make an effort to understand. And in order to understand a phenomenon and its effects you need to work back to the initial causes, by honest intellectual effort. We must try to do this because, after all, we are thinking beings. I haven't yet succeeded, as I told you, and I don't know if I shall succeed. But in any case, one has to start out favourably disposed – or at least, impartial; one has to keep an open mind – that's essential to a scientific mentality. Everything is logical. To understand is to justify.

BÉRENGER: You'll be siding with the rhinoceroses before long.

DUDARD: No, no, not at all. I wouldn't go that far. I'm simply trying to look the facts unemotionally in the face. I'm trying to be realistic. I also contend that there is no real evil in what occurs naturally. I don't believe in seeing evil in everything. I leave that to the inquisitors.

BÉRENGER: And you consider all this natural?

DUDARD: What could be more natural than a rhinoceros?

BÉRENGER: Yes, but for a man to turn into a rhinoceros is abnormal beyond question.

DUDARD: Well, of course, that's a matter of opinion...

BÉRENGER: It is beyond question – absolutely beyond question!

DUDARD: You seem very sure of yourself. Who can say where the normal stops and the abnormal begins? Can you personally define these conceptions of normality and abnormality? Nobody has solved this problem yet, either medically or philosophically. You ought to know that.

BÉRENGER: The problem may not be resolved philosophically, but in practice it's simple. They may prove there's no such thing as movement... and then you start walking... (*he starts walking up and down the room*) ...and you go on walking, and you say to yourself, like Galileo, "*E pur si muove*"—*

DUDARD: You're getting things all mixed up! Don't confuse the issue. In Galileo's case it was the opposite: theoretic and scientific thought proving itself superior to mass opinion and dogmatism.

BÉRENGER (*quite lost*): What does all that mean? Mass opinion, dogmatism – they're just words! I may be mixing everything up in my head, but you're losing yours. You don't know what's normal and what isn't any more. I couldn't care less about Galileo... I don't give a damn about Galileo.

DUDARD: You brought him up in the first place and raised the whole question, saying that practice always had the last word. Maybe it does, but only when it proceeds from theory! The history of thought and science proves that.

BÉRENGER (*more and more furious*): It doesn't prove anything of the sort! It's all gibberish, utter lunacy!

DUDARD: There again, we need to define exactly what we mean by lunacy...

BÉRENGER: Lunacy is lunacy, and that's all there is to it! Everybody knows what lunacy is. And what about the rhinoceroses – are they practice or are they theory?

DUDARD: Both!

BÉRENGER: How do you mean – both?

DUDARD: Both the one and the other, or one or the other. It's debatable!

BÉRENGER: Well, in that case... I refuse to think about it!

DUDARD: You're getting all het up. Our opinions may not exactly coincide, but we can still discuss the matter peaceably. These things should be discussed.

BÉRENGER (*distracted*): You think I'm getting all het up, do you? I might be Jean. Oh no, no, I don't want to become like him. I mustn't be like him. (*He calms down.*) I'm not very well up in philosophy. I've never studied; you've got all sorts of diplomas. That's why you're so at ease in discussion, whereas I never know what to answer – I'm so clumsy. (*Louder rhinoceros noises passing first under the upstage window and then the downstage.*) But I do feel you're in the wrong... I feel it instinctively – no, that's not what I mean, it's the rhinoceros which has instinct – I feel it intuitively, yes, that's the word, intuitively.

DUDARD: What do you understand by "intuitive"?

BÉRENGER: Intuitively means... well, just like that! I feel it, just like that. I think your excessive tolerance and your generous indulgence... believe me, they're really only weakness... just blind spots...

DUDARD: You're innocent enough to think that.

BÉRENGER: You'll always be able to dance rings round me. But you know what? I'm going to try and get hold of the Logician...

DUDARD: What logician?

BÉRENGER: The Logician – the philosopher, a logician, you know... you know better than I do what a logician is. A logician I met, who explained to me...

DUDARD: What did he explain to you?

BÉRENGER: He explained that the Asian rhinoceroses were African and the African ones Asian.

DUDARD: I don't follow you.

BÉRENGER: No... no... he proved the contrary – that the African ones were Asian and the Asian ones... I know what I mean.

That's not what I wanted to say. But you'll get on very well with him. He's your sort of person – a very good man, a very subtle mind, brilliant.

(*Increasing noise from the rhinoceroses. The words of the two men are drowned out by the animals passing under the windows; for a few moments the lips of* DUDARD *and* BÉRENGER *are seen to move without any words being heard.*)

There they go again! Will they never stop! (*He runs to the upstage window.*) Stop it! Stop it! You devils!

(*The rhinoceroses move away.* BÉRENGER *shakes his fist after them.*)

DUDARD (*seated*): I'd be happy to meet your Logician. If he can enlighten me on these obscure and delicate points, I'd be only too delighted.

BÉRENGER (*as he runs to the downstage window*): Yes, I'll bring him along – he'll talk to you. He's a very distinguished person, you'll see. (*To the rhinoceroses, from the window:*) You devils! (*Shakes his fist, as before.*)

DUDARD: Let them alone. And be more polite. You shouldn't talk to people like that...

BÉRENGER (*still at the window*): There they go again!

(*A boater pierced by a rhinoceros horn emerges from the orchestra pit under the window and passes swiftly from left to right.*)

There's a boater impaled on a rhinoceros horn. Oh, it's the Logician's hat! It's the Logician's! That's the bloody limit! The Logician's turned into a rhinoceros!

DUDARD: That's no reason to be coarse!

BÉRENGER: Dear Lord, who can you turn to – who? I ask you! The Logician... a rhinoceros!

DUDARD (*going to the window*): Where is he?

BÉRENGER (*pointing*): There, that one there, you see!

DUDARD: He's the only rhinoceros in a boater! That makes you think... You're sure it's your Logician?

BÉRENGER: The Logician... a rhinoceros!

DUDARD: He's still retained a vestige of his old individuality.

BÉRENGER (*shakes his fist again at the straw-hatted rhinoceros, which has disappeared*): I'll never join up with you! Not me!

DUDARD: If he was a genuine thinker, as you say, he couldn't have got carried away. He must have weighed all the pros and cons before deciding.

BÉRENGER (*still shouting after the ex-Logician and the other rhinoceroses, who have moved away*): I'll never join up with you!

DUDARD (*settling into the armchair*): Yes, that certainly makes you think!

(BÉRENGER *closes the downstage window, goes to the upstage window, where other rhinoceroses are passing, presumably making a tour of the house. He opens the window and shouts:*)

BÉRENGER: No, I'll never join up with you!

DUDARD (*aside, in his armchair*): They're going round and round the house. They're playing! Just big babies!

(DAISY *has been seen mounting the top stairs. She knocks on* BÉRENGER's *door. She is carrying a basket.*)

There's somebody at the door, Bérenger!

(*He takes* BÉRENGER, *who is still at the window, by the sleeve.*)

BÉRENGER (*shouting after the rhinoceroses*): It's a disgrace, masquerading like this, a disgrace!

DUDARD: There's someone knocking, Bérenger – can't you hear?

BÉRENGER: Open, then, if you want to! (*He continues to watch the rhinoceroses, whose noise is fading away.*)

(DUDARD *goes to open the door.*)

DAISY (*coming in*): Morning, Mr Dudard.

DUDARD: Oh, it's you, Miss Daisy.

DAISY: Is Bérenger here? Is he any better?

DUDARD: How nice to see you, my dear. Do you often visit Bérenger?

DAISY: Where is he?

DUDARD (*pointing*): There.

DAISY: He's all on his own, poor thing. And he's not very well at the moment – somebody has to give him a hand.

DUDARD: You're a good friend, Miss Daisy.

DAISY: That's just what I am: a good friend.

DUDARD: You've got a warm heart.

DAISY: I'm a good friend, that's all.

BÉRENGER (*turning, leaving the window open*): Oh Miss Daisy! How kind of you to come – how very kind!

DUDARD: It certainly is.

BÉRENGER: Did you know, Miss Daisy, that the Logician is a rhinoceros?

DAISY: Yes, I did. I caught sight of him in the street as I arrived. He was running very fast for someone his age! Are you feeling any better, Mr Bérenger?

BÉRENGER: My head's still bad! Still got a headache! Isn't it frightful? What do you think about it?

DAISY: I think you ought to be resting... you should take things quietly for a few more days.

DUDARD (*to* BÉRENGER *and* DAISY): I hope I'm not disturbing you!

BÉRENGER (*to* DAISY): I meant about the Logician...

DAISY (*to* DUDARD): Why should you be? (*To* BÉRENGER:) Oh, about the Logician? I don't think anything at all!

DUDARD (*to* DAISY): I thought I might be in the way!

DAISY (*to* BÉRENGER): What do you expect me to think? (*To both:*) I've got some news for you: Botard's a rhinoceros!

DUDARD: Well, well!

BÉRENGER: I don't believe it. He was against it. You must be mistaken. He protested. Dudard has just been telling me. Isn't that so, Dudard?

DUDARD: That is so.

DAISY: I know he was against it. But it didn't stop him turning, twenty-four hours after Mr Papillon.

DUDARD: Well, he must have changed his mind! Everybody has the right to do that.

BÉRENGER: Then obviously anything can happen!

DUDARD (*to* BÉRENGER): He was a very good man, according to you just now.

BÉRENGER (*to* DAISY): I just can't believe you. They must have lied to you.

DAISY: I saw him do it.

BÉRENGER: Then he must have been lying; he was just pretending.

DAISY: He seemed very sincere – sincerity itself.

BÉRENGER: Did he give any reasons?

DAISY: What he said was: we must move with the times! Those were his last human words.

DUDARD (*to* DAISY): I was almost certain I'd meet you here, Miss Daisy.

BÉRENGER: ...Move with the times! What a mentality! (*He makes a wide gesture.*)

DUDARD (*to* DAISY): Impossible to find you anywhere else since the office closed.

BÉRENGER (*continuing, aside*): What childishness! (*He repeats the same gesture.*)

DAISY (*to* DUDARD): If you wanted to see me, you only had to telephone.

DUDARD (*to* DAISY): Oh you know me, Miss Daisy – I'm discretion itself.

BÉRENGER: But now I come to think it over, Botard's behaviour doesn't surprise me. His firmness was only a pose. Which doesn't stop him from being a good man, of course. Good men make good rhinoceroses, unfortunately. It's because they are so good that they get taken in.

DAISY: Do you mind if I put this basket on the table? (*She does so.*)

BÉRENGER: But he was a good man with a lot of resentment...

DUDARD (*to* DAISY, *and hastening to help her with the basket*): Excuse me – excuse us both – we should have given you a hand before.

BÉRENGER (*continues*): He was riddled with hatred for his superiors, and he'd got an inferiority complex—

DUDARD (*to* BÉRENGER): Your argument doesn't hold water, because the example he followed was the Chief's – the very instrument of the people who exploited him, as he used to say. No, it seems to me that with him it was a case of community spirit triumphing over his anarchic impulses.

BÉRENGER: It's the rhinoceroses which are anarchic, because they're in the minority.

DUDARD: They are, it's true – for the moment.

DAISY: They're a pretty big minority, and getting bigger all the time. My cousin's a rhinoceros now, and his wife. Not to mention leading personalities like the Cardinal of Retz...

DUDARD: A prelate!

DAISY: Mazarin...

DUDARD: This is going to spread to other countries, you'll see.

BÉRENGER: And to think it all started with us!

DAISY: ...and some of the aristocracy. The Duke of St Simon.

BÉRENGER (*with uplifted arms*): All our great names!

DAISY: And others, too. Lots of others. Maybe a quarter of the whole town.

BÉRENGER: We're still in the majority. We must take advantage of that. We must do something before we're inundated.

DUDARD: They're very potent – very.

DAISY: Well, for the moment, let's eat. I've brought some food.

BÉRENGER: You're very kind, Miss Daisy.

DUDARD (*aside*): Very kind indeed.

BÉRENGER: I don't know how to thank you.

DAISY (*to* DUDARD): Would you care to stay with us?

DUDARD: I don't want to be a nuisance.

DAISY: Whatever do you mean, Mr Dudard? You know very well we'd love you to stay.

DUDARD: Well, you know, I'd hate to be in the way…

BÉRENGER: Of course – stay, Dudard. It's always a pleasure to talk to you.

DUDARD: As a matter of fact, I'm in a bit of a hurry. I have an appointment.

BÉRENGER: Just now you said you'd got nothing to do.

DAISY (*unpacking her basket*): You know, I had a lot of trouble finding food. The shops have been plundered; they just devour everything. And a lot of the shops are closed. It's written up outside: "Closed on account of transformation."

BÉRENGER: They should all be rounded up in a big enclosure, and kept under strict supervision.

DUDARD: That's easier said than done. The Animals' Protection League would be the first to object.

DAISY: And besides, everyone has a close relative or a friend among them, and that would make it even more difficult.

BÉRENGER: So everybody's mixed up in it!

DUDARD: Everybody's in the same boat!

BÉRENGER: But how can people be rhinoceroses? It doesn't bear thinking about! (*To* DAISY:) Shall I help you lay the table?

DAISY: No, don't bother. I know where the plates are. (*She goes to a cupboard and takes out the plates.*)

DUDARD (*aside*): She's obviously very familiar with the place…

DAISY (*to* DUDARD): I'm laying for three – all right? You are staying with us?

BÉRENGER (*to* DUDARD): Yes, of course you're staying.

DAISY (*to* BÉRENGER): You get used to it, you know. Nobody seems surprised any more to see herds of rhinoceros galloping through the streets. They just stand aside, and then carry on as if nothing had happened.

DUDARD: It's the wisest course to take.

BÉRENGER: Well, I can't get used to it.

DUDARD (*reflectively*): I wonder if one oughtn't to give it a try?

DAISY: Well, right now, let's have lunch.

BÉRENGER: I don't see how a legal man like yourself can—

(*A great noise of rhinoceroses travelling very fast is heard outside. Trumpets and drums are also heard.*)

What's going on?

(*They rush to the downstage window.*)

What is it?

(*The sound of a wall crumbling is heard. Dust covers part of the stage, enveloping, if possible, the characters. They are heard speaking through it.*)

BÉRENGER: You can't see a thing! What's happening?
DUDARD: You can't see, but you can hear all right.
BÉRENGER: That's no good!
DAISY: The plates will be all covered in dust.
BÉRENGER: How unhygienic!
DAISY: Let's hurry up and eat. We won't pay any attention to them.

(*The dust disperses.*)

BÉRENGER (*pointing into the auditorium*): They've demolished the walls of the fire station.
DUDARD: That's true – they've demolished them!
DAISY (*who, after moving from the window to near the table, holding the plate which she is endeavouring to clean, rushes to join the other two*): They're coming out.
BÉRENGER: All the firemen, a whole regiment of rhinoceros, led by drums.
DAISY: They're pouring up the streets!
BÉRENGER: It's gone too far, much too far!
DAISY: More rhinoceroses are streaming out of the courtyard.
BÉRENGER: And out of the houses...
DUDARD: And the windows as well!
DAISY: They're joining up with the others.

(*A man comes out of the landing door left and dashes downstairs at top speed; then another with a large horn on his nose; then a woman wearing an entire rhinoceros head.*)

DUDARD: There aren't enough of us left any more.

BÉRENGER: How many with one horn, and how many with two?

DUDARD: The statisticians are bound to be compiling statistics now. There'll be plenty of erudite controversy, you can be sure!

BÉRENGER: They can only calculate approximately. It's all happening so fast. It leaves them no time. No time to calculate.

DAISY: The best thing is to let the statisticians get on with it. Come and eat, my dear. That'll calm you down. You'll feel better afterwards. (*To* DUDARD:) And you, too.

(*They move away from the window.* DAISY *takes* BÉRENGER's *arm; he allows himself to be led meekly.* DUDARD *suddenly halts.*)

DUDARD: I don't feel very hungry – or rather, to be frank, I don't like tinned food very much. I feel like eating outside on the grass.

BÉRENGER: You mustn't do that. Think of the risk!

DUDARD: But, really, I don't want to put you to the trouble.

BÉRENGER: But we've already told you—

DUDARD (*interrupting* BÉRENGER): I really mean it.

DAISY (*to* DUDARD): Of course, if you really don't want to stay, we can't force you...

DUDARD: I didn't mean to offend you.

BÉRENGER (*to* DAISY): Don't let him go – he mustn't go.

DAISY: I'd like him to stay... but people must do as they please.

BÉRENGER (*to* DUDARD): Man is superior to the rhinoceros.

DUDARD: I didn't say he wasn't. But I'm not with you absolutely, either. I don't know – only experience can tell.

BÉRENGER (*to* DUDARD): You're weakening too, Dudard. It's just a passing phase which you'll regret.

DAISY: If it's just a passing phase then there's no great danger.

DUDARD: I feel certain scruples! I feel it's my duty to stick by my employers and my friends, through thick and thin.

BÉRENGER: It's not as if you were married to them.

DUDARD: I've renounced marriage. I prefer the great universal family to the little domestic one.

DAISY (*softly*): We shall miss you a lot, Dudard, but we can't do anything about it.

DUDARD: It's my duty to stick by them; I have to do my duty.

BÉRENGER: No you're wrong, your duty is to... you don't see where your real duty lies... your duty is to oppose them, with a firm, clear mind.

DUDARD: I shall keep my mind clear. (*He starts to move round the stage in circles.*) As clear as ever it was. But if you're going to criticize, it's better to do so from the inside. I'm not going to abandon them. I won't abandon them.

DAISY: He's very good-hearted.

BÉRENGER: He's too good-hearted. (*To* DUDARD, *then dashing to the door:*) You're too good-hearted – you're human. (*To* DAISY:) Don't let him go. He's making a mistake. He's human.

DAISY: What can I do?

(DUDARD *opens the door and runs off; he goes down the stairs at top speed, followed by* BÉRENGER, *who shouts after him from the landing.*)

BÉRENGER: Come back, Dudard! We're fond of you – don't go! It's too late! (*He comes back.*) Too late!

DAISY: We couldn't do anything. (*She closes the door behind* BÉRENGER, *who darts to the downstage window.*)

BÉRENGER: He's joined up with them. Where is he now?

DAISY (*moving to the window*): With them.

BÉRENGER: Which one is he?

DAISY: You can't tell. You can't recognize him any more.

BÉRENGER: They all look alike, all alike. (*To* DAISY:) He *did* hesitate. You should have held him back by force.

DAISY: I didn't dare to.

BÉRENGER: You should have been firmer with him; you should have insisted; he was in love with you, wasn't he?

DAISY: He never made me any official declaration.

BÉRENGER: Everybody knew he was. He's done this out of thwarted love. He was a shy man. He wanted to make a big gesture to impress you. Don't you feel like going after him?

DAISY: Not at all. Or I wouldn't be here!

BÉRENGER (*looking out of the window*): You can see nothing but them in the street. (*He darts to the upstage window.*) Nothing but them! You were wrong, Daisy. (*He looks through the downstage window again.*) Not a single human being as far as the eye can see. They're all over the street. Half with one horn and half with two, and that's the only distinction!

(*Powerful noises of moving rhinoceroses are heard, but somehow it is a musical sound. On the upstage wall stylized heads appear and disappear; they become more and more numerous from now on until the end of the play. Towards the end they stay fixed for longer and longer, until eventually they fill the entire back wall, remaining static. The heads, in spite of their monstrous appearance, seem to become more and more beautiful.*)

You don't feel let down, do you, Daisy? There's nothing you regret?

DAISY: No, no.

BÉRENGER: I want so much to be a comfort to you. I love you, Daisy; don't ever leave me.

DAISY: Shut the window, darling. They're making such a noise. And the dust is rising, even up to here. Everything will get filthy.

BÉRENGER: Yes, you're right. (*He closes the downstage window and* DAISY *closes the upstage one. They meet centre stage.*) I'm not afraid of anything, as long as we're together. I don't care what happens. You know, Daisy, I thought I'd never be able to fall in love again. (*He takes her hands, strokes her arms.*)

DAISY: Well, you see, everything is possible.

BÉRENGER: I want so much to make you happy. Do you think you can be happy with me?

DAISY: Why not? If you're happy, then I'll be happy, too. You say nothing scares you, but you're really frightened of everything. What can possibly happen to us?

BÉRENGER (*stammering*): My love, my dear love... let me kiss your lips. I never dreamt I could still feel such tremendous emotion!

DAISY: You must be more calm and more sure of yourself now.

BÉRENGER: I am; let me kiss you.

DAISY: I'm very tired, dear. Stay quiet and rest yourself. Sit in the armchair.

(BÉRENGER, *led by* DAISY, *sits in the armchair.*)

BÉRENGER: There was no point in Dudard quarrelling with Botard, as things turned out.

DAISY: Don't think about Dudard any more. I'm here with you. We've no right to interfere in other people's lives.

BÉRENGER: But you're interfering in mine. You know how to be firm with me.

DAISY: That's not the same thing; I never loved Dudard.

BÉRENGER: I see what you mean. If he'd stayed he'd always have been an obstacle between us. Ah, happiness is such an egotistical thing!

DAISY: You have to fight for happiness, don't you agree?

BÉRENGER: I adore you, Daisy; I admire you, as well.

DAISY: Maybe you won't say that when you get to know me better.

BÉRENGER: The more I know you the better you seem; and you're so beautiful, so very beautiful. (*More rhinoceroses are heard passing.*) Particularly compared to them... (*He points to the window.*) You probably think that's no compliment, but they make you seem more beautiful than ever...

DAISY: Have you been good today? You haven't had any brandy?

BÉRENGER: Oh yes, I've been good.

DAISY: Is that the truth?

BÉRENGER: Yes, it's the truth, I assure you.

DAISY: Can I believe you, I wonder?

BÉRENGER (*a little flustered*): Oh yes, you must believe me.

DAISY: Well, all right then, you can have a little glass. It'll buck you up.

(BÉRENGER *is about to leap up.*)

You stay where you are, dear. Where's the bottle?

BÉRENGER (*pointing to it*): There, on the little table.

DAISY (*going to the table and getting the bottle and glass*): You've hidden it well away.

BÉRENGER: It's out of the way of temptation.

DAISY (*pours a small glass and gives it to* BÉRENGER): You've been a good boy. You're making progress.

BÉRENGER: I'll make a lot more now I'm with you.

DAISY (*handing him the glass*): Here you are. That's your reward.

BÉRENGER (*downing it at one go*): Thank you. (*He holds up his empty glass to* DAISY.)

DAISY: Oh no, dear. That's enough for this morning. (*She takes his glass, puts it back on the table with the bottle.*) I don't want it to make you ill. (*She comes back to him.*) How's your head feel now?

BÉRENGER: Much better, darling.

DAISY: Then we'll take off the bandage. It doesn't suit you at all.

BÉRENGER: Oh no, don't touch it.

DAISY: Nonsense, we'll take it off now.

BÉRENGER: I'm frightened there might be something underneath.

DAISY (*removing the bandage in spite of his protests*): Always frightened, aren't you – always imagining the worst! There's nothing there, you see. Your forehead's as smooth as a baby's.

BÉRENGER (*feeling his brow*): You're right; you're getting rid of my complexes. (DAISY *kisses him on the brow.*) What should I do without you?

DAISY: I'll never leave you alone again.

BÉRENGER: I won't have any more fears now I'm with you.

DAISY: I'll keep them all at bay.

BÉRENGER: We'll read books together. I'll become clever.

DAISY: And when there aren't so many people about we'll go for long walks.

BÉRENGER: Yes, along the Seine, and in the Luxembourg Gardens...

DAISY: And to the Zoo.

BÉRENGER: I'll be brave and strong. I'll keep you safe from harm.

DAISY: You won't need to defend me, silly! We don't wish anyone any harm. And no one wishes us any, my dear.

BÉRENGER: Sometimes one does harm without meaning to – or rather, one allows it to go unchecked. I know you didn't like poor old Mr Papillon very much, but perhaps you shouldn't have spoken to him so harshly that day when Boeuf turned into a rhinoceros. You needn't have told him he had such horny hands.

DAISY: But it was true – he had!

BÉRENGER: I know he had, my dear. But you could have said so less bluntly and not hurt his feelings so much. It had a big effect on him.

DAISY: Do you think so?

BÉRENGER: He didn't show it – he was too proud for that – but the remark certainly went home. It must have influenced his decision. Perhaps you might have been the means of saving him.

DAISY: I couldn't possibly foresee what was going to happen to him... besides, he was so ill-mannered.

BÉRENGER: For my own part, I shall never forgive myself for not being nicer to Jean. I never managed to give him really solid proof of the friendship I felt for him. I wasn't sufficiently understanding with him.

DAISY: Don't worry about it. You did all you could. Nobody can do the impossible. There's no point in reproaching yourself now. Stop thinking about all those people. Forget about them. You must forget all those bad memories.

BÉRENGER: But they keep coming back to me. They're very real memories.

DAISY: I never knew you were such a realist – I thought you were more poetic. Where's your imagination? There are many sides to reality. Choose the one that's best for you. Escape into the world of the imagination.

BÉRENGER: It's easy to say that!

DAISY: Aren't I enough for you?

BÉRENGER: Oh yes, more than enough!

DAISY: You'll spoil everything if you go on having a bad conscience. Everybody has their faults, but you and I have got less than a lot of people.

BÉRENGER: Do you really think so?

DAISY: We're comparatively better than most. We're good, both of us.

BÉRENGER: That's true – you're good and I'm good. That's true.

DAISY: Well, then – we have the right to live. We even owe ourselves a duty to be happy in spite of everything. Guilt is a dangerous symptom. It shows a lack of purity.

BÉRENGER: You're right, it can lead to that… (*He points to the window, under which the rhinoceroses are passing, and to the upstage wall, where another rhinoceros head appears.*) A lot of them started like that!

DAISY: We must try and not feel guilty any more.

BÉRENGER: How right you are, my wonderful love… You're all my happiness; the light of my life… We are together, aren't we? No one can separate us. Our love is the only thing that's real. Nobody has the right to stop us from being happy – in fact, nobody could, could they?

(*The telephone rings.*)

Who could that be?

DAISY (*fearful*): Don't answer.

BÉRENGER: Why not?

DAISY: I don't know. I just feel it's better not to.

BÉRENGER: It might be Mr Papillon, or Botard, or Jean, or Dudard ringing to say they've had second thoughts. You did say it was probably only a passing phase.

DAISY: I don't think so. They wouldn't have changed their minds so quickly. They've not had time to think it over. They're bound to give it a fair trial.

BÉRENGER: Perhaps the authorities have decided to take action at last – maybe they're ringing to ask for our help in whatever measures they've decided to adopt.

DAISY: I'd be surprised if it was them.

(*The telephone rings again.*)

BÉRENGER: It is the authorities, I tell you – I recognize the ring – a long, drawn-out ring; I can't ignore an appeal from them. It can't be anyone else. (*He picks up the receiver.*) Hallo? (*Trumpeting is heard coming from the receiver.*) You hear that? Trumpeting! Listen!

(DAISY *puts the telephone to her ear, is shocked by the sound, quickly replaces the receiver.*)

DAISY (*frightened*): What's going on?

BÉRENGER: They're playing jokes now.

DAISY: Jokes in bad taste!

BÉRENGER: You see! What did I tell you?

DAISY: You didn't tell me anything.

BÉRENGER: I was expecting that; it was just what I'd predicted.

DAISY: You didn't predict anything. You never do. You can only predict things after they've happened.

BÉRENGER: Oh yes, I can – I can predict things, all right.

DAISY: That's not nice of them – in fact, it's very nasty. I don't like being made fun of.

BÉRENGER: They wouldn't dare make fun of you. It's me they're making fun of.

DAISY: And naturally I come in for it as well, because I'm with you. They're taking their revenge. But what have we done to them?

(*The telephone rings again.*)

   Pull the plug out.
BÉRENGER: The telephone authorities say you mustn't.
DAISY: Oh, you never dare to do anything – and you say you
   could defend me!
BÉRENGER (*darting to the radio*): Let's turn on the radio for
   the news!
DAISY: Yes, we must find out how things stand!

(*The sound of trumpeting comes from the radio.* BÉRENGER
*peremptorily switches it off. But in the distance other trumpeting,
like an echo, can be heard.*)

   Things are getting really serious! I tell you – frankly, I don't
   like it! (*She is trembling.*)
BÉRENGER (*very agitated*): Keep calm! Keep calm!
DAISY: They've taken over the radio stations!
BÉRENGER (*agitated and trembling*): Keep calm, keep calm!

(DAISY *runs to the upstage window, then to the downstage window
and looks out;* BÉRENGER *does the same in the opposite order,
then the two come and face each other centre stage.*)

DAISY: It's not a joke any longer. They mean business!
BÉRENGER: There's only them left now – nobody but them.
   Even the authorities have joined them.

(*They cross to the window as before, and meet again centre stage.*)

DAISY: Not a soul left anywhere.
BÉRENGER: We're all alone, we're left all alone.
DAISY: That's what you wanted.
BÉRENGER: You mean that's what you wanted!
DAISY: It was you!
BÉRENGER: You!

(*Noises come from everywhere at once. Rhinoceros heads fill the upstage wall. From left and right in the house, the noise of rushing feet and the panting breath of the animals. But all these disquieting sounds are nevertheless somehow rhythmical, making a kind of music. The loudest noises of all come from above; a noise of stamping. Plaster falls from the ceiling. The house shakes violently.*)

DAISY: The earth's trembling! (*She doesn't know where to run.*)

BÉRENGER: No, that's our neighbours, the perissodactyls! (*He shakes his fist to left and right and above.*) Stop it! You're preventing us from working! Noise is forbidden in these flats! Noise is forbidden!

DAISY: They'll never listen to you!

(*However, the noise does diminish, merely forming a sort of musical background.*)

BÉRENGER (*he, too, is afraid*): Don't be frightened, my dear. We're together – you're happy with me, aren't you? It's enough that I'm with you, isn't it? I'll chase all your fears away.

DAISY: Perhaps it's all our own fault.

BÉRENGER: Don't think about it any longer. We mustn't start feeling remorse. It's dangerous to start feeling guilty. We must just live our lives and be happy. We have the right to be happy. They're not spiteful, and we're not doing them any harm. They'll leave us in peace. You just keep calm and rest. Sit in the armchair. (*He leads her to the armchair.*) Just keep calm! (DAISY *sits in the armchair.*) Would you like a drop of brandy to pull you together?

DAISY: I've got a headache.

BÉRENGER (*taking up his bandage and binding* DAISY's *head*): I love you, my darling. Don't you worry, they'll get over it. It's just a passing phase.

DAISY: They won't get over it. It's for good.

BÉRENGER: I love you. I love you madly.

DAISY (*taking off the bandage*): Let things just take their course. What can we do about it?

BÉRENGER: They've all gone mad. The world is sick. They're all sick.

DAISY: We shan't be the ones to cure them.

BÉRENGER: How can we live in the same house with them?

DAISY (*calming down*): We must be sensible. We must adapt ourselves and try and get on with them.

BÉRENGER: They can't understand us.

DAISY: They must. There's no other way.

BÉRENGER: Do you understand them?

DAISY: Not yet. But we must try to understand the way their minds work, and learn their language.

BÉRENGER: They haven't got a language! Listen... do you call that a language?

DAISY: How do you know? You're no polyglot!

BÉRENGER: We'll talk about it later. We must have lunch first.

DAISY: I'm not hungry any more. It's all too much. I can't take any more.

BÉRENGER: But you're the strong one. You're not going to let it get you down? It's precisely for your courage that I admire you so.

DAISY: You said that before.

BÉRENGER: Do you feel sure of my love?

DAISY: Yes, of course.

BÉRENGER: I love you so.

DAISY: You keep saying the same thing, my dear.

BÉRENGER: Listen, Daisy, there *is* something we can do. We'll have children, and our children will have children – it'll take time, but together we can regenerate the human race.

DAISY: Regenerate the human race?

BÉRENGER: It happened once before.

DAISY: Ages ago. Adam and Eve... They had a lot of courage.

BÉRENGER: And we, too, can have courage. We don't need all that much. It happens automatically with time and patience.

DAISY: What's the use?

BÉRENGER: Of course we can – with a little bit of courage.

DAISY: I don't want to have children – it's a bore.

BÉRENGER: How can we save the world if you don't?

DAISY: Why bother to save it?

BÉRENGER: What a thing to say! Do it for me, Daisy. Let's save the world.

DAISY: After all, perhaps it's we who need saving. Perhaps we're the abnormal ones.

BÉRENGER: You're not yourself, Daisy – you've got a touch of fever.

DAISY: There aren't any more of our kind about anywhere, are there?

BÉRENGER: Daisy, you're not to talk like that!

(DAISY *looks all around at the rhinoceros heads on the walls, on the landing door, and now starting to appear along the footlights.*)

DAISY: Those are the real people. They look happy. They're content to be what they are. They don't look insane. They look very natural. They were right to do what they did.

BÉRENGER (*clasping his hands and looking despairingly at* DAISY): We're the ones who are doing right, Daisy, I assure you.

DAISY: That's very presumptuous of you!

BÉRENGER: You know perfectly well I'm right.

DAISY: There's no such thing as absolute right. It's the world that's right, not you and me.

BÉRENGER: I *am* right, Daisy. And the proof is that you understand me when I speak to you.

DAISY: What does that prove?

BÉRENGER: The proof is that I love you as much as it's possible for a man to love a woman.

DAISY: Funny sort of argument!

BÉRENGER: I don't understand you any longer, Daisy. You don't know what you're saying, darling. Think of our love! Our love...

DAISY: I feel a bit ashamed of what you call "love" – this morbid feeling, this male weakness. And female, too. It just doesn't compare with the ardour and the tremendous energy emanating from all these creatures around us.

BÉRENGER: Energy! You want some energy, do you? I can let you have some energy! (*He slaps her face.*)

DAISY: Oh! I never would have believed it possible... (*She sinks into the armchair.*)

BÉRENGER: Oh forgive me, my darling, please forgive me! (*He tries to embrace her; she evades him.*) Forgive me, my darling. I didn't mean it. I don't know what came over me, losing control like that!

DAISY: It's because you've run out of arguments, that's why.

BÉRENGER: Oh dear! In the space of a few minutes we've gone through twenty-five years of married life.

DAISY: I pity you. I understand you all too well...

BÉRENGER (*as* DAISY *weeps*): You're probably right in saying that I've run out of arguments. You think they're stronger than me – stronger than us. Maybe they are.

DAISY: Indeed they are.

BÉRENGER: Well, in spite of everything, I swear to you I'll never give in – never!

DAISY (*she rises, goes to* BÉRENGER, *puts her arms round his neck*): My poor darling, I'll help you to resist – to the very end.

BÉRENGER: Will you be capable of it?

DAISY: I give you my word. You can trust me.

(*The rhinoceros noises have become melodious.*)

Listen – they're singing!

BÉRENGER: They're not singing, they're roaring.

DAISY: They're singing.

BÉRENGER: They're roaring, I tell you.

DAISY: You're mad – they're singing.

BÉRENGER: You can't have a very musical ear, then.

DAISY: You don't know the first thing about music, poor dear – and look, they're playing as well, and dancing.

BÉRENGER: You call that dancing?

DAISY: It's their way of dancing. They're beautiful.

BÉRENGER: They're disgusting!

DAISY: You're not to say unpleasant things about them. It upsets me.

BÉRENGER: I'm sorry. We're not going to quarrel on their account.

DAISY: They're like gods.

BÉRENGER: You go too far, Daisy; take a good look at them.

DAISY: You mustn't be jealous, my dear.

(*She goes to* BÉRENGER *again and tries to embrace him. This time it is* BÉRENGER *who frees himself.*)

BÉRENGER: I can see our opinions are directly opposed. It's better not to discuss the matter.

DAISY: Now, you mustn't be nasty.

BÉRENGER: Then don't you be stupid!

DAISY (*to* BÉRENGER, *who turns his back on her. He looks at himself closely in the mirror*): It's no longer possible for us to live together.

(*As* BÉRENGER *continues to examine himself in the mirror, she goes quietly to the door, saying*:)

He isn't very nice, really, he isn't very nice. (*She goes out, and is seen slowly descending the stairs.*)

BÉRENGER (*still looking at himself in the mirror*): Men aren't so bad-looking, you know. And I'm not a particularly handsome specimen! Believe me, Daisy! (*He turns round.*) Daisy! Daisy! Where are you, Daisy? You can't do that to me! (*He darts to the door.*) Daisy! (*He gets to the landing and leans over the banister.*) Daisy! Come back! Come back, my dear! You haven't even had your lunch. Daisy, don't leave me alone! Remember your promise! Daisy! Daisy! (*He stops calling, makes a despairing gesture and comes back into the room.*) Well, it was obvious we weren't getting along together. The home was broken. It just wasn't working out. But she shouldn't have left like that with no explanation. (*He looks all around.*) She didn't even leave a message. That's no way to behave. Now I'm all on my own. (*He locks the door carefully, but angrily.*) But they won't get me. (*He carefully closes the windows.*) You won't get me! (*He addresses all the rhinoceros heads.*) I'm not joining you; I don't understand you! I'm staying as I am. I'm a human being. A human being. (*He sits in the armchair.*) It's an impossible situation. It's my fault she's gone. I meant everything to her. What'll become of her? That's one more person on my conscience. I can easily picture the worst, because the worst can easily happen. Poor little thing left all alone in this world of monsters! Nobody can help me find her – nobody, because there's nobody left.

(*Fresh trumpeting, hectic racings, clouds of dust.*)

I can't bear the sound of them any longer; I'm going to put cotton wool in my ears. (*He does so, and talks to himself in the mirror.*) The only solution is to convince them – but convince them of what? Are the changes reversible? That's the point! Are they reversible? It would be a labour of Hercules – far beyond me. In any case, to convince them you'd have to talk to them. And to talk to them I'd have to learn their language. Or they'd have to learn mine. But what language do I speak? What is my language? Am I talking French? Yes, it must be French. But what is French? I can call it French if I want, and nobody can say it isn't – I'm the only one who speaks it. What am I saying? Do I understand what I'm saying? Do I? (*He crosses to the middle of the room.*) And what if it's true what Daisy said, and they're the ones in the right? (*He turns back to the mirror.*) A man's not ugly to look at – not ugly at all! (*He examines himself, passing his hand over his face.*) What a funny-looking thing! What do I look like? What? (*He darts to a cupboard, takes out some photographs, which he examines.*) Photographs! Who are all these people? Is it Mr Papillon – or is it Daisy? And is that

Botard or Dudard or Jean? Or is it me? (*He rushes to the cupboard again and takes out two or three pictures.*) Now I recognize me: that's me, that's me! (*He hangs the pictures on the back wall, beside the rhinoceros heads.*) That's me, that's me!

(*When he hangs the pictures one sees that they are of an old man, a huge woman and another man. The ugliness of these pictures is in contrast to the rhinoceros heads, which have become very beautiful.* BÉRENGER *steps back to contemplate the pictures.*)

I'm not good-looking, I'm not good-looking. (*He takes down the pictures, throws them furiously to the ground and goes over to the mirror.*) They're the good-looking ones. I was wrong! Oh, how I wish I was like them! I haven't got any horns, more's the pity! A smooth brow looks so ugly. I need one or two horns to give my sagging face a lift. Perhaps one will grow and I needn't be ashamed any more – then I could go and join them. But it will never grow! (*He looks at the palms of his hands.*) My hands are so limp – oh, why won't they get rough! (*He takes his coat off, undoes his shirt to look at his chest in the mirror.*) My skin is so slack. I can't stand this white, hairy body. Oh, I'd love to have a hard skin in that wonderful dull-green colour – a skin that looks decent naked without any hair on it, like theirs! (*He listens to the trumpeting.*) Their song is charming – a bit raucous, perhaps, but it does have charm! I wish I could do it! (*He tries to imitate them.*) Ahh, Ahh, Brr! No, that's not it! Try again, louder! Ahh, Ahh, Brr! No, that's not it, it's too feeble – it's got no drive behind it. I'm not trumpeting at all; I'm just howling. Ahh, Ahh, Brr. There's a big difference between howling and trumpeting. I've only myself to blame; I should have gone with them while there was still time. Now it's too late! Now I'm a monster, just a monster. Now I'll never become a rhinoceros, never, never! I've gone past changing.

I want to, I really do, but I can't, I just can't. I can't stand the sight of myself. I'm too ashamed! (*He turns his back on the mirror.*) I'm so ugly! The Devil take those people who try to hang on to their individuality! (*He suddenly snaps out of it.*) Oh well – too bad! I'll take on the whole of them! I'll put up a fight against the lot of them – the whole lot of them! I'm the last man left, and I'm staying that way until the end. I'm not capitulating!

CURTAIN

EXIT THE KING

First produced in Paris by Jacques Mauclair
at the Théâtre de l'Alliance Française on
15th December 1962

Characters

BÉRENGER THE FIRST, the King
QUEEN MARGUERITE, First Wife to KING BÉRENGER THE FIRST
QUEEN MARIE, Second Wife to KING BÉRENGER THE FIRST
THE DOCTOR, who is also SURGEON, EXECUTIONER, BACTE-
    RIOLOGIST and ASTROLOGIST
JULIETTE, domestic help and registered nurse
THE GUARD

Ionesco's own suggested cuts are indicated throughout this play within square brackets.

The Set

The throne room, vaguely dilapidated, vaguely Gothic. In the centre of the stage, against the back wall, a few steps leading to the KING's throne. On either side, downstage, two smaller thrones – those of the two queens, his wives.

Upstage left, a small door leading to the KING's apartments. Upstage right, another small door. Also on the right, downstage, a large door. Between these two doors, a Gothic window. Another small window on the left of the stage; and another small door downstage, also on the left. Near the large door, an old GUARD with a halberd.

Before and during the rise of the curtain, and for a few minutes afterwards, you can hear a derisive rendering of regal music reminiscent of the King's Levée* in the 17th century.

GUARD (*announcing*): His Majesty King Bérenger the First. Long
live the King!

(*The* KING *enters from the little door on the right, wearing a
deep-crimson cloak, with a crown on his head and a sceptre in
his hand; he rapidly crosses the stage and goes off through the
upstage door on the left.*)

(*announcing*): Her Majesty Queen Marguerite, First Wife to
the King, followed by Juliette, domestic help and registered
nurse to their Majesties. Long live the Queen!

(MARGUERITE, *followed by* JULIETTE, *enters through the downstage door on the left, and they go out through the large door.*)

(*announcing*): Her Majesty Queen Marie, Second Wife to
the King, but first in affection, followed by Juliette, domestic help and registered nurse to their Majesties. Long live
the Queen!

(MARIE, *followed by* JULIETTE, *enters through the large
door on the right and goes out with* JULIETTE *through the
downstage door on the left.* MARIE *appears younger and
more beautiful than* MARGUERITE. *She has a crown and a
deep-crimson cloak. She is wearing jewels. Her cloak is of
more modern style and looks as if it comes from a high-
class couturier. The* DOCTOR *comes in through the upstage
door on the right.*)

(*announcing*): His Notability, Doctor to the King, Gentleman,
Court Surgeon, Bacteriologist, Executioner and Astrologist.

(*The* DOCTOR *comes to the centre of the stage and then, as though he had forgotten something, turns back the way he came and goes out through the same door. The* GUARD *remains silent for a few moments. He looks tired. He rests his halberd against the wall, and then blows into his hands to warm them*).

I don't know – this is just the time when it ought to be hot. Central heating, start up! Nothing doing, it's not working. Central heating, start up! The radiator's stone cold. It's not my fault. He never told me he'd taken away my job as Chief Firelighter. Not officially, anyway. You never know with them. (*Suddenly, he picks up his weapon. Queen Marguerite reappears through the upstage door on the right. She has a crown on her head and is wearing a deep-crimson cloak that is a bit shabby. She looks rather severe. She stops in the centre, downstage. She is followed by* JULIETTE.) Long live the Queen!

MARGUERITE (*to* JULIETTE, *looking around her*): There's a lot of dust about. And cigarette ends on the floor.

JULIETTE: I've just come from the stables, milking the cow, your Majesty. She's almost out of milk. I haven't had time to do the living room.

MARGUERITE: This is *not* the living room. It's the throne room. How often do I have to tell you?

JULIETTE: All right, the throne room, as your Majesty wishes. I haven't had time to do the living room.

MARGUERITE: It's cold.

GUARD: I've been trying to turn the heat on, your Majesty. Can't get the system to function. The radiators won't cooperate. The sky is overcast and the clouds don't seem to want to break up. The sun's late. And yet I heard the King order him to come out.

MARGUERITE: Is that so! The sun's already deaf to his commands.

GUARD: I heard a little rumble during the night. There's a crack in the wall.

MARGUERITE: Already? Things are moving fast. I wasn't expecting this so soon.

GUARD: Juliette and I tried to patch it up.

JULIETTE: He woke me in the middle of the night, when I was sound asleep!

GUARD: And now it's here again. Shall we have another try?

MARGUERITE: It's not worth it. We can't turn the clock back. (*To* JULIETTE.)

JULIETTE: Where's Queen Marie? She must still be dressing.

MARGUERITE: Naturally!

JULIETTE: She was awake before dawn.

MARGUERITE: Oh! Well, that's something!

JULIETTE: I heard her crying in her room.

MARGUERITE: Laugh or cry, that's all she can do. (*To* JULIETTE:) Let her be sent for at once. Go and fetch her.

(*Just at this minute,* QUEEN MARIE *appears, dressed as described above.*)

GUARD (*a moment before* QUEEN MARIE*'s entrance*): Long live the Queen!

MARGUERITE (*to* MARIE): Your eyes are quite red, my dear. It spoils your beauty.

MARIE: I know.

MARGUERITE: Don't start crying again!

MARIE: I can't really help it.

MARGUERITE: Don't go to pieces, whatever you do. What's the use? It's the normal course of events, isn't it? You were expecting it. Or had you stopped expecting it?

MARIE: *You've* been *waiting* for it!

MARGUERITE: A good thing, too. And now the moment's arrived. (*To* JULIETTE:) Well, why don't you give her another handkerchief?

MARIE: I was still hoping—

MARGUERITE: You're wasting your time. Hope! (*She shrugs her shoulders.*) Nothing but hope on their lips and tears in their eyes. What a way to behave!

MARIE: Have you seen the Doctor again? What did he say?

MARGUERITE: What you've heard already.

MARIE: Perhaps he's made a mistake.

MARGUERITE: Don't start hoping all over again! The signs are unmistakable.

MARIE: Perhaps he misinterpreted them.

MARGUERITE: There's no mistaking the signs if you look at them objectively. And you know it!

MARIE (*looking at the wall*): Oh! That crack!

MARGUERITE: Oh! You've seen it, have you? And that's not the only thing. It's your fault if he's not prepared. It's your fault if it takes him by surprise. You let him go his own way. You've even led him astray. Oh yes! Life was very sweet. With your fun and games, your dances, your processions, your official dinners, your winning ways and your firework displays, your silver spoons and your honeymoons! How many honeymoons have you had?

MARIE: They were to celebrate our wedding anniversaries.

MARGUERITE: You celebrated them four times a year! "We've got to *live*," you used to say... but one must never forget.

MARIE: He's so fond of parties.

MARGUERITE: People know and carry on as if they didn't. They know and they forget. But *he* is the King. *He* must not forget. He should have his eyes fixed in front of him, know every stage in the journey, know exactly how long the road, and never lose sight of his destination.

MARIE: My poor darling, my poor little King.

MARGUERITE (*to* JULIETTE): Give her another handkerchief. (*To* MARIE:) Be a little more cheerful, can't you? Tears are catching. He's weak enough already. What a pernicious influence you've had on him. But there! I'm afraid he liked you better than me! I wasn't at all jealous. I just realized he wasn't being very wise. And now you can't help him any more. Look at you! Bathed in tears. You're not defying me now. You've lost that challenging look. Where's it all gone, that brazen insolence, that sarcastic smile? Come on now, wake up! Take your proper place and try to straighten up. Think! You're still wearing your beautiful necklace! Come along! Take your place!

MARIE (*seated*): I'll never be able to tell him.

MARGUERITE: I'll see to that. I'm used to the chores.

MARIE: And don't *you* tell him either. No, no, please. Don't say a word, I beg you.

MARGUERITE: *Please* leave it to me. We'll still want you, you know, later – still need you during the ceremony. You like official functions.

MARIE: Not this one.

MARGUERITE (*to* JULIETTE): You spread our trains out properly.

JULIETTE: Yes, your Majesty. (JULIETTE *does so.*)

MARGUERITE: I agree it's not so amusing as all your charity balls. Those dances you get up for children, and old folks, and newly-weds. For victims of disaster or the honours lists. For lady novelists. Or charity balls for the organizers of charity balls. This one's just for the family, with no dancers and no dance.

MARIE: No, don't tell him. It's better if he doesn't notice anything.

MARGUERITE: And goes out like a light? That's impossible.

MARIE: You've no heart.

MARGUERITE: Oh yes, I have! It's beating.

MARIE: You're inhuman.

[MARGUERITE: What does that mean?

MARIE: It's terrible...] He's not prepared.

MARGUERITE: It's your fault if he isn't. He's been like one of those travellers who linger at every inn, forgetting each time that the inn is not the end of the journey. When I reminded you that in life we must never forget our ultimate fate, you told me I was a pompous bluestocking.

JULIETTE (*aside*): It *is* pompous, too!

MARIE: As it's inevitable, he must at least be told as tactfully as possible. Tactfully – with great tact. He ought always to have been prepared for it. He ought to have thought about it every day. The time he's wasted! (*To* JULIETTE:) What's the matter with you, goggling at us like that? You're not going to break down too, I hope? You can leave us; don't go too far away – we'll call you.

JULIETTE: So I don't have to sweep the living room now?

MARGUERITE: It's too late. Never mind. Leave us.

(JULIETTE *goes out on the left.*)

MARIE: Tell him gently, I implore you. Take your time. He might have a heart attack.

MARGUERITE: We haven't the time to take our time. This is the end of your happy days, your high jinks, your revelries and your striptease. It's all over. You've let things slide to the very last minute, and now we've not a minute to lose. Obviously. It's the last. We've a few moments to do what ought to have been done over a period of years. I'll tell you when to leave us alone. Then *I'll* help him.

MARIE: It's going to be so hard, so hard.

MARGUERITE: As hard for me as for you, and for him. Stop grizzling, I say! That's a piece of advice. That's an order.

MARIE: He won't do it.

MARGUERITE: Not at first.

MARIE: I'll hold him back.

MARGUERITE: Don't you dare! It's all got to take place decently. Let it be a success, a triumph. It's a long time since he had one. His palace is crumbling. His fields lie fallow. His mountains are sinking. The sea has broken the dykes and flooded the country. He's let it all go to rack and ruin. You've driven every thought from his mind with your perfumed embrace. Such bad taste! But that was him all over! Instead of conserving the soil, he's let acre upon acre plunge into the bowels of the earth.

MARIE: Expert advice on how to stop an earthquake! I've no patience with you!... He could still have planted conifers in the sand and cemented the threatened areas. But no! Now the kingdom's as full of holes as a gigantic Gruyère cheese.

MARIE: We couldn't fight against fate, against a natural phenomenon like erosion.

MARGUERITE: Not to mention all those disastrous wars. While his drunken soldiers were sleeping it off, at night or after a lavish lunch in barracks, our neighbours were pushing back our boundaries. Our national boundaries were shrinking. His soldiers didn't want to fight.

MARIE: They were conscientious objectors.

MARGUERITE: We called them conscientious objectors here at home. The victorious armies called them cowards and deserters, and they were shot. You can see the result: towns razed to the ground, burnt-out swimming pools, abandoned bistros. The young are leaving their homeland in hordes. At the start of his reign there were nine billion inhabitants.

MARIE: Too many. There wasn't room for them all.

MARGUERITE: And now only about a thousand old people left. Less. Even now, while I'm talking, they're passing away.

MARIE: There are forty-five *young* people, too.

MARGUERITE: No one else wants *them*. *We* didn't want them either; we were forced to take them back. Anyway, they're ageing fast. Repatriated at twenty-five, two days later and they're over eighty. You can't pretend that's the normal way to grow old.

MARIE: But the King, *he's* still young.

MARGUERITE: He *was* yesterday, he *was* last night. You'll see in a moment.

GUARD (*announcing*): His Notability, the Doctor, has returned. His Notability, His Notability!

(*The* DOCTOR *enters through the large door on the right, which opens and closes by itself. He looks like an astrologer and an executioner at one and the same time. On his head he is wearing a pointed hat with stars. He is dressed in red with a hood hanging from the collar, and holding a great telescope.*)

DOCTOR (*to* MARGUERITE): Good morning, your Majesty. (*To* MARIE:) Good morning, your Majesty. I hope your Majesties will forgive me for being rather late. I've come straight from the hospital, where I had to perform several surgical operations of the greatest import to science.

MARIE: You can't operate on the King!

MARGUERITE: You can't *now*, that's true.

DOCTOR (*looking at* MARGUERITE, *then at* MARIE): I know.
Not his Majesty.

MARIE: Doctor, is there anything new? He *is* a little better, isn't
he? Isn't he? He *could* show *some* improvement, couldn't he?

DOCTOR: He's in a typically critical condition that admits no
change.

MARIE: It's true, there's no hope, no hope. (*Looking at* MARGUER-
ITE.) She doesn't want me to hope – she won't allow it.

MARGUERITE: Many people have delusions of grandeur, but
you're deluded by triviality. There's never been a queen like you!
You make me ashamed for you. Oh! She's going to cry again.

DOCTOR: In point of fact, there *is*, if you like, *something* new
to report.

MARIE: What's that?

DOCTOR: Something that merely confirms the previous symptoms.
Mars and Saturn have collided.

MARGUERITE: As we expected.

DOCTOR: Both planets have exploded.

MARGUERITE: That's logical.

DOCTOR: The sun has lost between fifty and seventy-five per cent
of its strength.

MARGUERITE: That's natural.

DOCTOR: Snow is falling on the North Pole of the sun. The
Milky Way seems to be curdling. The comet is exhausted,
feeling its age, winding its tail round itself and curling up
like a dying dog.

MARIE: It's not true – you're exaggerating. You must be. Yes,
you're exaggerating.

DOCTOR: Do you wish to look through this telescope?

MARGUERITE (*to the* DOCTOR): There's no point. We believe
you. What else?

DOCTOR: Yesterday evening it was spring. It left us two hours and
thirty minutes ago. Now it's November. Outside our borders,
the grass is shooting up, the trees are turning green. All the
cows are calving twice a day. Once in the morning and again
in the afternoon, about five, or a quarter past. Yet in our own

country, the brittle leaves are peeling off. The trees are sighing
and dying. The earth is quaking rather more than usual.

GUARD (*announcing*): The Royal Meteorological Institute calls
attention to the bad weather conditions.

MARIE: I can feel the earth quaking, I can hear it. Yes, I'm afraid
I really can.

MARGUERITE: It's that crack. It's getting wider, it's spreading.

DOCTOR: The lightning's stuck in the sky, the clouds are raining frogs,
the thunder's mumbling. That's why we can't hear it. Twenty-five
of our countrymen have been liquefied. Twelve have lost their
heads. Decapitated. This time without my surgical intervention.

MARGUERITE: Those are the signs, all right.

DOCTOR: Whereas—

MARGUERITE (*interrupting him*): No need to go on. It's what
always happens in a case like this. We know.

GUARD (*announcing*): His Majesty, the King! (*Music.*) Attention
for His Majesty. Long live the King!

(*The* KING *enters through the upstage door on the left. He has bare
feet.* JULIETTE *comes in behind the* KING.)

MARGUERITE: Now where has he scattered his slippers?

JULIETTE: Sire, they are here.

MARGUERITE: It's a bad habit to walk about barefoot.

MARIE (*to* JULIETTE): Put his slippers on. Hurry up! He'll catch cold.

MARGUERITE: It's no longer of any importance if he catches cold.
It's just that it's a bad habit.

(*While* JULIETTE *is putting the* KING's *slippers on and* MARIE *moves
towards him, the royal music can still be heard.*)

DOCTOR (*with a humble and unctuous bow*): May I be allowed to
wish your Majesty a good day? And my very best wishes.

MARGUERITE: That's nothing now but a hollow formality.

KING (*to* MARIE, *and then to* MARGUERITE): Good morning,
Marie. Good morning, Marguerite. Still here? I mean, you're

here already! How do you feel? *I* feel awful! I don't know quite what's wrong with me. My legs are a bit stiff. I had a job to get up, and my feet hurt! I must get some new slippers. Perhaps I've been growing! I had a bad night's sleep, what with the earth quaking, the borders retreating, the cattle bellowing and the sirens screaming. There's far too much noise. I really must look into it. We'll see what we can do. Ouch, my ribs! (*To the* DOCTOR:) Good morning, Doctor. Is it lumbago? (*To the others*:) I'm expecting an engineer... from abroad. Ours are no good nowadays. They just don't care. Besides we haven't any. Why did we close the École Polytechnique? Oh yes! It fell through a hole in the ground. And why should we build more when they all disappear through a hole? On top of everything else, I've got a headache. And those clouds... I thought I'd banished the clouds. Clouds! We've had enough rain. Enough, I said! Enough rain. Enough, I said! Oh! Look at that! Off they go again! There's an idiotic cloud that can't restrain itself. Like an old man, weak in the bladder. (*To* JULIETTE:) What are you staring at me for? You look very red today. My bedroom's full of cobwebs. Go and brush them away.

JULIETTE: I removed them all while your Majesty was still asleep. I can't think where they spring from. They keep on coming back.

DOCTOR (*to* MARGUERITE): You see, your Majesty. This too confirms my diagnosis.

KING (*to* MARIE): What's wrong with you, my love?

MARIE (*stammering*): I don't know... nothing... nothing wrong.

KING: You've got rings round your eyes. Have you been crying? Why?

MARIE: Oh God!

KING (*to* MARGUERITE): I won't have anyone upset her. And why did she say "Oh God"?

MARGUERITE: It's an expression. (*To* JULIETTE:) Go and get rid of those cobwebs again.

KING: Oh yes! Those cobwebs – disgusting! They give you nightmares!

MARGUERITE (*to* JULIETTE): Hurry up – don't dawdle! Have you forgotten how to use a broom?

JULIETTE: Mine's all worn away. I need a new one. I could really do with twelve brooms. (JULIETTE *goes out.*)

KING: Why are you all staring at me like this? Is there something abnormal about me? Now it's so normal to be abnormal, there's no such thing as abnormality. So that's straightened that out.

MARIE (*rushing towards the* KING): My dear King, you're limping!

KING (*taking two or three paces with a slight limp*): Limping? *I'm* not limping. I *am* limping a little.

MARIE: Your leg hurts. I'm going to help you along.

KING: It doesn't hurt. Why should it hurt? Why yes, it *does* just a little. It's nothing. (*To* MARIE:) I don't need anyone to help me. Though I like being helped by you.

MARGUERITE (*moving towards the* KING): Sire, I have some news for you.

MARIE: No, be quiet!

MARGUERITE (*to* MARIE): Keep quiet yourself!

MARIE (*to the* KING): What she says isn't true.

KING: News about what? *What* isn't true? Marie, why do you look so sad? What's the matter with you?

MARGUERITE (*to the* KING): Sire, we have to inform you that you are going to die.

DOCTOR: Alas, yes, your Majesty.

KING: But I know that – of course I do! We *all* know it! You can remind me when the time comes. Marguerite, you have a mania for disagreeable conversation early in the morning.

MARGUERITE: It's midday already.

KING: It's not midday. Why yes, it is! It doesn't matter. For me, it's the morning. I haven't eaten anything yet. Let my breakfast be brought. To be honest, I'm not very hungry. Doctor, you'll have to give me some pills to stimulate my appetite and shake up my liver. My tongue's all coated, isn't it? (*He shows his tongue to the* DOCTOR.)

DOCTOR: Yes, indeed, your Majesty.

KING: My liver's all choked up. I had nothing to drink last night, but I've a nasty taste in my mouth.

DOCTOR: Your Majesty, Queen Marguerite has spoken the truth, you *are* going to die.

KING: What, again? You get on my nerves! I'll die, yes, I'll die all right. In forty, fifty, three hundred years. Or even later. When I want to, when I've got the time, when I make up my mind. Meanwhile, let's get on with affairs of state. (*He climbs the steps of the throne.*) Ouch! My legs! My back! I've caught a cold. This palace is so badly heated, full of draughts and gales. What about those broken window panes? Have they replaced those tiles on the roof? No one works any more. I shall have to see to it myself... but I've had other things to do. You can't count on anyone. (*To* MARIE, *who is trying to support him:*) No, I can manage. (*He helps himself up with his sceptre, using it as a stick.*) There's some use in this sceptre yet. (*He manages to sit down, painfully, helped, after all, by* MARIE.) No, I say, no, I can do it. That's it! At last! This throne's got very hard! We ought to have it upholstered. And how is my country this morning?

MARGUERITE: What remains of it...

KING: There are still a few titbits left. We've got to keep an eye on them, anyhow. And it'll give you something else to think about. Let us send for all our Ministers.

(JULIETTE *appears.*)

Go and fetch the Ministers. I expect they're still fast asleep. They imagine there's no more work to be done.

JULIETTE: They've gone off on their holidays. Not very far, because now the country's all squashed up. It's shrunk. They're at the opposite end of the kingdom – in other words, just round the corner, at the edge of the wood beside the stream. They've gone fishing. They hope to catch a few to feed the population.

KING: Go to the wood and fetch them.

JULIETTE: They won't come. They're off duty. But I'll go and see if you like.

(*She goes to look through the window.*)

KING: No discipline!

JULIETTE: They've fallen into the stream.

MARIE: Try and fish them out again.

(JULIETTE *goes out.*)

KING: If the country could produce any other political experts, I'd give those two the sack.

MARIE: We'll find some more.

DOCTOR: We won't find any more, your Majesty.

MARGUERITE: You won't find any more, Bérenger.

MARIE: Yes we will, among the schoolchildren, when they're grown up. We've a little time to wait, but once these two have been fished out, they can keep things going for a while.

DOCTOR: The only children you find in the schools today are a few congenital mental defectives, Mongoloids and hydrocephalies with goitres.

KING: I see the nation's not very fit. Try and cure them, Doctor, or improve their condition a bit. So at least they can learn the first four or five letters of the alphabet. In the old days, we used to kill them off.

DOCTOR: His Majesty could no longer allow himself that privilege. Or he'd have no more subjects left!

KING: Do something with them, anyway!

MARGUERITE: We can't improve anything now. We can't cure anyone. Even *you* are incurable now.

DOCTOR: Sire, you are now incurable.

KING: I am not ill.

MARIE: He feels quite well. (*To the* KING:) Don't you? A little stiffness, that's all. It's nothing. It's a lot better now, anyway.

MARIE: He says it's all right, you see, you see.

KING: Really, I feel fine.

MARGUERITE: You're going to die in an hour and a half; you're going to die at the end of the show.

KING: What did you say, my dear? That's not funny.

MARGUERITE: You're going to die at the end of the show.

MARIE: Oh God!

DOCTOR: Yes, Sire, you are going to die. You will not take your breakfast tomorrow morning. Nor will you dine tonight. The chef has shut off the gas. He's handing in his apron. He's putting the tablecloths and napkins away in the cupboard for ever.

MARIE: Don't speak so fast, don't speak so loud.

KING: And who can have given such orders, without my consent? I'm in good health. You're teasing me. Lies. (To MARGUERITE:) You've always wanted me dead. (To MARIE:) She's always wanted me dead. (To MARGUERITE:) I'll die when I want to. I'm the King. I'm the one to decide.

DOCTOR: You've lost the power to decide for yourself, your Majesty.

MARGUERITE: And now you can't even help falling ill.

KING: I'm not ill. (To MARIE:) Didn't you just say I wasn't ill? I'm still handsome.

MARGUERITE: And those pains of yours?

KING: All gone.

MARGUERITE: Move about a bit. You'll see!

KING (who has just sat down again, tries to stand up): Ouch!... That's because I wasn't mentally prepared. I didn't have time to think! I think and I am cured. The King can cure himself, but I was too engrossed in ruling my kingdom.

MARGUERITE: Your kingdom! What a state that's in! You can't govern it now. Really, you know you can't, but you won't admit it. You've lost your power now, over yourself and over the elements. You can't stop the rot and you've no more power over us.

MARIE: You'll always have power over me.

MARGUERITE: Not even you.

(JULIETTE *enters*.)

JULIETTE: It's too late to fish the Ministers out now. The stream they fell into, with all its banks and willows, has vanished into a bottomless pit.

KING: I see. It's a plot. You want me to abdicate.

MARGUERITE: That's the best way. A voluntary abdication.

DOCTOR: Abdicate, Sire. That would be best.

KING: Abdicate? Me?

MARGUERITE: Yes. Abdicate governmentally! And morally!

DOCTOR: And physically!

MARIE: Don't give your consent! Don't listen to them!

KING: They're mad. Or else they're traitors.

JULIETTE: Sire, Sire, my poor lord and master, Sire.

MARIE (*to the* KING): You must have them arrested.

KING (*to the* GUARD): Guard! Arrest them!

MARIE: Guard! Arrest them! (*To the* KING:) That's it. Give orders!

KING (*to the* GUARD): Arrest them all! Lock them up in the tower! No, the tower's collapsed. Take them away and lock them up in the cellar, in the dungeons, or in the rabbit-hutch. Arrest them, all of them! That's an order!

MARIE (*to the* GUARD): Arrest them!

GUARD (*without moving*): In the name of His Majesty, I... I... arrest... you.

MARIE (*to the* GUARD): Get moving, then!

JULIETTE: He's the one who's arrested.

KING (*to the* GUARD): Do it, then, Guard! Do it!

MARGUERITE: You see, now he can't move. He's got gout and rheumatism.

DOCTOR (*indicating the* GUARD): Sire, the army is paralysed. An unknown virus has crept into his brain to sabotage his strongpoints.

MARGUERITE (*to the* KING): Your Majesty, you can see for yourself, it's your own orders that paralyse him.

MARIE (*to the* KING): Don't you believe it. She's trying to hypnotize you. [It's a question of will-power. You can control the whole situation by will-power.]

GUARD: I... you... in the name of the King... I... you...

(*He stops speaking, his mouth wide open.*)

KING (*to the* GUARD): What's come over you? Speak! Advance! Do you think you're playing statues?

MARIE (*to the* KING): Don't ask him questions! Don't argue! Give orders! Sweep him off his feet in a whirlwind of will-power!

DOCTOR: You see, your Majesty, he can't move a muscle. He can't say a word; he's turned to stone. He's deaf to you already. It's a characteristic symptom. Very pronounced, medically speaking.

KING: Now we'll see if I've still any power or not.

MARIE (*to the* KING): Prove that you have! You can if you want to.

KING: I'll prove that I want to; I'll prove I can.

MARIE: Stand up, first!

KING: I stand up. (*He makes a great effort, grimacing.*)

MARIE: You see how easy it is!

KING: You see, both of you, how easy it is! You're a pair of humbugs! Conspirators, Bolsheviks! (*He walks to* MARIE, *who tries to help him.*) No, no, alone... because I can, all by myself. (*He falls.* JULIETTE *rushes forwards to pick him up.*) I can get up by myself. (*He does indeed get up by himself, but with difficulty.*)

GUARD: Long live the King! (*The* KING *falls down again.*) The King is dying.

MARIE: Long live the King! (*The* KING *stands up with difficulty, helping himself with his sceptre.*)

GUARD: Long live the King! (*The* KING *falls down again.*) The King is dead!

MARIE: Long live the King! Long live the King!

MARGUERITE: What a farce! (*The* KING *stands up again, painfully.*)

JULIETTE (*who has disappeared, reappears*): Long live the King! (*She disappears again. The* KING *falls down again.*)

GUARD: The King is dying!

MARIE: No! Long live the King! Stand up! Long live the King!

JULIETTE (*appearing, then disappearing again, while the* KING *stands up*): Long live the King! (*This scene should be played like a tragic Punch and Judy show.*)

GUARD: Long live the King!

MARIE: You see, he's better now.

MARGUERITE: It's his last burst of energy, isn't it, Doctor?

DOCTOR (*to* MARGUERITE): Just a final effort before his strength gives out.

KING: I tripped, that's all. It can happen to anyone. It does happen, you know. My crown! (*The crown had fallen to the ground when the* KING *collapsed.* MARIE *puts it back on his head again.*) That's a bad omen.

MARIE: Don't you believe it! (*The* KING'*s sceptre falls.*)

KING: That's another bad omen.

MARIE: Don't you believe it! (*She gives him his sceptre.*) Hold it firmly in your hand! Clench your fist!

GUARD: Long live... Long live... (*Then he falls silent.*)

DOCTOR (*to the* KING): Your Majesty...

MARGUERITE (*to the* DOCTOR, *indicating* MARIE): We must keep that woman quiet! She says anything that comes into her head. She's not to open her mouth again without our permission.

(MARIE *is motionless.*)

MARGUERITE (*to the* DOCTOR, *indicating the* KING): Now, try and make him understand.

DOCTOR (*to the* KING): Your Majesty, several decades, or even three days, ago, your empire was flourishing. In three days, you've lost all the wars you won. And those you lost you've lost again. [While our harvests rotted in the fields and our continent became a desert, our neighbours' land turned green again. And it was a wilderness last Thursday!] The rockets you want to fire can't even get off the ground. Or else they leave the pad and drop back to earth with a thud.

KING: A technical fault.

DOCTOR: There weren't any in the past.

MARGUERITE: Your triumphs are all over. You've got to realize that.

DOCTOR: Your pains, your stiffness...

KING: I've never had them before. This is the first time.

DOCTOR: Exactly. That's the sign. It really has happened all at once, hasn't it?

MARGUERITE: You should have expected it.

DOCTOR: It's happened all at once and you're no longer your own master. You must have noticed, Sire. Try and have the courage to look facts in the face! Just try!

KING: I picked myself up. You're lying. I *did* pick myself up.

DOCTOR: You're a very sick man, and you could never make that effort again.

MARGUERITE: Of course not. It won't be long now. (*To the* KING:) What can you still *do?* Can you give an order that's obeyed? Can you change anything? Just try and you'll see.

KING: It's because I never used my will-power that everything went to pieces. Sheer neglect. It can all be put right. It will all be restored and look like new. You'll soon see what I can do. Guard, move, approach!

MARGUERITE: He can't. He can only obey other people now. Guard, take two paces forwards! (*The* GUARD *advances two paces.*) Guard, two paces back! (*The* GUARD *takes two paces back.*)

KING: Off with that Guard's head, off with his head! (*The* GUARD's *head leans a little to the right, a little to the left.*) His head's toppling! It's going to fall!

MARGUERITE: No, it isn't. It wobbles a bit, that's all. No worse than it was before.

KING: Off with that Doctor's head, off with it at once! Right now, off!

MARGUERITE: That Doctor has a sound head on his shoulders. He's got it screwed on all right!

DOCTOR: I'm sorry, Sire; as you see, I feel quite ashamed.

KING: Off with Marguerite's crown! Knock it on the floor! (*It is the* KING'S *crown which again falls to the floor.* MARGUERITE *picks it up.*)

MARGUERITE: All right, I'll put it on again.

KING: Thank you. What *is* all this? Witchcraft? How have I lost my power over you? Don't imagine I'll let things go on like this. I'm going to get to the bottom of this. There must be rust in the machine. It stops the wheels from turning.

MARGUERITE (*to* MARIE): You can speak now. We give you permission.

MARIE (*to the* KING): Tell me to do something and I'll do it. Give me an order. Command me, Sire, command me! I'll obey you.

MARGUERITE (*to the* DOCTOR): She thinks that which she calls love can achieve the impossible. Sentimental superstition. Things have changed. That's out of the question now. We're past that stage already. A long way past.

MARIE (*who has retreated backwards to the left and is now near the window*): Your orders, my King? Your orders, my love? See how beautiful I am. Smell my perfume. Order me to come to you, to kiss you!

KING (*to* MARIE): Come to me, kiss me! (MARIE *does not move.*) Can you hear me?

MARIE: Why yes, I can hear you. I'll do it.

KING: Come to me then!

MARIE: I'd like to. I'm going to. I want to do it. But my arms fall to my side.

KING: Dance, then! (MARIE *does not move.*) Dance! Or at least, turn your head, go to the window, open it and close it again!

MARIE: I can't!

KING: I expect you've got a stiff neck. You must have a stiff neck. Step forwards – come closer to me!

MARIE: Yes, Sire.

KING: Come closer to me!

MARIE: Yes, Sire.

KING: And smile!

MARIE: I don't know what to do, how to walk. I've suddenly forgotten.

MARGUERITE: Take a few steps nearer! (MARIE *advances a little in the direction of the* KING.)

KING: You see, she's coming!

MARGUERITE: Because she listened to *me*. (*To* MARIE:) Stop! Stand still!

MARIE: Forgive me, your Majesty. It's not my fault.

MARGUERITE (*to the* KING): Do you need any more proof?

KING: I order trees to sprout from the floor. (*Pause.*) I order the roof to disappear. (*Pause.*) What? Nothing? I order rain to fall. (*Pause – still nothing happens.*) I order a thunderbolt, one I can hold in my hand. (*Pause.*) I order leaves to grow again. (*He goes to the window.*) What? Nothing? I order Juliette to come in through the great door. (JULIETTE *comes in through the small door upstage left*.) Not that way, this way! Go out by that door! (*He indicates the large door.* JULIETTE *goes out by the small door on the left, opposite. To* JULIETTE:) I order you to stay. (JULIETTE *has gone out.*) I order bugles to sound. I order bells to ring! A salute from a hundred and twenty-one guns in my honour. (*He listens.*) Nothing!... Wait! Yes!... I can hear something.

DOCTOR: It's only the buzzing in your ears, your Majesty.

MARGUERITE (*to the* KING): Don't try any more! You're making a fool of yourself.

MARIE (*to the* KING): You're... you're getting too tired, my dear little King. Don't despair. You're soaked in perspiration. Rest a little! After a while, we'll start again. Wait for an hour and then we'll manage it.

MARGUERITE (*to the* KING): In one hour and twenty-five minutes you're going to die.

DOCTOR: Yes, Sire. In one hour, twenty-four minutes and fifty seconds.

KING (*to* MARIE): Marie!

MARGUERITE: In one hour, twenty-four minutes and forty-one seconds. (*To the* KING:) Prepare yourself!

MARIE: Don't give in!

MARGUERITE (*to* MARIE): Stop trying to distract him! [Don't open your arms to him! He's slipping away already.] You can't hold him back now. The official programme must be followed, in every detail.

GUARD (*announcing*): The ceremony is about to commence!

(*General commotion. They all take up their positions, as if for some solemn ceremony. The* KING *is seated on his throne, with* MARIE *at his side.*)

KING: Let time turn back in its tracks.

MARIE: Let us be as we were twenty years ago.

KING: Let it be last week.

MARIE: Let it be yesterday evening. Turn back, time! Turn back! Time, stop!

MARGUERITE: There is no more time. Time has melted in his hands.

DOCTOR (*to* MARGUERITE, *after looking heavenwards through his telescope*): If you look through this telescope, which can see through roofs and walls, you will notice a gap in the sky that used to house the Royal Constellation. In the annals of the universe, his Majesty has been entered as deceased.

GUARD: The King is dead! Long live the King!

MARGUERITE (*to the* GUARD): Idiot! Can't you keep quiet!

DOCTOR: He is, indeed, far more dead than alive.

KING: I'm not. I don't want to die. Please don't let me die. Be kind to me, all of you – don't let me die! I don't want to.

[MARIE (*helplessly*): How can I give him the strength to resist? I'm weakening, myself. He doesn't believe *me* any more, he only believes *them*. (*To the* KING:) But don't give up hope, there's still hope!

MARGUERITE (*to* MARIE): Don't confuse him! You'll only make things worse for him now.]

KING: I don't want to, I don't want to.

DOCTOR: The crisis I was expecting. It's perfectly normal. The first breach in his defences, already.

MARGUERITE (*to* MARIE): The crisis will pass.

GUARD (*announcing*): The King is passing!

DOCTOR: We shall miss your Majesty greatly! And we shall say so publicly. That's a promise.

KING: I don't want to die.

MARIE: Oh dear, look! His hair has suddenly gone white. (*The* KING*'s hair has indeed turned white.*) The wrinkles are spreading across his forehead, over his face. All at once he looks fourteen centuries older.

MARGUERITE: Antiquated. And so suddenly too!

KING: Kings ought to be immortal.

MARGUERITE: They are. Provisionally.

KING: They promised me *I* could choose the time when I would die.

MARGUERITE: That's because they thought you'd have chosen long ago. But you acquired a taste for authority. Now you must be *made* to choose. You got stuck in the mud of life. You felt warm and cosy. (*Sharply:*) Now you're going to freeze.

KING: I've been trapped. I should have been warned, I've been trapped.

MARGUERITE: You were often warned.

KING: You warned me too soon. I won't die... I don't want to. Someone must save me, as I can't save myself.

MARGUERITE: [It's your fault if you've been taken unawares; you ought to have been prepared. You never had the time.] You'd been condemned, and you should have thought about that the very first day, and then day after day, five minutes every day. It wasn't much to give up. Five minutes every day. Then ten minutes, a quarter, half an hour. That's the way to train yourself.

KING: I *did* think about it.

MARGUERITE: Not seriously, not profoundly – never with all your heart and soul.

MARIE: He was alive.

MARGUERITE: Too much alive. (*To the* KING:) You ought to have had this thought permanently at the back of your mind.

DOCTOR: He never looked ahead; he's always lived from day to day, like most people.

MARGUERITE: You kept on putting it off. At twenty you said you'd wait till your fortieth year before you went into training. At forty—

KING: I was in such good health – I was so young!

MARGUERITE: At forty: why not wait till you were fifty? At fifty—

KING: I was full of life, wonderfully full of life!

MARGUERITE: At fifty, you wanted first to reach your sixties. And so you went on, from sixty to ninety to a hundred and twenty-five to two hundred, until you were four hundred years old. Instead of putting things off for ten years at a time, you put them off for fifty. Then you postponed them from century to century.

KING: But I was just about to start. Oh! If I could have a whole century before me, perhaps then I'd have time!

DOCTOR: All you have now is one hour, Sire. You must do it all in an hour.

MARIE: He'll never have enough time, it's impossible. He must be given more.

MARGUERITE: That *is* impossible. But an hour gives him all the time he needs.

DOCTOR: A well-spent hour's better than whole centuries of neglect and failure. Five minutes are enough – ten fully conscious seconds. We're giving him an hour! Sixty minutes, three thousand and six hundred seconds. He's in luck.

MARGUERITE: He's lingered too long by the wayside.

[MARIE: We've been ruling the kingdom. *He's* been working.

GUARD: The Labours of Hercules.

MARGUERITE: Pottering about.]

(*Enter* JULIETTE.)

JULIETTE: Poor Majesty; my poor master's been playing truant.

KING: I'm like a schoolboy who hasn't done his homework and sits for an exam without swotting up on the papers...

MARGUERITE: Don't let that worry you!

KING: …like an actor on the first night who doesn't know his lines and who dries up, up, up. Like an orator pushed onto a platform who's forgotten his speech and has no idea who he's meant to be addressing. I don't know this audience, and I don't want to. I've nothing to say to them. What a state I'm in!

GUARD (*announcing*): The King has just alluded to his State.

MARGUERITE: A state of ignorance.

JULIETTE: He'd like to go on playing truant for centuries to come.

KING: I'd like to resit the exam.

MARGUERITE: You'll take it now. No resits are allowed.

DOCTOR: There's nothing you can do, your Majesty. Neither can we. We only practise medical science; we can't perform miracles.

KING: Do the people know the news? Have you warned them? I want everyone to know that the King is going to die. (*He makes a rush to open the window, with a great effort, for his limp is getting worse.*) My good people, I am going to die! Hear me! Your King is going to die!

MARGUERITE (*to the* DOCTOR): They mustn't hear him. Stop him shouting!

KING: Hands off the King! I want everyone to know I'm going to die. (*He shouts.*)

DOCTOR: Scandalous!

KING: People, I've got to die!

MARGUERITE: What was once a king is now a pig that's being slaughtered.

MARIE: He's just a king. He's just a man.

DOCTOR: Your Majesty, think of the death of Louis XIV, of Philip II, or of the Emperor Charles V, who slept in his own coffin for twenty years. It is your Majesty's duty to die with dignity.*

KING: Die with dignity? (*At the window.*) Help! Your King is going to die.

MARIE: Poor dear King, my poor little King!

JULIETTE: Shouting won't help. (*A feeble echo can be heard in the distance:* "*The* KING *is going to die.*")

KING: Hear that?

MARIE: I hear, I can hear.

KING: They've answered me. Perhaps they're going to save me.

JULIETTE: There's no one there. (*The echo can be heard: "Help!"*)

DOCTOR: It's only the echo, a bit late in answering.

MARGUERITE: Late as usual, like everything else in this country. Nothing functions properly.

KING (*leaving the window*): It's impossible. (*Going back to the window.*) I'm frightened. It's impossible.

MARGUERITE: He imagines no one's ever died before.

MARIE: No one *has* died before.

MARGUERITE: It's all very painful.

JULIETTE: He's crying! Just like anyone else!

MARGUERITE: What a commonplace reaction! I hoped terror would have produced some fine ringing phrases. (*To the* DOCTOR:) I must put you in charge of the chronicles. We'll attribute to him the fine words spoken by others. We'll invent some new ones, if need be.

DOCTOR: We'll credit him with some edifying maxims. (*To* MARGUERITE:) We'll watch over his legend. (*To the* KING:) We'll watch over your legend, your Majesty.

KING (*at the window*): People, help!... Help, people!

MARGUERITE: Haven't you had enough, your Majesty? It's a waste of effort.

KING (*at the window*): Who will give me his life? Who will give his life for the King's? His life for the good old King's, his life for the poor old King's?

MARGUERITE: It's indecent!

MARIE: Let him try everything once.

JULIETTE: As there's no one left in the country to hear, why not? (*She goes out.*)

[MARGUERITE: The spies are still with us.

DOCTOR: Enemy ears listening at the borders.

MARGUERITE: He'll disgrace us all, panicking like this.]

DOCTOR: The echo's stopped answering. His voice doesn't carry any more. He can shout as much as he likes. It won't even reach as far as the garden wall.

MARGUERITE (*while the* KING *is wailing*): He's moaning.

DOCTOR: We're the only ones who can hear him now. He can't even hear himself. (*The* KING *turns round and takes a few steps towards the centre of the stage.*)

KING: I'm cold; I'm frightened; I'm crying.

MARIE: His legs are all stiff.

DOCTOR: He's riddled with rheumatism. (*To* MARGUERITE:) An injection to quieten him?

(JULIETTE *appears with an invalid chair on wheels, which has a crown and royal emblems on the back.*)

KING: I won't have an injection.

MARIE: No injection.

KING: I know what they mean! I've had injections given to other people before! (*To* JULIETTE:) I never told you to bring that chair. I'm going for a walk; I want to take the air. (JULIETTE *leaves the chair in a corner of the stage on the left and goes out.*)

MARGUERITE: Sit down in that chair or you'll fall. (*The* KING *is, in fact, staggering.*)

KING: I won't give in! I intend to stay on my feet.

(JULIETTE *returns with a blanket.*)

JULIETTE: You'd feel much better, Sire, much more comfortable, with a blanket over your knees and a hot-water bottle. (*She goes out.*)

KING: No, I want to stay on my feet – I want to scream. I want to scream. (*He screams.*)

GUARD (*announcing*): His Majesty is screaming!

DOCTOR (*to* MARGUERITE): He won't scream for long. I know the symptoms. He'll get tired. He'll stop, and then he'll listen to us.

(JULIETTE *comes in, bringing more warm clothing and a hot-water bottle.*)

KING (*to* JULIETTE): I won't have them!

MARGUERITE: Sit down now, sit down.

KING: I refuse! (*He tries to climb the steps of the throne and fails. He goes and sits down, all the same, collapsing on the* QUEEN'*s throne to the right.*) I can't help it; I nearly fell over.

(JULIETTE, *after following the* KING *with the objects mentioned above, goes and puts them on the invalid chair.*)

MARGUERITE (*to* JULIETTE): Take his sceptre; it's too heavy for him.

KING (*to* JULIETTE, *who is returning to him with a night cap*): I won't wear *that!*

JULIETTE: It's a sort of crown, but not so heavy.

KING: Let me keep my sceptre!

MARGUERITE: You've no longer the strength to hold it.

DOCTOR: It's no good trying to lean on it now. We'll carry you. We'll wheel you along in the chair.

KING: I want to keep it.

MARIE (*to* JULIETTE): Leave him his sceptre! He wants it. (JULIETTE *looks to* MARGUERITE *for her instructions.*)

MARGUERITE: After all, I don't see why not. (JULIETTE *gives the sceptre back to the* KING.)

KING: Perhaps it's not true. Tell me it's not true. Perhaps it's a nightmare. (*The others are silent.*) Perhaps there's a ten-to-one chance – one chance in a thousand. (*The others are silent. The* KING *is sobbing.*) I often used to win the sweepstake!

DOCTOR: Your Majesty!

KING: I can't listen to you any more, I'm too frightened. (*He is sobbing and moaning.*)

MARGUERITE: You must listen, Sire.

KING: I *won't* hear what you're saying. Your words frighten me. I won't hear any more talk. (*To* MARIE, *who is trying to approach him.*) Don't you come any nearer, either! You frighten me with your pity. (*He moans again.*)

[MARIE: He's like a small child. He's a little boy again.

MARGUERITE: An ugly little boy, with a beard and wrinkles. You're too lenient with him!

255

JULIETTE (*to* MARGUERITE): You don't try to put yourself in his place.]

KING: No, speak to me! I didn't mean it, speak to me! Stand by me, hold me! Help me up! No, I want to run away. (*He rises painfully to his feet and goes to sit down on the other small throne on the left.*)

JULIETTE: His legs can hardly carry him.

KING: It hurts to move my arms, too. Does that mean it's starting? No. Why was I born if it wasn't for ever? Damn my parents! What a joke, what a farce! I came into the world five minutes ago. I got married three minutes ago.

MARGUERITE: Two hundred and eighty-three years.

KING: I came to the throne two and a half minutes ago.

MARGUERITE: Two hundred and seventy-seven years and three months.

KING: Never had time to say bye! Never had time to get to know life.

MARGUERITE: He never even tried.

KING: It was like a brisk walk through a flowery lane, a promise that's broken, a smile that fades.

MARGUERITE (*to the* DOCTOR, *continuing*): Yet he had the greatest experts to tell him all about it. Theologians, people of experience, and books he never read.

KING: I never had the time.

MARGUERITE: You used to say you had all the time in the world.

KING: I never had the time, I never had the time, I never had the time.

[JULIETTE: He's going back to that again.

MARGUERITE (*to the* DOCTOR): All the time it's the same old story.]

DOCTOR: I'd say things were looking up. However much he moans and groans, he's started to reason things out. He's complaining, protesting, expressing himself. That means he's begun to resign himself to it.

KING: I shall never resign myself to it.

DOCTOR: As he says he won't, it's a sign that he *will*. He's posing the problem of resignation, raising the question.

MARGUERITE: At last!

DOCTOR: Your Majesty, you have made war one hundred and eighty times. You have led your armies into two thousand battles. First, on a white horse with a conspicuous red-and-white plume, and you never knew fear. Then, when you modernized the army, you would stand on top of a tank, or on the wing of a fighter plane, leading the formation.

MARIE: He was a hero.

DOCTOR: You have come near death a thousand times.

KING: I only came *near* it. I could tell it wasn't meant for me.

MARIE: You were a hero, do you hear? Remember that.

MARGUERITE: Aided and abetted by this doctor here, the Executioner, you ordered the assassination...

KING: Execution, not assassination.

DOCTOR (*to* MARGUERITE): Execution, your Majesty, not assassination. I was only obeying orders. I was a mere instrument – just an executor, not an executioner. It was all euthanasia to me. Anyhow, I'm sorry. Please forgive me.

MARGUERITE (*to the* KING): I tell you, you had my parents butchered, your own brothers, your rivals, our cousins and great-grand cousins, and all their families, friends and cattle. You massacred the lot and scorched all their lands.

DOCTOR: His Majesty used to say they were going to die one day, anyway.

KING: That was for reasons of State.

MARGUERITE: You're dying too because of your state.

KING: But I *am* the State.

JULIETTE: And what a state the poor man's in!

MARIE: He was the law – above the law.

[KING: I'm not the law any more.

DOCTOR: He admits it. Better and better.

MARGUERITE: That makes things easier.]

KING (*groaning*): I'm not above the law any more – not above the law any more.

GUARD (*announcing*): The King is no more above the law.

JULIETTE: The poor old boy's no more above the law. He's just like us, and not unlike my granddad!

MARIE: Poor little chap, poor child!

KING: Child! A child? Then I can make a fresh start! I want to start again. (*To* MARIE:) I want to be a baby, and you can be my mother. Then they won't come for me. I still don't know my reading, writing and arithmetic. [I want to go back to school and be with all my playmates.] What do two and two make?

JULIETTE: Two and two make four.

MARGUERITE (*to the* KING): You knew that already.

KING: She was only prompting me... Oh dear, it's no good trying to cheat! Oh dear, oh dear! There are so many people being born at this moment – numberless babies all over the world.

MARGUERITE: Not in *our* country.

DOCTOR: The birth rate's down to zero.

JULIETTE: Not a lettuce, not a grass that grows. Utter sterility, because of you!

MARIE: I won't have you blaming him!

JULIETTE: Perhaps everything will grow again.

MARGUERITE: When he's accepted the inevitable. When he's gone.

KING: When I've gone, when I've gone. They'll laugh and stuff themselves silly and dance on my tomb. As if I'd never existed. Oh, please make them all remember me! Make them weep and despair and perpetuate my memory in all their history books. Make everyone learn my life by heart. Make them all live it again. Let the schoolchildren and the scholars study nothing else but me, my kingdom and my exploits. Let them burn all the other books, destroy all the statues and set mine up in all the public squares. My portrait in every ministry, my photograph in every office of every town hall, including Rates and Taxes, and in *all* the hospitals. Let every car and pushcart, flying ship and steamplane be named after me. Make them forget all other captains and kings, poets, tenors and philosophers, and fill every conscious mind with memories of me. Let them learn to read by spelling out my name: B, E, BE for Bérenger. Let my likeness be on all the icons, me on the millions of crosses in all our churches. Make them say mass for me and let *me* be the Host. Let all the windows light up in the shape and colour of my eyes. And the rivers trace my profile on the plains! Let them cry my name throughout eternity, and beg me and implore me.

MARIE: Perhaps you'll come back again?

KING: Perhaps I will come back. Let them preserve my body in some palace, on a throne, and let them bring me food. Let musicians play for me and virgins grovel at my ice-cold feet.

(*The* KING *has risen in order to make this speech.*)

JULIETTE (*to* MARGUERITE): He's raving, Ma'am.

GUARD (*announcing*): His Majesty the King is delirious.

MARGUERITE: Not yet. There's too much sense in what he says. Too much, and not enough.

DOCTOR (*to the* KING): If such be your will, your Majesty, we will embalm your body and preserve it. As long as we can.

KING: Horror! I don't want to be embalmed. I want nothing to do with corpses. I don't want to be burnt. I don't want to be buried, I don't want to be thrown to the wild beasts or the vultures. I want to feel arms around me, warm arms, cool arms, soft arms, strong arms.

JULIETTE: He's not too sure what he *does* want.

MARGUERITE: We'll make his mind up for him. (*To* MARIE:) Now don't faint! (JULIETTE *is weeping.*) And there's another one! They're always the same!

KING: If I *am* remembered, I wonder for how long? Let them remember me until the end of time. And beyond the end of time, in twenty thousand years, in two hundred and fifty-five thousand million years, there'll be no one left to think of anyone then. They'll forget before that. Selfish, the lot of them. They only think of their own little lives, of their own skins. Not of mine. If the whole earth's going to wear out or melt away, it will. If every universe is going to explode, explode it will. It's all the same, whether it's tomorrow or in countless centuries to come. What's got to finish one day is finished now.

MARGUERITE: Everything is yesterday.

JULIETTE: Even "today" will be "yesterday".

DOCTOR: All things pass into the past.

MARIE: My darling King, there is no past, there is no future. Remember, there's only a present that goes right on to the end; everything is present. Be present, be the present!

KING: Alas! I'm only present in the past.

MARIE: No, you're not.

MARGUERITE: That's right, Bérenger, try and get things straight.

MARIE: Yes, my king, get things straight, my darling! Stop torturing yourself! "Exist" and "die" are just words, figments of our imagination. Once you realize that, nothing can touch you. [Forget our empty clichés. We can never know what it really means, "exist" or "die". Or if we think we do, our knowledge has deceived us. Stand firm; get a grip on yourself! Never lose sight of yourself again! Sweep everything else into oblivion! *Now* you exist, you *are*. Forget the rest. That's the only truth.] Just be an eternal question mark: what?... why?... how?... And remember: that you can't find the answers is an answer in itself. It's you, all the life in you, straining to break out. Dive into an endless maze of wonder and surprise – then you too will have no end, and can exist for ever. Everything is strange and undefinable. Let it dazzle and confound you! Tear your prison bars aside and batter down the walls! Escape from definitions and you will breathe again!

DOCTOR: He's choking!

MARGUERITE: Fear cramps his vision.

MARIE: Open the floodgates of joy and light to dazzle and confound you. Illuminating waves of joy will fill your veins with wonder. If you want them to.

JULIETTE: You bet he does.

MARIE (*in a tone of supplication*): I implore you to remember that morning in June we spent together by the sea, when happiness raced through you and inflamed you. You knew then what joy meant: rich, changeless and undying. If you knew it once, you can know it now. You found that fiery radiance within you. If it *was* there *once,* it is *still* there *now.* Find it again. Look for it in yourself.

KING: I don't understand.

MARIE: You don't understand any more.

MARGUERITE: He never did understand himself.

MARIE: Pull yourself together!

KING: How do I manage that? No one can or will help me. And *I* can't help myself. Oh help me, sun! Sun, chase away the shadows and hold back the night! Sun, sun, illumine every tomb, shine into every hole and corner, every nook and cranny! Creep deep inside me! Ah! Now my feet are turning cold. Come and warm me! Pierce my body, steal beneath my skin and blaze into my eyes! Restore their failing light and let me see, see see! Sun, sun, will you miss me? Good little sun, protect me! And if you're in need of some small sacrifice, then parch and wither up the world. Let every human creature die provided *I* can live for ever, even alone in a limitless desert. I'll come to terms with solitude. I'll keep alive the memory of others, and I'll miss them quite sincerely. But I can live in the void, in a vast and airy wasteland. It's better to miss one's friends than to be missed oneself. Besides, one never is. Light of our days, come and save me!

DOCTOR (*to* MARIE): This is not the light *you* meant. [This is not the timeless waste you wanted him to aim for! He didn't understand you – it's too much for his poor brain.]

MARGUERITE (*to* MARIE, *or referring to* MARIE): Love's labours lost. You're on the wrong track.

KING: Let me go on living, century after century, even with raging toothache. But I fear what must end one day has ended now.

[DOCTOR: Well, Sire, what are you waiting for?]

MARGUERITE: It's only his speeches that are never-ending! (*Indicating* MARIE *and* JULIETTE:) And these two weeping women. They only push him deeper in the mire, trap him, bind him and hold him up.

KING: No, there's not enough weeping, not enough lamentation. Not enough anguish. (*To* MARGUERITE:) Don't stop them weeping and wailing and pitying their king, their young king, old king, poor little king. *I* feel pity when I think how they'll miss me, never see me again and be left behind all alone. I'm still the one who thinks about others, about everyone. All the rest of you, be me, come inside me, come beneath my skin. I'm dying! You hear? I'm trying to tell you I'm dying, but I can't express it, unless I talk like a book and make literature of it.

[MARGUERITE: Is that what it is!

DOCTOR: It's not worth recording his words. Nothing new.

KING: They're all strangers to me. I thought they were my family. I'm frightened, I'm sinking, I'm drowning, I've gone blank, I've never existed. I'm dying.

MARGUERITE: Now that *is* literature!]

DOCTOR: And that's the way it goes on, to the bitter end. As long as we live, we turn everything into literature.

MARIE: If only it could console him!

GUARD (*announcing*): The King finds some consolation in literature!

KING: No, no. I know nothing can console me. It just wells up inside me, then drains away. Oh dear, oh dear, oh dear, oh dear, oh dear! (*Lamentations – then, without declamation, he goes on moaning gently to himself*) Help me, you countless thousands who died before me! Tell me how you managed to accept death and die. Then teach me! Let your example be a consolation to me; let me lean on you like crutches, like a brother's arms. Help me to cross the threshold you have crossed! Come back from the other side a while and help me! Assist me, you who were frightened and did not want to go! What was it like? Who held you up? Who dragged you there, who pushed you? Were you afraid to the very end? And you who were strong and courageous, who accepted death with indifference and serenity, teach me your indifference and serenity, teach me resignation!

(*The following dialogue should be spoken and acted as though it were ritual, with solemnity, almost chanted, accompanied by various movements, with the actors kneeling, holding out their arms, etc.*)

JULIETTE: You statues, you dark or shining phantoms, ancients and shades…

MARIE: Teach him serenity.

GUARD: Teach him indifference.

DOCTOR: Teach him resignation.

MARGUERITE: Make him see reason and set his mind at rest.

KING: You suicides, teach me how to feel disgust for life! Teach me lassitude! What drug must I take for that?

DOCTOR: I could prescribe euphoric pills or tranquillisers.

MARGUERITE: He'd vomit them up!

JULIETTE: You remembrances…

GUARD: You pictures of days gone by…

JULIETTE: …which no longer exist but in our memories of memories…

GUARD: Recollections of recollections…

MARGUERITE: He's got to learn how to let go and then surrender completely.

GUARD: …we invoke you.

MARIE: You morning mists and dews…

JULIETTE: You evening smoke and clouds…

MARIE: You saints, you wise and foolish virgins, help him! For *I* cannot.

JULIETTE: Help him!

KING: You who died blissfully, who looked death in the face, who remained conscious of your end…

JULIETTE: Help him!

MARIE: Help him, all of you, help him, I beg you! You who died happy, what face did you see close to yours? What smile gave you ease and made *you* smile? What were the last rays of light that brushed your face?

JULIETTE: Help him, you thousand millions of dead!

GUARD: Oh you, great Nothing, help the King!

KING: [Thousands and millions of the dead. They multiply my anguish.] I am the dying agony of them all. My death is manifold. So many worlds will flicker out in me.

MARGUERITE: Life is exile.

KING: I know, I know.

DOCTOR: In short, Majesty, you will return to your own country.

MARIE: You'll go back to where you came from when you were born. Don't be so frightened – you're sure to find something familiar there.

[KING: I like exile. I ran away from my homeland and I don't want to go back. What *was* that world like?

MARGUERITE: Try and remember.

KING: I can see nothing! I can see nothing.

MARGUERITE: Remember! Come along, think! Think carefully! Think, just think! You've never thought!

DOCTOR: He's never given it a second thought since then!]

MARIE: Other world – lost world, buried and forgotten world – rise again from the deep!

JULIETTE: Other plains, other valleys, other mountain chains...

MARIE: Remind them of your name.

[KING: No memories of that distant land.

JULIETTE: He can't remember his homeland.

DOCTOR: He's in no state to do so – he's too weak.

KING: No nostalgia, however dim or fleeting.]

MARGUERITE: Plunge into your memories, dive through the gaps in your memory into a world beyond memory. (*To the* DOCTOR:) *This* is the only world he really misses!

MARIE: Memories immemorial, appear before him! Help him!

[DOCTOR: You see, it's quite a problem to get him to take the plunge.

MARGUERITE: He'll have to do it.

GUARD: His Majesty's never been down in a diving bell. Pity he never had the training.

MARGUERITE: It's a job he'll have to learn.]

KING: When faced with death, even a little ant puts up a fight. Suddenly he's all alone, torn from his companions. In him, too, the universe flickers out. It's not natural to die, because no one ever wants to. I want to exist.

JULIETTE: That's all he knows. He wants to exist for ever.

[MARIE: It seems to him he always *has*.

264

MARGUERITE: He'll have to stop looking about him, stop clinging to pictures of the outside world. He must shut himself up and lock himself in. (*To the* KING:) Not another word – be quiet, stay inside! Stop looking around and it'll do you good!
KING: Not the sort of good *I* want.
DOCTOR (*to* MARGUERITE): We haven't quite got to that stage. He still can't manage that. Your Majesty should encourage him, of course, but don't push him too far – not yet.
MARGUERITE: It won't be easy, but we can be patient and wait.
DOCTOR: We're sure of the final result.]
KING: Doctor, Doctor, am I in the throes of death already?... No, you've made a mistake... not yet... not yet. (*A kind of sigh of relief.*) It hasn't started yet. I exist, I'm still here. I can see. There are walls and furniture here, there's air to breathe, I can watch people watching me and catch their voices, I'm alive, I can think, I can see, I can hear, I can still see and hear. A fanfare! (*A sort of fanfare can be heard far away in the distance. He starts walking.*)
GUARD: The King is walking! Long live the King!

(*The* KING *falls down.*)

JULIETTE: He's down.
GUARD: The King is down! The King is dying!

(*The* KING *gets up.*)

MARIE: He's up again!
GUARD: The King is up! Long live the King!
MARIE: He's up again!
KING: Long live the King! (*The* KING *falls down.*) The King is dead!
MARIE: He's up again! (*The* KING *does indeed get up again.*) He's still alive!
GUARD: Long live the King!

(*The* KING *makes for his throne.*)

JULIETTE: He wants to sit on his throne.

MARIE: The King still reigns! The King still reigns!

DOCTOR: And now for the delirium.

MARIE (to the KING, *who is trying to totter up the steps of his throne*): Don't let go, hang on! (*To* JULIETTE, *who is trying to help the* KING:) Leave him alone! He can do it alone!

(*The* KING *fails to climb the steps of the throne.*)

[KING: And yet I've still got my legs!

MARIE: Try again!]

MARGUERITE: We've got thirty-two minutes and thirty seconds left.

KING: I can still stand up.

DOCTOR (*to* MARGUERITE): It's the last convulsion but one.

(*The* KING *falls into the invalid chair, which* JULIETTE *has just brought forward. They cover him up and give him a hot-water bottle, while he is still saying:*)

KING: I can still stand up.

(*The hot-water bottle, the blankets, etc, are gradually brought into the following scene by* JULIETTE.)

MARIE: You're out of breath; you're tired. Have a rest and you can stand up again later.

MARGUERITE (*to* MARIE): Don't lie! That doesn't help him!

KING (*in his chair*): I used to like Mozart.

MARGUERITE: You'll forget all about it.

KING (*to* JULIETTE): Did you mend my trousers? Or do you think it's not worth the trouble now? There was a hole in my red cloak. Have you patched it? Have you sewn those buttons onto my pyjamas? Have you had my shoes re-soled?

JULIETTE: I never gave it another thought.

KING: You never gave it another thought! What *do* you think about? Talk to me! What does your husband do?

(JULIETTE *has now put on, or is putting on, her nurse's cap and white apron.*)

JULIETTE: I'm a widow.

KING: What do you think about when you do the housework?

JULIETTE: Nothing, your Majesty.

KING: Where do you come from? What's your family?

MARGUERITE (*to the* KING): You never took any interest before.

MARIE: He's never had time to ask her.

MARGUERITE (*to the* KING): And you're not really interested now.

DOCTOR: He wants more time.

KING (*to* JULIETTE): Tell me how you live. What sort of life do you have?

JULIETTE: A bad life, Sire.

KING: Life can never be bad. It's a contradiction in terms.

JULIETTE: Life's not very beautiful.

KING: Life is life.

JULIETTE: When I get up in the winter, it's still dark. And I'm cold as ice.

KING: So am I. But it's not the same cold. You don't like feeling cold?

JULIETTE: When I get up in the summer, it's only just beginning to get light. A pale sort of light.

KING (*rapturously*): A *pale* light! There are all sorts of light: blue and pink and white and green – and *pale*!

JULIETTE: I do all the palace laundry in the washhouse. It hurts my hands and cracks my skin.

KING (*rapturously*): And it hurts. One can feel one's skin. Haven't they bought you a washing machine yet? Marguerite! A palace, and no washing machine!

MARGUERITE: We had to pawn it to raise a State loan.

JULIETTE: I empty the chamber pots. I make the beds.

KING: She makes the beds! Where we lie down and go to sleep and then wake up again. Did you ever realize that every day you woke up? To wake up every day... Every morning one comes into the world.

JULIETTE: I polish the parquet floors and sweep, sweep, sweep! There's no end to it.

KING (*rapturously*): There's no end to it!

JULIETTE: It gives me backache.

KING: That's right. She has a back! We've all got backs!

JULIETTE: Pains in the kidneys.

KING: And kidneys too!

JULIETTE: And now we've no gardeners left, I dig and rake and sow.

KING: And then things grow!

JULIETTE: I get quite worn out, exhausted!

KING: You ought to have told us.

JULIETTE: I *did* tell you.

KING: That's true. Such a lot has escaped my notice. [I never got to know everything. I never went everywhere I could. My life could have been so full.]

JULIETTE: There's no window in my room.

KING (*rapturously again*): No window! You go out in search of light. You find it and then you smile. To go out, you turn the key in the door, open it, then close it again and turn the key to lock it. Where do you live?

JULIETTE: In the attic.

KING: To come down in the morning, you take the stairs, you go down one step, then another, down a step, down a step, down a step. And when you get dressed, you put on first your stockings, then your shoes.

JULIETTE: Down at heel!

KING: And a dress. It's amazing...

JULIETTE: A cheap one. A tatty old thing!

KING: You don't know what you're saying! It's beautiful, a tatty old dress!

JULIETTE: Once I had an abscess in the mouth and they pulled out one of my teeth!

KING: You're in terrible pain. But it starts to ease off and then disappears. It's a tremendous relief; it makes you feel wonderfully happy.

JULIETTE: I feel tired, tired, tired!

KING: So you take a rest. That's good.

JULIETTE: Not enough time off for that!

KING: You can still hope you'll have some, one day... You go out with a basket and do the shopping. You say good day to the grocer.

JULIETTE: He's enormous! Hideously fat! So ugly he frightens the birds and the cats away.

KING: Marvellous! You take out your purse, you pay and get your change. The market's a medley of green lettuce, red cherries, golden grapes and purple aubergines... all the colours of the rainbow!... It's extraordinary! Incredible! Like a fairy tale!

JULIETTE: And then I go home... the same way I came.

KING: You take the same road twice a day! With the sky above you! You can gaze at it twice a day. And you breathe the air. You never realize you're breathing. You must think about it! Remember! I'm sure it never crosses your mind. It's a miracle!

JULIETTE: And then... then I do the washing-up from the day before. Plates smothered in sticky fat! And then I have the cooking to do.

KING: Sublime!

JULIETTE: You're wrong. It's a bore. It makes me sick!

KING: It's a bore! Some people one can *never* understand! It's wonderful to feel bored, and *not* to feel bored, too, to lose one's temper, and *not* to lose one's temper, to be *dis*contented and to be content. To practise resignation and to insist on your rights. You get excited, you talk and people talk to you; you touch and they touch you. All this is magical, like some endless celebration.

JULIETTE: You're right there. There's no end to it! After that, I still have to wait at table.

KING (*still rapturously*): You wait at table! You wait at table! What do you serve at table?

JULIETTE: The meal I've just prepared.

KING: What, for example?

JULIETTE: I don't know, the main dish. Stew!

KING: Stew! Stew! (*Dreamily.*)

JULIETTE: It's a meal in itself.

KING: I used to be so fond of stew, with vegetables and potatoes, cabbage and carrots all mixed up with butter, crushed with a fork and mashed together.

JULIETTE: We could bring him some.

KING: Send for some stew!

MARGUERITE: No.

JULIETTE: But if he likes it...

DOCTOR: Bad for his health. He's on a diet.

KING: I want some stew.

DOCTOR: It's not what the Doctor orders for a dying man.

MARIE: But if it's his last wish...

MARGUERITE: He must detach himself.

KING: Gravy... hot potatoes... and carrots under my nose...

JULIETTE: He's still making jokes.

KING (*wearily*): Till now, I'd never noticed how beautiful carrots were. (*To* JULIETTE:) Quick! Go and kill the two spiders in my bedroom! I don't want them to survive me. No, don't kill them! Perhaps in *them* there's something still of *me*... it's dead, that stew... vanished from the universe. There never was such a thing as stew.

GUARD (*announcing*): Stew has been banished from the length and breadth of the land.

MARGUERITE: At last, something achieved! At least he's given *that* up! Of all the things we crave, the minor ones go first. Now we can begin. Gently, as you remove a dressing from an open sore, first lifting the corners, because they're farthest from the centre of the wound. (*Approaching the* KING.) Juliette, wipe the sweat from his face, he's dripping wet. (*To* MARIE:) No, not you!

DOCTOR (*to* MARGUERITE): It's panic oozing through his pores. (*He examines the sick man, while* MARIE *might kneel for a moment, covering her face with her hands.*) You see, his temperature's gone down, though there's not much sign of gooseflesh. His hair was standing on end before. Now it's resting and lying flat. He's not used to being so terrified yet, oh no! But now he can see the fear inside him; that's why he's dared to close his eyes. He'll open them again. He still looks tense, but see how the wrinkles of old age are settling on his face. Already he's letting things take their course. He'll still have a few setbacks. It's not as quick as all that. But he won't have the wind-up any more. That would have been too degrading. He'll still be subject to fright, but pure fright, without abdominal complications. We can't hope his death will be an example to others. But it will be fairly respectable. His *death* will kill him now, and not his fear. We'll have to help him all the same, your Majesty; he'll need a lot of help, till the very last second; till he's drawn his very last breath.

MARGUERITE: I'll help him. I'll drive it out of him. I'll cut him loose. I'll untie every knot and ravel out the tangled skein. I'll separate the wheat from the tenacious tares that cling to him and bind him.

[DOCTOR: It won't be easy.

MARGUERITE: Where on earth did he pick up all these weeds, these trailing creepers?

DOCTOR: They've grown up slowly, through the years.

MARGUERITE: You've settled down nicely now, your Majesty. Don't you feel more peaceful?

MARIE (*standing up, to the* KING): Until Death comes, you are still *here*. When Death is here, *you* will have gone. You won't meet her or see her.

MARGUERITE: The lies of life, those old fallacies! We've heard them all before. Death has always been here, present in the seed since the very first day. She is the shoot that grows, the flower that blows, the only fruit we know.

MARIE (*to* MARGUERITE): That's a basic truth too, and we've heard *that* before!

MARGUERITE: It's a basic truth. And the ultimate truth, isn't it, Doctor?

DOCTOR: What you both say is true. It depends on the point of view.

MARIE (*to the* KING): You used to believe me, once.

KING: I'm dying.

DOCTOR: He's changed *his* point of view. He's shifted his position.

MARIE: If you've to look at it from both sides, look at it from my side too.

KING: I'm dying. I can't. I'm dying.

MARIE: Oh! My power over him is going.]

MARGUERITE (*to* MARIE): Neither your charm nor your charms can bewitch the King any more.

GUARD (*announcing*): The Charm of Queen Marie no longer casts its spell over the King.

MARIE (*to the* KING): You used to love me; you love me still, as I have always loved you.

[MARGUERITE: She thinks of no one but herself.

JULIETTE: That's human nature.

MARIE: I've always loved you; I love you still.

KING: I don't know why, but that doesn't seem to help.

DOCTOR: Love is mad.

MARIE (*to the* KING): Love *is* mad. And if you're mad with love, if you love blindly, completely, death will steal away. If you love me, if you love everything, love will consume your fear. Love lifts you up, you let yourself go and fear lets go of you. The whole universe is one, everything lives again and the cup that was drained is full.

KING: I'm full, all right, but full of holes. I'm a honeycomb of cavities that are widening, deepening into bottomless pits. It makes me dizzy to look down the gaping gulfs inside me. I'm coming to an end.]

MARIE: There is no end. Others will take your place and gaze at the sky for *you*.

KING: I'm dying.

MARIE: Become these other beings, and live in them. There's always something here... something...

KING: What's that?

MARIE: Something that exists. *That* never perishes.

KING: And yet there's still... there's still... there's still so little left.

MARIE: The younger generation's expanding the universe.

KING: I'm dying.

MARIE: Conquering new constellations.

KING: I'm dying.

MARIE: Boldly battering at the gates of heaven.

KING: They can knock them flat for all I care!

DOCTOR: They've also started making elixirs of immortality.

KING (*to the* DOCTOR): Incompetent fool! Why didn't *you* discover them before?

MARIE: New suns are about to appear.

KING: It makes me wild!

MARIE: Brand new stars. Virgin stars.

KING: They'll fade away. Anyhow, I don't care!

GUARD (*announcing*): Constellations old or new no longer interest His Majesty, King Bérenger!

[MARIE: A new science is coming into being.

KING: *I'm* dying.

MARIE: A new wisdom's taking the place of the old, a stupidity and ignorance greater than before, different, of course, but still the same. Let that console you and rejoice your heart.

KING: I'm frightened, I'm dying.

MARIE: You laid the foundations for all this.

KING: I didn't do it on purpose.]

MARIE: You were a pioneer, a guide, a harbinger of all these new developments. You count. And you will be counted.

KING: And I'll never be the accountant. I'm dying.

MARIE: Everything that has been will be; everything that will be is; everything that will be has been. You are inscribed for ever in the Annals of the Universe.

KING: Who'll look up those old archives? I die, so let everything die! No, let everything stay as it is! No, let everything die, if my death won't resound through worlds without end! Let everything die! No, let everything remain!

GUARD: His Majesty the King wants the remains to remain.

KING: No, let it all die!

GUARD: His Majesty the King wants it all to die!

KING: Let it all die with me! No, let it all survive me! No, let it all stay, let it all die, stay, die!

MARGUERITE: He doesn't know *what* he wants.

JULIETTE: I don't think he knows what he wants *any more*.

DOCTOR: He no longer *knows* what he wants. His brain's degenerating, he's senile, gaga.

GUARD (*announcing*): His Majesty has gone ga—

MARGUERITE (*to the* GUARD, *interrupting him*): Idiot, be quiet! We want no more doctors' bulletins given to the press. [People would only laugh – those who are still here to laugh and to listen. The rest *of* the world can pick up your words by radio, and they're quite jubilant.]

GUARD (*announcing*): Doctors' bulletins are suspended, by order of Her Majesty Queen Marguerite.

MARIE (*to the* KING): My King, my little King...

KING: When I had nightmares and cried in my sleep, you would wake me up, kiss me and smooth away my fears.

MARGUERITE: She can't do that now!

KING: When I had sleepless nights and wandered out of my room, you would wake up too. In your pink-flowered dressing gown, you'd come and find me in the throne room, take me by the hand and lead me back to bed.

JULIETTE: It was just the same with my husband.

KING: I used to share my colds with you, and the flu.

MARGUERITE: You won't catch colds now!

KING: In the morning we used to open our eyes at the very same moment. I shall close them alone, or not have *you* beside me. We used to think the same things at the same time. And you'd finish a sentence I'd just started in my head. I'd call you to rub my back when I was in the bath. And you'd choose my ties for me. Though I didn't always like them. We used to fight about that. No one knew, and no one ever will.

[DOCTOR: A storm in a teacup.

MARGUERITE: How suburban! We'll have to draw a veil over *that*!

KING (*to* MARIE): You'd hate my hair to be untidy. You used to comb it for me.

JULIETTE: It's so romantic, all this.

MARGUERITE: Your hair won't be untidy now!

JULIETTE: But it's really very sad.

KING: Then you'd dust my crown and polish the pearls to make them shine.]

MARIE (*to the* KING): Do you love me? Do you love me? I've always loved *you*. Do you still love *me*? He *does* still love me. Do you love me today? Do you love me this minute? Here I am... Here... I'm here... Look! Look!... Take a good look!... Well, *look* at me!

KING: I've always loved myself; at least I can still love myself, feel myself, see myself, contemplate myself.

[MARGUERITE (*to* MARIE): That's enough! (*To the* KING:) You must stop looking back. That's a piece of advice. Or hurry and get it over. Soon this will be an order. (*To* MARIE:) I've told you before. From now on you can't do him anything but harm.]

DOCTOR (*looking at his watch*): He's running late... he's turned back in his tracks.

MARGUERITE: It's not serious. Don't worry, Doctor, Executioner. His little tricks, these kicks against the pricks... it was all to be expected, all part of the programme.

DOCTOR: If this was a good old heart attack, we wouldn't have had so much trouble...

MARGUERITE: Heart attacks are reserved for businessmen.

DOCTOR: ...or even double pneumonia!

MARGUERITE: That's for the poor, not for kings.

KING: I could decide not to die.

JULIETTE: You see, he's not cured yet.

KING: What if I decided to stop wanting things, to just stop wanting, and decided not to decide!

[MARGUERITE: We could decide for you.

GUARD (*announcing*): The Queen and the Doctor no longer owe the King obedience.

DOCTOR: We owe him *dis*obedience.

KING: Who except the King can release you from your duty to the King?

MARGUERITE: Force can do that – the force of events. First principles dictate their own commandments.

DOCTOR (*to* MARGUERITE): First principles and commandments are now invested in us.]

GUARD (*while* JULIETTE *starts pushing the* KING *round the stage in his invalid chair*): It was His Majesty, my Commander-in-Chief, who set the Thames on fire. It was he who invented gunpowder and stole fire from the gods. He nearly blew the whole place up. But he caught the pieces and tied them together again with string. I helped him, but it wasn't so easy. *He* wasn't so easy either. He was the one who fitted up the first forges on earth. He discovered the way to make steel. He used to work eighteen hours a day. And he made *us* work even harder. He was our chief engineer. As an engineer he made the first balloon, and then the Zeppelin. And finally, with his own hands, he built the first aeroplane. At first it wasn't a success. The first test pilots, Icarus and the rest, all fell into the sea. Till eventually he piloted the plane himself. I was his mechanic. Long before that, when he was only a little prince, he'd invented the wheelbarrow. I used to play with him. Then rails and railways and automobiles. He drew up the plans for the Eiffel Tower, not to mention his designs for the sickle and the plough, the harvesters and the tractors.

KING: Tractors! Good Heavens, yes! I'd forgotten.

GUARD: He extinguished volcanoes and caused new ones to erupt. He built Rome, New York, Moscow and Geneva. He *founded* Paris. He created revolutions, counter-revolutions, religion, reform and counter-reform.

JULIETTE: You wouldn't think so to look at him.

KING: What's an automobile?

JULIETTE (*still pushing him in his wheelchair*): It runs along by itself.

GUARD: He wrote tragedies and comedies under the name of Shakespeare.

JULIETTE: Oh, so that's who Shakespeare was!

DOCTOR (*to the* GUARD): You ought to have told us before! Think how long we've been racking our brains to find out!

GUARD: It was a secret. He wouldn't let me. He invented the telephone and the telegraph, and fixed them up himself. He did everything with his own hands.

JULIETTE: He was never any good with his hands! He used to call the plumber at the slightest sign of a leak!

GUARD: My Commander-in-Chief was a very handy man!

MARGUERITE: Now he can't even get his shoes on. Or off!

GUARD: Not so long ago he managed to split the atom.

JULIETTE: Now he can't even turn the light off. Or on!

GUARD: Majesty, Commander-in-Chief, Master, Managing Director...

MARGUERITE (*to the* GUARD): We know all about his earlier exploits. We don't need an inventory.

(*The* GUARD *returns to his post.*)

KING (*while he is being pushed around*): What's a horse?... Those are windows, those are walls and this is the floor.

KING: I've done such things! What do they say I did? I don't remember what I did. I forget, I forget. (*While he is still being pushed around*:) And that's a throne.

MARIE: Do you remember me? I'm here, I'm here.

KING: I'm here. I exist.

JULIETTE: He doesn't even remember what a horse is.

KING: I remember a little ginger cat.

MARIE: He remembers a cat.

KING: I used to have a little ginger cat. We called him our Wandering Jew. I had found him in a field, stolen from his mother, a real wild cat. He was two weeks old, or a little more, but he knew how to scratch and bite. He was quite fierce. I fed him and stroked him and took him home and he grew into the gentlest of cats. Once, Madame, he crept into the coat sleeve of a lady visitor. He was the politest of creatures, a natural politeness, like a prince. When we came home in the middle of the night he used to come and greet

277

us with his eyes full of sleep. Then he'd stumble off back to his box. In the morning he'd wake us up to crawl into our bed. [One day we'd shut the bedroom door. He tried so hard to open it, shoving his little behind against it. He got so angry and made a terrible row; he sulked for a week.] He was scared stiff of the vacuum cleaner. A bit of a coward, really, that cat; defenceless, a poet cat. We bought him a clockwork mouse. He started by sniffing it anxiously. When we wound it up and the mouse began to move, he spat at it, then took to his heels and crouched under the wardrobe. [When he'd grown up, his lady friends would pace round the house, courting and calling him. It used to frighten him silly, and he wouldn't move.] We tried to introduce him to the outside world. We put him down on the pavement near the window. He was terrified, afraid of the pigeons that hopped all round him. There he was, pressed against the wall, miaowing and crying to me in desperation. To him, other animals and cats were strange creatures he mistrusted or enemies he feared. He only felt at home with us. [We were his family. He was not afraid of men. He'd jump on their shoulders without warning, and lick their hair.] He thought *we* were cats and cats were something else. And yet, one fine day he must have felt the urge to go out on his own. The neighbour's big dog killed him. And there he was, like a toy cat, a twitching marionette with one eye gone and a paw torn off – yes, like a doll destroyed by a sadistic child.

[MARIE (*to* MARGUERITE): You shouldn't have left the door open; I warned you.

MARGUERITE: I hated that sentimental, timorous beast.

KING: How I missed him! He was good and beautiful and wise, all the virtues. He loved me, he loved me. My poor little cat, my one and only cat.] (*The lines about the cat should be spoken with as little emotion as possible: to say them, the* KING *should rather give an impression of being dazed, in a kind of dreamy stupor, except perhaps in this very last speech, which expresses a certain sorrow.*)

[DOCTOR: I tell you, he's running late.

MARGUERITE: I'm watching it. The timetable allows for hold-ups. Some delays were expected, you know.]

KING: I used to dream about him... that he was lying in the grate, on the glowing embers, and Marie was surprised he didn't burn. I told her, "Cats don't burn – they're fireproof." He came miaowing out of the fireplace in a cloud of thick smoke. But it wasn't him any more. What a transformation! It was a different cat – fat and ugly. An enormous she-cat. Like his mother, the wild cat. A bit like Marguerite. (*For a few moments* JULIETTE *leaves the* KING *in his wheelchair downstage in the centre, facing the audience.*)

JULIETTE: It's a great pity, I must say – a real shame! He was such a good king.

DOCTOR: Far from easy to please. Really quite wicked. Revengeful and cruel.

MARGUERITE: Vain.

JULIETTE: There have been worse.

MARIE: He was gentle; he was tender.

GUARD: We were rather fond of him.

DOCTOR (*to the* GUARD *and to* JULIETTE): You both complained about him, though.

JULIETTE: That's forgotten now.

[DOCTOR: Several times I had to intervene on your behalf.

MARGUERITE: He only listened to Queen Marie.

DOCTOR: He was hard and severe, and not even just.

JULIETTE: We saw him so little. And yet we *did* see him; we saw him quite often, really.

GUARD: He was strong. It's true he cut a few heads off.

JULIETTE: Not many.

GUARD: All for the public good.

DOCTOR: And the result? We're surrounded by enemies. You can hear us crumbling away. We've lost our borders already; only an ever-widening gulf cuts us off from our neighbours.

JULIETTE: It's better that way. Now they can't invade us. We're poised over a gaping chasm. Nothing but a growing void all round us.

GUARD: We're still clinging to the earth's crust.

MARGUERITE: Not for long!

MARIE: Better to perish with him!

MARGUERITE: There's nothing but the crust left. We'll soon be adrift in space.]

DOCTOR: And it's all his fault! He never cared what came after him. He never thought about his successors. After him, the deluge. Worse than the deluge – after him there's nothing! Selfish bungler!

JULIETTE: *De mortuis nihil nisi bene.** He was king of a great kingdom.

MARIE: He was the heart and centre of it.

JULIETTE: Its royal residence.

GUARD: A kingdom that stretched for thousands of miles around. You couldn't even glimpse its boundaries.

JULIETTE: Boundless in space.

MARGUERITE: But bounded in time. At once infinite and ephemeral.

JULIETTE: He was its Prince, its First Gentleman; he was its father and its son. He was crowned king at the very moment of his birth.

MARIE: He and his kingdom grew up together.

MARGUERITE: And vanish together.

[JULIETTE: He was the King, Master of all the Universe. An unwise master, who didn't know his own kingdom.

MARGUERITE: He knew very little of it.

MARIE: It was too extensive.

JULIETTE: The earth collapses with him. The suns are growing dim. Water, fire, air – ours and every universe – the whole lot disappears. In what warehouse or cellar, junk room or attic will there ever be room to store all this? It'll take up space, all right!]

DOCTOR: When Kings die, they clutch at the walls, the trees, the fountains, the moon. They pull themselves up...

MARGUERITE: But it all crashes down.

GUARD: And disintegrates.

DOCTOR: It melts and evaporates, till there's not a drop left – not a speck of dust, not the faintest shadow.

[JULIETTE: He drags it all with him into the abyss.

MARIE: He'd organized his world so well. He hadn't quite become master of it. But he would have been. He's dying too soon. He'd divided the year into four seasons. He was really getting on very nicely. He'd thought up the trees and the flowers, all the perfumes and colours.

GUARD: A world fit for a king.

MARIE: He'd invented the oceans and the mountains: nearly sixteen thousand feet for Mont Blanc. Over twenty-nine thousand for the Himalayas. The leaves fell from the trees, but they grew again.

JULIETTE: That was clever.]

MARIE: The very day he was born, he created the sun. And that wasn't enough. He had to have fire made too.

MARGUERITE: And there were wide open spaces, and there were stars, and the sky and oceans and mountains; and there were plains, there were cities, and people and faces and buildings and rooms and beds; and the light and the night; and there were wars and there was peace.

GUARD: And a throne.

MARIE: And his fingers.

MARGUERITE: The way he looked and the way he breathed...

JULIETTE: He's still breathing now.

MARIE: He's still breathing, because I'm here.

MARGUERITE (*to the* DOCTOR): Is he still breathing?

JULIETTE: Yes, your Majesty. He's still breathing, because we're here.

DOCTOR (*examining the invalid*): Yes, yes, no doubt about it. He's still breathing. His kidneys have stopped functioning, but the blood's still circulating. Going round and round. His heart is sound.

MARGUERITE: It'll have to stop soon. What's the good of a heart that's no reason to beat?

DOCTOR: You're right. His heart's gone berserk. D'you hear? (*You can hear the frantic beatings of the* KING*'s heart.*) There it is, racing away, then it slows down, then it's off again, as fast as it can go.

(*The beatings of the* KING's *heart shake the house. The crack in the wall widens and others appear. A stretch of wall could collapse or vanish from sight.*)

JULIETTE: Good God! Everything's falling to pieces!

MARGUERITE: A mad heart – a madman's heart!

DOCTOR: A heart in a panic. It's infectious. Anyone can catch it.

MARGUERITE (*to* JULIETTE): It'll all be quiet in a moment.

DOCTOR: We know every phase of the disease. It's always like this when a universe snuffs out.

MARGUERITE (*to* MARIE): It proves his universe is not unique.

JULIETTE: That never entered his head.

MARIE: He's forgetting me. At this very moment he's forgetting me. I can feel it – he's leaving me behind. I'm nothing if he forgets me. I can't go on living if I don't exist in his distracted heart. Hold tight, hold firm! Clench your fists with all your strength! Don't let go of me!

JULIETTE: Now his strength has left him.

MARIE: Cling to me, don't let go! It's I who keep you alive. I keep *you* alive, you keep *me* alive. D'you see? D'you understand? If you forget me, if you abandon me, I no longer exist, I am nothing.

DOCTOR: He will be a page in a book of ten thousand pages in one of a million libraries which has a million books.

JULIETTE: It won't be easy to find that page again.

[DOCTOR: Oh yes, you'll find it catalogued by subject matter, in alphabetical order... until the day comes when the paper's turned to dust... unless it's destroyed by fire. Libraries often go up in smoke.]

JULIETTE: He's clenching his fists. He's hanging on. He's still resisting. He's coming back to consciousness.

MARIE: He's not coming back to me.

JULIETTE (*to* MARIE): Your voice is waking him up, his eyes are open. He's looking at you.

DOCTOR: Yes, his heart's ticking over again.

[MARGUERITE: He's in a fine state! A dying man trapped in a thicket of thorns! A thicket of thorns! How can we pull him out? (*To the* KING:) You're stuck in the mud, caught in the brambles.

JULIETTE: And when he does get free, he'll leave his shoes behind.]
MARIE: Hold me tight as I hold you! Look at me, as I look at you!

(*The* KING *looks at her.*)

MARGUERITE: She's getting you all mixed up. Forget about her and you'll feel better.
DOCTOR: Give in, your Majesty. Abdicate, Majesty. You'd better abdicate, if you must.

(JULIETTE *pushes him round in his chair again and stops in front of* MARIE.)

KING: I can hear, I can see; who are you? Are you my mother? My sister? My wife? My daughter? My niece? My cousin?... I know *you*... I'm sure I *do* know you. (*They turn him to face* MARGUERITE.) You hateful, hideous woman! Why are you still with me? Why are you leaning over me? Go away, go away!
MARIE: Don't look at her! Turn your eyes on me, and keep them wide open! Hope! I'm here. Remember who you are! I'm Marie.
KING (*to* MARIE): Marie?
MARIE: If you don't remember, gaze at me and learn again that I am Marie. Look at my eyes, my face, my hair, my arms! And learn me off by heart!
MARGUERITE: You're upsetting him. He's past learning anything now.
MARIE (*to the* KING): If I can't hold you back, at least turn and look at me! I'm here! Keep this picture of me in your mind and take it with you!
MARGUERITE: He could never drag that around, he hasn't got the strength. It's too heavy for a ghost [and we can't let other ghosts oppress him. He'd collapse under the weight. His ghost would bleed to death. He wouldn't be able to move]. He's got to travel light. (*To the* KING:) Throw everything away, lighten the load.
DOCTOR: [It's time he began to get rid of the ballast.] Lighten the load, your Majesty.

(*The* KING *rises to his feet, but he has a different way of moving – his gestures are jerky – he already begins to look rather like a sleepwalker. The movements of a sleepwalker will become more and more pronounced.*)

KING: Marie?

MARGUERITE (*to* MARIE): You see, your name means nothing to him now.

GUARD: Marie's name now means nothing to the King.

KING: Marie! (*As he pronounces this name, he can stretch out his arms and then let them fall again.*)

MARIE: He's said it.

DOCTOR: Repeated it, but without understanding.

JULIETTE: Like a parrot. Sounds that are dead.

KING (*to* MARGUERITE, *turning towards her*): I don't know you; I don't love you.

JULIETTE: He knows what not knowing means.

MARGUERITE (*to* MARIE): He'll start his journey with a picture of *me* in his mind. That won't get in his way. [It will leave him when it has to.] It's fitted with a gadget that's worked by remote control. (*To the* KING:) Have another look!

(*The* KING *turns towards the audience.*)

MARIE: He can't see you.

MARGUERITE: He won't see *you* any more.

(*By some theatrical trick,* MARIE *suddenly disappears.*)

JULIETTE: He can't see any more.

DOCTOR (*examining the* KING): That's true – he's lost his sight. (*He has been moving his finger in front of the* KING*'s eyes; or perhaps a lit candle or a match or a cigarette lighter held in front of Bérenger's eyes. They stare out vacantly.*)

JULIETTE: He can't see any more. The Doctor has made an official pronouncement.

GUARD: His Majesty is officially blind.

[MARGUERITE: He'll see better if he looks inside himself.

KING: I can see things and faces and towns and forests; I can see space; I can see time.

MARGUERITE: Look a little farther.

KING: I can't see any farther.

JULIETTE: His horizon's closing in, blocking his view.

MARGUERITE: Cast your eyes beyond what you can see. Behind the road, through the mountain, away beyond that forest – the one you never cleared for cultivation.

KING: The ocean... I daren't go any farther; I can't swim.

DOCTOR: Not enough exercise!

MARGUERITE: That's only the surface of things. Look deep inside them.]

KING: There's a mirror in my entrails where everything's reflected; I can see more and more – I can see the world, I can see life slipping away.

MARGUERITE: Look beyond the reflection.

KING: I see myself. Behind everything, I exist. Nothing but me everywhere. [I am the earth, I am the sky, I am the wind, I am the fire.] Am I in every mirror or am I the mirror of everything?

JULIETTE: He loves himself too much.

DOCTOR: A well-known disease of the psyche: narcissism.

[MARGUERITE: Come nearer.

KING: There isn't a path.

JULIETTE: He can hear. He's turning his head as he speaks – he's trying to listen; he's stretching out an arm, and now the other.]

GUARD: What's he trying to take hold of?

JULIETTE: He wants something to lean on.

(*For a few moments the* KING *has been advancing like a blind man, with very unsteady steps.*)

KING: Where are the walls? Where are the arms? Where are the doors? Where are the windows?

JULIETTE: The walls are here, your Majesty; we are all here. Here's an arm for you.

(JULIETTE *leads the* KING *to the left, and helps him touch the wall.*)

KING: The wall is here. The sceptre!

(JULIETTE *gives it to him.*)

JULIETTE: Here it is!

KING: Guard, where are you? Answer me!

GUARD: Still yours to command, your Majesty. Yours to command. (*The* KING *takes a few steps towards the* GUARD. *He touches him.*) Yes, yes, I'm here. Yes, yes, I'm here.

JULIETTE: Your apartments are this way, your Majesty. I swear we'll never leave you, Majesty.

(*The* GUARD *suddenly disappears.*)

JULIETTE: We're here beside you; we'll stay with you.

(JULIETTE *suddenly disappears.*)

KING: Guard! Juliette! Answer me! I can't hear you any more. Doctor, Doctor, am I going deaf?

DOCTOR: No, your Majesty, not yet.

KING: Doctor!

DOCTOR: Forgive me, your Majesty, I must go. I'm afraid I have to. I'm very sorry – please forgive me. (*The* DOCTOR *retires. He goes out bowing, like a marionette, through the upstage door on the right. He has gone out backwards, with much bowing and scraping, still excusing himself.*)

KING: His voice is getting faint and the sound of his footsteps is fading... he's gone!

MARGUERITE: He's a doctor, with professional obligations.

KING (*stretching out his arms – before she left,* JULIETTE *must have pushed the wheelchair into a corner so it is not in the way*): Where are the others? (*The* KING *reaches the downstage door on the right, then makes for the downstage door on the left.*) They've gone and they've shut me in.

MARGUERITE: They were a nuisance, all those people. They were in your way, hanging round you, getting under your feet. Admit they got on your nerves!

(*The* KING *is walking rather more easily.*)

KING: I need their services.

MARGUERITE: I'll take their place. I'm the queen of all trades.

KING: I didn't give anyone leave to go. Make them come back – call them.

MARGUERITE: They've been cut off. It's what you wanted.

KING: It's not what I wanted.

MARGUERITE: They could never have gone away if you hadn't wanted them to. You can't go back on your decision now. You've dropped them.

KING: Let them come back!

MARGUERITE: You've even forgotten their names. What were they called? (*The* KING *is silent.*) How many were there?

KING: Who do you mean?... I don't like being shut in. Open the doors.

MARGUERITE: A little patience. And the doors will soon be open wide.

KING (*after a silence*): The doors... the doors... what doors?

MARGUERITE: Were there once some doors? Was there once a world? Were you ever alive?

KING: I am.

MARGUERITE: Keep still. Moving tires you. (*The* KING *does as she says.*)

KING: I am... Sounds, echoes, coming from a great distance, fainter and fainter, dying away. I am deaf.

MARGUERITE: You can still hear *me*; you'll hear me all the better. (*The* KING *is standing motionless, without a word.*) Sometimes you have a dream. And you get involved, you believe in it, you love it. In the morning, when you open your eyes, the two worlds are still confused. The brilliance of the light blurs the faces of the night. You'd like to remember; you'd like to hold them back. But they slip between your fingers – the brutal reality of day drives them away. What did I dream about, you ask yourself? What was it happened? Who was I kissing? Who did I love? What was I saying and what was I told? Then you find you're left with a vague regret for all those things that were or seemed to have been. You no longer know what it was that was there all round you. You no longer know.

KING: I no longer know what was there all round me. I know I was part of a world, and this world was all about me. I know it was me and what else was there, what else?

MARGUERITE: There are still some cords that bind you which I haven't yet untied. Or which I haven't cut. There are still some hands that cling to you and hold you back. (*Moving around the* KING, MARGUERITE *cuts the space, as though she had a pair of invisible scissors in her hand.*)

KING: Me. Me. Me.

MARGUERITE: This you is not the real you. It's an odd collection of bits and pieces, horrid things that live on you like parasites. The mistletoe that grows on the bough is not the bough, the ivy that climbs the wall is not the wall. You're sagging under the load, your shoulders are bent – that's what makes you feel so old. And it's that ball and chain dragging at your feet which make it so difficult to walk. (MARGUERITE *leans down and removes an invisible ball and chain from the* KING*'s feet, then, as she gets up, she looks as though she were making a great effort to lift the weight.*) A ton weight – they must weigh at least a ton. (*She pretends to be throwing them in the direction of the audience; then, freed of the weight, she straightens up.*) That's better! How did you manage to trail them around all your life! (*The* KING *tries to straighten up.*) And I used to wonder why you were so round-shouldered! It's because of that sack! (MARGUERITE *pretends to be taking a* *sack from the* KING's *shoulders and throws it away.*) And that heavy pack. (MARGUERITE *goes through the same motions for the pack.*) And that spare pair of army boots.

KING (*with a sort of grunt*): No.

MARGUERITE: Don't get so excited! You won't need an extra pair of boots any more. Or that rifle, or that machine gun. (*The same procedure as for the pack.*) Or that toolbox. (*Same procedure: protestations from the* KING.) He seems quite attached to it! A nasty rusty old sabre. (*She takes it off him, although the* KING *tries grumpily to stop her.*) Leave it all to me and be a good boy. (*She taps on the* KING's *hand.*) You don't need self-defence any more. No one wants to hurt you now. All those thorns and splinters in your cloak, those creepers and seaweed and slimy wet leaves. How they stick to you! I'll pick them off; I'll pull them away. What dirty marks they make! (*She goes through the motions of picking and pulling them off.*) The dreamer comes out of his dream. There you are! I've got rid of all those messy little things that worried you. Now your cloak's more beautiful – we've cleaned you up. You look much better for it. Now have a little walk. Give me your hand, give me your hand then! Don't be afraid any more – let yourself go; I'll see you don't fall. You don't dare!

KING (*in a kind of stammer*): Me.

MARGUERITE: Oh no! He imagines he's *everything!* He thinks *his* existence is *all* existence. I'll have to drive *that* out of his head! (*Then, as if to encourage him.*) Nothing will be forgotten. It's all quite safe in a mind that needs no memories. A grain of salt that dissolves in water doesn't disappear: it makes the water salty. Ah, that's it! Straighten up! Now you're not round-shouldered, no more pains in your back, no more stiffness! Wasn't it a heavy weight to bear? Now you feel better. You can go forwards now, go on! Come along, give me your hand! (*The* KING's *shoulders are slowly rounding again.*) Don't hunch your shoulders – you've no more loads to bear... Oh, those conditioned reflexes – so hard to shake off!... You've no more weight on your shoulders, I tell you. Stand up straight!

(*She helps him to straighten up.*) Your hand!... (*The* KING *is undecided.*) How disobedient he is! Don't clench your fists like that! Open your fingers out! What are you holding? (*She unclenches his fingers.*) He's holding the whole kingdom in his hand. In miniature: on microfilm... in tiny grains. (*To the* KING.) That grain won't grow again, it's bad seed! They're all mouldy! Drop them! Unclasp your fingers! I order you to loosen those fingers! Let go of the plains, let go of the mountains! Like this. They were only dust. (*She takes him by the hand and drags him away, in spite of some slight resistance still from the* KING.) Come along! Still trying to resist! Where does he find all this will-power? No, don't try to lie down! Don't sit down either! No reason why you should stumble. I'll guide you, don't be frightened. (*She guides him across the stage, holding him by the hand.*) You can do it now, can't you? It's easy, isn't it? I've had a gentle slope made for you. It gets steeper later on, but that doesn't matter. You'll have your strength back by then. Don't turn your head to see what you'll never see again; think hard, concentrate on your heart, keep right on, you must!

KING (*advancing with his eyes closed, still held by the hand*): The Empire... has there ever been another Empire like it? With two suns, two moons and two heavens to light it. And there's another sun rising, and there's another! A third firmament appearing, shooting up and fanning out! As one sun sets, others are rising... dawn and twilight all at once... Beyond the seven hundred and seventy-seven poles.

MARGUERITE: Go farther, farther, farther. Toddle on, toddle on, go on!

KING: Blue, blue.

MARGUERITE: He can still distinguish colours. (*To the* KING:) Give up this Empire too! And give your colours up! They're leading you astray, holding you back. You can't linger any longer, you can't stop again, you mustn't! (*She moves away from the* KING.) Walk by yourself! Don't be frightened! Go on! (MARGUERITE, *from one corner of the stage, is directing the* KING *at a distance.*) It's not the day now, or the night – there's no more day and no more night. Try and follow that wheel that's spinning round in front of you! Don't lose sight of it – follow it! But not too close – it's all in flames; you might get burnt. Go forwards! I'll move the undergrowth aside. Watch out! Don't bump into that phantom on your right... clutching hands, imploring hands, pitiful arms and hands, don't you come back – away with you! Don't touch him, or I'll strike you! (*To the* KING:) Don't turn your head! Skirt the precipice on your left, and don't be afraid of that howling wolf... his fangs are made of cardboard, he doesn't exist. (*To the wolf:*) Wolf, cease to exist! (*To the* KING:) Don't be afraid of the rats now either! They can't bite your toes. (*To the rats:*) Rats and vipers, cease to exist! (*To the* KING:) And don't start pitying that beggar who's holding out his hand!... Beware of that old woman coming towards you!... Don't take that glass of water she's offering! You're not thirsty. (*To the imaginary old woman:*) He's no need to quench his thirst, my good woman, he's not thirsty. Don't stand in his way! Vanish! (*To the* KING:) Climb over the fence... that big truck won't run you over – it's a mirage... cross now... Why no, daisies don't sing, even in the spring. I'll smother their cries. I'll obliterate them!... And stop listening to the babbling of that brook! It's not real, anyway, it's deceiving you... false voices, be still! (*To the* KING:) No one's calling you now. Smell that flower for the last time, then throw it away! Forget it's perfume! Now you've lost the power of speech. Who's left for you to talk to? Yes, that's right. Put your best foot forwards! Now the other! There's a footbridge. No, you won't feel giddy. (*The* KING *is advancing towards the steps of the throne.*) Hold yourself straight! You don't need your stick, besides you haven't got one. Don't bend down, and whatever you do don't fall! Up, up you go! (*The* KING *starts to climb the three or four steps to the throne.*) Higher – up again, up you go – still higher, higher, higher! (*The* KING *is quite close to the throne.*) Now turn and face me! Look at me! Look right through me! Gaze into my unreflecting mirror and stand up straight!... Give me your legs! The right one! Now the left! (*As she gives him these orders, the* KING *stiffens his legs.*) Give me a finger! Give me two fingers... three, four... five... all ten fingers! Now let me have your right arm! Your left arm! Your chest, your two shoulders and your stomach! (*The* KING *is motionless, still as a statue.*) There you are, you see! Now you've lost the power of speech, there's no need for your heart to beat, no more need to breathe. It was a lot of fuss about nothing, wasn't it? Now you can take your place.

(*Sudden disappearance of* QUEEN MARGUERITE *on the left. The* KING *is seated on his throne. During this final scene, the doors, windows, and walls of the throne room will have slowly disappeared. This part of the action is very important.*

Now there is nothing on the stage except the KING *on his throne in a greyish light. Then the* KING *and his throne also disappear.*

Finally, there is nothing but the grey light.

This disappearance of the windows, the doors and the walls, the KING *and the throne must be very marked, but happen slowly and gradually. The* KING, *sitting on his throne, should remain visible for a short time before fading into a kind of mist.*)

CURTAIN

A STROLL IN THE AIR

*To Madeleine Renaud
and Jean-Louis Barrault*

*First produced in Paris by Jean-Louis Barrault at
the Théâtre de l'Odéon on 8th February, 1963*

Characters

MONSIEUR BÉRENGER, the heavenly hiker
MADAME BÉRENGER, his wife, JOSÉPHINE
MLLE BÉRENGER, his daughter, MARTHE
THE JOURNALIST (English)
THE FIRST ENGLISHMAN, in his Sunday best (1ST MAN)
THE FIRST ENGLISHWOMAN, his wife (1ST WOMAN)
THE LITTLE BOY, their son
THE SECOND ENGLISHMAN, in his Sunday best (2ND MAN)
THE SECOND ENGLISHWOMAN, his wife (2ND WOMAN)
THE LITTLE GIRL, their daughter
JOHN BULL, chorus leader
FIRST OLD ENGLISH LADY (1ST LADY)
SECOND OLD ENGLISH LADY (2ND LADY)
THE DOCTOR-UNCLE
THE UNDERTAKER'S MAN (UNDERTAKER)
THE VISITOR FROM THE ANTI-WORLD
Members of the Court of Justice:
    The JUDGE
    Two ASSESSORS
    JOHN BULL, disguised as an EXECUTIONER (HANGMAN)
THE MAN IN WHITE (GREAT WHITE MAN)

The Set

On the extreme stage left, a small house in the country, English style: a cottage, realized a little in the manner of Douanier Rousseau or perhaps Utrillo or even Chagall,* according to the designer's taste. This little house, like the landscape described below, should have a dreamlike quality. In any case, the dream-like effect should be achieved rather by the methods used by a Primitive artist, consciously naive, than by those of a Surrealist artist, or one inspired by the technique of the Opéra or the Chatelet theatre. Everything is fully lit, and so there should be nothing dim, and no gauze, etc…

The rest of the stage represents a grassy down, very green and very fresh, overlooking a valley; at the back of the stage you can see the hill opposite. The top of the downs where the action takes place should be semicircular and give the feeling that we are almost on the edge of a cliff that drops away into a gorge, allowing a glimpse in the background stage right of the outlying houses of a small English country town, very white and drenched in April sunshine. The sky is very blue and very pure. A few trees can be seen on the stage: cherry trees and pear trees in blossom.

The very faint sound of trains can be heard passing down in the gorge, alongside a small navigable river, which is also invisible, of course, but whose presence can be suggested by the distant sound of ships' horns. You can see the cables of a telpher railway with two little red cabins going up and down.

Later, as the action advances, we shall see further props and changes in the setting. During the walk taken by BÉRENGER *and his family, for example, along the edge of the cliff, we shall see pink ruins smothered in flowers, infinite space beyond the precipice, a silver bridge, a rack railway on the hillside, opposite, etc.…*

(*When the curtain rises two old English ladies are taking a walk from stage right to stage left.*)

1ST LADY: Oh, yes.
2ND LADY: Yes, we're in England.
1ST LADY: In Gloucestershire.
2ND LADY: What lovely weather for a Sunday.

(*Church bells are heard.*)

They're the bells from the Catholic church.
1ST LADY: There was no Catholic church in my village.

(*At this moment the* SECOND OLD LADY *is struck by a ball and turns round as a little* ENGLISH BOY *arrives on the stage.*)

2ND LADY: Oh!
1ST LADY (*to the* LITTLE BOY): Oh! You naughty little boy!

(*The* FIRST ENGLISHMAN *appears – the father of the* LITTLE BOY.)

1ST MAN: So sorry – please excuse my little boy.
LITTLE BOY: I didn't do it on purpose.

(*The* FIRST ENGLISHWOMAN *arrives – the wife of the* FIRST ENGLISHMAN *and mother of the* LITTLE BOY.)

1ST WOMAN (*to the* LITTLE BOY): You must be more careful.
That's no way to behave. Go and tell the lady you're sorry.
LITTLE BOY: I'm sorry.
1ST MAN (*to the* LADIES): I'm really very sorry.

1ST WOMAN (*to the* LADIES): I'm really very sorry.

(*The two* OLD LADIES *and the parents greet one another, saying:* "*Sorry, we're so sorry.*" *They separate, continuing their walk in opposite directions, while a* LITTLE ENGLISH GIRL *arrives, picks up the* LITTLE BOY*'s ball and gives it back to him.*)

1ST WOMAN (*to the* LITTLE GIRL): You've been very well brought up, little girl.

(*The* LITTLE GIRL *bobs a curtsy and the* SECOND ENGLISHMAN *and his wife arrive – the parents of the* LITTLE GIRL.)

1ST WOMAN (*to the parents*): Your little girl is very well brought up.
1ST MAN (*to the* 2ND MAN): Your little girl is very well brought up.
2ND MAN (*to the* 1ST MAN): And I'm sure your little boy must be, too.
1ST WOMAN: He's not as polite as all that.
2ND WOMAN: Our little girl isn't always so polite either.

(*The two English couples greet each other in turns, saying:* "*So sorry, so sorry.*" *They turn away and continue their walk separately while the* 1ST WOMAN *delivers a parting shot at the* LITTLE BOY: "*You naughty boy!*" *The* LITTLE BOY *thumbs his nose at his parents on the sly.*)

LITTLE GIRL: Oh! What a naughty little boy!
1ST LADY (*who has seen what happened*): Oh! what a naughty little boy!
2ND LADY: Oh! You naughty boy!
LITTLE GIRL: I won't say anything. It's not nice to tell tales.

(*Enter the* JOURNALIST *from stage left, from behind* BÉRENGER*'s house.*)

JOURNALIST (*to the* 1ST MAN): Aoh! Good morning!
1ST WOMAN: Aoh! What a fine Sunday morning, isn't it!

1ST MAN: What a fine Sunday morning!

JOURNALIST: It's just the weather to spend Sunday in the country.

(*The English people go out, quietly continuing their walk. All except the* JOURNALIST, *who moves towards* BÉRENGER's *cottage. At this moment* BÉRENGER *puts his head through the window, looking at the sky and grass, and says:*)

BÉRENGER: What a fine Sunday morning!

JOURNALIST: Oh please, Monsieur Bérenger. You are Monsieur Bérenger, aren't you? Excuse me, I'm a journalist...

(BÉRENGER *makes as if to withdraw.*)

Please, don't go away.

(BÉRENGER's *head pops out again, in Punch and Judy style.*)

I only wanted to ask you a few questions.

(BÉRENGER's *head disappears.*)

Only some very simple questions. Please, Monsieur Bérenger. Just one question.

(BÉRENGER *pops his head out again.*)

BÉRENGER: I have decided, Monsieur, not to answer any more questions from newspapermen.

(*His head disappears again.*)

JOURNALIST: Only one question. It's not a question from a newspaperman – it's a question from the newspaper. I've been sent here specially to ask you this question. It's nothing serious, nothing serious, don't worry.

BÉRENGER (*popping his head out again*): I haven't got much time; I've work to do. Or perhaps I haven't any yet, or perhaps I'll find some – who knows? I've come to England from the Continent to rest, to get away from work…

JOURNALIST (*taking out his notebook*): Yes, we know. You've come to England, to Gloucestershire, and you live in a little prefabricated house, in the middle of this grassy field, right on top of the green downs, overlooking the gorge, where there's a small navigable river (*while he is talking, the* JOURNALIST *points to the different parts of the set*) flowing between two wooded hills… We've already obtained this information, Monsieur – forgive us for being so indiscreet. It was well meant.

BÉRENGER: It's not a secret. Besides, anyone can see.

JOURNALIST: My newspaper would like to ask you a question, dear Monsieur Bérenger.

BÉRENGER: I don't answer questions any more.

(BÉRENGER *makes as if to withdraw. His head disappears and reappears.*)

JOURNALIST: Don't go away, Monsieur Bérenger. It's a very simple question. You can answer how you like. It's to put on the front page – with a big photograph of you, half life-size.

BÉRENGER: Well, be quick about it. I haven't got much time. I'm having a rest.

JOURNALIST: Forgive me – I'm very sorry to disturb you. I'm going to ask you the usual question: when shall we see in the great theatres of the world one of your new masterpieces?

BÉRENGER: I don't want to answer that question.

JOURNALIST: Oh, please, Monsieur Bérenger.

BÉRENGER: I shall have to make you a confession. I've always known I never had any reason to write.

JOURNALIST: That's perfectly understandable. But that's not a reason to have no reason to write. There's no reason for anything, we all know that.

BÉRENGER: Of course we do. But people still do things, even though there's no reason for doing them. Anyway, the weaker brethren invent apparent reasons for their actions. They pretend to believe in them. We can't avoid doing something, they say. I'm not one of *them*. Once upon a time, though I'm really a nihilist, there was some strange force inside me that made me do things and made me write. I can't go on any longer.

JOURNALIST: I'll jot that down. You can't go on any longer.

BÉRENGER: No, I can't. For years it was a consolation to me to be able to say there was nothing *to* say. But now I feel far too sure I was right. I'm convinced of it. But not intellectually or psychologically. Now it's a deeply held conviction; it's got into my flesh and blood and bones; it's physiological. It paralyses me. Writing isn't a game for me any more, and it will never be a game again. It ought to lead to something else, but it doesn't.

JOURNALIST: What should it lead to?

BÉRENGER: If I knew that, there'd be no problem.

JOURNALIST: Give us a message.

BÉRENGER: They've all been given before. You've got them all to hand – as many as you want. The cafés and the newspaper offices are swarming with literary geniuses who have solved everything. Really in the know. There's nothing easier than a mechanical message. Luckily for them. They believe in the straight and narrow path of Historical Necessity, but History is really round the bend. For them, might is right, so Historical Necessity is the doctrine of the victorious party in power, whatever it may be; they believe that History is right. You can always find the best of reasons to justify a victorious ideology. But it's just when it's victorious and comes to power that it starts going wrong. You need discrimination, intellectual courage or penetrating insight if you're going to be able to resist what's with us now and foresee what will be, or even just feel that there ought to be something different.

JOURNALIST: Some people say it's really because you're afraid of rivals that you may be temporarily giving up the theatre.

BÉRENGER: I think it's rather because I need renovating inside. Shall I be able to renovate myself? In theory, yes – in theory I will, because I don't approve of the way things are going. The few people who disapprove of the way things are going are the only ones who can say anything new. The truth is to be found in a kind of neurosis... It's not there in a healthy mind – in neurosis lies the truth – tomorrow's truth, which contradicts the apparent truth of today. All writers, or almost all, and almost all the playwrights, are denouncing yesterday's evils, injustices, alienations, yesterday's diseases. They close their eyes to the evils of today. But it's no use denouncing an old evil. It's pointless to demystify what has been demystified already. That's just being conformist. All that it does is conceal the new disease, the new injustices, the new deceptions. Most contemporary writers think they're an advance guard, that History has really left them far behind. They are stupid – they're not courageous at all.

JOURNALIST: One moment, please... So your plays *are* plays with a message? Not like anybody else's message, but a message all the same... Your message—

BÉRENGER: I'm afraid it's against my principles, but I hope there's something else behind my apparent message – I still don't quite know what, but perhaps it will reveal itself... as the play goes on... through my imagination...

JOURNALIST: Let me take this down: down with the way things are... neurosis... cafés... discrimination... courage, intuition... diseases... writers are stupid.

BÉRENGER: And then, good or bad, the critics make me tired. And then the theatre makes me tired, and actors make me tired, and life makes me tired.

JOURNALIST: Got that: tired... tired... tired...

BÉRENGER: Sometimes, too, I wonder whether literature and the theatre can ever give a full account of reality – it's so complex so overwhelming. And I wonder if, nowadays, anyone can get a clear image of other people or of himself. We are living a horrible nightmare. Literature has never been so powerful, so vivid or so intense as life. And certainly not today. If it wants to be compared with life, literature ought to be a thousand times more cruel and terrifying than it is. However cruel it becomes, literature can only give a very dim and feeble picture of how cruel life is in reality, or how marvellous it can be too. Literature isn't knowledge, either, as it's nothing but a cliché: I mean, it gets stereotyped as soon as it becomes hidebound, set in its expression, which lags behind instead of leading the way. What must we do to make literature an exciting voyage of discovery? Even imagination is not enough. Orthodox men of letters – and all men of letters are orthodox – believe they know or reflect reality. But reality surpasses fiction; it cannot be grasped any more, even by the conscious mind...

JOURNALIST: I now put on record that it can no longer be recorded.

BÉRENGER: But I suppose we could put up with anything providing we were immortal. I am paralysed by the knowledge that I'm going to die. There's nothing new about that truth. But it's a truth we forget... so that we can *do* something. I don't want to *do* anything any more, I want to be cured of death. Au revoir, Monsieur.

JOURNALIST: That's fine. Thank you for that enlightening statement. I'm sure it will be of lively interest to our Sunday readers. Give them something really entertaining. I'd like to offer you a special vote of thanks for giving me something that will help to fill up my column.

BÉRENGER: Front page, with the photograph, please.

JOURNALIST: Of course, Monsieur. You'll receive the cheque tomorrow.

BÉRENGER: How much?

(*The* JOURNALIST *cups his hands and mentions an inaudible figure to* BÉRENGER.)

Right, that'll do, Monsieur. Au revoir, Monsieur.

(BÉRENGER's *head disappears. The* JOURNALIST *goes off stage right.*

The stage is empty for a few moments. In the distance you can hear the throbbing of a plane, which will go on increasing in volume during the following scene.

MME BÉRENGER — JOSÉPHINE — *dressed in a dark-blue peignoir with a white star-shaped pattern, comes in from the right.*

Behind her comes the DOCTOR-UNCLE, *followed in turn by the* UNDERTAKER's MAN. *The latter is wearing a black suit, black gloves and a black tie, and is carrying a black bowler hat. The* DOCTOR-UNCLE *is greying at the temples; he wears a grey suit with black crêpe on the lapel of the jacket.*)

DOCTOR-UNCLE (*catching* JOSÉPHINE *up*): Joséphine! Joséphine!
JOSÉPHINE (*turning round*): Is it you, Doctor-Uncle? I thought you were in Brazzaville...
DOCTOR-UNCLE: I've never been to Brazzaville.
UNDERTAKER: Madame Bérenger, Madame Bérenger...
JOSÉPHINE: What is it, Monsieur?
UNDERTAKER: Excuse me, Madame Bérenger; allow me to introduce myself: I'm the undertaker's man. I've some rather distressing news for you.
JOSÉPHINE: Oh! Heavens!
DOCTOR-UNCLE: It's not distressing news at all, don't worry, little Joséphine. On the contrary – it's very pleasant news.
UNDERTAKER: That depends on your point of view. Perhaps it is pleasant news, but it's distressing enough for us.
JOSÉPHINE: But what on earth has happened?
UNDERTAKER: Have no fear, Madame, it's quite terrible.
DOCTOR-UNCLE (*to the* UNDERTAKER): Let me break the news to my niece myself. I must be careful how I tell her. People can die of great joy and great sorrow. (*To* JOSÉPHINE:) My brother, your father—
JOSÉPHINE: I know, the poor man died in the war. They brought his body back.

DOCTOR-UNCLE: He's not dead any more, Joséphine.

JOSÉPHINE: Raised from the dead? Stop joking, Uncle.

DOCTOR-UNCLE: I don't know whether he's been raised from the dead, but he's alive all right, take my word as a doctor. Perhaps we've only believed he was dead. We were wrong. In any case, he's not far off – he'll be here any moment now.

JOSÉPHINE: It's impossible, impossible!

DOCTOR-UNCLE: I swear it's true!

JOSÉPHINE: How is he? Where is he? Has he lost weight? Is he tired? Is he ill? Is he sad? Is he happy?

UNDERTAKER: But what about us, Madame, what are *we* going to do? You've announced this gentleman's – your father's – decease officially, you've ordered an interment. Everything's ready; we've announced it in the newspapers; we've paid out all the expenses.

JOSÉPHINE: Oh! My poor father! It's so long since I saw him. Do you think I'll recognize him?

DOCTOR-UNCLE: He's younger than before his death was announced. He looks as he did in that old photo taken before he went off to the war. He's lost weight, yes, of course. He is pale. He has long hair. He's been wounded.

JOSÉPHINE: Father, where are you? I can't wait any longer – I want to see him at once.

UNDERTAKER: Don't be in such a hurry, Madame. You must regularize the situation first. This is very prejudicial to our financial and moral interests. The excellent reputation of our firm, founded in 1784, five years before your French Revolution—

DOCTOR-UNCLE: We must cancel the interment—

UNDERTAKER: And here I am, left with a funeral on my hands!

DOCTOR-UNCLE: It won't be wasted. There's quite a demand.

JOSÉPHINE: Oh yes, of course, we must cancel it.

DOCTOR-UNCLE: We'll pay you for everything.

UNDERTAKER: That's not good enough, sir.

DOCTOR-UNCLE: What's more, we offer you our apologies.

UNDERTAKER: I accept them, sir, but there's more than that at stake. We've sent in a public obituary notice, we've advertised it, and now the burial won't take place. Who will have confidence in us again?

JOSÉPHINE: All right, take us to court and we'll pay you all the necessary damages.

UNDERTAKER: There's never been a case like this before. We'll take it to the Chamber of Commerce. And then to the Court of Appeal. We'll make a precedent of it. I protest – I protest most vigorously. I'll have my lawyer on you, with the Judge and all the ushers.

JOSÉPHINE: Oh, Monsieur, don't get so angry. You're not going to upset my poor father again.

UNDERTAKER (*going off*): You'll hear more of this, you won't get away with it. I'll make a scandal, and it'll be in all the papers. (*He goes out.*)

DOCTOR-UNCLE: We'll see our lawyer about it – don't worry, it'll all be all right. Even if the papers do mention it, we can always say it was a miracle. And that our intentions were honourable.

JOSÉPHINE: We shouldn't have announced the funeral so quickly... Now we've got to start sending out resurrection cards – resurrection cards! But where is he?

DOCTOR-UNCLE (*pointing into space*): Here, he's over there.

JOSÉPHINE: Father, I want to kiss you – show yourself. I can't see him – I can't see you, where are you?

DOCTOR-UNCLE (*still pointing into space*): Over there – look, he's over there!

JOSÉPHINE: Show yourself, Father, show yourself. It doesn't matter if the undertakers are angry; that doesn't matter. Show yourself.

(*The noise of the plane has become deafening. It is so loud that it doubtless drowns out the inaudible dialogue between* JOSÉPHINE *and the* DOCTOR-UNCLE *which probably follows. For a few moments these two characters go on acting wordlessly in the uproar.*

The stage has been getting darker as the noise increased in volume, and now it is in darkness. Suddenly a bomb is heard exploding on BÉRENGER's *cottage, which, for a couple of seconds, we can see lit up in the flash of the explosion, and even in flames, if possible.*

Utter darkness again for a few very brief moments, and the throbbing of the plane gradually dying away. After the next four or five lines of dialogue that come, it will be heard no more.

Lights. BÉRENGER'*s cottage is a pile of smoking ruins.* BÉRENGER *is seen framed in the doorway, which alone has remained intact.*

JOSÉPHINE *is standing on the right, dressed in a sky-blue suit of rather classical cut, with a rose pinned on the lapel, carrying a black leather handbag. On her head, a little pink hat.*

Next to JOSÉPHINE *is* MLLE BÉRENGER, *whose Christian name is* MARTHE. *She is wearing a pink Sunday dress, white shoes, a little white embroidered collar round the neck, and she is carrying a small white handbag. She has long chestnut hair, gentle grey-green eyes and a good clear profile, if rather severe. She is wearing white stockings.*

The English characters are at the back of the stage with their back to the public.

Each of the two OLD LADIES *is right at one side of the stage. Nearer the centre of the stage, at the back, are the first and second couples, with their children. The* LITTLE BOY *and the* LITTLE GIRL *are both holding a croquet mallet. All the English characters are quite still, looking up at the sky as if they were following the aeroplane out of sight. At the back of the stage, dead centre, stands* JOHN BULL *in his characteristic and well-known costume.* JOHN BULL *is the only English character not to be watching the plane. You can see him, like an enormous puppet, slowly taking off his typical hat to wipe the sweat from the inside. Then he mops his brow with a large handkerchief, and puts the handkerchief back in his pocket and the hat back on his head, while he slowly turns to face the public. Once this movement has been accomplished, he stands with his legs wide apart and his arms behind his back.*

In their corner of the stage MME *and* MLLE BÉRENGER *are not watching the plane either. They are talking.*)

MARTHE: *Ma petite maman*, you're all upset. I wish I could dream of Grandpa, just to know what he was like. I wish I could meet him.

JOSÉPHINE: I'd forgotten I missed him so much. Now I remember how it hurt to see him go.

MARTHE: We've got Papa now.

BÉRENGER (*looking at the sky, to the English characters*): It's a German bomber. Left over from the last war.

(*The English characters turn round all together.*)

1ST WOMAN (*showing her LITTLE GIRL to the other English people*): She wants to be a prima donna.

JOSÉPHINE: Of course, but I'm afraid no one's replaceable. When someone disappears, it leaves a gap you can never quite fill.

BÉRENGER (*to the English characters*): It's a good thing I was in the doorway. I wanted to walk about in the fresh grass, under your blue sky, as beautiful as the sky in June, a beautiful English blue.

JOHN BULL (*to the LITTLE BOY*): And what do *you* want to be?

LITTLE BOY: A pilot.

2ND MAN (*to BÉRENGER*): Oh yes, spring's a lovely season here.

2ND LADY: It doesn't rain so much.

JOHN BULL (*to the LITTLE BOY*): And why a pilot, my child?

MARTHE (*to JOSÉPHINE*): Better not say a word to Papa, perhaps, about your dream.

LITTLE BOY (*to JOHN BULL*): To drop bombs on the houses.

1ST LADY (*to the 1ST WOMAN*): Let her sing us something.

JOHN BULL (*to the LITTLE GIRL*): Sing us a nice song, my child.

LITTLE GIRL: No!

ALL THE ENGLISH CHARACTERS (*together*): Sing us something.

MARTHE (*to JOSÉPHINE*): Oh! Look at the countryside... the valley... Look at those little English children.

THE ENGLISH PEOPLE (*to the LITTLE GIRL*): Sing us a nice song.

MARTHE (*to JOSÉPHINE*): Look – there's Papa; he's seen us.

(BÉRENGER *advances towards* JOSÉPHINE *and* MARTHE.)

Papa! Isn't this a lovely field!

2ND LADY (*pointing to* JOHN BULL): If you won't sing us a song, that man will eat you up.

BÉRENGER (*to his wife*): Did you see what's just happened to me?

1ST COUPLE (*to* the LITTLE GIRL): Sing, little girl!

JOSÉPHINE (*to* BÉRENGER): What did I tell you? You ought to be more careful.

2ND COUPLE: Sing, little daughter!

BÉRENGER: It's not *my* fault. I wasn't in the plane. How could I help it?

THE TWO LADIES: Sing, young Miss!

JOSÉPHINE: You ought to have bought a more solid house, not a cardboard shack like that, which collapses at the slightest bomb. It's made an awful mess of your notebooks.

MARTHE: Leave him alone, Maman. (*To* BÉRENGER:) We had a lovely journey down from London. It was all so green, and there were rivers and little towns like toy models and red and yellow cars on the roads. Was it nice and quiet for you to work?

BÉRENGER: Yes. If it hadn't been for the plane.

JOSÉPHINE: You couldn't have found a better excuse for not working.

(*The* LITTLE GIRL *suddenly starts singing. In fact, all she produces is a series of trills, just like a little mechanical nightingale.*)

MARTHE: Oh! It's the little English girl singing. (*Fresh trills.*) Doesn't she sing nicely? I wish I could sing like that.

JOHN BULL (*to the* LITTLE GIRL): Oh, that's very pretty.

2ND WOMAN: It's an old song from our part of the country.

1ST LADY: My Grandfather used to sing me that.

1ST MAN: My Grandfather used to sing it to me too.

JOHN BULL: It's known everywhere in England. But with us it was a little different. We used to sing it like this.

(*He sings. Again, like the trills of a mechanical nightingale, exactly the same as before.*

Then all the English characters sing the same trills in chorus. Only JOHN BULL*'s voice comes through a little lower, and the* LITTLE GIRL*'s voice a little higher.*

This musical sequence must be very short.

The production should not insist on this scene, or complicate it. The English characters must just have enough time to smile a couple of times while they sing. In fact, they will only open their mouths, as a mechanical nightingale will be hidden somewhere to sing for them.

The LITTLE BOY *pulls the* LITTLE GIRL*'s pigtails and she appears quite bald.)*

THE BÉRENGER FAMILY: Oh!

2ND WOMAN: Well, yes, our little girl is the little bald prima donna.*

(None of the English characters or the BÉRENGER *family are the slightest bit surprised by this and it passes off quite naturally. All that happens is that the* LITTLE BOY*'s mother snatches the* LITTLE GIRL*'s wig and gives it to her father, who hands it over to her mother, who passes it back to her.*

The LITTLE BOY*'s father smacks his son on the hand and signs to him to go up to the* LITTLE GIRL. *The* LITTLE BOY *goes and kisses the* LITTLE GIRL, *then the two English children go and play croquet in the left-hand corner of the stage, from which they will disappear into the wings.*

JOHN BULL *has a few words with the two couples in turn, then with the* OLD LADIES, *and slowly, one after the other, they all pass into the wings; later they will appear again in groups, cross the stage and disappear again – sometimes a few of them, sometimes a larger number – in order to provide a kind of moving background. All these directions apply to the moves of these characters during the following scene. The English characters will appear together again only when they are wanted, and this will be indicated.)*

MARTHE *(conversing, therefore, with* JOSÉPHINE *and* BÉRENGER, *against a background of English people walking* slowly *about, to emphasize the gentle country atmosphere*): Look at Maman's pretty hat!

BÉRENGER (*to* JOSÉPHINE): It suits you very well, *chérie,* and tones with your sky-blue dress.

MARTHE: Maman's little dress is quite classic. The classic cut suits her very well. Doesn't she look sweet in it? Look, Papa, have you noticed? She's got a rose pinned to the lapel – a red rose. Do you see?

BÉRENGER: I'm not so absent-minded as you all think.

JOSÉPHINE: If Marthe hadn't drawn your attention to it you'd never have noticed.

MARTHE: Oh, Maman, please! (*Then to* BÉRENGER:) The colours go very well together. She's got very good taste, Maman.

BÉRENGER: Indeed she has. It's all very nice. Except for the black leather handbag, which doesn't quite go with the rest.

JOSÉPHINE: I can't buy everything all at once – you know that quite well. It's too expensive.

MARTHE: We saw a lovely bag for Maman in the window of a shop in Piccadilly: a light colour – I'm not quite sure what shade – with flowers on it that moved and closed and opened and closed again, like real flowers; you'd really think they *were* flowers.

BÉRENGER: Perhaps they were real flowers...

MARTHE: Yes, perhaps real flowers, or perhaps little hands like fans. It was so pretty. I don't know why, but it makes me feel happy, a thing like that. I did so want that bag for Maman. You'll give it to her as a present, won't you? For her birthday?

BÉRENGER: Tomorrow, if she likes.

JOSÉPHINE: There's no hurry. For my birthday, if you like. We mustn't spend everything all at once. I'll make do with this one for now: we've got your house to build again. Where are you going to work now?

BÉRENGER: Don't worry about that. There's no shortage of houses – you find them in all the towns, all the villages, along all the roads and even in the depths of the country. And even on the water. Nothing but houses. And to think there are people who complain they don't know where to live.

JOSÉPHINE: There are more people than houses.

BÉRENGER: Not in the countryside.

JOSÉPHINE: Oh, you can't count.

MARTHE: All the people could take it in turns to use them.

BÉRENGER: Don't worry about your dream. It's only a dream, that's all.

JOSÉPHINE: You really think so?

BÉRENGER: Why yes, why yes, I'm sure it was.

MARTHE (*to* JOSÉPHINE): You shouldn't have told him about it.

JOSÉPHINE (*to* BÉRENGER): I can't help it upsetting me. It was my father.

BÉRENGER: Of course, I understand. But that only means you were very fond of your father, that you very much wish he was still alive and that you realize it's not possible – it's just not possible. It's when we dream about our loved ones that we really notice how much we miss them, how very much we miss them.

JOSÉPHINE: That's exactly what I was saying just now.

BÉRENGER: In the daytime we forget. We don't think about it. If we were as sharply conscious of things all the time as we are in our dreams, we couldn't go on living. It's at night we remember. The daytime is made for forgetting. Don't let your dream upset you – just have a look at this grass…

MARTHE: Don't cry, Maman. Papa's right.

BÉRENGER: Look at the grass, and look at those woods opposite, on the other side of the gorge. Enjoy it all. Turn round…

MARTHE (*to* JOSÉPHINE): Turn round…

JOSÉPHINE (*turning round*): All right, all right, I can turn round on my own…

BÉRENGER: Better look at those white walls of the first houses in the town…

MARTHE: They look as if they're going to melt in the light.

JOSÉPHINE: It's very pretty.

MARTHE: It's more than pretty.

BÉRENGER: Look at the sky!

MARTHE: Look at it!

JOSÉPHINE: But I *am* looking – what else do you want?

BÉRENGER: Look, look at it! Let the light be enough to make you happy. Have you ever seen anything so gentle, so pure and fresh?

JOSÉPHINE: Yes, I'm still thinking of…

MARTHE: Stop thinking, Maman, stop thinking. Enjoy yourself!

JOSÉPHINE: I'll enjoy myself, if you like.

BÉRENGER: There's a very beautiful view from the edge of the gorge. I'll take you both by the hand and we'll go for a lovely walk.

MARTHE (*giving her hand to* BÉRENGER *and to* JOSÉPHINE): Give him your hand.

BÉRENGER (*to* JOSÉPHINE): Come on, hand in hand, and you'll forget your worries.

(JOSÉPHINE *gives her hand hesitantly to* BÉRENGER *– or rather, it is* BÉRENGER *who takes hers in his.*)

JOSÉPHINE: There's so much waiting to be done at home. The pancakes and the salad for the week…

MARTHE: Come on, Maman, it's Sunday. Sunday is a day of rest.

(*The English characters now come on the stage from the left, one by one or in pairs, as is indicated subsequently, and go out on the right. They can return in the opposite direction if necessary.*

Meanwhile a curtain or screen, with the various items to be mentioned, will move in the same direction as the English characters are walking. The BÉRENGER *family will walk in the opposite direction to the screen at the back – or rather, will pretend to be walking.*

At the front of the stage the two children playing croquet will move in the opposite direction to the English parents. They will leave the stage and then come back. Or perhaps they can just move from the one side of the stage to the other and then back again in the opposite direction, up to the moment when they finally disappear.)

1ST LADY (*appearing with the* 2ND LADY): I felt like a prisoner in this country and there was no escape. I'd been living there quite a long time. I was so frightened I never really wanted to leave it, but when I found out I wasn't allowed to leave it, I was even more frightened. I could see nothing but walls all round me. Walls everywhere. I had a nervous breakdown. Claustrophobia. It's not being unable to leave that's so bad, it's *knowing* that you *can't*.

2ND LADY: I quite understand, my dear.

(*The two* OLD LADIES *go out.* BÉRENGER, JOSÉPHINE *and* MARTHE *go to the right-hand side of the stage and start walking at the back from right to left. You can hear the distant sound of a train and the whistle from the engine. A tiny little train can be seen in the distance, with red carriages.*)

MARTHE: Oh, look, Papa, look, Maman, what a pretty little train! It's like a toy one.

BÉRENGER: Joséphine, look, you'd think it *was* a toy...

(*They can stop walking for a moment and have a good look round them before continuing their stroll.*)

1ST MAN (*appearing with the* 2ND MAN): I've wasted my whole life trying to make up my mind to change it. When I lay awake at night, I used to say to myself: "Tomorrow I'll break with everything and I *will* change."

2ND MAN: Change what?

1ST MAN: Life, *my* life; the life *I've* been leading is someone else's life.

2ND MAN: And did you keep your promise?

BÉRENGER: That's the kind of train I should like to have had when I was a child. But I'm afraid the children of today don't want them any more – all they like is rockets. And a train like that is just a museum piece – all right for archaeologists. No one can understand it any more without a lot of phoney historical reconstruction.

MARTHE: I'd like to have a doll, too, that walks all by itself, makes wee-wee and talks.

JOSÉPHINE: You're too big to play with dolls now. Did you finish your homework for tomorrow?

2ND MAN: Did you keep your promise?

1ST MAN: I did when I first woke up in the morning… but after breakfast I felt much too heavy. I put it off to the next day. And so on, for years and years and years and years.

2ND MAN: You oughtn't to have had any breakfast.

1ST MAN: Now it's too late. But I'm still trying. How many breakfasts do you have in thirty years?

2ND MAN: Easy enough to calculate.

(*They go out.*)

BÉRENGER: What's the good of regretting what might have been? What's the good of it?

JOSÉPHINE: We all have our regrets. But they don't do us any good.

MARTHE: Maman's quite right – it doesn't do us any good regretting the past.

BÉRENGER: Yes, that's true. Especially when it's a lovely day like today.

1ST WOMAN (*appearing with the* 2ND WOMAN): How can I describe it to you? That town was so sad and ugly. You know what I mean?

2ND WOMAN: Nothing surprising about that.

1ST WOMAN: Quite by chance I found this street. A beautiful street it was – so beautiful I could have wept. In all that ghastly town, just one beautiful street, empty and beautiful, and no one knew about it. You believe me, don't you? And right at the end, a castle keep. Heavens, how beautiful it was. Indescribably beautiful. How can I tell you, how can I tell you…

2ND WOMAN: Don't say a word.

1ST WOMAN: When it's too beautiful, it's heartbreaking.

(*Enter* JOHN BULL.)

BÉRENGER: It's the river that starts somewhere near Bath. You see, it's making for the Ocean. (*Pointing.*) The sea is in that direction, and the port... It's a bigger port than Liverpool, but there's nothing gloomy about it. It's the only English city with colours like the Mediterranean. Look down there – the ships are taking their merchandise.

(*Melodious sounds are heard, voices or something resembling voices singing.*)

Listen!

JOHN BULL: It appears we should pay great attention to what the poets say. They are often right. That's what I've been told. They prophesy and their prophecies come true. I prefer sausages. I'd rather have my dog.

(JOHN BULL *goes off.*)

JOSÉPHINE: I can't hear anything.

(*Enter the* JOURNALIST.)

MARTHE: Why yes, listen...

JOURNALIST: I ought to give it up. (*He stops and faces the public.*) I ought to give it up. After all, up to what age can you go on being interested in art? Art and literature – that's kid's stuff. Art has lost its power; if it ever had any.

(*The* JOURNALIST *goes off.*)

JOSÉPHINE: Why yes! What *is* that music? Those lovely voices?
BÉRENGER: They're sirens' voices from the ships.
JOSÉPHINE: Ships' sirens, yes. But it's the sailors who start them up.

(*They continue their walk and see on the opposite side a fantastic turreted palace in the middle of the woods, and fields with motionless grazing cows; a train with different coloured carriages going up the rack railway; the screen at the back goes on moving, and on the hilltop opposite you can see a little Eiffel Tower, a red balloon floating away, a blue lake and a waterfall, the terminus of a telpher railway and a little rocket passing in a shower of sparks, etc... and then woods again and trees in blossom.*

The three BÉRENGERS *make no comment as they watch the scenery and the props, just a few exclamations: "Oh! Ah! Look – isn't it beautiful!"*

Meanwhile, walking in the opposite direction without looking at the landscape, the English characters are talking to one another.)

1ST WOMAN: It was black, black, black. You can't imagine how black it was. Black as snow in London. I'm not the author of that expression.

2ND WOMAN: Sometimes I dreamt, too, that I was walking about in a dreamlike city. All alone, absolutely alone.

(The two WOMEN *go out. Enter the* JOURNALIST *and* JOHN BULL.)

MARTHE: Oh! Isn't it wonderful!

JOURNALIST: There's the contemplative man: the man who wants to be in harmony with the world. And the man of action: that's the man who wants to bring the world into harmony with himself. Which is the right solution?

JOHN BULL: He and the world must each play his part. Each go a part of the way to meet the other.

(They both go out.)

JOSÉPHINE: It's marvellous.

1ST MAN *(reappearing with the* 2ND MAN*)*: In the old days it took a long time to go to those little islands! The road to the Isles! The voyage lasted weeks. You gradually got used to all the different climates. They spoke unfamiliar languages and had surprising faces. And how long it used to take, even by rail! There was some space in the world in those days – plenty of it.

2ND MAN: Now we have to look for it somewhere else. (*They both go out.*)

BÉRENGER: Oh!

1ST LADY (*reappearing with the* 2ND LADY): And the faces all look the same. Just like geese.

2ND LADY: And it seems you never *feel* any older. You have to rely on other people *telling* you. You're always just there, at the centre of things; you look all around you but you don't know. And when it happens, someone else has to tell you. *I* want to *know.*

1ST LADY: You have to get used to dying. It's more decent that way. You must be polite when you go. You must have time to say your goodbyes. Without too many tears.

JOSÉPHINE (*looking through her lorgnette*): Oh!

2ND LADY: My dear, it seems it's terribly easy. You get used to it so quickly. It's really quite amazing. You can give up everything straight away, all at once, just like that.

THE BÉRENGER FAMILY (*together*): Oh! Oh! Oh! Look – isn't it beautiful!

1ST LADY: It's incredible. Do you think it's true?

JOSÉPHINE (*looking at the countryside*): It's incredible.

2ND LADY: I'm sure it is, it's very easy. You only have to close your eyes. And everything slips gently away.

BÉRENGER (*looking at the countryside*): Oh!

MARTHE (*looking at the countryside*): Oh! Ah!

1ST LADY: No, I can't get used to it. Perhaps you're right, perhaps… But I can't get used to it. I suppose the time hasn't come for me yet; I'll get used to it later on. When I'm old.

(*They both go out.*)

JOSÉPHINE (*stopping and still looking through her lorgnette*): I must say, it's really very pretty.

(*All the English people who had gone out return, half from the left and half from the right of the stage. Among them, at first hidden by the others, on the left, is the* VISITOR FROM THE ANTI-WORLD, *dressed in the old style, with white side-whiskers.*

Meanwhile, a bench appears on the right and the BÉRENGER *family go and sit down facing the public, with* BÉRENGER *in the middle, all with their hands on their knees like a provincial family photograph at the beginning of the century.*

The English people meet in the centre of the stage and they exchange greetings. The children follow their parents out. Those who pass the bench as they go off greet the BÉRENGER *family.*

Now only the BÉRENGER *family is onstage, with the* VISITOR FROM THE ANTI-WORLD, *whom no one has noticed.* THE VISITOR *moves slowly towards the bench, with a pipe upside down in his mouth.*)

MARTHE: Look, that gentleman's different from the others.
JOSÉPHINE: What gentleman?
MARTHE: That gentleman all by himself.
BÉRENGER: So he is.

(*While* THE VISITOR *quietly draws nearer.*)

He's dressed in the old style.
JOSÉPHINE: But what gentleman are you talking about?
MARTHE: That old gentleman with white side-whiskers.
BÉRENGER: Yes, he has got white side-whiskers.

(THE VISITOR *is quite near the* BÉRENGERS; *he approaches them without appearing to have noticed them, and brushes so close to them that all except* JOSÉPHINE *draw back to make room and move their feet under the bench.*)

BÉRENGER: Look out!
MARTHE: He's not a very polite man, is he? He might have said he was sorry. English people are usually more polite.

(*Still walking at the same pace and without appearing to have noticed the* BÉRENGER *family,* THE VISITOR *returns to the side of the stage he came from.*)

JOSÉPHINE: But who is this gentleman you're talking about? You must be seeing things.
MARTHE: No, we're not. Didn't you see him with his pipe upside down? And the smoke going down instead of up?
BÉRENGER: Ah yes! I know.

(THE VISITOR *goes towards the back of the stage and suddenly disappears above the valley.*)

MARTHE: He's melted into thin air.
JOSÉPHINE: There you are! You really are seeing things.
BÉRENGER: Yes and no, yes and no.
MARTHE: Perhaps he fell over?

(*The three* BÉRENGERS *have already come to their feet and moved a few paces towards* THE VISITOR *before he disappears.*)

BÉRENGER: He didn't melt into the air and he didn't fall over. You can say he "fell" from the blue, if you like. He's going on with his walk, but we can't follow him any more. He's not a creature of this world. Although he moves among us, he's not one of us. He's from the Anti-World; he's gone right through the wall.
JOSÉPHINE: What wall?
BÉRENGER: Through the invisible wall. It's invisible, but we can't see through it.

(THE VISITOR FROM THE ANTI-WORLD *appears again for a brief moment above the gorge. He puts his hands behind his back and then disappears again.*)

MARTHE: There he is again! Look!
BÉRENGER: Did you see him this time?

JOSÉPHINE: You'll send me out of my mind, the two of you.

MARTHE: He's disappeared again!

BÉRENGER: He's passed the border. He's gone home.

JOSÉPHINE: Where's his home, then? And who do you mean?

BÉRENGER: The Gentleman from the Anti-World. He's gone back to his own world, the Anti-World. I see him sometimes in the mornings; he must take a walk every day at the same time, and I suppose he goes past some place where there's a crack in the Anti-World – a kind of gap, or no-man's-land, between two worlds. (*To* MARTHE:) Now you understand why he can't see us, and that's why he didn't say sorry when he passed in front of us.

JOSÉPHINE: Anyway, we can't take him at all seriously. Even if he really did exist he'd never be a useful person to know.

MARTHE: Papa, what is the Anti-World?

BÉRENGER: The Anti-World, the Anti-World... how can I explain it? There's no proof that it exists, but when you think about it, you can find it in your own thoughts. The evidence is in your mind. There's not just one anti-world. There are several universes, and they're all interlocking.

MARTHE: How many are there?

BÉRENGER: There are numbers and numbers of them. An unknown quantity of numbers. These worlds interlink and interlock, without touching one another, for they can all co-exist in the same space.

JOSÉPHINE: How's that?

BÉRENGER: I know it's difficult to imagine. But that's how it is.

MARTHE: That's what he says, so that's how it is.

JOSÉPHINE: Well, how can you see an inhabitant of one of these worlds?

BÉRENGER: It is, indeed, a very exceptional case – I know it must be due to some error of adjustment.

MARTHE: Anyone in the world can make an error of adjustment... in any world.

(*The* 1ST WOMAN *enters from the right.*)

JOSÉPHINE: It's just not good enough. Isn't there any other proof?

BÉRENGER: But I tell you, the proof lies in our own minds, in what we discover when we think.

MARTHE: We discover them when we think – we think these universes – that's what he says; don't you hear?

1ST WOMAN: You're looking for proof, aren't you? Forgive me interfering in your conversation. I thought I could help you. There is visual proof, you know.

JOSÉPHINE: Thank you.

1ST WOMAN: In Ireland and in Scotland, I myself have seen in mirrors the outline of a landscape that is not of our world.

MARTHE: Is that really true?

BÉRENGER: You see?

JOSÉPHINE: And what's it like, this landscape? Could you describe it to us?

1ST WOMAN: It is indescribable.

JOSÉPHINE: You should have brought one of these mirrors along with you.

1ST WOMAN: What good would that do? The images can only be reflected because of a certain quality in the air of Ireland, or in the water of Scotland. If one looks in these mirrors anywhere else but Ireland or Scotland, this strange phenomenon never occurs.

JOSÉPHINE: It's very peculiar. But I suppose you're right. And yet these disappearances, and these appearances that disappear again…

BÉRENGER: If we want a more detailed explanation, we shall have to ask a scientist. It's all quite beyond me.

(*The* 1ST MAN *enters from the left.*)

1ST WOMAN: Here's my husband. (*To her husband:*) Show them your little mirror from Ireland.

(*The* 1ST MAN *takes a mirror from his pocket. The other characters look at him, standing two or three paces away.*)

JOSÉPHINE: I can't see anything.

BÉRENGER: Of course you can't see anything. That just proves you've got to go to Ireland to see this indescribable landscape in the mirrors. So it also proves that it can be proved.

MARTHE: Of course it does, it's the proof you were asking for. (*The* IST MAN *and his wife go* up on the left, calling their little boy.)

IST WOMAN: Tony, be a good boy. Stop pulling the little soprano's hair!

IST MAN: If you don't, I'll pull your ears.

(*They go out. The* BÉRENGER *family go on with their walk. They walk very slowly; it is the screen at the back that is moving. At exactly the same moment as the English people go out, there appears, on the opposite side of the stage, the profile, the pipe and the arm of* THE VISITOR FROM THE ANTI-WORLD, *who disappears at once.*)

JOSÉPHINE: Look! Is that who you meant? I saw him!

MARTHE: Yes, that's him.

BÉRENGER: Oh, so you saw him this time, did you?

JOSÉPHINE: But he was quite clear. I could even describe him. I can't think why that Englishwoman said what she saw was indescribable. This is a proof that goes against her. So her proof wasn't a proper one. What I saw had an arm, a pipe, a profile, a cap—

MARTHE: No, not a cap. A tall hat.

BÉRENGER: Now be careful, this character is not like the one we saw. We can't possibly know what he's really like. (*Enter* JOHN BULL *from the left. He crosses the stage to go out on the right, smoking his fat cigar and without saying a word.*) Even if he's from the anti-world the nearest to our own, he still can't have white hair, it must be black. The only picture we can see is like a negative. If he seems old to us, perhaps it's because he's really young, and then what do "actually" and "really" really mean? Let's stick to our own world.

(*As he says the last two words, he looks at his daughter.*)

JOSÉPHINE: It's better that way.

BÉRENGER: You're still too young to understand all this. Anyway, Sunday's not the time for philosophy.

MARTHE: Is this gentleman what people call a ghost?

(*The two* OLD LADIES *come in from the right.*)

BÉRENGER: It's a popular belief that when people die they go to the Anti-World.

1ST LADY: There are a few little facts that seem to confirm this belief. As soon as someone passes on and is put into a coffin, the dead body disappears.

2ND LADY: And that explains why coffins weigh so little. What happens to the bodies?

(*The 2nd English couple enter from the right.*)

2ND MAN: What happens to the bodies? There's no such thing as ghosts.

(*The 1st English couple appear from the left.*)

1ST WOMAN: There's no such thing as ghosts.

BÉRENGER: Those who leave us settle down, so to speak, for good in the Anti-World, and they have anti-heads—

2ND WOMAN: They have anti-heads.

(*Enter* JOHN BULL *from the right.*)

JOHN BULL: Anti-heads, anti-limbs, anti-clothes, anti-feelings and anti-hearts.

BÉRENGER: If we catch a glimpse of one, it's only by accident – like that pseudo-gentleman just now, who was just a casual visitor.

1ST WOMAN: So if there's no such thing as ghosts, we can still have casual visitors.

2ND LADY: Or re-visitors.

1ST LADY: So they just pass through one little corner of our universe by mistake, for a few seconds, almost without realizing.

1ST WOMAN: Perhaps at this very moment *we* are paying *them* a visit.

2ND WOMAN: Without knowing it.

JOHN BULL: But in that case, how do we appear to them? Like nothing on earth.

JOSÉPHINE: These visitors arc just fancies blown up by the winds.

THE ENGLISH CHARACTERS (*together, talking among themselves*): It seems these visitors are fancies blown up by the winds.

1ST WOMAN: Fancies blown up by the winds.

(*The English characters disperse and leave from both sides of the stage.*)

BÉRENGER: No, no, it's not true – the negative of our universe *does* exist, and we have proof of it – or rather, it's our language that suggests the proof.

JOSÉPHINE: What proof does language suggest?

BÉRENGER: Well, for example, the expression "the world turned upside down" comes from there... although most people don't know its origin...

(BÉRENGER, *with* JOSÉPHINE *and* MARTHE, *is now at the centre of the stage. The objects that are now indicated by* BÉRENGER *will appear either at the front of the stage, between* BÉRENGER *and the audience, or behind* BÉRENGER, *in front of the screen at the back, carried along on rail.*)

BÉRENGER: ...Perhaps we can get a vague idea of this world when we see the turrets of a castle reflected in the water, or a fly upside down on the ceiling, or handwriting that you read from right to left or up the page, or an anagram (*this can be represented by a placard showing capital letters all jumbled up*), or a juggler or an acrobat, or the sun's rays shining through a crystal prism, reflected and broken up, disintegrating into a patchwork of colours and then put together again, you see, on this wall, on that screen, on your face, like a dazzling white light... as though turned inside out... It's a good thing the centre of our universe doesn't collide with the centre of the Anti-World...

MARTHE: What would happen then?

BÉRENGER: Then there'd be disintegration and annihilation for both. Pessimists even think that all the universes might destroy one another. The end of everything may come about like that.

MARTHE: Do you think so? That's terrible. And then what? There'd be nothing left?

BÉRENGER: We'd have to start again from the beginning.

JOSÉPHINE: Listen, *chéri*, I've been thinking! For quite a time now you've been drinking too much. It stops you working.

BÉRENGER: No, it doesn't. What do you think I'm doing now?

JOSÉPHINE: Well, the best you can say is that it inspires you to write purple patches like the one you've just been reciting.

MARTHE: Oh, leave him alone! He's free to do as he likes.

JOSÉPHINE: Come along! Instead of rambling on with all that nonsense, we'd better all go for a walk on the downs. The grass will freshen up your ideas.

BÉRENGER: Let's go for a stroll – yes, let's go for a stroll.

(*He takes* JOSÉPHINE *and* MARTHE *by the hand; all three make for the back of the stage, where there is a bush or a tree in blossom.* JOSÉPHINE *is on* BÉRENGER'*s left,* MARTHE *on his right. Suddenly, to the left of* JOSÉPHINE, *a small, pink, flower-covered column rises from the ground.*)

JOSÉPHINE (*slightly alarmed*): What on earth is that?

BÉRENGER: You can see it's a column, can't you?

MARTHE: It's wobbling about.

BÉRENGER: It's learning how to stand up straight.

JOSÉPHINE: It wasn't there a moment ago.

BÉRENGER: Of course not, it's just emerged from the void. You see, it's still quite fresh.

JOSÉPHINE: And what is the void?
BÉRENGER: It's a working hypothesis of the cosmos.

(*While he is talking,* MARTHE *is picking daisies round about.*)

You can't say it really exists, for if it existed, it wouldn't be void any longer. It's a kind of box. Every world and every-thing in these worlds goes into it and comes out of it, and yet it's very tiny – tinier than the tiniest cavity, tinier than the tiniest hollow in dice, tinier than tininess itself – because it has no dimension at all. You see, ruins like these, a relic of palaces that have ceased to exist, will be entirely swept away, of course, but perhaps, perhaps – and that's where there's a glimmer of hope – when they've passed through the void, they'll all be reconstructed and restored on the other side; inside out, naturally, as it's on the other side. Perhaps the rebuilding has already started; the stones and the ruins that disappear are being put together again out there. And the same with everything. And everything's aware of this, and that's what explains the happiness all about us, this feeling of victory (*he indicates both sides of the stage*), the beauty of the day.

(*The tree which had appeared at the back, and which the* BÉRENGER *family were making for, suddenly disappears.*)

MARTHE: There's no tree any more. What's happened to the tree?
BÉRENGER: I expect it's been sucked back into the void.
JOSÉPHINE: That's really going a bit too far!...
BÉRENGER: No, it's quite natural.
JOSÉPHINE: How do you explain it, then?
BÉRENGER: It's to restore the balance of things.
JOSÉPHINE: What balance?
BÉRENGER: Balance? I mean the balance that exists between the world and the outer worlds. If one thing leaves us (*the column disappears again*), another must return (*the tree reappears*).

For all these objects are the properties of the cosmos; they are all accounted for; there may be several infinities, but there are finite things within the infinite... the limits of infinity.

MARTHE: Why yes, Maman. I understand. Papa's explaining the accountancy of a multiple universe.

(*Fresh disappearance of the tree and fresh reappearance of the column.*)

BÉRENGER: The accountants are playing a game: one (*disappearance of the column*), two (*appearance of the tree*). One, two. (*The trick is repeated.*)

MARTHE: Oh! Isn't that funny!

JOSÉPHINE: You think so, do you?

BÉRENGER: One. (*The tree and the column have disappeared at the same time.*) Well I never! Two. (*The tree and the column appear at the same time.*) An error in calculation – the accountant has made a mistake... unless it's the property man.

(*Appearance of the figure of the* VISITOR FROM THE ANTI-WORLD.)

MARTHE: It's all because of him; it's his fault that everything's got mixed up.

JOSÉPHINE: There's no sense in it at all.

(*Disappearance of the* VISITOR FROM THE ANTI-WORLD; *disappearance also of the tree and the column.*)

There, you see: there are no rules; you can't make any rules for it.

BÉRENGER: Oh yes, you can.

JOSÉPHINE: Oh no, you can't – you can see for yourself.

(*Reappearance of the tree.*)

BÉRENGER: Oh yes, you can – you can see for yourself – what did I tell you?

MARTHE: What did Papa tell you?

(*Two or three successive disappearances and reappearances first of the tree, then of the column.*)

JOSÉPHINE: They get on my nerves, anyway. What do they think they're doing?

BÉRENGER: They're waiting for you to choose. Just make up your mind, that's all. Which do you prefer?

JOSÉPHINE: I'd rather have this one.

(*She indicates the column, which now remains.*)

BÉRENGER: Well, keep the column then. I'll make you a present of it.

JOSÉPHINE: Thanks. But what do I have to do to make it stay?

MARTHE: It's when you want it, you make it stay!

BÉRENGER: The borders of the void are invisible; you can easily step the other side. Look!

(*The leg of the* VISITOR FROM THE ANTI-WORLD *and his pipe appear and then disappear.*)

Look!

(*Reappearance and fresh disappearance of the same character – this time headless and pipeless.*)

Look!

JOSÉPHINE: You're not going to bring him into it again! I told you I didn't want to see him any more.

BÉRENGER (*aside*): And to think there are people who imagine the void is like a huge black hole, a bottomless pit; and yet the void is neither black nor white, and to be bottomless, it would need acres and acres and acres of space.

JOSÉPHINE: I told you I never wanted to see that gentleman again. Whether he's from our world or any other world, he gets on my nerves – he and his blessed pipe.

BÉRENGER (*still aside*): Yes. The void is neither white nor black; it doesn't exist, it's everywhere.

JOSÉPHINE: My dear man, are you with us? In the void or in the next world? I'm talking to you and you don't answer.

BÉRENGER: How do you manage to read my thoughts?

JOSÉPHINE: Because I'm an attentive wife. I was listening to you. I *do* listen to you, you know.

BÉRENGER: But I wasn't thinking out loud. I never even moved my lips.

JOSÉPHINE: That doesn't stop people from hearing if they really try.

MARTHE (*coming up to them with her bunch of daisies*): One's only got to look at you to guess everything you're thinking. You've got such an expressive face. You ought to be a film actor, or a mime or a monkey. Do you like my flowers?

BÉRENGER: They're so full of life you can hear them breathe.

MARTHE: Would you like one?

(*She puts a flower in his buttonhole.*)

It's the most beautiful one. (*Turning to* JOSÉPHINE:) Would you like one, or two?

(MARTHE *puts the flower on* JOSÉPHINE's *hat*.)

BÉRENGER: I never could resist a loving gesture. Ah! If only everyone was like you! Then we'd all be so gentle. Life would be possible and we'd even die peacefully, without regrets. If you live happily, you can die happily. We always ought to love one another.

JOSÉPHINE: It does happen occasionally, after all.

MARTHE: I'm always full of love.

BÉRENGER: What do you love?

MARTHE: I love... I don't know what I love... But I'm full of love. Everything you can see around you is so beautiful.

BÉRENGER: You're right. But we forget. Most of the time we forget. Remind me again when you see us looking worried, your mother and me.

JOSÉPHINE (*to* MARTHE): Mind you don't drop your flowers. (*To* BÉRENGER:) Where are we going to put this column? On the balcony or in the courtyard?

BÉRENGER: I've never been so relaxed; I've never been so happy. I've never felt so light, so weightless. What's happening to me?

(*While he is speaking to* MARTHE, *the scenery changes; the column quietly disappears.*)

It's all because of you. You were right, you know.

JOSÉPHINE: I think it's the air that does you good. The oxygen. You ought to live more often in the country. The Doctor's told you before. And then it's the walking, too, everyone knows that.

BÉRENGER: I suppose it's that, I suppose it must be that. When I look around me, it's as though I was seeing everything for the first time. As though I'd just been born.

JOSÉPHINE: Well, now you know. In the future you've only got to keep your eyes open.

BÉRENGER: It's... how can I explain it? Like some feeling of joy that's been forgotten – forgotten yet still familiar – like something that's belonged to me from the beginning of time. You lose it every day and yet it's never really lost. And the proof is that you can find it again, that you can recognize it. That's what it is.

JOSÉPHINE: Don't get so excited. There's no need to go hopping about like a child.

MARTHE: Oh, it doesn't matter. No one can see him. There are no English people about.

JOSÉPHINE (*to* BÉRENGER): It's all a bit abstract, what you're saying.

BÉRENGER: No, on the contrary, it's all very concrete. This happiness is something physical. I can feel it *here*. The air that fills my lungs is more rarefied than air. It gives off vapours that are going to my head. A sort of divine intoxication! Divinely intoxicated! Can you feel it too? Do you feel it too?

JOSÉPHINE: A little, perhaps.

MARTHE: I do, quite a lot.

JOSÉPHINE: Isn't it rather disturbing? I'm afraid I find it rather disturbing.

BÉRENGER: At the moment, no. I have no more worries. No worries at all.

JOSÉPHINE: Well then, *you're* all right! So long as it lasts!

BÉRENGER: My head is reeling with conviction.

JOSÉPHINE: What conviction?

MARTHE: Don't ask him any more questions, Maman – it might shake his convictions.

BÉRENGER: Conviction, conviction. I don't know what conviction, but I'm convinced it *is* a conviction.

JOSÉPHINE: Well, it can't be a conviction. If it's so vague and imprecise, it's a very unconvincing conviction. It's in the nature of a conviction to be precise.

BÉRENGER: For me, for me, once a conviction's been limited by definition, it isn't one any more. Give it some boundaries and it's invaded by doubt and denial. Anyway, there's nothing more imprecise than precision.

JOSÉPHINE: You ought to read Descartes again.*

BÉRENGER: What is the precise meaning of precision?

JOSÉPHINE: You speak a very peculiar language of your own. With you words no longer mean anything. They're quite unrecognizable.

MARTHE: Not to me.

JOSÉPHINE: Oh, be quiet! You don't have to agree with everything he says, without thinking, just because he's your father. (*To* BÉRENGER:) No one can understand you but yourself. And I sometimes wonder!

MARTHE: *I* understand him.

JOSÉPHINE: That's just your luck!

BÉRENGER: Even if I don't understand myself, what's it matter? I wouldn't be so happy if I understood.

JOSÉPHINE: Anyway, there must be some reason for it.

BÉRENGER: Yes, there may be a reason, after all. Let's go on with our walk.

JOSÉPHINE: Let's walk, then; that won't do us any harm.

MARTHE: Let's walk. Give me your hand, Papa, and yours, Maman.

(*They turn round, take each other by the hand and take a few steps towards the back of the stage. A very large silver bridge appears on the screen, which has gone on moving occasionally during the conversation, showing various different landscapes.*)

BÉRENGER: That's it – that's the reason for it – it's all because of that. Look! Look at it!

(BÉRENGER *runs a few steps away from the others towards the bridge.*)

JOSÉPHINE: Where are you going?
MARTHE: Wait for us. Where are you running to? Don't go away!
JOSÉPHINE: Wait for us!

(*Then, seeing the silver bridge,* JOSÉPHINE *and* MARTHE *both cry out:*)

JOSÉPHINE AND MARTHE: Oh! How beautiful!
JOSÉPHINE: It's magnificent!
MARTHE: You see, he *was* right.
JOSÉPHINE: That's true, Bérenger, you weren't wrong after all.

(*The silver bridge, dazzlingly brilliant, joins the two sides of the gorge above the abyss. It is like a ship in the shape of an arch, which seems to be suspended very high in the air above the river, leaping from one gleaming hilltop to the other.*

MARTHE *and* JOSÉPHINE *have also gone closer to the back of the stage and gaze at it.*

The English characters, with their children, have come in from left and right. They also gaze at the bridge. But they are more phlegmatic – much more phlegmatic – and their reactions are more reasonable.)

BÉRENGER: I understand, now I understand why I feel so happy. That's why I felt so light and airy just now.

1ST MAN (*entering from the left*): Oh!

1ST WOMAN: Ah!

2ND MAN (*entering from the opposite side to the* 1ST MAN): Ah!

2ND WOMAN: Oh!

JOHN BULL (*entering from* the *left*): Ahoh!

LITTLE BOY (*who is coming with his parents*): What is that great big thing?

1ST LADY: You mustn't call it a "great big thing". You see, we call it a great silver bridge.

JOURNALIST (*coming in from the left*): Ah! There you are, Monsieur Bérenger; could you say a few words about this bridge?

JOSÉPHINE: Leave him alone, Monsieur – he's not an engineer, he's not an architect, he knows nothing about structures.

JOURNALIST: I beg your pardon, Madame, I apologize.

(*He withdraws.*)

MARTHE: Now we can't see anything. All these English people have gone and stood in the way.

JOSÉPHINE: Mesdames, Messieurs, do you mind moving aside? *We* saw it first.

(*All the English people, one after the other, say "I'm sorry" and move aside. The* LITTLE GIRL *says "I'm sorry" too, but not the* LITTLE BOY.)

1ST WOMAN: Will you say sorry, or I'll slap your behind!

LITTLE BOY: I don't want to say I'm sorry.

1ST WOMAN (*to* JOSÉPHINE): I *am* sorry.

(*The silver bridge, which was hidden for a time by the English people, reappears, still more brilliant and beautiful. On the hillside opposite, on either side of the bridge, you can see the stations of the rack railway and the cable card moving backwards and forwards, all in different colours. The silver arch should catch and reflect the sun's rays and the brilliance of the sky, dazzlingly intensified.)*

JOSÉPHINE: Why do they seem so surprised? It's *their* bridge – it's in their own country – they can look at it every day.
1ST MAN: We only look at it on our days off, that's quite enough.
2ND MAN: In France, no one would look at it at all.

(Little motor cars start crossing the bridge at full speed. The light is reflected in the car windows and flashes back, broken into a thousand rainbow-coloured fragments.)

MARTHE: What are those moving lights? You'd think they were diamonds flashing along.
BÉRENGER: I expect they're those famous particles of light that scientists call "photons".
JOURNALIST: Although they say the French love to stand and stare.
MARTHE: Is that true?
1ST WOMAN: There are some enormous bridges in America too, but the Americans cross them with their eyes shut.
JOSÉPHINE: You'll make her more stupid than she already is. She takes you seriously, you know.
2ND LADY: That's why there are so many accidents – that's why they crash over the top.
MARTHE: I know he's only joking.
1ST LADY: There are some in Russia too.
JOHN BULL: I've seen two in Australia as well.
JOSÉPHINE: When does he ever stop joking? Still, I suppose it's better when he is. It's only when he's miserable that he stops talking nonsense.
1ST LADY: But no one looks at them there. No one takes much interest, it appears.
JOHN BULL: People are only interested in their practical utility.
MARTHE: Are you often miserable? Oh! it makes me feel miserable to know you're miserable.

1ST WOMAN: And that means the bridge no longer exists.

2ND MAN: It's destructive to be too practical.

BÉRENGER (*gaily, jumping up and down*): I feel miserable when I think of the years going by like a lot of sacks we send back empty. I feel miserable when I think we're all going to leave one another and even take leave of ourselves. But hollow hours are made for sorrow. And today I'm filled with joy, overflowing with happiness.

(BÉRENGER *goes on jumping up and down while he says this and makes sweeping gestures with his arms, like wings.*)

2ND WOMAN: Destructive of what?

2ND MAN: Destructive of everything.

JOHN BULL: It's an admirable piece of English construction.

JOURNALIST: It dates from the time of Mary Stuart.*

JOSÉPHINE (*using her lorgnette to cover her embarrassment*): Mind what you're doing! They're looking at you.

(*The English characters have indeed turned round to face the public and they gaze at* BÉRENGER, *vaguely disapproving.*)

Don't get so excited! You get too carried away. Your excitability's much too Latin for their latitude. It's not nice. It's ridiculous.

JOURNALIST: But it had to be restored.

1ST LADY: They don't make any like it nowadays.

BÉRENGER (*hopping and jumping up and down*): Forgive me, Joséphine, I can't help it. Forgive me, ladies and gentlemen, I feel so gay I can't control it. I'm overflowing.

JOHN BULL: He feels so gay he can't control it.

1ST MAN: He's overflowing.

BÉRENGER: I'm transported, carried away.

THE ENGLISHMEN: Transported!

THE ENGLISHWOMEN: Carried away!

1ST WOMAN (*to the* LITTLE BOY): This gentleman's French, you see.

LITTLE GIRL: Why is that gentleman hopping up and down?

BÉRENGER: I'm overflowing, transported, carried away, lifted right off the ground.

(BÉRENGER's *feet have indeed lifted a few inches from the ground.*)

JOSÉPHINE: Don't talk so loud, Bérenger. ·

BÉRENGER: The soles of my shoes are just brushing the top of the grass!

JOSÉPHINE: But what on earth do you think you're doing? Stop it!

BÉRENGER (*to the English characters*): Have you noticed anything?

1ST MAN: He looks happy enough.

1ST WOMAN: What's he doing?

JOURNALIST: He's walking very fast.

2ND WOMAN: It looks as if he's gliding. Yes, he is gliding.

2ND MAN: I think he's pretending to ski or to skate.

1ST LADY: He's enjoying himself because it's Sunday.

2ND LADY: We ought to enjoy ourselves on Sundays. But there's no need to caper about like a mad thing.

JOSÉPHINE: They say you must be mad.

LITTLE BOY: You'd almost think he'd grown. Grown-ups can grow too. (*To his mother:*) Do you still go on growing when you're grown up?

JOHN BULL: Perhaps. Perhaps he *has* grown – an inch or two at the most. In England, there's nothing very strange about that. (*To* JOSÉPHINE:) Don't let it worry you, Madame.

JOSÉPHINE: It's impossible. It's crazy.

JOURNALIST: It's hardly noticeable to us. We're usually very tall. Much taller than that.

2ND MAN: He'll never be as tall as us.

1ST MAN: Or, at any rate, not for long.

(BÉRENGER *has his feet on the ground again.*)

You see, he's just average height again now.

(BÉRENGER *is again lifted from the ground.*)

MARTHE: Isn't it funny! Papa's walking above the grass. He's really walking over the top of the grass.

JOSÉPHINE: Oh, be quiet! You're mad. They'll start making fun of us.

(*The two children start hopping about.*)

1ST WOMAN (*to her son*): Now, be a good boy! What do you think you're doing?

2ND MAN (*to his daughter*): You mustn't hop about like that, – it's no way to behave.

1ST MAN: It's the terrible education they get at school. It's not like it used to be.

JOSÉPHINE: Now look here, Bérenger, you're setting a very bad example.

MARTHE: But he is – yes he is – he's walking just above the grass.

(JOSÉPHINE *gazes at* BÉRENGER'*s feet with her lorgnette.*)

Look at the grass, and look at his feet!

JOSÉPHINE: But you're quite right. It's perfectly true. (*To* BÉRENGER:) It's not respectable, do you hear? What on earth do you think you're doing? Herbert, have you finished?

1ST LADY: It's his way of showing he's happy. (*To* JOSÉPHINE:) Leave him alone, Madame, and let him enjoy himself.

JOHN BULL: There are a thousand ways of showing you're happy. But there's no need to show it at all.

2ND MAN: We'd rather be reserved.

JOURNALIST: It's one aspect of his personality. I'll make a note of that.

1ST WOMAN: He's an artist.

1ST LADY: I find it rather charming and original.

JOHN BULL: That is not my opinion.

1ST MAN: After all, he *is* a guest.

JOSÉPHINE: Herbert! Herbert!

1ST MAN: As he's a guest, let's say no more about it.

JOSÉPHINE: He's almost a foot above the ground! We'll be a laughing stock! You'll make us all look ridiculous.

JOHN BULL: I can't help thinking he's rather ill-bred.

(*The two* OLD ENGLISH LADIES *start hopping about like our feathered friends.*)

1ST MAN: It's odd for someone from the Continent. He ought to have his feet on the ground.

2ND MAN: Perhaps it's that disease they call St Vitus's dance.

1ST MAN (*to the* JOURNALIST): What do you make of it?

JOURNALIST: Modern man is quite unbalanced. As you can see in behaviour like this.

JOHN BULL (*looking at the* OLD LADIES): And as for them, they look like a lot of old hens. You see, it's infectious, too.

1ST WOMAN: I can't think how people can let themselves go like that and make an exhibition of themselves.

(*She starts hopping about like a bird too, and says to the* LITTLE BOY, *who is now quite still:*)

That's enough! I tell you, that's enough!

2ND WOMAN: Neither can I. (*She also begins to hop about.*)

1ST MAN: Our wives are light in the head.

2ND MAN: They're unforgivably light on their feet.

(*The two Englishmen also start hopping about.*)

2ND WOMAN (*hopping about; to the* LITTLE GIRL, *who is now quite still*): That's enough now! That's enough!

JOURNALIST: We ought to put these foreigners from the Continent in quarantine, or at least vaccinate them before we let them in. (*He too begins to hop about.*)

JOHN BULL: That's what happens when you let your body get out of hand. It's very infectious.

(*He lumbers about with the others.* BÉRENGER *and his family are now the only ones who are not hopping about; the children and the others still go on with it for a few moments.*)

JOSÉPHINE (*to* BÉRENGER): Everyone says the same thing. They'll all think you've been badly brought up. (*To* MARTHE:) Whatever you do, don't you start.

MARTHE: Everyone's trying to do the same. But they can't. Papa's the most graceful.

JOSÉPHINE: They're only doing it out of politeness. (*To* BÉRENGER:) You look so badly brought up.

JOHN BULL (*with a thick, rather sing-song voice*): No, no, you look so badly brought up.

BÉRENGER: I'll bring myself up a bit higher in a minute.

JOSÉPHINE: They'll attack you in the newspapers. You'll never get another English visa.

(*The other English characters sing in chorus:* "No, no, you've been so badly brought up". *All movement ceases.*)

BÉRENGER: I feel elevated and overwhelmed by a sense of joy.

JOSÉPHINE (*to* MARTHE): What did he say?

MARTHE: Didn't you hear? He's been flooded. Elevated and overwhelmed by a sense of joy.

(*All the following passage is sung.*)

JOHN BULL: What did he say?

TWO LADIES: What did he say?

THE TWO ENGLISHMEN AND THE JOURNALIST: What did he say?

LITTLE GIRL (*solo*): He's been elevated and overwhelmed by a sense of joy.

There's nothing wrong with that.

(BÉRENGER *leaps about, looking as though he was gliding through the water. End of the sung section.*)

1ST LADY: He's walking way above the ground...

2ND LADY: And you'd almost think he was gliding through the water, prancing along on his sea horse, on a gigantic hippocampus.*

1ST WOMAN: Along the bottom of the ocean.

JOURNALIST: The air this morning is almost as heavy as water.

2ND MAN: And the blue sky...

JOHN BULL (*singing*): And our English sky is a deep-sea navy blue.

JOSÉPHINE: You might at least explain it to us.

JOURNALIST: That strange habit of his – those eccentric movements demand an explanation.

2ND MAN (*to* BÉRENGER): Excuse me, Monsieur, but I can't help thinking you ought to explain yourself.

1ST WOMAN: He's going to explain.

THE ENGLISH CHARACTERS (*in spoken chorus*): The foreign visitor wants to explain himself.

JOSÉPHINE: Well go on, Herbert, explain yourself!

THE TWO OLD LADIES: Explain yourself, Monsieur, my good guest.

THE ENGLISHMEN: Explain yourself, Mr Foreigner!

THE ENGLISHWOMEN: Explain yourself!

JOURNALIST: Are you bringing us a new epidemic?

(BÉRENGER *seems to be having great difficulty in keeping to the surface of the ground. From time to time he makes a few easy little leaps.*)

BÉRENGER: No, you can see for yourself – I'm flying.

JOURNALIST: He says he's flying.

BÉRENGER: I've found the way to do it again – the way we'd all forgotten.

(*He leaps three feet into the air.*)

1ST MAN: He says he's found the way to do it again.

1ST WOMAN: What has he found the way to do?

JOURNALIST: He says he's found the way to fly again.

(BÉRENGER *makes a leap of six feet into the air.*)

JOSÉPHINE: Now you've gone far enough. You're not a butterfly.

JOHN BULL: It's not natural.

MARTHE: He's not a caterpillar either.

1ST MAN: No, it's not natural.

BÉRENGER: I promise you, it's all quite spontaneous. It just happens all by itself.

1ST LADY: If it just happens, perhaps it's natural after all.

JOSÉPHINE: You're out of your mind.

BÉRENGER (*standing still*): Man has a crying need to fly.

JOHN BULL: I don't believe you.

BÉRENGER: It's as necessary and as natural as breathing.

1ST MAN: You mean we've a crying need to *eat*.

2ND MAN: And then to drink.

JOURNALIST: And then to philosophize.

1ST WOMAN: And then if there's any time left…

2ND WOMAN: Then perhaps we'll fly, just for fun.

JOSÉPHINE: Everyone thinks you're wrong.

BÉRENGER: But I'm not, I'm not – everyone knows how to fly. It's an innate gift, but everyone forgets. How could I have forgotten the way it's done? It's so simple, so dear, so childish. It would be better for us to starve than not to fly. I expect that's why we all feel so unhappy.

1ST MAN: I don't feel in the least unhappy.

1ST WOMAN: It's true we'd save lots of money if we knew how to fly.

JOHN BULL: It would be the end of industry.

BÉRENGER: You *are* unhappy, but you don't know it. That's what's wrong with mankind: we've forgotten how to fly. What would you say if we'd forgotten how to swim or walk or sit or stand?

JOHN BULL: Sitting's good enough for me. But I like standing too. Or lying flat on my tum with my backside as a blanket.

2ND LADY: Supposing we did know how to do it once, Monsieur, we'd never be able to learn how to fly again now – it's too late.

JOSÉPHINE: It's too late.

BÉRENGER: It's never too late. Besides, all you have to do is remember.

JOURNALIST: Nowadays science won't let us rely entirely on our memory. It's even better not to rely on it at all. It's not reliable. It's misleading.

1ST MAN: If there really are people who fly, they must all be mad.

JOURNALIST: And worse!

2ND MAN: Not all of them, anyway.

JOURNALIST: People who've gone right round the bend.

JOHN BULL: The incurable, the hopeless cases.

JOSÉPHINE: I've never seen him do this before. Believe me, he can still surprise me, even after all these years of married life.

BÉRENGER: If most of the time I've forgotten how to fly, I still feel I ought to be able to. I know what it is that's missing and makes me suffer. It's like not keeping fit. If we don't fly, it's because we're not healthy enough.

1ST LADY: I must say, ladies and gentlemen, it would seem that if we invent rockets and aeroplanes and interspatial machines, it must be because men feel they *ought* to fly.

2ND LADY: We're trying to fulfil a crying need.

JOURNALIST: Technology has adequately and brilliantly fulfilled that need already.

JOSÉPHINE: You can't do better than technology.

BÉRENGER: Does a cripple in a wheelchair really walk?

MARTHE: No, he's pushed along.

BÉRENGER: Does a motorist walk?

JOURNALIST: He rolls along on wheels, Monsieur.

BÉRENGER: He rolls along, shut up in a little box. It's the box that rolls *him* along.

1ST MAN: But a pilot, a pilot – you mean to say a pilot doesn't fly?

1ST WOMAN: That's right, that's what my husband says. You can't say a pilot doesn't fly?

BÉRENGER: He doesn't fly.

LITTLE BOY: Yes, Monsieur, he does.

1ST MAN: Shut up!

1ST WOMAN: It's not polite to interrupt grown-ups when they're talking.

BÉRENGER: No, he doesn't fly. It's his machine that flies.

JOSÉPHINE: You'll never be able to compete with aviation.

JOHN BULL: He'd like us to break up all our planes and sink all our ships.

2ND WOMAN (*to the* JOURNALIST): Perhaps he's a spy in England, an enemy agent.

1ST MAN: Where will it all lead us, anyway?

2ND MAN: To the calamity of calamities.

BÉRENGER: It's as easy to fly as to breathe.

JOURNALIST: No, it's certainly not as easy to fly as to breathe.

BÉRENGER: Oh yes, it is!

MARTHE: I think it's just as easy to fly as to breathe.

JOSÉPHINE: Don't be silly, of course it isn't!

JOHN BULL: Even if it was, we oughtn't to.

2ND LADY: Why not, as it's natural?

1ST LADY: I'm not at all sure it *is* natural, my dear.

2ND LADY: And everything that's natural is nice.

JOHN BULL: We should rise above our instincts.

BÉRENGER: We rise above them when we fly over them. We ought to have our own means of flying, our own means.

1ST MAN: No, we shouldn't.

1ST LADY: Perhaps we should.

2ND MAN: No, madam.

LITTLE GIRL: Yes.

2ND MAN: No.

1ST LADY: Yes.

JOHN BULL: No.

THE TWO OLD LADIES (*together*): Yes, yes.

THE ENGLISHMEN: No.

THE TWO OLD LADIES: Of course we should.

THE ENGLISHWOMEN: Perhaps we should.

JOURNALIST: But what if we really could? We've just seen – it would only help us to jump across roads and gardens and rivers—

1ST MAN: —and bushes and one-storey houses—

2ND MAN: —like a wretched little cricket.

JOHN BULL: Man is not a cricket.

BÉRENGER: Man can fly much higher than a cricket. In the old days he used to. We've just got to catch the habit again, I tell you, get back into the habit.

MARTHE: Perhaps we only lost it because we're lazy.

BÉRENGER: I don't call it progress to walk on crutches. If we're not careful we'll forget how to walk too. It's started already, anyway. We're losing all our natural powers.

JOURNALIST: On the contrary, technology multiplies them.

BÉRENGER: There's nothing on the roads now but cars.

1ST LADY: It's true, there are very few pedestrians left.

2ND LADY: And no one thinks much of *them*!

1ST LADY: Soon they'll have all disappeared.

2ND LADY: We'll have all disappeared.

BÉRENGER: I want to remain a pedestrian and a pedestrian in the air. (*He takes a leap.*) I want to stroll in the air without any artificial mechanical aid. (*He takes another leap.*)

1ST WOMAN: Good Heavens! He's off again!

MARTHE: How do you do it? Teach me!

JOURNALIST: He'll never go any higher.

1ST MAN: He's shown us all he's able to do.

2ND MAN: And that's not much.

JOHN BULL: All right, if he thinks he can go any higher, he can prove it to us.

JOSÉPHINE: Everyone says you can't go any higher. So don't try – it's not worth it. Relax.

BÉRENGER: Oh yes, I can. So can you all – we can all do it. I'll tell you what you must do.

1ST LADY: He's going to tell us what we must do.

2ND LADY: What did he say?

1ST LADY: He said he's going to tell us what we must do.

JOHN BULL: In so far as politeness permits, permit me to permit us all to laugh.

BÉRENGER: It's perfectly simple. All you need is the will to do it. You've got to have confidence. You only come down when you lose confidence. You may have noticed that when you come down you never drop like a stone.

2ND LADY: That's true. I remember that.

JOURNALIST: You mean you *seem* to remember it.

BÉRENGER: It's just another proof that it's perfectly natural to fly. And when you're in full flight, away above the highest trees or over a lake or a hilltop, you never feel frightened. Whereas, in an aeroplane, you often *do*.

1ST WOMAN: And even in a cable car.

1ST LADY: I'm even afraid on my balcony – I get so dizzy.

BÉRENGER: But, of course, sometimes you feel terribly surprised to be flying right over the cathedral, the roofs and the mountains.

2ND MAN: What happens if you start feeling too surprised?

BÉRENGER: Once you start thinking it's not normal to stay up there in the air without wings and a propeller, then your faith is shaken, you lose height and you come down, but no faster than a lift. Sometimes you can shoot up and climb again by an effort of will, as though you were throwing out ballast. But not for long. It only needs a little crack in your will-power and you start gliding right down to earth. Whenever I've found the secret again in myself, how many times have I said as I threw myself into the air: "Now I know and I'll always know; I'll never forget, any more than I can forget how to look or to listen."

(*A child's red balloon can be seen coming gently down from the flies to the stage.*)

This time I really won't forget. I'll be careful; I'll remember; I'll jot down all my movements in a notebook, then I can reproduce them whenever I like. (*He leaps very easily into the air.*) I can't stay down any longer. I'm longing to take the air and go higher and higher up. I'm going to fly right over this valley. I want to see what there is in the other valleys – the other side of those hills.

1ST LADY: He can hardly hold himself down.

1ST WOMAN: He's like a restless horse pawing the ground.

2ND WOMAN: Look at him! He's only touching the ground with the tips of his toes.

1ST WOMAN: He's going up.

(BÉRENGER *rises nearly a couple of feet and comes down again.*)

1ST MAN: He's coming down again.

2ND LADY: He's going up again.

2ND MAN: He's coming down again.

JOSÉPHINE (*to* MARTHE): Tell him to stop. He won't listen to *me*.
(*To* BÉRENGER:) Herbert, let's go home, or we'll miss the train.

MARTHE (*to her father*): How do you do it?

BÉRENGER: It's very easy – I'll show you.

JOSÉPHINE: That would be the last straw.

BÉRENGER: You'll see. It's a game. A children's game. Of course, there are a few rules to obey, but they're simple ones. There are all sorts of little tricks. Let's see now – which shall I choose? You can swim in the air. But that's tiring. You can float on the air, but you don't go very high. If you know how to ride a bicycle, you can cycle up too. It's another machine, I know, but we've got so used to this one, it's the best way for beginners to learn. Machines are taking over the functions of men. Let's use one of these substitutes to rediscover one of man's lost functions.

(*A white circus bicycle is thrown on from the wings.* BÉRENGER *catches it.*

At the same moment tiers of seats appear, like a circus, and the English characters and JOSÉPHINE *go and take their places there. They have become the audience at a circus.*

MARTHE *is on the right, at the front of the stage, with her back to the seats.*

It is not necessary for the circus to be constructed. It can be suggested by a few items. A platform, sloping upwards to the wings, could slide on from the left and acrobat rings can appear

347

over the heads of the spectators, unless nylon wires are used to raise the acrobat.

While BÉRENGER *explains what must be done, he does it. He gets on the bicycle.)*

BÉRENGER: Look: you move your legs as though you're going to set the wheels in motion. You sit very straight, as though you've got a saddle. With your hands in front of you, as though they were on the handlebars. After seven or eight turns of the pedals, you gradually move off.

(BÉRENGER *goes round the arena.*)

JOSÉPHINE: Move a bit farther away – no one can see properly.
JOHN BULL: It's very easy.
JOURNALIST: Let's wait for what comes next.
BÉRENGER: And suddenly you find you're as high as a wardrobe... a young cherry tree... an older cherry tree...
LITTLE BOY: Is that gentleman a balloon?
THE ENGLISHWOMEN: Oh!

(BÉRENGER *will cycle round the stage right above the heads of the spectators, who will have to look up to see him. He could ride up the sloping platform, disappear in the wings and then reappear still above the characters, possibly replaced by a trained acrobat.*

Acrobatic turn; the bicycle has only one wheel; then there are no handlebars. BÉRENGER *goes on moving round in circles, still pedalling like a cyclist. Then he comes down again. And when he does the platform and the rings disappear.*)

BÉRENGER: ...and then a much older cherry tree. Like this... There you are. Understand? Try it.

(*While* BÉRENGER *is circling round on high in a clockwise direction,* MARTHE *is circling round below on another bicycle in an anticlockwise direction.*)

JOSÉPHINE: Look out! Be careful! Don't listen to him! (*When the two bicycles have disappeared and the circus turn is over, the English characters applaud;* BÉRENGER *acknowledges the applause by raising* his *hands above his head like a champion.*)

LITTLE BOY: Encore!

BÉRENGER (*to* MARTHE): You see, flying's as easy as riding a bike.

1ST MAN: You've got to know how to ride one first. And I don't.

1ST LADY: I know how.

LITTLE GIRL: You can learn at any age.

BÉRENGER (*to all*): You simply have to keep your balance.

JOHN BULL: I don't know how to ride a bike either.

1ST WOMAN: You know how to ride a horse.

2ND MAN: Not all horses have wings.

2ND LADY: But a lot of them have. My husband had two in his stables with wings.

JOSÉPHINE: And he really used to go flying with them?

2ND LADY: No, they were only ornamental.

JOHN BULL: I've never seen a horse with wings! And I've owned plenty of horses.

2ND MAN: But it seems they really exist.

JOURNALIST: It's a special breed, but they're dying out.

(*The circus props have disappeared. The English characters have been getting up while they spoke.*

Once again it is the countryside, bathed in a dazzling light. The silver arch can still be seen. No more scenes in the background. Just a kind of sky or blue void.

The English surround BÉRENGER, *but all keep a fair distance between one another and* BÉRENGER *himself.*)

JOHN BULL: In fact, he uses mechanical aids like anyone else.

1ST MAN: A bicycle! That's not very smart!

2ND MAN: Lots of people can ride a bike. And what's more, I don't envy them.

1ST WOMAN: It's a pseudo-bicycle.

JOHN BULL: And that's even more uninteresting.

1ST MAN: Even a flying bicycle is still a nasty creeping thing on wheels.

JOURNALIST: An unreal bicycle's no better than a real one.

BÉRENGER: There is a more natural method.

1ST LADY: He says there's a more natural way.

BÉRENGER: A gymnastic method. (*To* MARTHE:) Watch closely.

(*Trapezes descend from the flies, in nylon if possible, unless* BÉRENGER *is to be raised with nylon wires. As before,* BÉRENGER *will act out his explanations.*)

MARTHE: Yes, Papa.

BÉRENGER: Here we go! You leap in the air as high as you can, lifting your arms right up. And then, instead of jumping down again, you hang on to an imaginary branch, as though you were going to climb a tree.

(*He jumps and remains about three feet above the ground.*)

Then you pull yourself up by the strength of your wrists and catch on to another branch a little higher. (*He does this.*) And so you climb from branch to imaginary branch.

(*He rises up in successive jerks.*)

You can climb as high as you like. For the imaginary tree is high as you want it to be. It's even infinitely high, if you like. If you can do it, you never stop climbing! Try it.

(MARTHE *tries it.*)

MARTHE: It's so difficult. I can't.

JOSÉPHINE: It's much too hard for her. She hasn't had any training. She's never been good at gym. (*The* LITTLE BOY *tries, but he can't do it either.*)

BÉRENGER: Like this.

(*He jerks himself up a little higher, then slowly comes down again.*)

Of course, it's hard to start with, and it's tiring, but the higher you climb, the easier it is. Some force pushes you up; you don't feel your own weight any more. You can scramble up with one hand. Or one finger. And then just thinking does it. (*One more easy leap; then* BÉRENGER *comes down again.*) Where there's a will there's a way. Where there's a will there's a way.

JOHN BULL: It's easy.

2ND LADY: Do it then, if you can.

JOHN BULL: You've only got to be lighter than air. That's the only rule. But it's beneath my dignity.

JOURNALIST: What's more, it's risky, it's dangerous. The natural resistance of the air tries to stop you rising. And you shouldn't fight against it.

1ST MAN: You shouldn't weaken the forces that bring you down or you might get light-headed. You can get just as drunk at high altitudes as you can in the lower depths.

2ND WOMAN: You might disappear for good.

1ST MAN: We mustn't destroy any of the forces of nature.

BÉRENGER: We mustn't resist them either, we mustn't resist them either. (*To everybody:*) You want to have a go? You want to try it? Do you want to fly with me?

(*The English characters move away, protesting, except for the English children, whose parents are tugging them away by the hand.*)

Don't be afraid! (*To* JOSÉPHINE *and to* MARTHE:) I can take each of you under one arm if you don't want to fly by yourselves.

JOSÉPHINE: But you're not going to take us by force.

1ST MAN: You're not going to take this lady by force.

MARTHE: Well, I don't know... I'd rather like to.

JOSÉPHINE: I absolutely forbid it.

JOURNALIST: We object.

JOHN BULL: With all our weight.

THE ENGLISH (*in chorus*): We object with all our weight.

(*Suddenly* BÉRENGER, *hitting the ground a little too hard with his feet, takes flight and rapidly disappears in a flash into the flies.*

JOSÉPHINE: He didn't do it on purpose. This time I'm sure he didn't do it on purpose.

MARTHE: Yes, he *did* do it on purpose.

THE ENGLISH PEOPLE (*together, gaze at him in the air*): Oh! Ah! Oh!

(*The* LITTLE GIRL *starts singing a kind of English hymn.*)

1ST LADY: He hit the ground with his foot harder than he intended.

1ST WOMAN: Look, he's going up very quickly!

2ND MAN: I expect he's been sucked up by some rising current in the atmosphere.

JOSÉPHINE: He's mad. He's mad.

MARTHE (*to* JOSÉPHINE): Don't get so excited!

2ND LADY: He's been swept up in a whirlwind.

1ST MAN: He's slowing down.

2ND MAN: He's going off at a tangent.

1ST WOMAN: He's reached the calm waters of the air.

2ND WOMAN: He's flying parallel with the arch.

LITTLE BOY: He's a balloon. He's a balloon.

1ST LADY: But high above it.

2ND LADY: Very much higher.

JOURNALIST: He doesn't need to make complicated movements now.

1ST MAN: He's not making any movements at all.

1ST WOMAN: He's holding himself quite straight; he's motionless in the air.

JOHN BULL: What's he doing? What's he doing?

JOSÉPHINE: What *can* he be doing?

1ST LADY: He's slowly making for that hill over there.

1ST MAN: How does he manage to keep on the right course?

2ND LADY: He just looks ahead. It's the way he looks that takes him in the right direction.

MARTHE: That's very good, Papa – bravo!

JOURNALIST: He's going higher still.

1ST MAN: He's floating on his back.

2ND MAN: He's flying very fast in a horizontal position.

1ST WOMAN: He's veering to the right.

2ND WOMAN: He's disappeared to the right.

1ST LADY: Now he's coming back on the left.

2ND LADY: There he is, straight ahead.

(*The English characters move their heads and turn completely round, very fast and comically, in order to follow him in his course.*)

JOURNALIST: He's disappeared again.

1ST MAN: Now he's over there.

2ND LADY: There he is again.

JOURNALIST (*to* JOSÉPHINE): And what do you make of your husband's exploits, Madame?

JOSÉPHINE: It upsets me. But I've every confidence.

ENGLISHMEN AND WOMEN: He's disappeared. He's reappeared. He's disappeared. He's circling round again.

(*In the background can be seen a sort of glowing ball or rocket, which appears and disappears, going from right to left and from left to right, faster and faster.*)

JOHN BULL: That's thirty-six times he's been round. thirty-six times.

2ND WOMAN: forty-five.

1ST LADY: ninety-seven.

1ST MAN: No, ninety-five.

1ST LADY: ninety-seven.

2ND WOMAN: We've all lost count. He's made a complete circuit more than two hundred times.

MARTHE: He's going so fast you'd think he'd stopped moving. (*The ball stops a moment in the centre of the sky.*)

JOHN BULL: It's true, he's stopped going round. He's rising straight up. He's halfway between the two hills.

(*The ball does what he says.*)

1ST MAN: He's stopping. You'd think he was stopping.

1ST WOMAN: Yes, he is stopping.

1ST LADY: He's stopped to have a look round.

(*The ball has gone from sight; so has he. Or perhaps there is a tiny doll-like figure of* BÉRENGER.)

2ND LADY: At the four corners of the earth.

JOURNALIST: He's dominating the earth.

JOSÉPHINE (*half anxious, half admiring*): I'd never have thought him capable of this. He really is someone after all. But it's very risky.

2ND MAN: He's going higher still!

2ND WOMAN: Higher still!

1ST MAN: Higher still!

2ND WOMAN: Higher still!

LITTLE BOY: He's a balloon, he's a balloon.

1ST LADY: He's giving out distress signals.

JOSÉPHINE: Oh dear! Is he going to fall?

MARTHE: Don't worry. You know very well he said he couldn't fall.

JOURNALIST: He's not losing height, he's not falling.

2ND LADY: Something's gone wrong.

(BÉRENGER, *the little doll, gets bigger.*)

1ST LADY: What's he seen?

JOHN BULL: He doesn't look very pleased.

1ST LADY: What's he seen?

JOSÉPHINE: What on earth *can* he have seen?

1ST MAN: What's he seen?

2ND LADY: He's vanished from sight.

JOSÉPHINE: He's vanished from sight. He's disappeared.

(*Gradually the stage darkens. Blood-red glimmering lights and great rumbles of thunder or bombardment. In the silence and half-light that follows, a spotlight picks out and isolates* JOSÉPHINE, *lighting her dimly at first.*)

JOSÉPHINE: He's got a positive mania for leaving me alone! He takes every opportunity to abandon me. Yet he knows I get frightened… He knows perfectly well. I've no one in the world – nobody, nobody, nobody.

MARTHE (*rather to one side, and more in the shadow than* JOSÉPHINE): You've got Papa.

JOSÉPHINE: I'm alone. I'm quite alone, cast off into the darkness and abandoned.

MARTHE: But look, Maman, I'm here.

JOSÉPHINE: I'm all alone in a great big forest, far away from everything. I'm frightened.

(*The* JOURNALIST *and the* 2ND ENGLISHMAN *cross the stage. They are transformed completely enough for us to be astonished at the change, but still recognizable; they look slightly distorted, as in a dream. Perhaps the lighting can suggest this change. Or perhaps they could wear masks representing their own faces. This may be the best solution. In any case, the lighting can tone down the colour of their clothes. They are talking:*)

JOURNALIST: You see, friendship… friendship was a snare and a delusion. Besides, it slowly sucks the life out of you. Loathing is better. It provides the most favourable background for life. It's the only thing can give us strength. Loathing means energy. It's energy itself.

2ND MAN: So we ought to loathe each other? Can I loathe you and still be polite?

JOURNALIST: It's more relaxing that way. But we've always loathed each other. Friendship was what we used to cover up our weakness; we were too timid and repressed our loathing of one another. Nowadays we're living through an age of science and cerebration. We must take a good look at ourselves, gaze straight in the face of ourselves and the truth. And to get a true perspective we must keep a certain distance apart... (*As he walks, he knocks into the* 2ND MAN *with his elbow.*) Oh, sorry! I knocked into you. So, sorry!

2ND MAN: It's nothing, really! Please don't apologize!

JOURNALIST: See what I mean?... All this sentimentality in our day and age... We can't believe in that now – we're not children any more. Friendship's a ludicrous word, hypocritical; now it's gone for good.

2ND MAN: I think you must be right, old man.

(*They go out.*)

MARTHE: I'm here, I tell you. Can't you hear me?

JOSÉPHINE: Nobody.

MARTHE: Don't you want to hear me? Maman, I'm here. And there are all the others.

JOSÉPHINE: Yes, yes, I can hear. Don't shout like that!

MARTHE: All the other people.

JOSÉPHINE: What people?

MARTHE: Friends, we've got lots of friends.

JOSÉPHINE: And you call them friends? What am I to them? And what are they to me? No, no, they're not friends. Empty vessels in a desert. Monstrously indifferent, selfish, cruel and enigmatic. Each confined in his own little shell.

MARTHE: Oh!

JOSÉPHINE: No, no, Marthe, not you, of course. But what can you do? You're only a little girl... What can you do?... And I'm so tiny in this gigantic world of ours. I'm like a frightened little ant that's lost her way, looking for her companions. My father's dead, my mother's dead, all my family are dead.

The neighbours who used to know us have left the town where I was born, and scattered all over the world. I've never heard from them since. There's no one left, not a soul in the world.

MARTHE: There's all the rest, all the other people. There are lots of people.

JOSÉPHINE: I don't know them and they don't know me. They're strangers... Once I had my parents, who were big and strong. And they took me by the hand to guide me through life. Nothing frightened *them*. They just marched straight on. With them I had nothing to fear... In those days I had nothing to fear, nothing to fear... except the fear of losing them. All the time I used to think that I would have to lose them. That was inevitable. I knew it, I knew it. And then very quickly that day came – too quickly, I'm afraid! It's a long time, such a long time now, since I've been all alone – such a long time since they left me by myself... And I've never got used to them not being here. And I never shall. Never, never... I've been left all alone, and I'm frightened, so frightened. I'm lost and I just wander about... No one knows me and no one loves me; I mean nothing to other people. For them I don't count. For them I just don't count.

MARTHE: I'm growing up. I'll soon be as strong as your mother was. I'll protect you.

JOSÉPHINE: I fight to protect myself, in my despair, as best I can. Fear has taught me how. The clawing fingers of fear have driven me on. And I fight tooth and nail.

MARTHE: You must love people. If you love them, they won't he strangers to you any more. If you stop being afraid of them, they won't be monsters any more. Deep down in their shells, they're frightened too. Love them. Then hell will exist no more.

(MARTHE *is no longer visible. In the semi-darkness a wall can be seen. A terrified child, rather like the little English boy, dashes to the wall and tries to climb it. Without success. A large fat character appears, not unlike John Bull, chasing the child. It is, in fact,* JOHN BULL *and the* LITTLE BOY, *also slightly transformed, as in a dream.*)

FAT MAN: You stinking little brat!

CHILD: Let me go, sir... I'm sorry, sir.

FAT MAN: Filthy little swine! So you'd get away from us, would you? Trying to escape! Why? Just tell me why!

CHILD: I'm very sorry, sir. I wanted to go for a walk in the light. I wanted lots of sky.

FAT MAN: Greedy child. Hooligan. (*He slaps the boy and pulls the weeping child away by his ear.*) You thought I couldn't catch you, did you?...

CHILD: Not the cell, sir; I won't go back to that cell!

FAT MAN: Stupid brat, you've got to learn that the light's a lot more beautiful when it's seen from the bottom of a nice black hole. And a clear blue sky's a lot purer when you look at it through a high barred window.

CHILD: Not the cell, sir; I won't go back to that cell!

FAT MAN (*pulling him off*): We'll teach you. We'll educate you. You'll understand one day... or you'll learn to put up with it.

(*They go out. Strange apparitions can be seen, which are then recognizable as the* 1ST ENGLISHMAN *and the* 1ST ENGLISHWOMAN, *the* 2ND ENGLISHMAN *and the* JOURNALIST, *slightly transformed, as if somewhat caricatured, and with exaggerated gestures. They go up to* JOSÉPHINE.)

JOURNALIST: Oh Madame, Madame, all our hearts are with you.

THE THREE ENGLISHMEN (*together*): All our hearts are with you. All our hearts are with you.

1ST MAN: If there's anything we can do...

2ND MAN: We'd do anything for you.

JOSÉPHINE: You're very kind, Madame, Messieurs.

1ST WOMAN: I know what it's like to be all alone in a foreign country. We've had the same experience. My husband will help you and all our lovers are at your service.

JOSÉPHINE: Oh, you're so kind – you're much too kind.

JOURNALIST: We're entirely at your service.

JOSÉPHINE: Thank you, I'm covered with confusion.

1ST MAN: What did she say?

2ND MAN: She said she's covered with confusion. Imagine that? She said she's covered with confusion.

(*The three* ENGLISHMEN *and the* ENGLISHWOMAN *leave the stage, saying:*)

1ST WOMAN: She's covered with confusion – she told you she was covered with confusion?

JOURNALIST: Yes, she said "Thank you, thank you, I'm covered with confusion."

1ST MAN (*imitating* JOSÉPHINE): Thank you, I'm covered with confusion.

2ND MAN: The lady's so naive, she's a very stupid Eve.

JOURNALIST: That's why she's covered with confusion. Hee hee!

THE TWO MEN: Hee hee!

1ST WOMAN: You could take advantage of the situation, yes?

JOURNALIST: There's no advantage there, I guess.

(*Before they go off, they turn towards her for the last time, and laughingly take their farewell, making grotesque gestures and grimaces.*

JOSÉPHINE, *who has her back turned to them, does not notice.*

JOSÉPHINE *remains alone; she is on the extreme right of the stage.*)

JOSÉPHINE (*in a different tone*): And what about him – where's he always off to? What's he doing? *He* could have helped me. He ought to help me... He abandons me, like all the rest, he doesn't think about me... No one thinks about me...

(*A gigantic character appears in crimson light, dressed in a long red robe with a square red cap on his head. The character could be from seven to ten feet tall, and he can be raised up on a platform hidden by his red robe; he is a judge... He could have an enormous doll's head; he is terrifying, of course, but that need not prevent the audience from laughing.*

They can laugh and be frightened at the same time, as when the enormous boots of the dead body appear at the end of Amédée, or How to Get Rid of It.* *Laughter will not weaken the effect.*

This monumental judge advances, on rollers, towards JOSÉPHINE, *until she is quite near, just facing him; to look at him, she has to raise her head.*

To the right and left of the Judge there are two assessors, also dressed in red, but not nearly so tall; they are, in any case, seated; only the Judge remains standing.

This is a Court of Law, already set up, which is brought forwards on rails. They first glide slowly up to JOSÉPHINE, *and will later retire in the same way, being drawn backwards.*

Just as they arrive in front of JOSÉPHINE, *one of the assessors, fat and purple-faced, is ringing a little bell. The other one has a hood over his head. The platform stops.*)

JOSÉPHINE: I haven't done anything wrong, your honour... Why do I have to appear before you? What am I accused of? I haven't done anything.

MARTHE (*or the voice of* MARTHE): Don't be frightened, Maman. It's a vision, it's a nightmare. It's not real. It's only real if you believe in it. It's real if you think it is. It's real if you want it to be. Don't believe it.

JOSÉPHINE: Yes, it is. It's the Judge. I recognize him.

MARTHE: You've never seen him before. He doesn't exist.

JOSÉPHINE: I'm afraid he does. It's the Judge.

MARTHE: I promise you it's an hallucination – it's an image in a dream... Wake up. Wake up and he'll disappear.

JOSÉPHINE: No, no... he's real.

MARTHE: He *isn't* real, my poor little Maman – you're dreaming... You're *dreaming,* I tell you – believe me. (MARTHE *disappears again.*)

JOSÉPHINE: I've done no harm to anyone, your honour... Why have you come? What do you want with me?

1ST ASSESSOR (*ringing his bell*): Silence! It's we who ask the questions, and you must answer.

JOSÉPHINE: I've nothing to say. It doesn't matter how much I search my conscience, I've nothing to tell you, I've nothing to hide, I swear I haven't, I don't understand, I don't understand...

(*The Court is silent.*)

If everyone's got to be judged, why start with me? Why did you choose me, when there are so many others?... Why make me the scapegoat?... I suppose it's because I'm not so well defended as the others. I haven't a lawyer.

(*The Court is silent.*)

My conscience is clear. Is that why I'm vulnerable? I'm not guilty of anything; it's not my fault. I have no faults. Tell the executioner not to kill me, your honour.

(*The Court is silent.*)

What can I possibly have done? What can you hold against me? There's nothing you can hold against me. I've always been a virtuous and faithful wife... I've done my duty, always. I've never left my post. I've always stayed at my post and been good, and sad and resigned and unhappy... (*She starts sobbing.*) And unhappy... Do you want to punish me because I've been unhappy? You want to condemn me for being good? No, it can't be that, can it? No, it really can't be that?... I don't understand you, I don't understand you, your honour. Punish the wolves, if you like, but *I'm* a lamb.

(*The Judge points his first finger threateningly at* JOSÉPHINE. *The two assessors shake their heads approvingly. The head shaking of the assessor who wears the hood is more violent and more grotesque.*)

They're going to condemn me. They don't believe me...
No, no, no.

MARTHE: It's not real, don't be frightened – you only see these
figures because you're afraid. It's not true, I swear it isn't.
Convince yourself it's not true, all this. You're imagining it,
you're inventing it...

JOSÉPHINE: I don't want to... I don't want to... What have I done?
I haven't done any harm. (*She is sobbing.*)

MARTHE (*kissing* JOSÉPHINE): Poor little Maman, hide your head
in my arms and you won't see them any more.

JOSÉPHINE: No, no, no, it's impossible. I don't want to.

MARTHE: But of course it's impossible... Of course it's not real.
(*The second assessor takes off his hood: it is* JOHN BULL.)

JOHN BULL: The reasons of the heart are not those of real justice and logic. If justice seems to you unjust, it is because it
is impartial.

(*The Court of Law is pulled backwards, slowly and silently, and
disappears into the wings on the left.*)

MARTHE: What did I tell you? It's just a vision. It can't do any
harm. Now the wicked judges have all gone... Calm yourself,
Mother, calm yourself, my child...

(JOHN BULL *appears from the right with a machine gun that
makes no noise when he fires it. He is accompanied by the two*
ENGLISHMEN *and the* JOURNALIST. *The little English children
appear from the left, with their mothers on either side, followed
by the* UNDERTAKER'S MAN *and the* DOCTOR *who appeared at
the start of the play.*)

JOHN BULL: It's better to be a few years early than two minutes
too late... Isn't it, ladies?

1ST WOMAN: You're right.

2ND WOMAN: I entirely agree, Mr John Bull. You're perfectly
right, Mr John Bull.

(*The* 2ND LADY *appears from the left, looking very agitated*.)

2ND LADY: Don't think I'm afraid, because I'm not. I'm just indignant – terribly indignant.

JOHN BULL (*to the two* ENGLISHMEN *and the* JOURNALIST): Well then, since your wives share your own opinions (*to the* JOURNALIST) and everything's all right... let's get on with it.

JOURNALIST: Carry on, then.

UNDERTAKER: Carry on, then.

1ST MAN: As it's got to be, you might as well do it.

2ND MAN: Yes, you might as well do it.

2ND LADY: I strongly protest...

UNDERTAKER: Better now at that age than later... Now, they won't realize what's happening. Later on, they'd suffer and they'd resist.

JOURNALIST: It's for their own good.

JOHN BULL (*taking aim with his rifle or machine gun*): Ladies, close your eyes.

1ST WOMAN: Let's close our eyes.

2ND LADY: I protest.

JOHN BULL (*to the* OLD LADY): Get out of the way. It's too late for you now.

(JOHN BULL *takes aim, and fires. The two* CHILDREN *fall to the ground*.)

2ND LADY (*who had moved away*): I protest most violently...

JOHN BULL: Ladies, open your eyes.

1ST WOMAN: Is it over already?

2ND WOMAN: How quick you are!

UNDERTAKER: It's like a mercy killing. It's not exactly mercy killing, but you could say it's preventative mercy killing.

2ND LADY: I protest most strongly, most violently.

JOURNALIST (*to the* ENGLISHWOMEN): Now you can pick up your children.

UNDERTAKER: It's not worth the trouble, ladies. Leave it to me. That's my job. I'll take care of it…

2ND WOMAN: We've only done our duty.

JOHN BULL: And we've done ours. (*To the* DOCTOR:) Doctor, will you verify that these children are well and truly defunct?

2ND LADY: I protest. It's absolutely disgraceful. It shouldn't be allowed. (*To the* DOCTOR-UNCLE:) You call yourself a doctor, and you accept it all, just like that?

DOCTOR-UNCLE: I don't accept it. I'm resigned to it.

JOSÉPHINE: What, is it you, Doctor-Uncle? You're not in this too?

DOCTOR-UNCLE (*to* JOSÉPHINE): This way, you see, I shall avoid being judged myself…

JOHN BULL (*to the* ENGLISHWOMEN, *with a certain gallantry*): Since you have no more children to bring up, I wonder, ladies, if you'd mind… taking your turn?

1ST WOMAN: We don't mind at all.

JOSÉPHINE (*to the* DOCTOR): I'd never have thought you could behave so contemptibly.

DOCTOR-UNCLE: What do you expect, my poor Joséphine? We all acquire wisdom in time. Besides, it's better that way. In any case, it was bound to happen. It's all over much quicker this way. It's better sooner than later – much better to be thirty years early than two seconds too late.

JOSÉPHINE: You… you who've saved so many human lives, thousands of children…

DOCTOR-UNCLE: This is how I redeem myself.

JOHN BULL (*to the* ENGLISHWOMEN): And your husbands, too. Your husbands will follow you. (*To the* ENGLISHMEN:) After you, gentlemen, if you don't mind.

(*Slight, discreet hesitation on the part of the* ENGLISHMEN. *The* ENGLISHWOMEN *advance with* JOHN BULL *behind, holding his machine gun.*)

MARTHE (*to* JOSÉPHINE): It's not real, don't get so upset… none of it is real.

(*The* UNDERTAKER'S MAN *picks up the children, one under each arm. The* OLD LADY, *the children, the* DOCTOR-UNCLE, *the* UNDERTAKER'S MAN, *the* ENGLISHMEN *and* WOMEN, JOHN BULL *and the* JOURNALIST, *all disappear from both sides of the stage.*

The GREAT WHITE MAN *appears. Same apparatus and installation as for the Court of Law. On the right of the* GREAT WHITE MAN, *a hangman in white with a white hood. To the right of the hangman, a gibbet.*

In the background there is a twilight sky with a red sun. As soon as this group approaches JOSÉPHINE, *they stop and remain silent for a few moments.*)

JOSÉPHINE: No, no.

MARTHE (*to* JOSÉPHINE): Don't take any notice. All you have to do is not believe in them.

THE MAN IN WHITE (*indicating the gibbet to* JOSÉPHINE): Madame, wouldn't you like to? Make up your mind.

(JOSÉPHINE, *in her terror, still keeps up the polite habits of society, and so does the* MAN IN WHITE: *nightmare and drawing-room manners.*)

JOSÉPHINE: No, please don't ask me. I'm terribly sorry, Monsieur. I don't feel like it, I'd really rather not.

MAN IN WHITE: You would, if you took my advice.

MARTHE: She doesn't want to, I tell you. And if she's said she doesn't want to—

MAN IN WHITE (*to* JOSÉPHINE): Think carefully. You really won't? Take your courage in both hands!

JOSÉPHINE: Oh no, oh no, really, not now.

MAN IN WHITE: In any case, you won't be able to put it off indefinitely.

JOSÉPHINE: No, no. We'll see – perhaps tomorrow. Oh please, no, not now – the day after tomorrow. Not today. I really don't feel like it just now.

MARTHE: You see, she really doesn't feel like it.

HANGMAN (*to* JOSÉPHINE): Madame, why put off till tomorrow what you might just as well do today? Why not get it over with?

MARTHE (*to the* HANGMAN): Mind your own business and don't interrupt our conversation. Leave her alone.

JOSÉPHINE: No.

MAN IN WHITE: You know very well you can't escape. You know very well that everyone goes the same way. You don't gain anything really, only a little time.

JOSÉPHINE: Tomorrow, tomorrow, tomorrow. Give me a little longer, Monsieur Man-in-White… Give me a little longer, Monsieur Hangman.

MAN IN WHITE: If you really insist. But it's a mistake. However, if you really don't want to, we're not in a desperate hurry yet.

HANGMAN: They're all alike – they're so stupid. Just try and get them to see reason… (*To* JOSÉPHINE:) And yet you've just seen for yourself, the English people all agreed. Even the children.

MARTHE: You didn't ask their consent. You didn't ask their consent!

(*The* MAN IN WHITE *makes a sign: gibbet, hangman, then the* MAN IN WHITE *himself, all slowly disappear to the left.*)

You see, Maman, it wasn't real. If you don't want it to be, it isn't real. It all depends on you. Now stop having nightmares. Promise me you won't have any more nightmares… No more nightmares… They've gone, they didn't really exist!

JOSÉPHINE: I'm not so sure.

(*Change in the lighting: the* ENGLISHMEN, *the* ENGLISHWOMEN, JOHN BULL *and the* JOURNALIST *reappear, as they did at the beginning.*)

MARTHE: You see, the little English Children are still here.

(*The stage gradually darkens. It glows blood-red with great sounds of thunder or bombardment. Light returns to the stage again;*

but this time it is a different light, which makes the landscape look grey and sad, a kind of twilight; perhaps in the background you could see a few smoking ruins, a cathedral, a smoking volcano. You can also hear:)

THE VOICE OF BÉRENGER (*despairing*): I can see, I'm afraid I can see everything! And there's no more hope. It's impossible, it's just impossible. And yet, perhaps, if it were only a dream. No, no, it's not a dream. Oh God!

1ST LADY: He's spinning slowly round.

JOHN BULL: Like a top that's running down.

2ND LADY: He looks as though he's coming down.

2ND WOMAN: He *is* coming down.

MARTHE (*to* JOSÉPHINE): You see, he's coming down. He's coming.

JOSÉPHINE: A good thing too. I don't feel quite so anxious.

1ST WOMAN: He could have stayed up there as long as he liked.

1ST LADY; I wouldn't have come down.

2ND WOMAN: But the man's got a family.

1ST MAN: He's coming closer. You can see him better.

2ND MAN: He's gesticulating. You'd think he was talking.

1ST LADY: Though we can't hear him.

JOURNALIST: He's coming down very gently.

2ND LADY (*to* JOSÉPHINE): You must be proud of your husband.

MARTHE: He's coming down so sadly. He looks so depressed.

1ST LADY (*giving the* LITTLE GIRL *a bouquet of flowers*): You must give the gentleman this bunch of flowers.

JOSÉPHINE (*to* MARTHE): Why do you think he seems sad? He's been very successful.

2ND LADY (*giving a rather torn and dirty flag to the* LITTLE BOY): And you can march in front of him when he arrives with this.

JOHN BULL: It's not much of a triumph in my opinion.

MARTHE: Yes, he is sad. You can tell that from his movements, from the general look of him.

1ST MAN: He's coming nearer and nearer.

(*The sounds heard just now have got gradually fainter. Now there is nothing but the sound of firecrackers, and there is a kind of twilight – red, perhaps. You can see a few firecrackers exploding with brief flashes of blood-red. Through the spluttering sound, you can also hear in the distance a kind of 14th of July dance music, derisively triumphant.*)*

1ST WOMAN: He's coming down step by step.
1ST LADY: It's as though he was coming down an invisible staircase.
2ND LADY: There he is. (*To* JOSÉPHINE:) There's your husband, Madame.
2ND WOMAN: Where can you see him?
1ST MAN (*pointing with his finger*): There! At the end of my finger.
1ST WOMAN: He's brushing the top of that tree.
2ND MAN: He's not in a hurry. He's picking a leaf.
JOURNALIST: Automatically.

(*The leaf can be seen fluttering down.*)

JOHN BULL: Here he is.
2ND LADY: Bravo, Madame Bérenger!

(BÉRENGER *reappears, alighting gently on the stage. They all go towards him.*)

LITTLE GIRL: Bravo, Monsieur Bérenger!

(*The* LITTLE BOY *has got a kind of trombone, which he blows into in an effort to play a victory march. He has already given his flag to* BÉRENGER, *who drops it at once.* BÉRENGER *has not taken the flowers from the* LITTLE GIRL *either; they too drop on the stage.*)

　　Bravo!
JOSÉPHINE: He's quite deflated. (*To* BÉRENGER:) What did you see up there? Are you tired?

(*The* ENGLISHWOMEN *wave their coloured handkerchiefs and clap their hands, shouting "Hurrah for Bérenger!" The* ENGLISHMEN *are silent. It should be pointed out that, before his feet touched the grass again,* BÉRENGER, *in his descent, just grazed the heads of the* ENGLISHMEN, *who had to move out of the way.*)

JOURNALIST: Tell us all your impressions, Monsieur Bérenger.

JOSÉPHINE: I'm so glad you're back. I must say, I was really frightened, after all. You ought to have warned me. Tell the Journalist all your impressions.

BÉRENGER: I... I... (*He falls silent.*)

JOHN BULL: Monsieur, may I ask you how you did it?

1ST MAN: And what you did?

2ND LADY: You saw for yourself – he's been flying.

BÉRENGER: I have been flying, yes, I've been flying all right...

1ST LADY: But you saw for yourself.

JOURNALIST: Why have you been flying?

BÉRENGER: I don't know... I couldn't help myself.

JOHN BULL: What we mean is "Why do you *fly*?" What do you hope to achieve with an exploit like that?

1ST MAN: It's not true. You weren't really flying at all. We were watching carefully: you were walking over an invisible arch. On something solid.

1ST WOMAN: Oh, no! There wasn't any arch!

1ST LADY: There was no invisible arch.

JOURNALIST: There could have been. If the air solidifies, it does make an invisible arch.

2ND MAN: Anyone could have done that.

2ND WOMAN (*to her husband*): Don't exaggerate!

1ST LADY: Why don't you try, then?

2ND LADY: That's true, you could at least try.

2ND MAN: Anyone can do the same. Absolutely anyone.

1ST MAN: All we need is for you to tell us the exact position of that invisible air-bridge.

BÉRENGER: There isn't any arch apart from the silver bridge. I was just flying, that's all – I promise I was flying.

JOHN BULL (*to the other English characters*): In any case, there's nothing very extraordinary about his achievement.

2ND MAN: That's right. A flying kite does exactly the same.

2ND WOMAN: Well, it's something, anyway, for a man to be a flying kite.

JOHN BULL: Why give yourself all that trouble when you can reach the other side of the valley in a few seconds by crossing the bridge in a car?

1ST MAN: Or in one of our planes.

2ND MAN: Or in one of our rockets.

JOURNALIST: It took him a good five minutes just to cover half the distance.

1ST LADY (*to* JOSÉPHINE): They're too critical. Don't listen to them, Madame.

2ND LADY: People are so envious.

JOURNALIST: Five minutes at least, or even six! It's much too long! It's a terrible waste of time.

1ST MAN: And we haven't any time to waste.

JOHN BULL (*to* BÉRENGER): We're not prepared to patent your system.

JOURNALIST: Anyway, just to keep my professional conscience quiet, I'm going to ask you to give us your impressions.

BÉRENGER: What can I tell you? What on earth can I tell you?

2ND WOMAN (*to* JOHN BULL): I think we ought to – we ought to patent it.

1ST MAN: Technology does far better, Madame. Technology does better. It's against all the principles of progress and the development of the human mind to return to natural laws.

MARTHE: Bravo, Papa, bravo, bravo! Oh! But he really does look deflated.

JOSÉPHINE: What's the matter with you?

2ND MAN (*to the* 1ST WOMAN): I assure you, Madame, it may be a brave thing to do, but it's nothing out of the ordinary. Absolutely any Englishman, with a little training, a little training…

JOSÉPHINE: What's the matter with you? You ought to be proud of yourself! What a character! You don't look satisfied – you never look satisfied.

2ND WOMAN: Defend yourself, Monsieur, explain yourself.

1ST LADY: Tell them how important this is.

1ST WOMAN: You have all our admiration.

JOSÉPHINE (*to* BÉRENGER): You see.

JOHN BULL (*to the English characters*): Now listen to me: the whole incident presents no interest at all.

JOURNALIST: Puerile! The only height he's scaled is the height of ridicule.

JOSÉPHINE: Believe me, it is a success – there will always be someone to criticize.

2ND LADY: Anyone who's been as high as you have won't be put off by a little thing like that.

1ST WOMAN: Say something, Monsieur, say something.

MARTHE: He's frightened, he's tired. His eyes look quite wild...

JOSÉPHINE: Oh God! What a look! What can you have seen on the other side?

1ST MAN: He can't have seen anything at all, going at such a speed, and with no precision instrument.

1ST WOMAN: What did you see, Monsieur, on the other side? Tell us. What did you see?

THE ENGLISHWOMEN (*together*): What did you *see?*

BÉRENGER: I saw... I saw... some geese...

JOHN BULL: He saw some geese. He's a practical joker.

BÉRENGER: Men with the heads of geese.

JOURNALIST: Is that all? That's not much.

BÉRENGER: Men licking the monkeys' behinds and drinking the sows' piss.

JOURNALIST: Monsieur, Monsieur! Don't be indecent!

JOHN BULL: Little children have delicate ears.

1ST MAN: What depravity!

JOSÉPHINE: Herbert, watch your language!

(*On hearing* BÉRENGER'*s words, the* LITTLE BOY *says:* "Hear what he said?" *And the* LITTLE GIRL *replies:* "He said the monkeys' behinds and the sows' piss".)

BÉRENGER: I saw columns of guillotined men, marching along without their heads, columns of guillotined men... crossing enormous plains. And then, and then, I don't know, giant grasshoppers and fallen angels, and archangels gone astray.

JOHN BULL: He's an old humbug.

JOURNALIST: He hasn't seen anything at all. He simply read that in the Apocalypse.

1ST WOMAN (to the LITTLE BOY): No, you *can't* have it. It's not a children's book.

BÉRENGER: I saw whole continents of paradise all in flames. And all the blessed were being burned alive.

JOURNALIST: If that's all you've got to tell us, Monsieur, it's not worth taking notes.

2ND WOMAN: Make an effort, Monsieur Bérenger, just to please us. We admire you. Tell us all about your journey.

BÉRENGER: I'm trying to.

1ST WOMAN: Something more interesting, more up to date.

BÉRENGER: I saw some knives, I saw some graves—

1ST MAN: And he thinks we'll be amazed at that. We've got steel-works and cemeteries all over the place.

JOSÉPHINE: But where else did you go? What else did you see?...

BÉRENGER: In another place, the earth was cracking... the mountains were caving in and there were oceans of blood... of mud and blood and mud...

JOHN BULL: Not much imagination. If that's literature, I don't think much of it.

JOURNALIST: Compare it with *our* poets!

1ST MAN: And even with *foreign* poets! You don't have to look any further than Dante.

2ND MAN: There's not much of interest here.

2ND LADY: And yet, I must say it impresses me – it quite moves me.

MARTHE: But when you went higher up? When you were right in the air?

JOSÉPHINE: What else did you see up there?

BÉRENGER: I went such a long way up. To see what was going on towards the other points of the compass.

JOURNALIST: And when you got there, what did you see?

JOHN BULL: Did you see anything more exciting?

1ST MAN: Not so vulgar?

2ND MAN: A bit more cheerful?

BÉRENGER: I reached the ridge of the invisible roof where space and time come together, and I touched it with my head; I gazed to the right, to the left, behind and in front of me.

(*While he has been saying the last sentence, the* 1ST MAN *has remarked to his wife: "It's getting late for the little one."*)

1ST WOMAN (*taking the child by the hand*): Come along, let's go home.

(*The* 1ST MAN *and the* LITTLE BOY *move away slowly to the left, where the vague cracklings and feeble glimmerings of a firework display suggest some gloomy celebration.*)

BÉRENGER: Bottomless pits, bombardments, bombardments, bottomless pits opening over the plains, already ravaged and deserted centuries ago.

2ND MAN (*taking his wife and little daughter by the hand*): We don't want this nonsense to give her a bad impression.

(*They stroll slowly away on the opposite side – that is to say to the right, watching the celebrations, which are similar to those on the other side.*)

BÉRENGER: And then, and then, and then...

JOHN BULL: If he wanted us to believe him, he might have brought a fox back with him, or one of his old sows.

JOURNALIST (*to* JOHN BULL): The pub's open. Coming?

(*They walk slowly to the back of the stage, and then too quietly disappear with all the others, one by one.*)

1ST LADY (*to the* 2ND LADY): It's getting very late.

BÉRENGER: ...millions of vanishing universes, millions of exploding stars.

2ND LADY: I'm cold. Let's have a cup of tea.

(THE TWO OLD LADIES *also go off quietly, and everyone will have disappeared by the end of* BÉRENGER*'s speech.*)

BÉRENGER: And then, and then infinite wastes of ice instead of unending fire, then the fire and the ice again. Deserts of ice, deserts of fire battling with each other and all coming slowly towards us... nearer and nearer and nearer.

JOSÉPHINE: You must tell everyone – tell them quickly what you've seen! Listen to what he's saying!

MARTHE: They're not listening.

BÉRENGER: No one would believe me. I was sure no one would believe me... mud and fire and blood... tremendous curtains of flames...

MARTHE: *I* believe you. *We* believe you.

BÉRENGER: And even if they did believe me, even if they did believe me...

JOSÉPHINE: Well, what are you waiting for? Take us one under each arm, now you've proved you can do it, and fly us away.

MARTHE: Quickly, fly us away!

BÉRENGER: But where to?

JOSÉPHINE: Fly us away, much farther away – far on the other side of hell.

BÉRENGER: I'm afraid I can't, my darlings. After that, there's nothing.

JOSÉPHINE: What do you mean, nothing?

BÉRENGER: Nothing. After that there's nothing – nothing but abysmal space... abysmal space.

(*The evening falls blood red, the spluttering of firecrackers can be heard, followed by fleeting red glows.*)

MARTHE: Can you hear? Can you see? I'm frightened.
BÉRENGER: It's nothing, my darlings, not yet. There's nothing yet but the celebrations, it's a kind of English Fourteenth of July.

(*With lowered heads* BÉRENGER, JOSÉPHINE *and* MARTHE *make for the red lights of the town and go out.*)

It's nothing, not just yet. It's nothing, not just yet.
MARTHE: Perhaps that's all that's going to happen – just firecrackers... Perhaps it will all come right in the end... Perhaps the flames will die down, perhaps the ice will melt, perhaps the depths will rise. Perhaps the... the gardens... the gardens...

(*They go out.*)

CURTAIN

Notes

p. 3, *The Killer*: An attempt has been made to reach a compromise between American and British English, but in the event of production, producers should feel themselves free to change any word that would obviously offend an audience. Two cases in point would be elevator/lift and prefect/monitor (TRANSLATOR'S NOTE).

p. 35, *clochard*: "Vagrant" (French).

p. 43, *earn your living... says*: See Genesis 3:19.

p. 50, *blue-blooded critic... Hobson*: There is a pun here in the original on the name of the French writer and dramatic critic Morvan Lebesque. Harold Hobson is a natural choice in England for his well-known admiration of French drama. American readers might like to pun on the name of an American critic (TRANSLATOR'S NOTE).

p. 115, *Épicerie*: "Grocery" (French).

p. 142, *two horns... African rhinoceros*: Of the five extant species of rhinoceros, two are native to Africa and three to Southern Asia. Jean has confused the species, however: the African species have two horns, while the Asian species have a single horn, as Bérenger points out.

p. 154, *The colour bar*: A system by which organizations, employers, etc. would deny access based on race.

p. 195, *Judge not lest ye be judged*: See Matthew 7:1.

p. 197, *You're a Don Quixote*: Don Quixote, the main character in the celebrated eponymous novel by Miguel de Cervantes (1547–1616), does not see the world for what it is.

p. 201, *Galileo... si muove*: "And yet it moves" (Italian); a phrase attributed to Galileo Galilei (1564–1642), which was supposedly spoken after he was forced to recant his theory that the earth moves around the sun, rather than the reverse.

p. 228, *the King's Levée*: The *Levée*, or "Rising" (French), was a ceremony that took place upon a king's waking-up, where visitors of note were granted an audience.

p. 252, *the death... with dignity*: The kings Louis XIV of France (1638–1715) and Philip II of Spain (1527–98), and the Holy Roman Emperor Charles V (1500–58) are all thought to have suffered greatly before their deaths – with diabetes, dental abscesses and gout, cancer and malaria respectively.

p. 280, *De mortuis nihil nisi bene*: "Of the dead, nothing but good" (Latin), equivalent to the expression "Do not speak ill of the dead".

p. 295, *Douanier Rousseau... Chagall*: Henri Rousseau (1844–1910), also known after his job as a customs officer, "le Douanier", Maurice Utrillo (1883–1955) and Marc Chagall (1887–1985) were French painters, whose works were often landscapes, and notable for their modernist style.

p. 310, *our little... prima donna*: A reference to Ionesco's 1950 play, *La Cantatrice chauve* (*The Bald Prima Donna*), in which, unlike here, where nobody is "the slightest bit surprised by this and it passes off quite naturally", the mention of the bald prima donna has an unsettling effect on the characters.

p. 332, *read Descartes again*: An allusion to the work of the French philosopher René Descartes (1596–1650), which brought into question the notion of reality.

p. 336, *the time of Mary Stewart*: Mary, Queen of Scots, reigned 1542–67.

p. 341, *hippocampus*: "Any of various fishes considered to have a head and neck resembling those of a horse" (*OED*).

p. 360, *dead body... Rid of It*: A reference to Ionesco's 1954 play about a dead body.

p. 368, *14th of July... triumphant*: The French celebrate the Storming of the Bastille on this date.